D0598552

Oracle Database 10g: A Beginner's Guide

Ian Abramson
Michael S. Abbey
Michael Corey

McGraw-Hill/Osborne

New York   Chicago   San Francisco
Lisbon   London   Madrid   Mexico City   Milan
New Delhi   San Juan   Seoul   Singapore   Sydney   Toronto

The McGraw·Hill Companies

McGraw-Hill/Osborne
2100 Powell Street, 10th Floor
Emeryville, California 94608
U.S.A.

To arrange bulk purchase discounts for sales promotions, premiums, or fund-raisers, please contact **McGraw-Hill**/Osborne at the above address. For information on translations or book distributors outside the U.S.A., please see the International Contact Information page immediately following the index of this book.

Oracle Database 10*g*: A Beginner's Guide

567890 FGR FGR 0198

ISBN 0-07-223078-9

Publisher
Brandon A. Nordin

Vice President & Associate Publisher
Scott Rogers

Acquisitions Editor
Lisa McClain

Project Editor
Emily K. Wolman

Project Manager
LeeAnn Pickrell

Acquisitions Coordinator
Athena Honore

Technical Editor
Carl Dudley

Copy Editor
Mike McGee

Proofreader
Susie Elkind

Indexer
Valerie Perry

Composition
Jean Butterfield, Dick Schwartz

Illustrators
Kathleen Edwards, Melinda Lytle

Series Design
Jani Beckwith, Jean Butterfield, Peter F. Hancik

Cover Designer
Damore Johann Design, Inc.

This book was composed with Corel VENTURA™ Publisher.

About the Authors

Ian Abramson is the CTO of Red Sky Data, a Toronto-based company that has been building a results-based track record for delivering high-quality Data Warehouse and Oracle solutions to its clients around the world.

Ian is coauthor of several Oracle titles including books on Data Warehousing, on Tuning, and, of course, in the Oracle Beginner's Guide series. He is very active in the Oracle user community and is the International Oracle Users Group's Director of Education and Programming. Ian is also well known for his lively seminars and technical training classes. While Ian is busy during the day building Oracle Data Warehouses and applications, by night he continues to engage in his dreams of being a professional hockey goalie. Ian may be contacted at ian.abramson@redskydata.com.

Michael S. Abbey is a frequent presenter at many Oracle user group events. He has been working with the software since the mid '80s, having had the pleasure of experiencing versions 3 through 10*g*. Michael has been very active in the International Oracle Users Group, a Chicago-based voice for the Oracle software user community. Michael's forté is anything related to installation, configuration, backup/recovery, and management of very large databases. He is recognized in many circles as an expert in many facets of the Oracle technology. He is the owner of two 1970s Fender Precision bass guitars, evidence of one of his other passions—loud, grinding rock music.

Michael Corey, an entrepreneur, author, and recognized expert on relational databases and Data Warehousing, founded Ntirety Technologies in May 2001. As CEO, he leverages his extensive experience and business savvy to manage and expand the premier Remote Administration Services firm in New England. Corey is a frequent speaker at technology conferences throughout the world and has written numerous articles and books (published by McGraw-Hill/Osborne) on topics such as SQL Server 7 Data Warehousing, and Oracle8 and Oracle8*i* Data Warehousing; he's also contributed to several Beginner's Guides. Corey also founded and is actively involved in numerous Oracle associations and industry user groups.

About the Contributing Authors

Steve Jones is a founding partner of Red Sky Data (www.redskydata.com), a consulting firm specializing in Data Warehousing and business intelligence implementations. Steve has been working with Oracle databases for a number of years in large-scale Data Warehousing environments such as insurance and telecommunications. His involvement on projects has spanned all phases of the development lifecycle including analysis, design and architecture, development, and testing. Steve lives in Toronto and can be reached at steve.jones@redskydata.com.

After developing a solid foundation of Oracle skills in his native Ottawa during the '90s, **Mark Kerzner** moved with his wife, Arlene, and their four children to the warmer climate of Phoenix, Arizona, in 1998. Mark works for the Pharma division of NDC Health and has served in both lead software engineer and project manager roles for them since moving to Phoenix. Currently, he is the technical lead for the Data Warehouse Solutions group. In 2001, Mark earned a Project Management Professional (PMP) designation from the Project Management Institute. You can contact him by e-mail at kerz@cox.net.

Michael Mallia, an Oracle expert in the National Capital region around Ottawa, is a recognized expert in the utilization of XML and the Oracle RDBMS for "Near Real Time" data integration. Michael is the senior data architect and founding member of Xteoma, Inc. He can be reached at mmallia@xteoma.com.

Tim Quinlan is an Oracle Certified Database Administrator with over 10 years of Oracle experience; he has worked with databases since 1981. Tim has performed the roles of DBA, architect, designer, and implementer of enterprise-wide Data Warehouse and transactional databases. This work has been performed in many business sectors including government, financial, insurance, pharmaceutical, energy, and telecommunications. Tim has spoken at many conferences, taught database courses, and written feature articles for leading database publications. His main (professional) interest is designing and implementing very large, high-performance, high-availability database systems.

George Trujillo is the president and CEO of Trubix, Inc., the largest third-party provider of Oracle education materials in the world. Trubix focuses on integrating leading-edge technologies such as Java, Web Services, Oracle, and XML. George Trujillo is internationally recognized and has been selected as a keynote and master presenter at numerous technical and business conferences. He has over 17 years of Oracle DBA and developer consulting experience.

Contents

ACKNOWLEDGMENTS xv
INTRODUCTION xvi

I Database Fundamentals I
  Critical Skill 1.1 Define a Database 2
  Critical Skill 1.2 Learn the Oracle Database 10g Architecture 3
    The Control Files 4
    The Online Redo Logs 4
    The SYSTEM Tablespace 5
    The SYSAUX Tablespace 5
    Default Temporary Tablespace 5
    Undo Tablespace 5
    The System Parameter File 6
    Background Processes 6
    Project 1-1 Reviewing the Oracle Database 10g Architecture 8
    The Database Administrator 9
  Critical Skill 1.3 Learn the Basic Oracle Database 10g Data Types ... 10
    varchar2 10
    number 10
    date 11
    timestamp 11
    clob 12
    blob 12
  Critical Skill 1.4 Work with Tables 12
    Tables Related to part_master 13
  Critical Skill 1.5 Work with Stored Objects 14
    Views 15
    Triggers 16
    Procedures 16
    Functions 16
    Packages 17

Critical Skill 1.6 Become Familiar with Other Important Items
in the Oracle Database 10*g* 19
Indexes 19
Users 20
Tablespace Quotas 20
Synonyms 21
Roles 22
Default User Environments 22
Critical Skill 1.7 Work with Object and System Privileges 23
Select 23
Insert 23
Update 24
Delete 24
System Privileges 24
Critical Skill 1.8 Introduce Yourself to the Grid 25
Critical Skill 1.9 Tie It All Together 28
Chapter 1 Mastery Check 30

2 SQL: Structured Query Language **33**
Critical Skill 2.1 Learn the SQL Statement Components 34
DDL 34
DML 35
Critical Skill 2.2 Use Basic insert and select Statements 36
insert 36
select 37
Critical Skill 2.3 Use Simple where Clauses 39
The where Clause with NOT 42
The where Clause with a Range Search 42
The where Clause with a Search List 43
The where Clause with a Pattern Search 44
The where Clause: Common Operators 44
Critical Skill 2.4 Use Basic update and delete Statements 46
update 46
delete 48
Critical Skill 2.5 Order Data 50
Critical Skill 2.6 Employ Functions: String, Numeric,
Aggregate (No Grouping) 51
String Functions 51
Numeric Functions 52
Aggregate Functions 53
Critical Skill 2.7 Use Dates and Data Functions
(Formatting and Chronological) 54
Date Functions 54

    Special Formats with the Date Data Type 55
    Nested Functions 56
Critical Skill 2.8 Employ Joins (ANSI vs. Oracle):
    Inner, Outer, Self 57
    Inner Joins 57
    Outer Joins 61
    Project 2-1 Joining Data Using Inner and Outer Joins 62
    Project 2-2 Joining Data Using ANSI SQL Joins 65
    Self-Joins 66
Critical Skill 2.9 Learn the group by and having Clauses 67
    group by 67
    having 68
    Project 2-3 Grouping Data in Your select Statements 69
Critical Skill 2.10 Learn Subqueries: Simple and Correlated
    Comparison with Joins 72
    Simple Subquery 72
    Correlated Subqueries with Joins 73
Critical Skill 2.11 Use Set Operators: Union, Intersect, Minus 74
    union 74
    union all 75
    intersect 75
    minus 76
    Project 2-4 Using the union Function in Your SQL 76
Critical Skill 2.12 Use Views 78
Critical Skill 2.13 Learn Sequences: Just Simple Stuff 79
Critical Skill 2.14 Employ Constraints: Linkage to Entity Models,
    Types, Deferred, Enforced, Gathering Exceptions 80
    Linkage to Entity Models 81
    Types 82
    Deferred 83
Critical Skill 2.15 Format Your Output with SQL*Plus 83
    Page and Line Size 83
    Page Titles 84
    Page Footers 84
    Formatting Columns 84
    Project 2-5 Formatting Your SQL Output 84
    Writing SQL*Plus Output to a File 87
Chapter 2 Mastery Check 87

3 The Database Administrator **89**
Critical Skill 3.1 Learn the Job of the DBA 90
Critical Skill 3.2 Understand the Oracle Database 10g
    DBA Skill Set 90

Critical Skill 3.3 Perform Day-to-Day Operations   91
   Architecture and Design   91
   Capacity Planning   91
   Backup and Recovery   91
   Security   92
   Performance and Tuning   92
   Managing Database Objects   92
   Storage Management   92
   Change Management   93
   Schedule Jobs   93
   Network Management   93
   Troubleshooting   93
Critical Skill 3.4 Understand the Oracle Database 10*g* Infrastructure . .   93
   Schemas   94
   Storage Structures   97
Critical Skill 3.5 Operate Modes of an Oracle Database 10*g*   97
   Modes of Operation   98
   Database and Instance Shutdown   99
Critical Skill 3.6 Get Started with Oracle Enterprise Manager 101
   Instance Configuration 102
   User Sessions 102
   Resource Consumer Groups 102
   Schema, Security, and Storage Management 103
   Distributed Management 104
   Warehouse Features 105
   Other Tools 105
Critical Skill 3.7 Manage Database Objects 106
   Controlfiles 106
   Redo Logs 106
   Undo Management 107
   Schema Objects 108
Critical Skill 3.8 Manage Space 109
   Archive Logs 110
   Tablespaces and Datafiles 110
Critical Skill 3.9 Manage Users 112
   Create a User 113
   Edit Users 114
Critical Skill 3.10 Manage Privileges for Database Users 115
   Grant Authority 115
   Roles 116
   Profiles 117
   In Conclusion 118

Project 3-1 Creating Essential Objects 118
Chapter 3 Mastery Check 120

4 Networking **121**
Critical Skill 4.1 Use Oracle Net Services 122
   Network Protocols 123
   Optimize Network Bandwidth 124
   Character Sets 125
   Connections 125
   Maintain Connections 126
   Define a Location 127
Critical Skill 4.2 Learn the Difference Between Dedicated
   and Shared Server Architectures 127
   Dedicated Server 128
   Shared Server 129
   Set Dispatchers 131
   Views to Monitor the Shared Server 133
Critical Skill 4.3 Define Connections 134
   A Connect Descriptor 134
   Define a Connect Descriptor 134
   The Oracle Connection Manager 135
   Session Multiplexing 136
   Firewall Access Control 136
Critical Skill 4.4 Use the Oracle Net Listener 137
   Password Authentication 139
   Multiple Listeners 140
   Connection Pooling 140
Critical Skill 4.5 Learn Naming Methods 140
   Directory Naming Method 141
   Directory Information Trees 141
   Distinguished Names 142
   How to Find the Directory Naming Information 142
   Net Service Alias Entries 143
   The Local Naming Method 143
   The Easy Naming Method 143
   The External Naming Method 144
   Which Naming Method to Use 144
Critical Skill 4.6 Use Oracle Configuration Files 144
   Syntax for Configuration Files 144
Critical Skill 4.7 Use Administration Tools 146
   The Oracle Enterprise Manager 146
   The Oracle Net Manager 147
   The OEM Console 148

The OEM Components   148
The Oracle Net Configuration Assistant   148
The Oracle Internet Directory Configuration Assistant   149
Command-Line Utilities   149
The Oracle Advanced Security Option   151
Dispatchers   151
Project 4-1 Testing a Connection   152
Critical Skill 4.8 Use Profiles   154
Control Access   154
Critical Skill 4.9 Network in a Multitiered Environment   155
Chapter 4 Mastery Check   156

5 Backup and Recovery **157**
Critical Skill 5.1 Oracle Backup and Recovery Fundamentals   158
Where Do I Start?   158
Backup Architecture   159
Oracle Binaries   160
The Parameter Files   160
Control Files   160
Redo Logs   161
Undo Segments   161
Checkpoints   161
Archive Logs   162
Datafiles, Tablespaces, Segments, Extents, and Blocks   162
Trace Files   163
Critical Skill 5.2 Learn about Oracle User-Managed Backup
and Recovery   164
Types of User-Managed Backups   164
Cold Backups   164
Hot Backups   165
Recovery from a Cold Backup   167
Recovery from a Hot Backup   168
Seven Steps to Recovery   169
Recovery Using Backup Control Files   169
Critical Skill 5.3 Write a Database Backup   170
Critical Skill 5.4 Back Up Archived Redo Logs   172
Critical Skill 5.5 Get Started with Oracle Data Pump   173
Critical Skill 5.6 Use Oracle Data Pump Export   174
Some Export Examples   177
Critical Skill 5.7 Work with Oracle Data Pump Import   178
A Data Pump Export and Import Example   181
Critical Skill 5.8 Use Traditional Export and Import   183
How to Run the Original Utilities   183
Examples Using Original Export and Import   184

Critical Skill 5.9 Get Started with Recovery Manager 185
   RMAN Architecture 186
   Set Up a Recovery Catalog and Target Database 188
   Key RMAN Features 189
   Backups 192
   Performing Backups 193
   Restore and Recovery 194
  Project 5-1   RMAN End-to-End 195
Chapter 5 Mastery Check 197

6 PL/SQL **199**
Critical Skill 6.1 Define PL/SQL and Why We Use It 200
Critical Skill 6.2 Describe the Basic PL/SQL Program Structure 202
Critical Skill 6.3 Define PL/SQL Data Types 204
   The PL/SQL Character Set 204
Critical Skill 6.4 Write PL/SQL Programs in SQL*Plus 210
  Project 6-1 Creating a PL/SQL Program 212
   SQL in Your PL/SQL Programs 213
   The Cursor FOR Loop 215
Critical Skill 6.5 Handle Error Conditions in PL/SQL 217
   Error Handling Oracle-Supplied Variables 220
Critical Skill 6.6 Include Conditions in Your Programs 222
   Program Control 223
  Project 6-2 Using Conditions and Loops in PL/SQL 231
Critical Skill 6.7 Create Stored Procedures—How and Why 232
Critical Skill 6.8 Create and Use Functions 237
  Project 6-3 Creating and Using a Function 237
Critical Skill 6.9 Call PL/SQL Programs 239
Chapter 6 Mastery Check 240

7 Java **241**
Java Server Fundamentals 242
Critical Skill 7.1 What Does Java Mean to an Oracle DBA? 242
Critical Skill 7.2 Overview of Java 245
   Platform Independence 247
   Java in All Three Tiers 247
   Java 2 Platform, Standard Edition 248
   Java 2 Platform, Enterprise Edition 248
   The J2EE Server 249
   Different Types of Java Programs 249
   Standalone Applications 250
   Applets 250
   JavaBeans 250
   JavaServer Pages and Servlets 250

Enterprise JavaBeans 251
Advantages of N-Tiered Architectures 251
Java, XML, Web Services, and Oracle 10*g* 252
Opportunities for Oracle DBAs 252
Critical Skill 7.3 Configure Java for Oracle 254
Java Initialization Parameters 254
Environmental Variables 255
Critical Skill 7.4 Java in Oracle 256
Native Compilation 256
Garbage Collection 257
Things to Watch Out For 257
Main Components of the JVM 257
Critical Skill 7.5 JDBC Drivers 258
JDBC Thin Driver 258
JDBC Thick Driver 258
JDBC Server-Side Driver 258
Use the Proper JDBC Driver 258
Critical Skill 7.6 Use JDBC 259
How to Write Database Programs 259
Project 7-1 Accessing the Database with Java 260
Critical Skill 7.7 Use SQLJ 261
SQLJ Translator 261
Sample SQLJ Code 262
SQLJ Directions 262
Critical Skill 7.8 Java-Stored Procedures 262
Java Utilities for DBAs 263
loadjava and dropjava Examples 263
ojvmjava Examples 263
Privileges 264
Resolver Specifications 264
Project 7-2 Creating a Java-Stored Procedure 264
Critical Skill 7.9 Create Java Objects in Oracle 266
create java class 266
create java source 266
create java resource 266
Critical Skill 7.10 Understand Oracle Java Products 267
Oracle Application Server 10*g* 267
Oracle JDeveloper 10*g* 267
Chapter 7 Mastery Check 269

8 XML **271**
Critical Skill 8.1 Understand XML 272
Critical Skill 8.2 XML DB: Use XML in the Database 273

Critical Skill 8.3 SQLX: Create XML from Data Stored in Oracle 276
   The SQL/XML Standard 276
   xmlelement() 277
   xmlattributes() 277
   xmlforest() 277
   xmlagg() 279
   Project 8-1 Creating an XML Listing 281
Critical Skill 8.4 Store XML in Oracle XML DB 283
   The Native XMLType 283
   The XML DB Repository 284
   Registering an XML Schema 284
   Loading XML Data 286
   Project 8-2 Storing XML 287
   Use the RESOURCE_VIEW 288
   Path-Based Access 289
   Update the XML Document 290
Critical Skill 8.5 Use Simple Queries 291
   Project 8-3 Using Simple Queries 293
Critical Skill 8.6 Create a Relational View from XML 294
Critical Skill 8.7 Learn Programmatic Access Using XSLT 296
Chapter 8 Mastery Check 297

9 Large Database Features **299**
Critical Skill 9.1 What Is a Large Database? 300
Critical Skill 9.2 Why and How to Use Data Partitioning 301
   Why Use Data Partitioning 301
   Implement Data Partitioning 305
   Project 9-1 Creating a Range-Partitioned Table and a Local
     Partitioned Index 320
Critical Skill 9.3 Compress Your Data 323
   Data Compression 324
   Index Key Compression 326
Critical Skill 9.4 Use Parallel Processing to Improve Performance 327
   Parallel Processing Database Components 327
   Parallel Processing Configuration 328
   Invoke Parallel Execution 330
Critical Skill 9.5 Use Materialized Views 331
   Uses for Materialized Views 332
   Query Rewrite 333
   When to Create Materialized Views 334
   Create Materialized Views 335
Critical Skill 9.6 Real Application Clusters: A Primer 336
   RAC Architecture 337

Critical Skill 9.7 Automatic Storage Management: Another Primer 338
    ASM Architecture 338
Critical Skill 9.8 Grid Computing: The "*g*" in Oracle Database 10*g* ... 340
    Self-Managing Databases 341
Critical Skill 9.9 Use SQL Aggregate and Analysis Functions 343
    Aggregation Functions 344
    Analysis Functions 346
    Other Functions 354
Critical Skill 9.10 Create SQL Models 355
    Project 9-2 Using Analytic SQL Functions and Models 358
Chapter 9 Mastery Check 360

A Mastery Check Answers **363**

Index **381**

Acknowledgments

an Abramson: I would like to thank my wife, Susan (who is the best decorator in the world), and my children, Baila and Jillian. We are strongest as one, we all draw strength from each other. Thanks also to my coauthors: you have helped to make this book a great project! YATFG to all! I would also like to thank the people who I work with and the people who I play with, so thanks to ReMax All-Stars hockey, Red Sky Data hockey, David Stanford, Paul Herron, Rob Snoyer and Ted Falcon, Jack Chadirjian, and, of course, my dad, Joe, who has taught me about what is truly important in life—family. Thank you to all, I could not have done it without you, and I share this book with each of you!

Michael Abbey: I would like to recognize my immediate and extended families, who have always helped me find ways to advance my career and satisfy my voracious appetite for Oracle's technology.

Michael Corey: Thanks to my family, and to my friends Mike Abbey and Ian Abramson, for all of their understanding and support. Thanks also to my good friends Ed Marram and Les Charm for all their help and support. To bring this book to press required a lot of time and effort from a lot of great people at McGraw-Hill/Osborne— thank you once again.

Steve Jones: I would like to thank my wife, Sandra, for her unwavering support and encouragement, as well as her patience and understanding. Thanks also to my loving kids, Devon, Spencer, and Matthew, for keeping me young and reminding me of the important things in life. Last but not least, I would like to thank coauthor Ian Abramson for his advice and support, and for giving me the opportunity to contribute to this book.

Mark Kerzner: Thank you to my wife, Arlene, and our four children, Marissa, Amanda, Shane and Dalia, whose excitement about this opportunity rivaled mine. They support every step I take, and for that I am deeply grateful. To my parents for their unconditional love and support. To my mentors, Ian Abramson and Michael Abbey, who launched my IT career and have always been there to encourage and support me. To the many friends I have made over the years, especially the JPL friends who are my Arizona family. You all have contributed to whom I have become.

Michael Mallia: First and foremost, to my soulmate, Shauna. Without her, our house would not be a home. Secondly, to my four-year-old's Godfather and his number-one birthday party invitee, MichaelAbbey (MichaelAbbey is one word!), for the dedication and love he obviously has for my family. May we know each other until I change my belt size.

Tim Quinlan: Special thanks to Helen, Ryan, and Brendan for supporting and helping me with this work.

George Trujillo: I would like to say a special thanks to my wife, Karen, and kids, Cole, Madison, and Gage, for their love and patience during all the long nights and early mornings while writing course materials.

Introduction

Oracle Database 10*g* marks the latest release by a company that has experienced a meteoric rise to success over the past 25-plus years. They have been grossing many billions of dollars annually for many years, vending a suite of solutions powered by their flagship product—the Oracle database. It has gone through many changes in names—v6, Oracle7, Oracle8*i*, Oracle9*i*, and now Oracle 10*g*. Regardless of what it is called, the Oracle server has been catapulted to the forefront of our Internet-savvy society, playing a role as the primary data server on a web site in your neighborhood. This book is your introduction to the Oracle Database 10*g* technology. It is the start of your journey—a quick start to a complex and popular technology.

Oracle Database 10*g* is the culmination of thousands upon thousands of person hours building an infrastructure to deliver data to a hungry, worldwide community, just as electricity is delivered to a three-prong outlet near you. Larry Ellison, CEO of Oracle Corporation, is a visionary steering Oracle's product set in directions unheard of before. You cannot read any public relations or technical material from Oracle Corporation without hearing that four letter word—*grid*. With grid computing, the industry envisions a computational grid where machines all the way from the Intel-based server to the high-end servers from HP, IBM, and Sun are interlaced with one another is a massively scalable and sharable environment.

There have been many advances in the processing power of computer chips over the past few decades, and grid computing is seen as allowing applications to harness that power. Idle processor time is deliberately consumed by shared applications. The analogy to the electricity grid is an interesting one. When you plug your iron into a socket in your basement, you neither know nor care where the electricity is coming from—it's just there and taken for granted. With Oracle Database 10*g* grid computing, transparent access is provided to a wide network of remote computers. Unbeknownst to application users, processing is shared between widely disparate sites, where the location of nodes responsible for data delivery is dynamic—hence the likeness to the electrical grid. The Far East is anywhere from eight to 12½ hours ahead of most geographic locations in North America. Imagine if the computing power from the quiet time (11 P.M. to 7 A.M. EST) in North America can be absorbed by users in India, Pakistan, and Sri Lanka.

You are reading *Oracle Database 10g: A Beginner's Guide* for one of many reasons. Perhaps you are a neophyte to the database arena and are looking for a way to fast-track your knowledge. Maybe you have been working in the industry for a number of years and are moving with your company into the Oracle product line. Some developers have been writing application code for years and are now being given the opportunity to roll up their sleeves and get their hands dirty with the technology under the covers. If someone has walked into your office and uttered what some feel are the most dreaded six words in the English language—"So, you're the new database administrator"—reading this book is the perfect place to be.

Oracle Database 10g: A Beginner's Guide features the following elements, which enable you to check your progress and sync your understanding of the concepts and details of the product:

- *Critical skills,* listed at the beginning of each chapter, highlight what you will learn by the end of the chapter.

- *Step-by-step projects* reinforce the concepts and skills learned in each chapter, enabling you to apply your newly acquired knowledge and skills immediately.

- *Ask the Expert* Q&As appear throughout the chapters to make the subject more interactive and personal.

- *Progress Checks* are quick, numbered, self-assessment sections where readers can easily check their progress by answering questions relating to the current chapter.

- *Mastery Checks*, at the end of each chapter, test proficiency in concepts and technology details covered in the chapter through multiple-choice, fill-in-the blank, true/false, and short-answer questions.

We start out by giving you an overview of database fundamentals with an Oracle Database 10g flavor, then move into the Structured Query Language (SQL), the delivery mechanism coming to a computer screen on your desktop. Next, we look at the job of the Oracle Database 10g gatekeeper—the DBA, or database administrator. Then come chapters on networking in the Oracle Database 10g world, backup and recovery, PL/SQL, Java, and XML. We finish the journey with a look at very large database features of Oracle Database 10g. This is an area Oracle has spent some time developing over the past few releases. Information repositories can be likened to jumbo jets—the bigger they are, the more difficult they are to maneuver.

There is one thing you must keep in mind as you travel around the pages of this book: Oracle Database 10*g* is a huge product with many, many more bells and whistles that we could discuss but chose not to. Other than the product name, the word *Beginner* in the book title is important. A Beginner's Guide is supposed to do the following:

- Introduce the concepts of the software.

- Discuss the major roles people play as they mind and interact with the software.

- Guide the reader through the vast assortment of tools imbedded in the software, highlighting the most useful.

- Provide the reader with opportunities to test-drive the software in a small, close, protected environment.

- Point the user in the right direction such that their interests steer them to the meat of the product and allow them to expand their knowledge after a quick jumpstart.

This list is by no means complete, but it drives the way we have organized the following nine chapters for your reading enjoyment. Please fasten your seatbelts as we begin the descent into the wild and wonderful world of Oracle Database 10*g*!

CHAPTER

1

Database Fundamentals

CRITICAL SKILLS

1.1 Define a Database

1.2 Learn the Oracle Database 10*g* Architecture

1.3 Learn the Basic Oracle Database 10*g* Data Types

1.4 Work with Tables

1.5 Work with Stored Objects

1.6 Become Familiar with Other Important Items in the Oracle Database 10*g*

1.7 Work with Object and System Privileges

1.8 Introduce Yourself to the Grid

1.9 Tie It All Together

his chapter is your first one on your Oracle Database 10*g* journey. From here on out, we will walk you through the skills that you need to begin working with the Oracle Database 10*g*. We'll begin at the core of this product, with the fundamentals of a database. This chapter will also help you form an understanding of the contents of your database and prepare you to move into the complex areas of Oracle Database 10*g* technology.

Define a Database

Oracle Database 10*g*—the latest offering from a software giant in northern California. Perhaps you have heard a lot of hype about Oracle Database 10*g*, perhaps not. Regardless of your experience, 10*g* is a rich, full-featured software intended to revolutionize the way many companies do their database business. *Database* you say—now there's a word you hear all the time! In a nutshell, a database is an electronic collection of information designed to meet a handful of needs:

1. Databases provide one-stop shopping for all your data storage requirements, be they in diverse areas such as human resources, finance, inventory, or sales and then some. The database contains any amount of data, from the small to the huge. Data volumes in excess of many hundreds of gigabytes are commonplace in this day and age, where a gigabyte is 1,073,741,824 bytes.

2. Databases must provide mechanisms to retrieve data quickly as applications interact with their contents. It is one thing to store tax information for the 300 million citizens of a country, but it's another kettle of fish to retrieve that data, as required, in a short time period.

3. Databases allow the sharing of corporate data such that personnel data is shared amongst one's payroll, benefits, and pension systems. A familiar adage in the database industry is "write once, read many." Databases are a manifestation of that saying—one's name, address, and other tombstone personnel information are stored in one place and read by as many systems requiring these details.

There is a great deal of academic interest in the database industry, the theory of the relational database being founded in relational algebra. As data is entered into and stored in the Oracle Database 10*g*, the relationships it has to other data are defined as well. This allows the assembling of required data as applications run. These relationships can be described in plain English for a fictitious computer parts store as follows:

■ Each geographical location within which the store does business is uniquely identified by a **quad_id**.

■ Each manufacturer that supplies parts is uniquely identified by a ten-character **manufacturer_id**. When a new manufacturer is registered with the system, it is assigned a **quad_id** based on its location.

■ Each item in the store's inventory is uniquely identified by a ten-character **part_id**, and must be associated with a valid **manufacturer_id**.

Based on these three points, practitioners commonly develop statements similar to the following to describe the relationships between locations, manufacturers, and parts:

■ There is a one-to-many relationship between locations and manufacturers—more than one manufacturer can reside in a specified location.

■ There is a one-to-many relationship between manufacturers and computer parts—the store purchases many different parts from each manufacturer.

These two relationships are established as data is captured in the store's database and other relationships can be deduced as a result—for example, one can safely say "parts are manufactured in one or more locations based on the fact that there are many manufacturers supplying many different products." Oracle has always been a relational database product, commanding a significant percentage of market share compared to its major competition. Let's get started and look at the Oracle Database 10g architecture.

CRITICAL SKILL 1.2

Learn the Oracle Database 10g Architecture

As with many new software experiences, there is some jargon that we should get out of the way before starting this section.

■ Oracle Database 10g is said to be *started* when the appropriate commands have been invoked to make it accessible on a day-to-day basis to applications.

■ The act of stopping Oracle Database 10g is called *shutdown*. When Oracle Database 10g is shut down, nobody can access the data in its files.

■ An *instance* is a set of processes that run in a computer's memory and provide access to the many files that come together to define themselves as Oracle Database 10g.

■ A *background process* supports access to a started Oracle Database 10g, playing a vital role in Oracle's database implementation. Various background processes are spawned when starting the database and each performs a handful of tasks until a database is shut down.

Let's now look at the assortment of files and background processes that support the Oracle Database 10g.

NOTE
In order to work with the code snippets and the sample schemas we discuss throughout this book, you will need to have the Oracle Database 10g software installed and the first database successfully created. The Database Configuration Assistant (dbca) is the fastest way to set up your first database. Most of the time you simply accept the defaults suggested on the dbca screens. If you have any problems with either the software installation or the dbca, please consult either a more senior colleague or surf MetaLink (http://metalink.oracle.com) to get assistance, after supplying appropriate login credentials.

The Control Files

These are binary files containing information about the assortment of files that come together to support the Oracle Database 10g. They contain information that describes the names, locations, and sizes of the database files. Oracle insists there is one control file, but savvy technicians have two or three and sometimes more. As the Oracle Database 10g is started, the control files are read and the files described therein are opened to support the running database.

The Online Redo Logs

As sessions interact with the Oracle Database 10g, the details of their activities are recorded in the online redo logs. Many think of these as the transaction logs. A *transaction* is a unit of work, passed to the database for processing. The following shows a few activities that can be referred to as two transactions.

```
-- Begin of transaction #1
create some new information
update some existing information
create some more new information
delete some information
save all the work that has been accomplished
-- End of transaction #1
-- Begin transaction #2
update some information
back out the update by not saving the changed data
-- End transaction #2
```

Oracle Database 10g insists that there are at least two online redo logs to support the instance. In fact, most databases have two or more redo log groups with each group having the same number of equally sized members.

The SYSTEM Tablespace

Tablespace is a fancy Oracle Database 10*g* name for a database file. Think of it as a *space* where a *table* resides. As an Oracle Database 10*g* is created, a **system** tablespace is built that contains Oracle's data dictionary. As Oracle Database 10*g* operates, it continually gets operational information out of its data dictionary and, as records are created, this **system** tablespace defines attributes of the data it stores, such as:

- The *data type* of pieces of information. Are they numeric, alphanumeric, or perhaps binary of some video or audio format?

- The maximum allowable size of fields as they are populated by the applications. This is where, for example, a country description is defined as from one to 30 characters long, and containing only letters.

- Who owns the information as the database data files are populated?

- Who is allowed to look at each other's data and what types of activities each user of the database can perform on that data?

The **system** tablespace is a very close cousin of the **sysaux** tablespace discussed next.

The SYSAUX Tablespace

Many of the tools and options that support the Oracle Database 10*g* activities store their objects in this **sysaux** tablespace. This is mandatory as a database is created. The Oracle Enterprise Manager (OEM) Grid Control repository used to go in its own **oem_repository** tablespace, but with Oracle Database 10*g* its objects now reside in **sysaux**.

Default Temporary Tablespace

As the dbca does its thing, a tablespace is created that serves as the default location for intermediary objects Oracle Database 10*g* builds as it processes SQL statements. *SQL* stands for the structured query language, an industry standard in the database arena, used to retrieve, create, change, and update data. Most of the work Oracle does to assemble a result set for a query operation is done in memory. A *result set* is a collection of data that qualifies for inclusion in a query passed to Oracle. If the amount of memory allocated for query processing is insufficient to accommodate all the activities required to assemble data, Oracle uses this default temporary tablespace as its secondary work area for many activities including sorting.

Undo Tablespace

As sessions interact with the Oracle Database 10*g*, they create, change, and delete data. Undo is the act of restoring data to a previous state. Suppose one's address is changed from 123 Any Street to 456 New Street via a screen in the personnel application.

The user who is making the change has not yet saved the transaction. Until that transaction is saved (referred to as *committed* in the world of Oracle Database 10*g*) or abandoned (referred to as *rolled back* in the same world), Oracle maintains a copy of the changed row in its *undo tablespace*.

The System Parameter File

Oracle Database 10*g* sometimes calls the system parameter file its *spfile*. This is where its startup parameters are defined and values in this file determine the environment within which the database operates. As one starts an Oracle instance, the spfile is read and various memory structures are allocated based on its contents.

Background Processes

Essentially, background processes facilitate access to the Oracle Database 10*g* and support the instance while it is running. These are the main background processes, many of their names not having changed over the past few releases prior to Oracle Database 10*g*.

- Database writer (dbwr) processes are responsible for writing the contents of database buffers to disk. As sessions interact with the Oracle Database 10*g*, all the information they use passes through Oracle's database buffers, a segment of memory allocated for this activity.

- The log writer (lgwr) process manages the writing of information to the online redo logs. A log buffer area is set aside in memory where information destined for the online redo logs is staged. The transfer of this information from memory to disk is handled by the *lgwr* process.

- The checkpoint process (ckpt) is responsible for updating information in Oracle Database 10*g*'s files during a checkpoint activity. A *checkpoint* is the activity of writing information from memory to the appropriate locations in the Oracle Database 10*g*. Think of a checkpoint as a stake in the ground allowing the restoration of a system to a specific point in time. The checkpoint process may trigger lgwr and dbwr to do their specialized tasks.

- The system monitor (smon) process is the gatekeeper of consistency as the Oracle Database 10*g* runs. *Consistency* defines the interrelatedness of the database components with one another. A consistent instance must be established every time the Oracle Database 10*g* starts and it is smon's job to continually enforce and reestablish this consistency. Plainly put—an inconsistent database is trouble!

- The process monitor (pmon) is responsible for cleaning up any resources that may have been tied up by aborted sessions interacting with the database. The famous CTRL-ALT-DEL that people tend to use to reboot a personal computer can leave resources tied up in the Oracle Database 10*g*. It is pmon's job to free up these resources.

■ The job queue coordination (cjq0) process is responsible for spawning job processes from Oracle Database 10*g*'s internal job queue. Oracle Database 10*g* does some self-management using its job queue, and users of the database can create jobs and have them submitted to this cjq0 coordinator.

■ The archiver (arc0) process is responsible for copying online redo logs to a secondary storage location before they are reused by the next set of transactions. In the "Online Redo Logs" section of this chapter, we discuss how Oracle Database 10*g* insists there are at least two online redo logs. Suppose we call these groups A and B. Oracle Database 10*g* uses these two groups in a cyclical fashion, moving back and forth from A to B to A to B and so on. The arc0 process, when and if instructed, will make a copy of a file from log group A before allowing it to be reused.

Figure 1-1 illustrates the way the architecture components we have described come together to support the Oracle Database 10*g*. The Oracle Database 10*g* is started, the control files are read to get its bearings. Then the online redo logs and the assortment of tablespaces listed in the control files are acquired. As the instance comes to life, the background processes take over and manage the operations of the database from there.

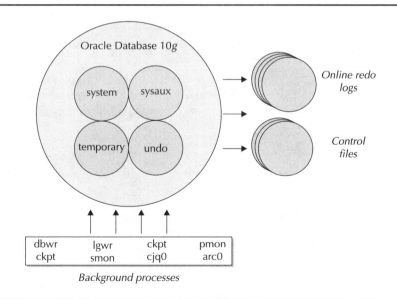

FIGURE 1-1.   *The Oracle Database 10*g *architecture*

Project 1-1	Reviewing the Oracle Database 10g Architecture

There are many types of files that come together to support the Oracle Database 10g. In this section, we have discussed control files, online redo logs, the **system** tablespace, and an assortment of tablespaces that support the database. As well, we have looked at the series of background processes that allow users to interact with Oracle Database 10g. In this brief project, you will apply what you have learned about the processes that support the Oracle Database 10g. As you descend into the land of Oracle Database 10g, this information is crucial to your understanding of this remarkable software solution.

Step by Step

1. There are a few pieces missing in the following diagram of the infrastructure of files that support the Oracle Database 10g. Fill in the missing text where required. You can confirm your answers by reviewing BEGP1-1a.tif online.

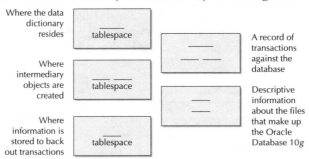

2. The second diagram shows a partial makeup of the background processes with Oracle Database 10g. Complete the missing text where indicated by broken lines. Again, you can check your answers online by viewing BEGP1-2a.tif.

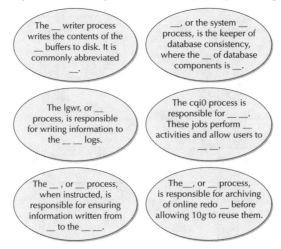

Project Summary

The reader need not master the Oracle Database 10g architecture to become fluent with the software. Just as an electrician needs the assistance of a good set of blueprints, the Oracle Database 10g technical person should understand some of the inner workings of the software. A peek under the covers, as brief as it may have been in this section, is a good path to follow while becoming familiar with what Oracle Database 10g is all about.

Before moving on to discuss Oracle Database 10g data types, let's spend a minute looking at the database administrator, the ultimate director of the operations of the database.

The Database Administrator

This privileged user of the Oracle Database 10g is commonly the most experienced technician in the shop, with some exceptions. Often, recent adopters of the Oracle technology have little or no in-house experience, and one or more employees may find themselves targets of the familiar directive "So, you're the new Oracle Database 10g DBA!" One scrambles to find sources for technical knowledge when thrust into this role and, what better place to be than reading *Oracle Database 10g: A Beginner's Guide?* The following list outlines common responsibilities of the Oracle Database 10g DBA:

- Install and configure the Oracle Database 10g software.

- Create tablespaces within which application data will reside.

- Create and manage accounts.

- Tweak the environment within which the Oracle Database 10g operates by adjusting initialization parameters using the system parameter file.

- Configure backups and carry out recovery tests to ensure the usability and integrity of system backups.

- Work with developers to ensure the code they write is optimal, and use the server's resources as efficiently as possible.

- Keep abreast of the emerging technology and be involved in scoping out future direction based on enhancements delivered with new software releases.

- Work with Oracle Support Services, initiating technical assistance requests (*i*TARs) to engage support analysts in problem-solving endeavors. The front-end to the *i*TAR creation process is called *MetaLink*.

- Tune the Oracle Database 10g so applications can coexist with one another on the same server and share that machine's resources efficiently.

- Work with the system administrators to ensure the appropriate disk space and processor power are available and properly utilized.

As with most lists, after reading the preceding bullet points, you may wonder what else DBAs do with their time. As you work with the Oracle Database 10*g*, you will experience other activities that will plug the loopholes that may exist in the previous list.

CRITICAL SKILL 1.3

Learn the Basic Oracle Database 10*g* Data Types

Very early in one's journey through the world of Oracle Database 10*g*, it becomes time to learn its common data types. Regardless of one's past experiences in information technology, data types are nothing new. Let's look at the most common type of data that can be stored in the Oracle Database 10*g*, keeping in mind that the list is much longer than the one we present here.

varchar2

By far the most common data type, varchar2 allows storage of just about any character that can be entered from a computer keyboard. In earlier software solutions, we commonly referred to this as *alphanumeric* data. The maximum length of varchar2 is 4000 bytes or characters. It is possible to store numeric data in this data type. This is a variable length character string, with no storing of trailing insignificant white space. Thus, if "Turkey   " is passed to a column defined as varchar2, it will store the text as "Turkey". The following listing shows a few sample varchar2 data definitions.

```
create table ... (
    name        varchar2(30),
    city        varchar2(30),
    ...
    ...
    state       varchar2(2));
```

If a program or SQL statement tries to store a set of characters in a varchar2 field that is longer than the field's specification, an error is returned and the statement abends.

number

The number data type allows the storing of integer as well as integer/decimal digits. When noninteger data is stored, the portion to the left of the decimal is referred to as *precision,* and that to the right as *scale.* The maximum precision is 38 and the maximum scale is 127. The confusing part of the specification of number data type comes into play when storing noninteger information. Table 1-1 illustrates this concept.

Number Specification	Column Length	Decimal Digits
(3,2)	3	2
(6,3)	6	3
(17,12)	17	12

TABLE 1-1.   *Number Data Type Specification*

The secret here is that the integer portion of a number data type where decimal places are specified is the difference between the two numbers. As Table 1-1 illustrates, the specification (9,4) allows for five, not nine, integer digits. If more decimal digits are received than the column definition permits, it rounds the value before storage.

date

The date data type stores time and date information, with the time component rounded to the nearest full second. There are many, many functions performed on date fields as they are extracted from an Oracle Database 10g. Even though we supposedly learned something during the millennium issues associated with the year 2000, we still commonly use a two-digit year designator.

As date columns are extracted from the Oracle Database 10g, it is common to perform a function on their values to make them more readable. By default, the time component of a date column is not displayed without manipulating its contents using a to_char function described in Chapter 2.

timestamp

The timestamp data type is a close relative of date. There is a time component in this data type, displayed with the data without the need for the to_char function. This listing illustrates this concept:

```
SQL> create table timestamp_test (ts timestamp);
Table created.
SQL> insert into timestamp_test values (sysdate);
1 row created.
SQL> select * from timestamp_test;
TS
----------------------------------------------------------------------
14-DEC-06 05.25.07.000000 PM
SQL> create table date_test (d date);
Table created.
SQL> insert into date_test values (sysdate);
1 row created.
```

```
SQL> select * from date_test;
TS
---------
14-DEC-06
```

clob

The clob data type allows storage of very large objects in excess of four gigabytes in size. Since this is a true character data type, it is very similar to the varchar2 data type except for its much larger maximum size.

blob

The blob data type permits storage of large unstructured binary objects. Sound and video are examples of blob data.

It's now time to have a look at the most common object in the Oracle Database 10*g*—the table. After that, we will have a look at a few types of programming units written using SQL, which a person can store in the Oracle Database 10*g*.

CRITICAL SKILL 1.4

Work with Tables

The best way to think of a table in a relational database such as Oracle Database 10*g* is to see it as a spreadsheet with rows and columns. With this in mind, note the following:

- Rows are often referred to as *records*.

- Each column has a name unique to the table within which it resides.

- The intersection of each row and column, referred to as a cell in a spreadsheet, is called a *field* in Oracle Database 10*g*.

Picture the following SQL statement that creates a table (the line numbers are not part of the code):

```
1- create table part_master (
2-    id                  number(8) not null,
3-    manufacturer_code   number(4) not null,
4-    inception           date not null,
5-    description         varchar2(60) not null,
6-    unit_price          number(6,2) not null,
7-    in_stock            varchar2(1));
```

Let's pick apart the code and highlight the main points in Table 1-2.

Table 1-2 mentions the concept of a relational database. Let's inspect a few other tables and see how they are related to one another.

Line	Important Points
1	The table has a unique name, from one to 30 characters. It is stored in Oracle Database 10g's data dictionary in uppercase.
2	The ID column is numeric with anywhere from one to eight digits. The application that creates and keeps track of parts may insist that the first character of the ID be a digit between 1 and 9. Since the field is defined as numeric, if the leading digit were a 0, the part ID would only be seven digits long.
3	The **manufacturer_code** is the only manufacturer information stored in **part_master**. Further information about who made the product is in a related table—hence, the terminology relational database.
4	**inception**, being a date field, contains a date and time specification, though it will display with a default month abbreviation and a two-character year unless some manual manipulation is performed (for example, 12-NOV-05).
5	**description** is a free form field with a variable length of up to 30 characters.
6	**unit_price** can accommodate up to four integer and two decimal digits.
7	**in_stock** is a one-character flag of sorts—thus, the system designers can decide to use an indicator like a "1" or "X" to represent items that are in stock. Notice how this is the only one of seven fields in the PART_MASTER table that can be left blank.

TABLE 1-2. *part_master Table Definitions*

Tables Related to part_master

The **manufacturer_code** column in **part_master** points to a record in **manufacturer**. As well, some columns in **manufacturer** may end up being related to column values in other tables. Figure 1-2 illustrates these relationship concepts, the heart of the Oracle Database 10g implementation.

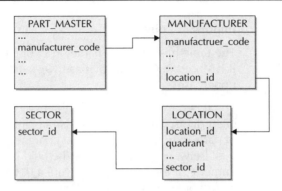

FIGURE 1-2. *Relationships to **part_master***

Suppose someone wanted to know where in the country a certain part was manufactured. By looking at Figure 1-2, that information is not readily available in **part_master**. However, **part_master** has a **manufacturer_code**. So, a person would traverse to **manufacturer** using **manufacturer_code** to get a **location_id**. Armed with that value, one then proceeds to **location** to get a **quadrant** column value. After this navigation is complete, a person would know where a specific part is built. Table 1-3 maps out this journey.

As illustrated in Table 1-3, we can deduce that part 33499909 comes from the Pacific Northwest—a deduction that is made by following the relationships between matching columns in the three tables in question.

CRITICAL SKILL 1.5

Work with Stored Objects

Oracle Database 10*g* offers the ability to store user-defined programming units in the data dictionary, called *stored objects.* These programming units are written in PL/SQL, the topic of Chapter 7. Without worrying about what goes inside these objects, let's do an overview of what they are all about.

Table	Part Number	Column Value	Related Column Value
part_master	33499909	manufacturer_code	3490
manufacturer	3490	location_id	5
location	5	quadrant	Pacific Northwest

TABLE 1-3. *Following Relationships Between Tables*

Ask the Expert

Q: What is the major difference between the clob and blob data types in Oracle Database 10*g*?

A: The clob stores only alphanumeric data, whereas the blob can accommodate any type of data, including sound and video.

Q: When specifying the number data type, how is the total length of the field determined?

A: The total length of a numeric field is determined by the digit(s) to the left of the comma if the specification includes an integer and decimal component. For example, *number(4,1)* denotes a maximum of four digits, of which one digit can be stored to the right of the decimal point.

Q: Which of the Oracle Database 10*g* background processes is responsible for writing information from memory into the database files?

A: This is the job of the database writer, or dbwr, process.

Q: Where does Oracle Database 10*g* read its environment from as it is started?

A: The startup parameters are read from the system parameter file, which can be a binary file stored in the Oracle Database 10*g*.

Q: As sessions interact with the data in the Oracle Database 10*g*, what role does the undo tablespace play in the architecture of the software?

A: When transactions change the contents of information in Oracle Database 10*g*'s tables, this special tablespace keeps a "before image" of the changes in case the operator decides to back out before saving newly entered information.

Views

Views are predefined subsets of data from an Oracle Database 10*g* table. The SQL query that builds the view is stored in the data dictionary and need not be reassembled every time the view is used. Suppose a personnel application stores the location of all employees in its EMPLOYEE_MASTER table in the **loc_id** column. With Oracle Database 10*g*, you can define a view called **emp_hq** as follows:

```
create or replace view emp_hq
as select * from employee_master
where loc_id = '2';
```

EMP_HQ becomes a valid object of the *select* statement just as if it were a table of its own.

Triggers

Just as their name implies, triggers are stored objects that fire based on the execution of certain events. Suppose a payroll application wants to audit salary increases. A trigger is created that fires when the **salary** column in **hr_master** is updated. The trigger could do the following:

1. Create a record in **sal_audit**.

2. Trap the time and date of the transaction.

3. Place the user's login ID in the **doer** column.

4. Place the old salary value in the **old_sal** column.

5. Place the new salary value in **new_sal** column.

Code in the trigger traps the event by specifying *on update.* While triggers are commonly used for auditing, the types of activities they can initiate are endless.

 NOTE
Triggers cannot exist independent of an Oracle Database 10g table. They are associated with one and only one table and, if a table is dropped, so is the trigger.

Triggers, as well as procedures, packages, and functions described next, are most commonly written using PL/SQL. The PL/SQL programming language is the topic of Chapter 6.

Procedures

Procedures perform specific tasks as applications interact with the Oracle Database 10*g*. If there are a number of interrelated activities to carry out in one place, a procedure is an ideal way to do this. Procedures can accept parameters when invoked and can interact with objects in the Oracle Database 10*g*. They encapsulate related activities into single programming units that simplify logic and share data values as they perform various activities. They offer extremely flexible features, many of which are not available with triggers.

Functions

Functions are very close relatives of procedures, except that they return a value to the code that called them. Oracle Database 10*g* delivers many functions out of the box and developers create their own functions to augment what is delivered with the software. Suppose one wants to strip all the vowels out of a name with a function. One passes in a name (for instance, Bellissimo) and gets back the text "Bllssm" when the function completes its work. Let's look at the **get_age** function which operates based on the following logic:

```
given a date of birth (format DD-MON-YYYY)
using an SQL function
get the months between today's date and the date passed in
divide the number of months by 12
truncate the results (giving the span in years between the 2 dates)
pass integer back
```

Packages

Packages roll functions and procedures together into a cohesive programming unit. Often, developers like to bundle like functionality together since it makes logical sense to call one larger unit and have it perform a series of tasks. Let's look at the CREATE_EMPLOYEE package in Table 1-4.

Component Name	Type	Work Accomplished
give_holidays	Procedure	Creates the default holiday quota based on the new person's rank in the company.
notify_benefits	Procedure	Creates a record in the BEN_QUEUE table to alert the benefits people of the new employee.
is_under_25	Function	Returns a "1" if the new employee is under 25 years old as of December 31 of the year they were hired.
is_over_59	Function	Returns a "1" if the new employee is 60 years old or older as of the calendar date of hire.

TABLE 1-4. *Members of the CREATE_EMPLOYEE Package*

Progress Check ⏱

1. Oracle Database 10*g* is referred to as a *relational database.* Why is the word *relational* used?

2. What is the maximum length of a varchar2 data type that can be stored in the Oracle Database 10*g*?

3. What is data consistency when referred to as a feature of the Oracle Database 10*g*? Give an example.

4. What types of stored objects can be encapsulated into an Oracle Database 10*g* package?

5. What is the fundamental difference between a procedure and a function in the Oracle Database 10*g*?

6. Data in the system tablespace is often referred to as *metadata*—data about data. Name at least two types of metadata in the system tablespace.

7. What is the difference between the timestamp and date data types?

8. What type of information and data ends up being stored in the SYSAUX tablespace?

Progress Check Answers

1. The word *relational* is used since Oracle Database 10*g* defines the relationships between tables. It is these relationships that allow applications to navigate an assortment of tables and assemble results from more than one table.

2. The varchar2 data type can accommodate up to 4000 characters.

3. Data consistency refers to the ability to ensure that related items of information are manipulated in a similar fashion. Suppose an application assigns a department to a new employee as a two-digit number field. Sometime down the road, due to company growth, the department identifier is changed to three digits. All the data where this used-to-be two-character identifier is stored must be changed to reflect the expansion of the department codes.

4. Packages can contain a mixture of one or more functions and procedures.

5. A procedure receives from zero to many parameters as it is invoked, and goes about its business until the end of its code segment. A function, on the other hand, accepts one or more parameters as it is called and returns a value to the code from where it was invoked. The procedure passes nothing back to its caller.

6. Metadata defines items such as the names of tables in the database, who owns the tables, the data types of the columns in each table, and who is allowed to look at what data.

7. When columns are displayed, they use the date data type, containing a day/month/year component, whereas, by default, the timestamp data type columns contain a time-of-day component as well.

8. The SYSAUX tablespace contains tables required to manage the Oracle Database 10*g*, such as the items required to support OEM Grid Control.

CRITICAL SKILL 1.6

Become Familiar with Other Important Items in the Oracle Database 10*g*

So far, we have had a brief look at tables, views, tablespaces, and a handful of stored objects—views, triggers, procedures, packages, and functions. Let's round out this introduction to Oracle Database 10*g* architecture by covering a few other items commonly encountered from day one. This discussion is a hodge-podge of things that are necessary for a person's understanding of the Oracle Database 10*g* architecture and operations. We must spend a bit of time first looking at the database administrator, affectionately called the *DBA*, the gatekeeper of the database and the person responsible for its smooth operation. There is a more detailed look at the DBA in Chapter 3, with more information on how DBAs go about carrying out their administrative chores.

Indexes

Tables are made up of rows and columns, being the baseline of all objects in the Oracle Database 10*g*. As applications interact with the database, they often retrieve vast amounts of data. Suppose MyYP, a fictitious Internet company, provided Yellow Pages listings for North America, and the data was stored primarily in a table called YP_MASTER. Each row in the YP_MASTER table is uniquely identified by a combination of company name, municipality, and geographic location (state or province). As words are retrieved from the database to satisfy online queries, indexes would provide a quick access path to the qualifying data. These characteristics about indexes are relevant to the power they deliver in the Oracle Database 10*g*. For instance:

- They are built on one or more columns in a table using simple SQL statements.

- They are separate from the tables upon which they are built, and can be dropped without affecting the data in the table itself. On the contrary, when a table is dropped, any indexes it has disappear with the table.

- The function they perform can be likened to the index in a book. If one were looking for a specific topic in a textbook, the best place to start would be the index—it provides a shortcut to the information being sought. If one imagined that YP_MASTER were a book rather than a table, finding Y&M Plumbing in Pensacola, Florida would be faster using the index than reading the book from the start into the entries for the 25th letter of the alphabet. The names on the corner of the pages in a phone book are like an index.

- Indexes occupy space in the database and, even though there are ways to keep their space to a minimum, extra space is required and must be preallocated.

Users

Most of us are familiar with accounts' usernames and passwords from our experience logging into corporate networks and other secure systems. Oracle Database 10*g* implements the same mechanism with login credentials and privileges given out by the database administrator. Once accounts are created, people initiate connections to the Oracle Database 10*g* and work with their own data and other users' data where the appropriate privileges have been given out. We discuss object privileges in the "Work with Object and System Privileges" section immediately following this one.

NOTE
With Oracle Database 10g, the terminology user, account, *and* schema *are used synonymously.*

Once an account is created, it is often given the rights to occupy space in one or more Oracle Database 10*g* tablespaces. This is discussed next.

Tablespace Quotas

As additional non-**system** tablespaces are created, the database administrator gives out quotas that allow users to occupy space therein. Tablespace quotas are given out using an SQL statement with three parts:

- The username to whom the quota is being given.

- The name of the tablespace within which the username is being permitted to create tables.

- The amount of that quota—be it mentioned in absolute bytes (for example, 500,000) or more commonly in quantities of megabytes (500MB, for instance). Unlimited quotas can be allowed using the keyword *unlimited.*

Regardless of how a quota is given out, the SQL statement passed to Oracle Database 10*g* resembles the following:

```
SQL*Plus: Release 10.1.0.1.0 - Production on Sun Mar 11 10:29:42 2007
Copyright (c) 1982, 2003, Oracle.  All rights reserved.
Connected to:
Oracle10g Enterprise Edition Release 10.1.0.1.0 - Production
With the Partitioning, OLAP and Data Mining options

SQL> alter user hr quota 500m on hr_data;
User altered.
SQL> alter user ap quota unlimited on ap_idx;
User altered.
```

Synonyms

Remember in the "Work with Tables" section where we discussed creating tables that the key was passing Oracle Database 10g the *create table* keywords? In a nutshell, table creation is undertaken after establishing a successful connection to the database, and then, with appropriate privileges in place, defining a table. One of the key concepts with all database management systems is sharing data. Since it is key to only have one copy of a table and have its contents shared amongst applications, *synonyms* are a way to reference other people's data.

Suppose we wanted to use the PART_MASTER table in an application owned by a user other than the owner. That owner would permit us to work with the table's data, and then we would create a synonym to reference its contents. The code would resemble the following:

```
SQL*Plus: Release 10.1.0.1.0 - Production on Sun Mar 11 10:29:42 2007
Copyright (c) 1982, 2003, Oracle.  All rights reserved.
Connected to:
Oracle10g Enterprise Edition Release 10.1.0.1.0 - Production
With the Partitioning, OLAP and Data Mining options
SQL> create synonym part_master for inv.part_master;
Synonym created.
SQL> select count(*)
  2  from part_master
  3  where in_stock is not null;
    COUNT(*)
-------------
       13442
```

The preceding SQL statement references an object called **part_master**. The owner of the table references it using its name, and others using their synonym. There are actually two kinds of synonyms:

- *Private synonyms* are created in one account and are only usable by the creator.

- *Public synonyms* are created by a central privileged user and are available to anyone able to connect to the Oracle Database 10g.

NOTE
One needs the appropriate object privileges to be able to work with someone else's data using a private or public synonym. The synonym itself does not imply that the appropriate privileges can be circumvented.

Roles

Often it makes sense to group similar users together somehow to streamline the organization of people who use the Oracle Database 10*g*. Using roles, the DBA can logically lump personnel together and give out object privileges to roles rather than individual users. Roles can be password protected, though in most implementations they do not have this level of complexity.

Default User Environments

As accounts are created by the DBA, users are given a default environment to use unless some specifics are coded as they interact with the Oracle Database 10*g*. Users are commonly set up with the following default environment settings:

- The *default tablespace* is where tables are placed unless the *create table* statement explicitly points at a nondefault tablespace upon which the user has a quota.

- *Temporary tablespaces* are the tablespaces where users perform sort and merge operations while the Oracle Database 10*g* engine is processing queries.

Users can be given membership in one or more roles and have their default profile changed as well. As users are created, they do not automatically inherit a default tablespace; one must be manually given out during or following the user creation statement. Users do automatically point at a temporary tablespace, as discussed in the "Default Temporary Tablespace" section of this chapter, unless manually pointed elsewhere.

Progress Check

1. Name at least four tasks handled by the Oracle Database 10*g* administrator?

2. What is the difference between *public* and *private* synonyms?

3. What is meant by a user's default tablespace?

4. What two units of measurement are commonly used to specify a tablespace quota?

5. Where do DBAs go to create *i*TARs where assistance is requested from Oracle's support organization?

6. Which of the following—*procedures, packages,* and *triggers*—cannot exist independent of a table to which they belong?

CRITICAL SKILL 1.7

Work with Object and System Privileges

It's next to impossible to work with data in the Oracle Database 10*g* without looking at object privileges. In this section, we are going to look at these privileges as well as a suite of system privileges closely related to managing the Oracle Database 10*g*. The four main object privileges are **select**, **insert**, **update**, and **delete**, discussed in the next four sections. Oracle Database 10*g* uses the term *grant* when referring to giving out both object and system privileges.

Select

This is the primary and most commonly used privilege, permitting other users to view your data. There are three parts to grant statements:

1. The keywords grant select on.

2. The name of the object upon which the privileges are being given out.

3. The recipient of the grant.

Once the **select** privilege has been given out, the recipients, using a private or public synonym as described earlier in the "Synonyms" section of this chapter, can reference your objects in their SQL statements.

Insert

This privilege allows users to create rows in tables belonging to other users. The creator of new rows in other users' objects is bound by the same rules used if they owned the objects themselves. They must adhere to the boundaries defined by the data types of the columns in the rows they create. For example, when rows are inserted into a table that has a column defined as type DATE, they must ensure that valid date type data is placed in the column so defined. As rows are created in an Oracle Database 10*g* table, the transaction must be committed to the database before the row becomes part of the information available to other users. With Oracle Database 10*g*, we use the term *commit* synonymously with *save* with other types of software.

Progress Check Answers

1. Installation, upgrades, tuning, and environment setup are four of many tasks performed by the DBA.

2. A private synonym can only be referenced in an SQL statement by the account who created and owns the synonym. A public synonym, created by a centralized user such as a DBA, is available to all users.

3. The default tablespace is the one within which users occupy space by default, unless another tablespace is mentioned as a table is created.

4. Quota on tablespaces is usually given out using bytes or megabytes as units of measurement.

5. The DBA goes to MetaLink to request assistance from Oracle's support organization.

6. Triggers cannot exist on their own without association with an Oracle Database 10*g* table.

Update

This privilege allows a person to change the contents of columns in rows belonging to other tables. The SQL **update** statement can change the value of data in one or more columns. As with **insert** activity, the **update** transactions need to commit their work to make it permanent in the Oracle Database 10*g* files.

Delete

Delete operations interact with one or more rows in Oracle Database 10*g* tables and must be followed by a commit as well to write the results of the transaction to the database files.

   We will see more in Chapter 2 about how SQL statements are constructed using the four keywords in the previous sections. SQL statements are subject to rigorous syntax requirements which, if not followed, return an assortment of Oracle errors. Just as with other programming languages you may be familiar with, the SQL statement processing engine is very strict with reserved words and the placement of the pieces that come together to form an SQL transaction. Let's briefly discuss system privileges that allow certain users of the Oracle Database 10*g* to perform secure activities.

System Privileges

We have mentioned the database administrator in a number of places in this introductory chapter. Classically, secure operations are performed by the DBAs, however one can grant system privileges to specified users so they can perform selected activities themselves. The following list illustrates a few examples of these secure operations of which we speak.

- There are a number of modes within which the Oracle Database 10*g* can operate. The modes are toggled using the **alter system** command. This privilege can be given out to Jane by issuing the command **grant alter system to jane;**.

- Often, the DBA wants to partition some of the user creation activities between a handful of users of the Oracle Database 10*g*. This is done by giving out the **create user** system privilege. Once new users are created, we often want to tweak their environment, along the lines of what we spoke about in a few places around this chapter. This can be accomplished by issuing the **grant alter user** statement to one or more users of the database.

- Sometimes when new users are created, they are given the **create session** system privilege which allows them to connect to the Oracle Database 10*g*. In many cases, depending on how new users are created, they are not allowed to build any objects until they receive the **create table** system privilege. As well, many users are not capable of defining triggers until they receive the **create trigger** system privilege.

Ask the Expert

Q: Name the four main object privileges used in the Oracle Database 10g.

A: The four most common privileges are **select**, **insert**, **update**, and **delete**.

Q: Placing an Oracle Database 10g in a state where it can be accessed by applications is referred to as what activity?

A: Putting an Oracle Database 10g in a normal operating mode for day-to-day access by a company's applications is referred to as *startup*.

Q: How many integer and decimal digits can a field defined in the data dictionary as *number(10,2)* accommodate?

A: The field would be able to store up to eight integer digits and two decimal digits.

Q: When Oracle Database 10g is passed the value "Beginner   " for storage in a varchar2 column, how does it deal with trailing insignificant spaces?

A: The trailing spaces are trimmed before the information is stored in the database. Though not as common as varchar2, the char data type can be used to store trailing spaces.

Q: What would Oracle Database 10g store as a value in a number(6,2) field when passed the value 9.8882?

A: It would store 9.89 in a *number(6,2)* field when passed 9.8882.

System privileges were introduced with early releases of Oracle7 (circa 1993) and have played a useful role in the division of labor in the database since their inception. Now it's time to get into the meat of the seventh letter of the alphabet, *g,* that throughout this chapter has followed the two-digit version number of this software release—10.

CRITICAL SKILL 1.8

Introduce Yourself to the Grid

As many have heard, the "*g*" in Oracle Database 10g stands for *grid*. Grid computing is a technology that allows for seamless and massively scalable access to a distributed network of diverse yet homogenous computer types. Oracle Database 10g is the glue permitting different vendors' computers to work together providing a seemingly endless supply of shared computer resources. Oracle sees the grid as revolutionizing the way companies go about doing their business. Grid computing targets the delivery of information as a utility, similar to the way electrical and telephone services are currently delivered to the public—hence the term *grid.* The industry as a whole, but Oracle in particular, sees a delivery method from the grid such that consumers will only pay for what they use. Interlaced computers will allow idle capacity to be leveraged by the grid to provide for a form of parallel processing on steroids. The following are the major players that enable the Oracle grid technology:

- **Real Application Clusters (RAC)** Involves a suite of networked computers sharing a common Oracle Database 10*g* and running platform independent clusterware, the glue that makes the interconnect between the clustered nodes so transparent.

- **Automatic Storage Management (ASM)** A front-end management system that can group disks from an assortment of manufacturers together to form a suite of disks that is available to all computers on the grid. ASM encapsulates the complete life cycle of disk management and allocation into a centralized GUI interface.

- **Oracle Resource Manager** Provides a framework within which administrators can control the computing resources of nodes on the grid.

- **Oracle Scheduler** Allows the handing out of jobs to members of the grid to facilitate the execution of business tasks anywhere and everywhere where idle resources exist.

- **Oracle Streams** Assists the processing requirements where copies of data need to be streamed between nodes in the grid and provide the mechanisms to keep data in sync on one database with the database from which the data originated. Oracle Stream's tight integration with the Oracle Database 10*g* engine facilitates this synchronization and delivers a preferred method of replication.

Figure 1-3 illustrates the primary differences between grid computing and traditional approaches to providing computer services.

The following points reinforce the details of the two scenarios depicted in Figure 1-3:

- The three applications at the top each have a dedicated server, each with their own dedicated disk. If the Linux server were to go out of service, the pension application would grind to a halt. There is no built-in mechanism for pension system processing to carry on another server.

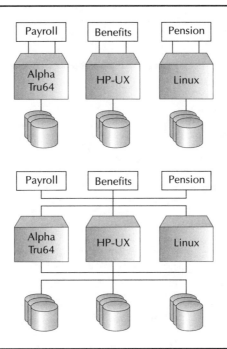

FIGURE 1-3. *Differences between traditional and grid computing*

■ The three applications at the bottom are interlaced with one another. The benefits application can be hosted on from one to three of the available servers. As well, the database files that support these three applications can reside upon, and be read from, any of the nine disks in the grid's disk farm.

The browser-based OEM Grid Control holds the whole thing together. With the implementation of the ASM component of Oracle Database 10g, disks are managed by OEM, database instances are managed by OEM, clusterware is managed through OEM, and the list is endless. Figure 1-4 shows the first OEM screen that appears after entering appropriate login credentials.

NOTE
There is an OEM configuration program (called emca) that must be successfully run before you can access the browser-based OEM. The screen shown in your version of Oracle Database 10g may be somewhat different than that shown in Figure 1-4. The look and feel of the OEM Grid Control screens can change significantly between minor releases of the software.

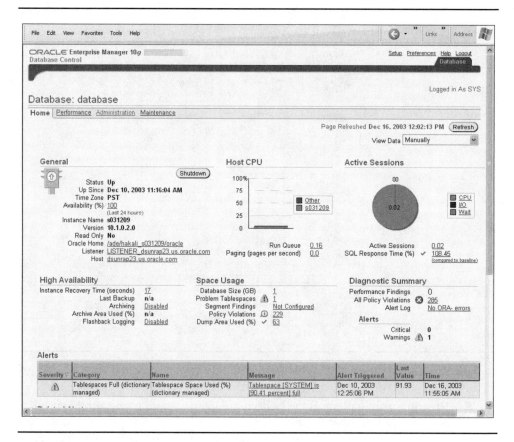

FIGURE 1-4. *OEM Startup*

Tie It All Together

Now that was quite a journey! We have covered database fundamentals, with an Oracle Database 10*g* flavor. Relational database management systems have been around for a few decades, and the release of Oracle Database 10*g* is a landmark in the industry. There have been many academic discussions about the grid technology— some claim Oracle Database 10*g* is a grid implementation, some don't. Regardless of which side of the fence you're on, Oracle Database 10*g* is a big step. Let's pull it all together and spend a bit of time on the big picture.

Oracle Database 10*g* is a collection of special files created using its database configuration assistant, then completing the work using OEM Grid Control. Access to these database files is facilitated by a set of shared memory processes referred to as an *instance*. Many technicians use this term synonymously with *database*. There is nothing wrong with that since, even though they are technically different pieces, they cannot survive without each other.

Relationships between objects in the database are defined in the data dictionary—hence the familiar term *relational database*. It is these relationships that provide the power and allow Oracle Database 10*g* to store vast amounts of data. Storing that data is one thing—retrieving it for applications in a quick and complete fashion is another story. Data retrieval is one of the strengths of the Oracle Database 10*g* engine.

Over the next eight chapters, we will be delving into more details of the Oracle Database 10*g* offering, paying specific attention to the following:

- **SQL—Structured Query Language**   This is the way we communicate with the Oracle Database 10*g*. Whatever the programming language (from COBOL to Java), SQL is all the database engine understands.

- **The Database Administrator**   The person who is the gatekeeper of the Oracle Database 10*g* and the one responsible for its smooth operation and optimal performance.

- **Networking**   The glue that holds many systems together and allows computers to communicate with one another in widely diverse and separated locations.

- **Backup and Recovery**   Two areas intimate to the smooth operation of the Oracle Database 10*g*. Oracle Database 10*g*'s Recovery Manager (referred to as *RMAN*) is the fundamental building block in its disaster recovery implementation.

- **PL/SQL**   A programming language native to the Oracle Database 10*g* engine, providing more procedural capabilities that amplify and enhance the functionality of SQL.

- **Java**   An increasingly popular development environment which, according to the likes of Sun Microsystems, powers the Internet. Many of the "sexy" features you enjoy on the Internet are courtesy of this.

- **XML**   Extensible Markup Language (XML) which offers a flexible way to format text. The Oracle Database 10*g* stores XML objects in their native format. XML has become an industry standard; very popular when exchanging information on the Internet and other electronic information exchange media.

- **Large Database Features**   Oracle Database 10*g* expands on an already solid offering in this area. With Oracle9*i*, they boasted the ability to support a database of up to 500 petabytes. Oracle Database 10*g* expands that upper limit to many exabytes, a staggering number, to say the least—where an exabyte is 1,152,921,504,606,846,976 bytes—or about one trillion million!

☑ Chapter 1 Mastery Check

1. The _____ background process is primarily responsible for writing information to the Oracle Database 10*g* files.

2. How many online redo log groups are required to start an Oracle Database 10*g*?

   A. 3

   B. 2

   C. 4

   D. 1

3. Of the following four items of information, which one is not stored in Oracle Database 10*g*'s control files?

   A. The name of the database files

   B. The creator of the database

   C. The location of the database files

   D. The sizes of the database files

4. What is the function of a default temporary tablespace in the support of the Oracle Database 10*g*?

5. Differentiate between an Oracle Database 10*g* and instance.

6. Activities such as allocating space in the database and user management are commonly performed by the DBA. What feature in the Oracle Database 10*g* allows some of these secure operations to be carried out by non-DBA users? How are these rights given out?

7. As a user of the Oracle Database 10*g* is created, we often specify a default tablespace. In this context, *default tablespace* means?

   A. The **system** tablespace

   B. A tablespace the user can occupy space in without a private or public synonym

   C. The tablespace within which objects are created if a location (tablespace) is not explicitly mentioned as a table is created

8. The _____ GUI interface is used to create a new database.

9. What happens when one tries to store the text "Madagascar" in a field with a specification of varchar2(8)?

10. What is the most common way one uses triggers in the Oracle Database 10*g*? Give an example of this activity.

11. What programming language, native to the Oracle Database 10*g*, is used to create stored objects such as triggers and functions?

    A. SQL*Plus

    B. OEM Grid Control

    C. Basic

    D. PL/SQL

12. What is the role of the **sysaux** tablespace in the Oracle Database 10*g*?

13. The clob and blob data types differ in all but one of the following three ways. Which one does not apply to the differences between the two data types?

    A. The clob holds standard alphanumeric data, whereas the blob may store binary information.

    B. The blob contains a time (hour/minute) component, but the clob does not.

    C. The blob contains unstructured free-form data, whereas the rules governing the type of information that can be stored in the clob are more stringent.

14. There are many ways to replicate data from one node to another. What main feature does Oracle Streams provide that is missing from many other methods?

15. What does the acronym SQL stand for?

    A. Structured Query Language

    B. Simple Query Language

    C. Straightforward Question-based Learning

CHAPTER 2

SQL: Structured Query Language

CRITICAL SKILLS

2.1 Learn the SQL Statement Components

2.2 Use Basic insert and select Statements

2.3 Use Simple where Clauses

2.4 Use Basic update and delete Statements

2.5 Order Data

2.6 Employ Functions: String, Numeric, Aggregate (No Grouping)

2.7 Use Dates and Data Functions (Formatting and Chronological)

2.8 Employ Joins (ANSI vs. Oracle): Inner, Outer, Self

2.9 Learn the group by and having Clauses

2.10 Learn Subqueries: Simple and Correlated Comparison with Joins

2.11 Use Set Operators: Union, Intersect, Minus

2.12 Use Views

2.13 Learn Sequences: Just Simple Stuff

2.14 Employ Constraints: Linkage to Entity Models, Types, Deferred, Enforced, Gathering Exceptions

2.15 Format Your Output with SQL*Plus

QL is the fundamental access tool of the Oracle database; in fact, it is the fundamental access tool of all relational databases. SQL is used to build database objects and it is also used to query and manipulate both these objects and the data they may contain. You cannot insert a row of data into an Oracle database unless you have first issued some basic SQL statements to create the underlying tables. While Oracle provides SQL*Plus, a SQL tool that enables you to interact with the database, there are also many GUI tools that can be used, which then issue SQL statements on your behalf behind the scenes.

CRITICAL SKILL 2.1

Learn the SQL Statement Components

Before learning many of the SQL commands that you will use frequently, first let's take a look at the two different categories into which SQL statements are classified. They are DDL, or *data definition language*, and DML, or *data manipulation language*. The majority of this chapter will deal with the latter.

DDL

DDL is the set of SQL statements that define or delete database objects such as tables or views. For the purposes of this chapter, we will concentrate on dealing with tables. Examples of DDL are any SQL statements that begin with **create**, **alter**, **drop**, and **grant**. Table 2-1 is a sample list of some DDL statements. It does not completely represent the many varied statements that all have a unique purpose and value.

SQL Command	Purpose
create table	Creates a table
create index	Creates an index
alter table	Adds a column, redefines an existing column, changes storage allocation
drop table	Drops a table
grant	Grants privileges or roles to a user or another role
truncate	Removes all rows from a table
revoke	Removes privileges from a user or a role
analyze	Gathers performance statistics on database objects for use by the cost-based optimizer

TABLE 2-1. *Common Formats of Date Type Data*

The following SQL statements are examples of DDL **create** and **drop** statements in action:

```
SQL> create table b
  2  (colb char(1));

SQL> drop table b;
Table dropped.

SQL> create table state
  2    (state_cd   char(2) not null,
  3     state_name varchar2(30));
Table created.
```

After you have created your table, you should confirm that it was created as you expected. To display a description of a table, the **describe** command is used. Experience suggests that you will find it very useful to be able to describe tables within the database after you create or any time you need to know the exact nature of the table. Let's take a closer look at the state table that we created in the previous example:

```
SQL> desc state;

Name                                      Null?    Type
----------------------------------------- -------- --------------------
STATE_CD                                  NOT NULL CHAR(2)
STATE_NAME                                         VARCHAR2(30)
```

DML

DML is any SQL statement that begins with **select**, **insert**, **update**, or **delete**. The remainder of this chapter will deal primarily with DML. Every DML SQL statement consists of a few basic components. The following three items form the basic foundation of most DML statements:

- Each DML statement begins with either a **select**, **insert**, **update** or **delete** command:

    - **select** is used when you want to retrieve data from an Oracle database. It is the most common SQL statement you will see.

    - **insert** is used when you want to add rows into an Oracle table.

    - **update** commands are used to change one or more records in a table.

    - **delete** commands are issued when you want to remove one or more records from a table.

■ All DML commands require reference to an object that will be manipulated. More often than not, the object being referenced is a table.

■ A conditional statement can be added to any **select**, **update**, or **delete** command. Absence of a conditional statement means that the command will be performed against every record in the object. A conditional statement is used when the DML command is intended to only act upon a group of records that meet a specific condition. The **where** clause will be discussed a little later in this chapter.

More optional DML statements will be described later in this chapter. For now, let's concentrate on understanding the fundamental structure of each DML statement starting with the **insert** and **select** statements.

CRITICAL SKILL 2.2

Use Basic insert and select Statements

Getting data into and out of a database are two of the most important features of a database. Oracle provides two basic features that help you do just that. To get data into the database, use the **insert** command; to get it back out, use the **select** command. You must master these commands, as they form the basic of most data access to your Oracle database. This section talks first about how to get data into your database, and then how to get data out.

insert

Using the state table created in the DDL example, the following is an illustration of using the **insert** statement in its simplest form:

```
SQL> insert into state values ('AZ','Arizona');
1 row created.
```

Each time you execute an **insert** command, you receive the message "1 row created." Thus, you get immediate feedback that you are populating the given table with data. When you load data into a table, you may also specify the column to load it into. This ensures that there is no mistaking where you want the data to be placed. In the next example, the columns are specified after the **insert** command:

```
SQL> insert into state (state_cd, state_name) values ('NJ','New Jersey');
1 row created.

SQL> insert into state (state_cd, state_name) values ('CA','California');
1 row created.

SQL> insert into state (state_cd, state_name) values ('TX','Texas');
```

```
1 row created.

SQL> insert into state (state_cd, state_name) values ('FL','Florida');
1 row created.

SQL> insert into state (state_cd, state_name) values ('MN','Maine');
1 row created.
```

select

As mentioned earlier, the **select** statement is used to retrieve data from the database. This is the commonest SQL statement you will use. The five basic parts of the SQL statement are as follows:

- First is the keyword **select** followed by what you want to retrieve from the database. The names of the columns to be retrieved are listed here. The **select** command is mandatory.

- The word **from** is the next part of the SQL statement. Reference to the object that the data is being retrieved from is made here. This is usually a table name. The **from** command is mandatory.

- As mentioned before, a conditional statement is optional for select statements. The word **where** followed by the conditions would be the next part of the SQL statement. See Critical Skill 2.3 for more details on the **where** clause.

- A **group by** statement is another optional component of the **select** statement. This topic will be covered in more detail in Critical Skill 2.8 once we have had the opportunity to discuss functions.

- The final component of a **select** statement is the **order by** statement. This will also be discussed in more detail later on in this chapter. This is an optional component, which will sort the results of the query before they are presented back to you.

Let's issue our first select statement against the state table we just populated in the **insert** command examples:

```
SQL> select *
  2  from    state;

ST STATE_NAME
-- -----------------------------
AZ Arizona
NJ New Jersey
CA California
TX Texas
```

```
FL Florida
MN Maine

6 rows selected.
```

Notice the use of the asterisk in the **select** statement. The asterisk means "retrieve data from all the columns" of a given table.

Rather than using the asterisk as we did in the previous example, we can specify one or more columns after the **select** command in a comma-separated list. Let's rewrite the previous query and only select the **state_name** column:

```
SQL> select state_name
  2  from    state;

STATE_NAME
------------------------------
Arizona
New Jersey
California
Texas
Florida
Maine

6 rows selected.
```

The semicolons in the two SQL examples force the immediate execution of the SQL statement within SQL*Plus. There are two ways in SQL*Plus to signify you have finished and that the SQL statement can be executed:

- The semicolon at the end of a line
- The slash on a separate line

Until SQL*Plus encounters either of these characters, it assumes you need an additional line. The following example highlights this point. Notice the use of the slash and semicolon.

```
SQL> select *
  2  from    a;

SQL> select *
  2  from    a
  3  /
```

The absence of the semicolon in the second example resulted in a new line. In these cases, the semicolon and slash on a separate line would force the execution of the statement.

CRITICAL SKILL 2.3

Use Simple where Clauses

Up to now, you have seen how the **select** command can be used to retrieve records from a table. However, our basic examples have all retrieved every record from the table. If you want to see only certain rows, you must add a **where** clause.

Since our previous examples returned every record in the table, we created a simple table with a few rows in it for illustration purposes. Had we chosen to illustrate the **select** command against the large sample tables provided by Oracle, we would have returned thousands of rows—far too many for listing in this chapter. Now that we are introducing the **where** clause, we will be able to control the output. As a result, the remaining examples in this chapter will now use the customers, products, sales, and costs tables that are part of the Oracle sample database. Let's describe each of these tables.

```
SQL> desc customers;
 Name                                      Null?     Type
 ----------------------------------------- --------  -------------------
 CUST_ID                                   NOT NULL  NUMBER
 CUST_FIRST_NAME                           NOT NULL  VARCHAR2(20)
 CUST_LAST_NAME                            NOT NULL  VARCHAR2(40)
 CUST_GENDER                               NOT NULL  CHAR(1)
 CUST_YEAR_OF_BIRTH                        NOT NULL  NUMBER(4)
 CUST_MARITAL_STATUS                                 VARCHAR2(20)
 CUST_STREET_ADDRESS                       NOT NULL  VARCHAR2(40)
 CUST_POSTAL_CODE                          NOT NULL  VARCHAR2(10)
 CUST_CITY                                 NOT NULL  VARCHAR2(30)
 CUST_CITY_ID                              NOT NULL  NUMBER
 CUST_STATE_PROVINCE                       NOT NULL  VARCHAR2(40)
 CUST_STATE_PROVINCE_ID                    NOT NULL  NUMBER
 COUNTRY_ID                                NOT NULL  NUMBER
 CUST_MAIN_PHONE_NUMBER                    NOT NULL  VARCHAR2(25)
 CUST_INCOME_LEVEL                                   VARCHAR2(30)
 CUST_CREDIT_LIMIT                                   NUMBER
 CUST_EMAIL                                          VARCHAR2(30)
 CUST_TOTAL                                NOT NULL  VARCHAR2(14)
 CUST_TOTAL_ID                             NOT NULL  NUMBER
 CUST_SRC_ID                                         NUMBER
 CUST_EFF_FROM                                       DATE
 CUST_EFF_TO                                         DATE
 CUST_VALID                                          VARCHAR2(1)

SQL> desc products;
 Name                                      Null?     Type
 ----------------------------------------- --------  -------------------
 PROD_ID                                   NOT NULL  NUMBER(6)
 PROD_NAME                                 NOT NULL  VARCHAR2(50)
```

```
    PROD_DESC                                NOT NULL VARCHAR2(4000)
    PROD_SUBCATEGORY                         NOT NULL VARCHAR2(50)
    PROD_SUBCATEGORY_ID                      NOT NULL NUMBER
    PROD_SUBCATEGORY_DESC                    NOT NULL VARCHAR2(2000)
    PROD_CATEGORY                            NOT NULL VARCHAR2(50)
    PROD_CATEGORY_ID                         NOT NULL NUMBER
    PROD_CATEGORY_DESC                       NOT NULL VARCHAR2(2000)
    PROD_WEIGHT_CLASS                        NOT NULL NUMBER(3)
    PROD_UNIT_OF_MEASURE                              VARCHAR2(20)
    PROD_PACK_SIZE                           NOT NULL VARCHAR2(30)
    SUPPLIER_ID                              NOT NULL NUMBER(6)
    PROD_STATUS                              NOT NULL VARCHAR2(20)
    PROD_LIST_PRICE                          NOT NULL NUMBER(8,2)
    PROD_MIN_PRICE                           NOT NULL NUMBER(8,2)
    PROD_TOTAL                               NOT NULL VARCHAR2(13)
    PROD_TOTAL_ID                            NOT NULL NUMBER
    PROD_SRC_ID                                       NUMBER
    PROD_EFF_FROM                                     DATE
    PROD_EFF_TO                                       DATE
    PROD_VALID                                        VARCHAR2(1)

SQL> desc sales;
 Name                                      Null?    Type
 ----------------------------------------- -------- --------------------
    PROD_ID                                NOT NULL NUMBER
    CUST_ID                                NOT NULL NUMBER
    TIME_ID                                NOT NULL DATE
    CHANNEL_ID                             NOT NULL NUMBER
    PROMO_ID                               NOT NULL NUMBER
    QUANTITY_SOLD                          NOT NULL NUMBER(10,2)
    AMOUNT_SOLD                            NOT NULL NUMBER(10,2)

SQL> desc costs;
 Name                                      Null?    Type
 ----------------------------------------- -------- --------------------
    PROD_ID                                NOT NULL NUMBER
    TIME_ID                                NOT NULL DATE
    PROMO_ID                               NOT NULL NUMBER
    CHANNEL_ID                             NOT NULL NUMBER
    UNIT_COST                              NOT NULL NUMBER(10,2)
    UNIT_PRICE                             NOT NULL NUMBER(10,2)

SQL> desc promotions
 Name                                      Null?    Type
 ----------------------------------------- -------- --------------------
    PROMO_ID                               NOT NULL NUMBER(6)
    PROMO_NAME                             NOT NULL VARCHAR2(30)
    PROMO_SUBCATEGORY                      NOT NULL VARCHAR2(30)
    PROMO_SUBCATEGORY_ID                   NOT NULL NUMBER
    PROMO_CATEGORY                         NOT NULL VARCHAR2(30)
```

```
    PROMO_CATEGORY_ID                           NOT NULL NUMBER
    PROMO_COST                                  NOT NULL NUMBER(10,2)
    PROMO_BEGIN_DATE                            NOT NULL DATE
    PROMO_END_DATE                              NOT NULL DATE
    PROMO_TOTAL                                 NOT NULL VARCHAR2(15)
    PROMO_TOTAL_ID                              NOT NULL NUMBER
```

The PRODUCTS table contains more than 70 products for sale. The following **select** statement will retrieve only one record for product ID **(prod_id) 117**.

```
SQL> select prod_id, prod_name, prod_category, prod_list_price
  2  from    products
  3  where   prod_id = 117;

    PROD_ID PROD_NAME
---------- --------------------------------------------------
PROD_CATEGORY                                        PROD_LIST_PRICE
-------------------------------------------------- ---------------
        117 CD-R, Professional Grade, Pack of 10
Software/Other                                             8.99
  (2)A where Clause with and/or
```

A **where** clause instructs Oracle to search the data in a table and return only those rows that meet your criteria. In the preceding example, we searched the products table for one specific record with a product ID equal to 117. This was accomplished with **where prod_id = 117;**.

You will often be interested in retrieving rows that meet multiple criteria—for example, if you want to retrieve a list of customers from Utah who have a credit limit greater than $10,000. The SQL statement and results would produce the following output:

```
SQL> select cust_id, cust_state_province, cust_credit_limit
  2  from    customers
  3  where   cust_state_province = 'UT'
  4  and     cust_credit_limit > 10000;

    CUST_ID CUST_STATE_PROVINCE                       CUST_CREDIT_LIMIT
---------- ------------------------------------------ -----------------
      50601 UT                                                    11000
      24830 UT                                                    15000
      28983 UT                                                    15000
     100267 UT                                                    11000
     100207 UT                                                    11000
     103007 UT                                                    15000

6 rows selected.
```

In the previous example, we retrieved records that met all the criteria. You may be interested in retrieving records that meet one criteria or another. For example, if you wanted to find all the product IDs in the products table that are either in the Hardware product category or have a weight class of 4, you would generate the following SQL statement and output:

```
SQL> select prod_id, prod_category, prod_weight_class
  2  from    products
  3  where   prod_category = 'Hardware'
  4  or      prod_weight_class = 4;

   PROD_ID PROD_CATEGORY
PROD_WEIGHT_CLASS
---------- -------------------------------------------------- ---------
        15 Hardware
1
        18 Hardware
1
       139 Electronics
4
```

The **and** and **or** are known as logical operators. They are used to tell the query how the multiple criteria affect each other. Compound conditions connected by the **and** keyword all have to evaluate to true for records to be retrieved. Records are returned by compound conditions connected by the **or** keyword when either one of the conditions are true.

The where Clause with NOT

The ability also exists within Oracle to retrieve records with negative criteria. The "not equals" operator is **!=**. For example, you might want to see all the products that are not in weight class 1. The following query and its output illustrate this example:

```
SQL> select prod_id, prod_category, prod_weight_class
  2  from    products
  3  where   prod_weight_class != 1;

   PROD_ID PROD_CATEGORY
PROD_WEIGHT_CLASS
---------- -------------------------------------------------- ---------
       139 Electronics
4
```

The where Clause with a Range Search

Oracle also supports range searches so you can query for records that are between two values. If you want to find all male customers in Connecticut who were born between 1936 and 1939, you would write a query with three conditions joined by

Ask the Expert

Q: Why is *hardware* in quotes in the sample statement?

A: When a character column is used in a **where** clause, it is necessary to use the single quotes around the value to be compared.

the **and** keyword (all three need to evaluate to true) and one of the conditions would use the range search **between** keyword. The following example illustrates the query and resulting output:

```
SQL> select cust_id, cust_gender, cust_year_of_birth
  2  from   customers
  3  where  cust_state_province = 'CT'
  4  and    cust_gender = 'M'
  5  and    cust_year_of_birth between 1936 and 1939;

  CUST_ID C CUST_YEAR_OF_BIRTH
---------- - ------------------
    20058 M               1937
    17139 M               1936
     1218 M               1938
     3985 M               1939
```

The where Clause with a Search List

Oracle also supports searching for records that meet criteria within a list. If you wanted to find all customers in Utah and Connecticut with a credit limit of $15,000, this can be done with a search list. The following query represents a search list condition:

```
SQL> select cust_id, cust_state_province, cust_credit_limit
  2  from   customers
  3  where  cust_credit_limit = 15000
  4  and    cust_state_province in ('UT','CT');

  CUST_ID CUST_STATE_PROVINCE                    CUST_CREDIT_LIMIT
---------- ------------------------------------- -----------------
    24830 UT                                                15000
    28983 UT                                                15000
```

```
101798 CT                                                15000
103171 CT                                                15000
102579 CT                                                15000
102238 CT                                                15000
101515 CT                                                15000
103007 UT                                                15000
104381 CT                                                15000
```

```
9 rows selected.
```

The where Clause with a Pattern Search

The **like** command exists within Oracle to search for records that match a pattern. The wildcard operator for pattern searches is the % sign. To search for all customers whose last name begins with the letter Q, the following query would produce these results:

```
SQL> select cust_last_name, cust_credit_limit
  2  from   customers
  3  where  cust_last_name like 'Q%';

CUST_LAST_NAME                          CUST_CREDIT_LIMIT
--------------------------------------- -----------------
Quinlan                                              9000
Quinn                                              11000
```

You could also ask Oracle to retrieve customers whose last names contain "inl" by using the wildcard at the beginning and end of the pattern search. The query and output would resemble the following:

```
SQL> select cust_last_name
  2  from   customers
  3  where  cust_last_name like '%inl%';

CUST_LAST_NAME
---------------------------------------
Quinlan
```

The where Clause: Common Operators

As you can see from the preceding examples, Oracle has a very powerful set of operators when it comes to restricting the rows retrieved. Table 2-2 is a partial list of operators you can use in the **where** clause.

Ask the Expert

Q: Are character searches case-sensitive?

A: Yes. Character columns can contain upper- or lowercase alphas. If we searched the CUSTOMERS table for all instances of "INL" in the last names, we would not have retrieved any records.

Q: The percent (%) sign appears to be a multicharacter wildcard. Is there a single character wildcard available for pattern searches?

A: Yes. The underscore (_) symbol serves as the single character wildcard.

Operator	Purpose	Example
=	Tests for equality.	select * from customers where cust_state_province = 'UT';
!=	Tests for inequality.	select * from customers where cust_state_province != 'UT';
^=	Same as !=.	select * from customers where cust_state_province ^= 'UT';
<>	Same as !=.	select * from customers where cust_state_province <> 'UT';
<	Less than.	select * from sales where amount_sold < 100;
>	Greater than.	
<=	Less than or equal to.	select * from sales where amount_sold <= 500;
>=	Greater than or equal to.	select * from sales where amount_sold >= 600;
In	Equal to any member in parentheses.	select * from customers where cust_state_province is in ('UT','CA','TX');
not in	Not equal to any member in parentheses.	select * from customers where cust_state_province is not in ('UT','CA','TX');

TABLE 2-2. *Common Comparison Operators*

Operator	Purpose	Example
between A and B	Greater than or equal to A and less than or equal to B.	select * from sales where amount_sold is between 100 and 500;
not between A and B	Not greater than or equal to A, and not less than or equal to B.	select * from sales where amount_sold is not between 100 and 500;
like '%tin%'	Contains given text (for example, 'tin').	select * from customer where cust_last_name is like '%tin%';

TABLE 2-2. *Common Comparison Operators* (continued)

CRITICAL SKILL 2.4

Use Basic update and delete Statements

While **select** will likely be the command you use the most; you'll use the **update** and **delete** commands regularly, too. As you will in Chapter 6, your programs will have a mixture of DML statements. In this section, we'll take a closer look at the **update** and **delete** commands.

update

It is often necessary to change data stored within a table. This is done using the **update** command. There are three parts to this command:

1. The word **update** followed by the table to which you want to apply the change. This part is mandatory.

2. The word **set** followed by one or more columns in which you want to change the values. This part is also mandatory.

3. A **where** clause followed by selection criteria. This is optional.

Let's imagine that one of our customers has requested an increase in their credit limit and our accounting department has approved it. An update statement will have to be executed to alter the credit limit. For illustration purposes, a customer record will be displayed before and after the update. The following example illustrates a simple update for one customer:

```
SQL> select cust_id, cust_credit_limit
  2  from   customers
```

```
 3  where  cust_id = 28983;

  CUST_ID CUST_CREDIT_LIMIT
---------- ----------------
    28983            15000

SQL> update customers
  2  set    cust_credit_limit = 20000
  3  where  cust_id = 28983;

1 row updated.

SQL> select cust_id, cust_credit_limit
  2  from    customers
  3  where cust_id = 28983;

  CUST_ID CUST_CREDIT_LIMIT
---------- ----------------
    28983            20000
```

This example reveals that customer 28983 had a $15,000 credit limit before the **update** statement was executed. The **update** statement is written against the CUSTOMERS table with a **set** clause issued against the column to be changed, cust_credit_limit, and a **where** clause to make the change only for customer 28983. After the command is executed, a **select** statement reveals that the customer now has a credit limit of $20,000. The **update** statement is a very powerful tool. It can be used against one record, multiple records meeting simple or complex criteria, or all records in a table.

Ask the Expert

Q: Can you use a where **clause with every type of DML statement?**

A: The **where** clause can be used only with **select**, **update**, and **delete** statements. The **insert** statement can never have a **where** clause.

Q: You mentioned that a where **clause is optional for** update **statements. What would happen if one isn't used during an update?**

A: If a **where** clause isn't used with an **update** statement, every record in the table will be updated.

delete

Use the **delete** statement when you want to remove one or more rows of data from a table. The command has two parts:

1. The keywords **delete from** followed by the table name you want to remove records from. This is mandatory.

2. A **where** clause followed by the record selection criteria. This is optional. As with the update, absence of a **where** clause will remove every record from the table.

   If you want to remove all the customers from the CUSTOMERS table, you would issue the SQL statement **delete from customer;**. As you become more familiar with Oracle, you will learn that the **trunc** command will also remove every record but this doesn't allow you to **rollback** the changes if you make a mistake. It's very easy to accidentally drop all the records in a table. As with the **update** statement, be very careful when issuing the **delete** or **truncate** commands.

   Let us now illustrate a deletion of all customers in the province of Delhi. The code listing will first show a count of customers in Delhi, introducing **count(*)** for the first time. This is being used to illustrate the number of records we expect to delete when we issue the command. The second SQL statement issues the **delete from** command, which confirms the number of records deleted. The final SQL statement is a repeat of the first one to illustrate that there are no records remaining for the province of Delhi. In order to continue to use these records for later examples, I will **rollback** the changes so they never get permanently committed to the database and re-run the first SQL statement one more time to confirm that the records have been restored.

```
SQL> select count(*)
  2  from    customers
  3  where   cust_state_province = 'Delhi';

COUNT(*)
----------
        34

SQL> delete from customers
  2  where cust_state_province = 'Delhi';

34 rows deleted.

SQL> select count(*)
  2  from    customers
  3  where   cust_state_province = 'Delhi';

COUNT(*)
```

```
         ----------
                  0

SQL> rollback;

Rollback complete.

SQL> select count(*)
  2  from    customers
  3  where   cust_state_province = 'Delhi';

  COUNT(*)
----------
        34
```

Progress Check

1. Of the following four items, which one is not a DML keyword?

   A. select

   B. insert

   C. create

   D. update

2. How can the defined columns of the CUSTOMERS table be displayed?

3. In order to retrieve data from the database, there are two keywords that are mandatory. Name them.

4. Write a SQL statement to select the customer last name and city for all customers in Utah with a credit limit less than 5000.

Progress Check Answers

1. C. The four DML keywords are **select**, **insert**, **update**, and **delete**.

2. The following code listing displays the defined columns for the CUSTOMERS table:
```
desc customers;
```

3. Every SQL statement that retrieves data from the database will have both the **select** and **from** keywords.

4. The following SQL statement is a correct answer:
```
SQL> select cust_last_name, cust_city
  2  from    customers
  3  where   cust_state_province = 'UT'
  4  and     cust_credit_limit < 5000;
```

Order Data

So far, all of our **select** queries have returned records in random order. Earlier, we selected records from the customer table where the customer was located in either Connecticut or Utah and had a credit limit of $15,000. The results came back in no apparent order. It is often desirable to order the result set on one or more of the selected columns. In this case, it probably would have been easier to interpret the results if they were sorted by state, and within that state were then sorted by customer ID. Let's take a look at the query syntax and resulting output:

```
SQL> select cust_id, cust_state_province, cust_credit_limit
  2  from    customers
  3  where   cust_credit_limit = 15000
  4  and     cust_state_province in ('UT','CT')
  5  order by cust_state_province, cust_id;

    CUST_ID CUST_STATE_PROVINCE                       CUST_CREDIT_LIMIT
 ---------- ------------------------------------- ------------------
     101515 CT                                                15000
     101798 CT                                                15000
     102238 CT                                                15000
     102579 CT                                                15000
     103171 CT                                                15000
     104381 CT                                                15000
      24830 UT                                                15000
     103007 UT                                                15000

8 rows selected.
```

Any column specified in the **order by** statement could either be sorted in ascending or descending order. By default, Oracle will sort each column in ascending order. In order to sort a column in descending order, the use of **desc** following the **order by** column will accomplish this. Let's look at the previous example one more time with the customer IDs sorted in descending order:

```
SQL> select cust_id, cust_state_province, cust_credit_limit
  2  from    customers
  3  where   cust_credit_limit = 15000
  4  and     cust_state_province in ('UT','CT')
  5  order by cust_state_province, cust_id desc;

    CUST_ID CUST_STATE_PROVINCE                       CUST_CREDIT_LIMIT
 ---------- ------------------------------------- ------------------
     104381 CT                                                15000
     103171 CT                                                15000
     102579 CT                                                15000
```

```
        102238 CT                                          15000
        101798 CT                                          15000
        101515 CT                                          15000
        103007 UT                                          15000
         24830 UT                                          15000

   8 rows selected.
```

CRITICAL SKILL **2.6**

Employ Functions: String, Numeric, Aggregate (No Grouping)

Up to now, we have illustrated a number of fairly simplistic DML statements. We've selected some records from different tables using criteria, we've updated existing rows, and we've even inserted and deleted some records.

Oracle provides us with many functions that allow us to analyze and aggregate the data, returning results that differ greatly from the result sets we've seen so far. A function manipulates the contents of a column in a SQL statement. We can find what the largest credit limit is in the CUSTOMERS table, we can round numbers or pad results with characters. In fact, when we ran a count of customers that were in the province of 'Delhi' before and after deleting these records, we took a sneak peek ahead at functions.

This section will introduce you to three different types of functions: string (or character), numeric, and aggregate.

String Functions

String functions, also known as character functions, can be categorized in two types: those that return character values and those that return numeric values.

Table 2-3 represents the most common functions you will perform with the character data type. It is only a partial list. The examples that follow all use the "dual" table. The "dual" table is an internal Oracle table and is useful in SQL and PL/SQL to perform functions that return a single row. It can be used to return the current system date and time, to perform arithmetic functions or to obtain a generated sequential number (more on this later in the chapter).

Function	Action	Example	Displays
lower(*char*)	Converts the entire string to lowercase.	select lower('DAliA') from dual;	dalia
replace(*char,str1,str2*)	Replaces every occurrence of *str1* in *char* with *str2*.	select replace('Scott', 'S', 'Boy') from dual;	Boycott

TABLE 2-3. *Common String Functions*

Function	Action	Example	Displays
substr(*char,m,n*)	Extracts the characters from *char* starting in position *m* for *n* characters.	select substr('ABCDEF',4,2) from dual;	DE
length(*char*)	Returns the length of *char*.	select length('Marissa') from dual;	7
rpad(*expr1,n,expr2*)	Pads *expr1* with *expr2* to the right for *n* characters. Often used for space padding in the creation of a fixed length record.	select rpad('Amanda', 10, '1') from dual;	Amanda1111
initcap(*char*)	Changes the first character of each element in *char* to uppercase.	select initcap('shane k.') from dual;	Shane K.

TABLE 2-3. *Common String Functions* (continued)

Numeric Functions

Table 2-4 illustrates some common numeric functions, their syntax, and the results they produce. These are only a few of the many functions available.

Function	Action	Example	Displays
ceil(*n*)	Returns nearest whole number greater than or equal to *n*.	select ceil(12.3) from dual;	13
floor(*n*)	Returns nearest whole number less than or equal to *n*.	select floor(127.6) from dual;	127
round(*n,m*)	Rounds *n* to *m* places to the right of the decimal point.	select round(579.34886,3) from dual;	579.349
power(*m,n*)	Multiplies *m* to the power *n*.	select power(5,3) from dual;	125
mod(*m,n*)	Returns the remainder of the division of *m* by *n*. If *n*=0, then 0 is returned. If *n>m*, then *m* is returned.	select mod(9,5) from dual; select mod(10,5) from dual; select mod(6,7) from dual;	4 0 6
sqrt(*n*)	Returns the square root of *n*.	select sqrt(9) from dual;	3

TABLE 2-4. *Common Numeric Functions*

Aggregate Functions

Unlike the character or numeric functions, which act on a single row, aggregate functions act on an entire column of data. Aggregate functions save the developer from having to write a lot of code to determine the maximum column value in a set of records or an average, for example. A single result row is returned by aggregate functions based on the group of rows. Table 2-5 illustrates the more commonly used aggregate functions but is only a partial list. As simple as these are, we're sure you'll agree that they are indeed quite powerful.

Function	Action	Example	Displays
count(*expr*)	Returns a count of non-null column values for each row retrieved.	select count(cust_id) from customers where cust_state_ province = 'NY';	694
avg(*expr*)	Returns the average for the column values and rows selected.	select avg(amount_sold) from sales where prod_id = 117;	9.92712978
sum(*expr*)	Returns the sum of the column values for all the retrieved rows.	select sum(amount_sold) from sales where prod_id = 117;	170270.13
min(*expr*)	Returns the minimum value for the column and rows retrieved.	select min(prod_list_price) from products;	6.99
max(*expr*)	Returns the maximum value for the column and rows retrieved.	select max(prod_list_price) from products;	1299.99

TABLE 2-5. *Common Aggregate Functions*

Use Dates and Data Functions (Formatting and Chronological)

Date is the next commonest type of data you'll find in an Oracle database after character and numeric data. The date data type consists of two principal elements: date and time. It's important to keep in mind that the date data type includes time when comparing two dates with each other for equality.

The default date format in many Oracle databases is DD-MON-YY, where DD represents the day, MON is the month and YY is the two-digit year. A date can be inserted into a table without specifying either the four-digit year or a value for the time element. Oracle will default the century to '20' for years '00–49' and '19' for years '50–99'. Without a specific time being specified during an insert, the time will default to midnight, which is represented as '00:00:00'.

Date Functions

As with the numeric and character data types, Oracle has provided many date functions to help with the manipulation of date data. If you were to routinely print customized letters to your best customers offering them a special deal that expires on the last day of the month, the last_day function could be used to automatically generate the expiration date for the offer. Table 2-6 shows the commonest date functions.

Function	Action	Example	Displays
Sysdate	Returns current system date. Time could also be retrieved using the to_char function, which is discussed in the next section.	select sysdate from dual;	17-MAR-04 on March 17, 2004
last_day(*date*)	Returns last day of the month for *date*.	select last_day('17-MAR-04') from dual;	31-MAR-04

TABLE 2-6. *Common Date Functions*

Function	Action	Example	Displays
add_months(*d,n*)	Adds *n* or subtracts *-n* months from date *d*.	select add_ months('21-APR-04', 2) from dual;	21-JUN-04
months_between(*d1,d2*)	Returns difference in months between date *d1* and date *d2*.	select months_ between('17-MAR-61', '21-APR-62') from dual;	-13.129032
next_day(*d,day*)	Returns the date that corresponds with the *day* of the week after date *d*.	select next_day('01-FEB-04','Sat urday') from dual;	07-FEB-04

TABLE 2-6. *Common Date Functions* (continued)

Special Formats with the Date Data Type

Date formats are used to change the display format of a date. This is done using the **to_char** conversion function along with the date and format mask. Table 2-7 shows a sample of the commoner date formats and their output.

Format Mask	Returns	Example	Displays
Y or YY or YYY	Last one, two, or three digits of year	select to_ char(sysdate,'YYY') from dual;	004 for all dates in 2004
YEAR	Year spelled out	select to_char(sysdate,'YEAR') from dual;	TWO THOUSAND FOUR in 2004
Q	Quarter of year	select to_char(sysdate,'Q') from dual;	3 for all dates in August
MM	Month	select to_char(sysdate,'MM') from dual;	12 for all dates in December

TABLE 2-7. *Common Formats of Date Type Data*

Format Mask	Returns	Example	Displays
Month	Name of month as a nine-character name	select to_char(sysdate,'Month') from dual;	March followed by 4 spaces for all dates in March
WW	Week of year	select to_char(sysdate,'WW') from dual;	29 on July 15, 2004
W	Week of the month	select to_char(sysdate,'W') from dual;	3 on May 15, 2004
DDD	Day of the year	select to_char(sysdate,'DDD') from dual;	359 on December 25 in non leap years
DD	Day of the month	select to_char(sysdate,'DD') from dual;	09 on September 9 in any year
D	Day of the week (1 through 7)	select to_char(sysdate,'D') from dual;	5 on January 29, 2004

TABLE 2-7. *Common Formats of Date Type Data* (continued)

Nested Functions

It is also common to nest functions within functions. Using the **months_between** example from Table 2-7, it would be possible to **round** the number of months between the two dates. The following statement and output illustrates this example.

```
SQL> select round(months_between('17-MAR-61','21-APR-62'))
  2  from dual;

ROUND(MONTHS_BETWEEN('17-MAR-61','21-APR-62'))
---------------------------------------------
                                          -13
```

The inner function is evaluated first, and then the outer function is evaluated second. This is true for all nested functions and as this example illustrates, different function types can be combined. Pay special notice to the parentheses for the outer and inner functions. For illustration purposes, this example nests only one function within another. However, it is possible to nest many functions within each other. Just be careful; the order of the functions is important, and the complexity of debugging nested functions increases with each additional nested function.

CRITICAL SKILL 2.8

Employ Joins (ANSI vs. Oracle): Inner, Outer, Self

Up until now, all of the examples in this chapter have selected data from only one table. In actual fact, much of the data that we need is in two or more tables. The true power of a relational database (and the source of its name) comes from the ability to relate different tables and their data together. Understanding this concept is critical to harvesting the information held within the database. This is more commonly known as *joining* two or more tables.

With Oracle Database 10*g*, queries can be written using either Oracle's SQL syntax or ANSI syntax. While Oracle hasn't made ANSI syntax available until recently, it has been used in non-Oracle environments for some time. Many third-party tools accept ANSI SQL and, as you'll see shortly, the joins are quite different.

Inner Joins

An inner join, also known simply as join, occurs when records are selected from two tables and the values in one column from the first table are also found in a similar column in the second table. In effect, two or more tables are joined together based on common fields. These common fields are known as *keys*. There are two types of keys:

- A *primary key* is what makes a row of data unique within a table. In the CUSTOMERS table, CUST_ID is the primary key.

- A *foreign key* is the primary key of one table that is stored inside another table. The foreign key connects the two tables together. The SALES table also contains CUST_ID, which in the case of the SALES table, is a foreign key back to the CUSTOMERS table.

Oracle Inner Joins

The tables to be joined are listed in the **from** clause and then related together in the **where** clause. Whenever two or more tables are found in the **from** clause, a join happens. Additional conditions can still be specified in the **where** clause to limit which rows will be returned by the join. For example, when we queried the SALES table on its own, the only customer information available to us was the CUST_ID. However, if we join each record, we retrieve from the SALES table by the CUST_ID to the same column in the CUSTOMERS table, and all the customer information becomes available to us instantly.

This first join example displays both the city and state details for each customer who has purchased a particular product under a specific promotion. The product ID and quantity sold is also displayed:

```
SQL> select prod_id, quantity_sold, cust_city, cust_state_province
  2  from    sales, customers
  3  where   sales.cust_id = customers.cust_id
  4  and     prod_id = 117;

   PROD_ID QUANTITY_SOLD CUST_CITY
---------- ------------- -----------------------------
CUST_STATE_PROVINCE
----------------------------------------
       117             1 Fort Klamath
OR

       117             1 San Mateo
CA

       117             1 Frederick
CO

. . .
```

The **from** clause identified two tables and the **where** clause joins them with **table_name.column_name** syntax. In this output, since the length of the CUST_CITY and CUST_STATE_PROVINCE columns are too wide for the display, the column headings and results wrap over two lines. Later on in this chapter, we'll take a brief look at the report formatting capabilities of SQL*Plus, which will allow us to control the look of the output.

NOTE
*The reason we must adopt the **table_name.column_name** construct is to tell Oracle exactly which tables and columns to join. This is to avoid any ambiguity when different tables have columns that are named the same.*

SQL statements can become quite confusing once you start joining tables, especially when you're joining more than two. Oracle also allows you to give the tables an alternate name known as a table alias. Let's present this query again using "s" as the table alias for the SALES table and "c" as the table alias for the CUSTOMERS table.

```
select prod_id, quantity_sold, cust_city, cust_state_province
from    sales s, customers c
where   s.cust_id = c.cust_id
and     prod_id = 117
```

Let's take this join example one step further. **cust_id** is the column with which we are joining the two tables, and therefore it is found in both the SALES and CUSTOMERS tables. If we want to display cust_id as part of the select list, we would need to prefix it with the table alias:

```
select s.prod_id, s.quantity_sold, c.cust_id,

    c.cust_city, c.cust_state_province
from    sales s, customers c
where   s.cust_id = c.cust_id
and     s.prod_id = 117
```

All the column names in this example were prefixed with the table alias qualifier. While it's only necessary for columns that appear in more than one table, it enhances the readability of the SQL statement as the statements become more complex and include more than one table join.

This leads us into the final example, which presents the concept of joining more than two tables. In addition to joining the CUSTOMERS table to the SALES table as we have in all of the preceding examples, we are also joining the CUSTOMERS table to the PRODUCTS and PROMOTIONS tables so we can pull in columns from those tables, as well.

```
select c.country_id, p1.promo_name, p2.prod_category, s.quantity_sold,
from    sales s,
        customers c,
        promotions p1,
        products p2
where   s.cust_id = c.cust_id
and     s.promo_id = p1.promo_id
and     s.prod_id = p2.prod_id
and     s.prod_id = 117
```

It's that simple to join a bunch of tables together. Name each of the tables in the **from** clause, alias them, and then join them to each other in your **where** clause using the foreign key relationships.

ANSI Inner Joins

With ANSI joins, the join criteria is found in the **from** portion of the SQL statement. The **where** clause only lists the selection criteria for the rows. There are a couple of different ways to join the tables together with ANSI syntax.

ANSI on/using   A simple join can be specified with an **on** or **using** statement. The columns to be joined on will be listed, and the **where** clause can list additional selection criteria. The following two examples illustrate the **on** syntax followed by the **using** syntax:

```
select c.cust_id, c.cust_state_province,
       s.quantity_sold, s.prod_category
```

```
from sales s join customers c
  on s.cust_id = c.cust_id
where prod_id = 117;
```

```
select cust_id, c.cust_state_province,
       s.quantity_sold, s.prod_category
from sales s join customers c
  using (cust_id)
where prod_id = 117;
```

The ANSI syntax also allows for two or more tables to be joined. This can be accomplished with multiple **join on** or multiple **join using** statements in the **from** section of the SQL statement. The following are two examples:

```
select c.cust_id, c.cust_state_province,
       s.quantity_sold, p.prod_name
from   sales s
  join customers c
    on s.cust_id = c.cust_id
  join products
    on s.prod_id = p.prod_id
where p.prod_id = 117
and c.country_id = 52790;
```

```
select cust_id, c.cust_state_province,
       s.quantity_sold, p.prod_name
from   sales s
  join customers c using (cust_id)
  join products p using (prod_id)
where p.prod_id = 117
and c.country_id = 52790;
```

Ask the Expert

Q: Why does the cust_id column in the ANSI on join have a table prefix qualifier while the cust_id column in the ANSI using join does not?

A: The **on** join syntax tells Oracle which columns to use in the table join. Like the Oracle inner join examples, the table prefix is required for cust_id within both the **select** list of columns and the table join. The **using** syntax declares only the column name and allows Oracle to resolve the join. The table qualifiers for the cust_id column are absent from the join portion of the SQL statement and need to be kept out of the select list as well. If you forget, don't worry, Oracle will return an "ORA-25154: column part of USING clause cannot have a qualifier" error message.

ANSI Natural Join   ANSI SQL also gives us a third join alternative, the **natural join**. In this case, the columns to be joined are not specified but rather are resolved by Oracle. They must be similarly named in the tables to be joined. As always, additional selection criteria can be specified in the **where** clause.

```
select cust_id, c.cust_state_province,
        s.quantity_sold, p.prod_name
from sales s
    natural join customers c
    natural join products p
where prod_id = 117;
```

As we found out with the **using** syntax, we couldn't use the table alias qualifier on the cust_id column. If we did, we would get an *"ORA-25155: column used in NATURAL join cannot have qualifier"* error message.

Although it would be very poor database design, it's entirely possible that a similarly named column could exist in different tables but have no relationship to each other. Be careful while naturally joining tables to make sure that it makes sense to join them. While this could just as easily happen with a regular Oracle join, the simple act of having to specify which columns to join could force you to go through this thought process. It's an important fact to know your tables and what you want to accomplish with the joins.

Outer Joins

Unlike an inner join, which only returned records that had matching values for a specific column in both tables, an outer join can return results from one table where the corresponding table did not have a matching value.

In our sample set of data, there are a number of customers that haven't recorded any sales. There are also a number of products that haven't been sold either. These examples will be used in the following explanation of Oracle and ANSI outer joins.

Oracle Outer Joins

In order to find rows from one table that don't match rows in another, known as an outer join, Oracle presented us with the "(+)" notation. The "(+)" is used in the **where** clause on either of the tables where nonmatching rows are to be returned.

In order to illustrate this, we have found that cust_id = 1 does not have any sales, while cust_id = 80 has exactly two. Let's take a look at what happens when we select these two customers from the CUSTOMERS table and request some SALES table details if they exist:

```
SQL> select  c.cust_id, c.cust_last_name, s.prod_id, s.quantity_sold
  2  from    customers c, sales s
  3  where   c.cust_id = s.cust_id(+)
  4  and     c.cust_id in (1,80);
```

```
    CUST_ID CUST_LAST_NAME                       PROD_ID QUANTITY_SOLD
---------- ------------------------------    ---------- -------------
         1 Kessel
        80 Carpenter                                127             1
        80 Carpenter                                 36             1
```

The *outer join* allows us to display the CUSTOMERS columns alongside the nulls for the non-matched rows SALES records. A simple join would have only returned the two records for **cust_id 80**.

Project 2-1   Joining Data Using Inner and Outer Joins

With the sample tables Oracle has provided, there are no *outer join* examples. When we learn about referential integrity and constraints later in this chapter, this will become a little clearer. Suffice it to say that the customers, products, and promotions in the sales table all exist in their respective tables. In this project, we're going to create our own simple tables where we can better demonstrate *outer joins*. Once we discuss the ANSI version of joins, we'll revisit this project and introduce a new concept available only with the ANSI syntax.

Step by Step

Let's start by creating and populating two very simple tables that will join on a common column. Open up a SQL*Plus session and issue the following commands:

1. **create table temp1 (id number(3), desc1 char(5));**

2. **create table temp2 (id number(3), desc2 char(5));**

3. **insert into temp1 values (123, 'ABCDE');**

4. **insert into temp1 values (456, 'FGHIJ');**

5. **insert into temp2 values (456, 'ZZZZZ');**

6. **insert into temp2 values (789, 'MMMMM');**

Both table temp1 and temp2 each have two records. The two tables join with each other on the "ID" column, and they have one ID in common: 456. Let's continue now by displaying all the records from temp1 and temp 2 followed by writing an *inner, right outer,* and *left outer join*. In SQL*Plus, enter the code from the following code listings and check that you get the same output.

1. Display the records from temp1 (remember to use **select *** when doing so):

```
        ID DESC1
---------- -----
       123 ABCDE
       456 FGHIJ
```

2. Next, display the records from temp2:

```
        ID DESC2
---------- -----
       456 ZZZZZ
       789 MMMMM
```

3. Use an inner join to join the two:

```
SQL> select a.id, a.desc1, b.desc2
  2  from   temp1 a, temp2 b
  3  where  a.id = b.id;

        ID DESC1 DESC2
---------- ----- -----
       456 FGHIJ ZZZZZ
```

4. Create an outer join table called temp2, as in the following:

```
SQL> select a.id, a.desc1, b.id, b.desc2
  2  from   temp1 a, temp2  b
  3  where  a.id = b.id(+);

        ID DESC1         ID DESC2
---------- ----- ---------- -----
       123 ABCDE
       456 FGHIJ        456 ZZZZZ
```

5. Generate outer join table temp1:

```
SQL> select a.id, a.desc1, b.id, b.desc2
  2  from   temp1 a, temp2  b
  3  where  a.id(+) = b.id;

        ID DESC1         ID DESC2
---------- ----- ---------- -----
       456 FGHIJ        456 ZZZZZ
                        789 MMMMM
```

6. Now, outer join both sides, as in the following:

```
SQL> select a.id, a.desc1, b.id, b.desc2
  2  from   temp1 a, temp2  b
  3  where  a.id(+) = b.id(+);
where  a.id(+) = b.id(+)
               *
ERROR at line 3:
ORA-01468: a predicate may reference only one outer-joined table
```

(continued)

Project Summary

The *outer join* of table temp2 returned all records from temp1 even if they had nonmatching rows in temp2. The *outer join* of table temp1 returned all records from temp2 whether or not they had matching rows in temp1. Lastly, we tried an outer join on both sides to see what would happen. This syntax would not work, and Oracle gave us a helpful error message (that's not always the case!). When we learn the **union** critical point later on in this chapter, we'll see that there's a way to do this with Oracle's syntax. However, let's move on to the ANSI outer join examples now, and we'll see that it is possible without writing a lot of code (that's a good thing!).

ANSI Outer Joins

With Oracle9*i*, Oracle began down the journey to fully support ANSI SQL standards. To meet this goal, Oracle started the support of ANSI joins as discussed previously. We now present to you ANSI Outer Joins. As we just alluded to in Project 2.1, the ANSI outer join syntax allows us to perform *right outer joins, left outer joins,* and *full outer joins.*

ANSI Right Outer Joins   As with the ANSI *inner joins,* the ANSI *outer joins* have moved the join to the **from** clause. A *right outer join* can be written with keywords **right outer join** or **right join** since **outer** is redundant. Rewriting our SALES and CUSTOMERS example from before with the ANSI syntax would produce the following:

```
SQL> select c.cust_id, c.cust_last_name, s.prod_id, s.quantity_sold
  2  from sales s right join customers c
  3       on c.cust_id = s.cust_id
  4  where c.cust_id in (1,80);

   CUST_ID CUST_LAST_NAME                          PROD_ID QUANTITY_SOLD
---------- ----------------------------------- ---------- -------------
         1 Kessel
        80 Carpenter                               127             1
        80 Carpenter                                36             1
```

As with the Oracle example, the SALES table nonmatched rows are returned. The main difference was that s.cust_id had the (+) notation before, and now we state that SALES will be right joined to CUSTOMERS. The join syntax is in the **from** clause, and the **where** clause contains only the selection criteria (in this case, only customer 1's and 80's records). This query can also be written with **using** or **natural right join** ANSI syntax. Go ahead and try that on your own. Make sure you get the exact same results as we did with the **on** example from the preceding example.

ANSI Left Outer Joins   The ANSI *left outer join* works exactly the same as the *right outer join* and can be written using either **left outer join** or **left join**. As with the *right outer join,* the **join on**, **join using**, or **natural left join** styles are all available.

Any of the combinations will produce exactly the same results. Let's hold off on the *left outer join* example until we revisit the outer join idea later in Project 2-4.

ANSI Full Outer Joins A *full outer join* is possible when using the ANSI syntax without having to write too much code. With a *full outer join,* you will be able to return both the *right outer join* and *left outer join* results from the same query.

The *full outer join* queries can be written as **full outer join** or **full join** and once again, the **on**, **using**, or **natural** joins are all possible. Let's revisit the Outer Joins Project and try the ANSI syntax out.

Project 2-2 Joining Data Using ANSI SQL Joins

Using the temp1 and temp2 tables we created and populated, let's try out the ANSI *right, left,* and *full outer joins.*

Step by Step

We've just learned that you can write the ANSI *outer joins* with or without the **outer** keyword in each of the ANSI *right, left,* and *full outer joins.* We also learned that the ANSI **on**, **using**, and **natural** join syntax is available as well. The following step-by-step instructions use a combination of these for illustration purposes. Feel free to try alternate syntax, but we encourage you to adopt a consistent style to allow your code to be self-documenting and traceable by other developers.

1. Use the ANSI right outer join:

```
SQL> select id, desc1, desc2
  2  from    temp2 right outer join temp1
  3              using (id);

        ID DESC1 DESC2
---------- ----- -----
       456 EFGH  ZZZZ
       123 ABCD
```

2. Use the ANSI left outer join, shown in the following:

```
SQL> select id, desc1, desc2
  2  from    temp2 b natural left join temp1 a;

        ID DESC1 DESC2
---------- ----- -----
       456 EFGH  ZZZZ
       789       MMMM
```

3. Use the ANSI full outer join to complete the syntax:

```
SQL> select a.id, a.desc1, b.id, b.desc2
  2  from    temp1 a full join temp2 b
  3              on a.id = b.id;
```

(continued)

```
    ID DESC1        ID DESC2
---------- -----  ---------- -----
       456 EFGH          456 ZZZZ
       123 ABCD

                         789 MMMM
```

Project Summary

The three examples in this project show an alternate way of performing outer joins using ANSI SQL. Our first join, the right outer join, returns all of the rows from the table listed on the right side of the **from** clause, TEMP1, regardless of whether or not they match to a row from the other table, TEMP2.

The second example switches the logic. The table on the left, TEMP2, returns all rows with a left outer join specified as natural left join.

Our final example introduces the full outer join concept available with ANSI SQL. In this case, all rows are returned from each table regardless of whether or not a match was made.

Self-Joins

A self-join is used for a relationship within a single table. Rows are joined back to the same table instead of joining them to a related second table as we have seen with the many CUSTOMERS and SALES tables examples throughout this chapter.

A common example involves hierarchical relationships where all of the records and related records are stored within the same table. A family tree is one such hierarchy that best illustrates the self-join. Let's take a look at the FAMILY table that we have created for this concept:

```
SQL> desc family
 Name                                      Null?    Type
 ----------------------------------------- -------- --------------
 NAME                                      NOT NULL CHAR(10)
 BIRTH_YEAR                                NOT NULL NUMBER(4)
 FATHER                                             CHAR(10)
```

The table contains columns for a person's name and birth year as well as their father's names. The fathers each have their own row in the table with their respective birth years and names. This table could be filled out with every known relationship in the family tree. For our example, Isaac, born in 1894, has a son, Edward, who was born in 1935. Edward has three children: Mark, born in 1961; Beth, born in 1964; and Cari, born in 1966. The following example first takes a look at all of the records in the table followed by our hierarchical self-join example:

```
SQL> select * from family;

NAME       BIRTH_YEAR FATHER
---------- ---------- ----------
Isaac            1894
Edward           1935 Isaac
```

```
Mark               1961 Edward
Beth               1964 Edward
Cari               1966 Edward

SQL> select a.name, a.birth_year,
  2          a.father, b.birth_year
  3  from    family a, family b, family c
  4  where   a.father = b.name;

NAME         BIRTH_YEAR FATHER       BIRTH_YEAR
---------- ---------- ---------- ----------
Edward            1935 Isaac            1894
Mark              1961 Edward           1935
Beth              1964 Edward           1935
Cari              1966 Edward           1935
```

The FAMILY table is found in the **from** clause twice with table aliases of a and b. The table is joined back to itself to retrieve the father's details. In order to accomplish this, the value found in the father column for each retrieved record (a.father) is joined back to the table to obtain a match on the name column (b.name), which will return the father's details—in this case, his year of birth (b.birth_year).

CRITICAL SKILL 2.9

Learn the group by and having Clauses

Earlier, we learned about functions that can work on sets of rows. We can also group sets of rows to lump similar types of information together and return summary information, also referred to as aggregated information. A large number of queries you write will perform group functions as the data is retrieved from the database. Mastering the use of functions and grouping is fundamental to understanding the full power of SQL.

group by

You can use many of the functions we presented earlier with or without the **group by** clause, but when you use them without it, Oracle treats all of the selected rows as one group. For example, the following query when written without a **group by** clause, returns the average amount sold for products within the Electronics category.

```
SQL> select avg(amount_sold)
  2  from    sales s, products p
  3  where   s.prod_id = p.prod_id
  4  and     prod_category = 'Electronics';

AVG(AMOUNT_SOLD)
----------------
      125.551667
```

The entire Electronics category was treated as one group. If we wanted to see the average amount sold for each subcategory within the Electronics category, we will need to use a **group by** clause in our query, lumping each of the Electronics subcategories together before calculating the average. Each **group by** clause is accomplished by putting the column or columns to group by in the **select** list followed by one or more functions. A **group by** statement follows the **where** clause, and it must include each of the select list columns that are not acted upon by a group function. Let's take a look at an example:

```
SQL> select prod_subcategory, avg(amount_sold)
  2  from    sales s, products p
  3  where   s.prod_id = p.prod_id
  4  and     prod_category = 'Electronics'
  5  group by prod_subcategory;

PROD_SUBCATEGORY                                    AVG(AMOUNT_SOLD)
-------------------------------------------------- ----------------
Game Consoles                                            300.523928
Home Audio                                               582.175922
Y Box Accessories                                        18.7803303
Y Box Games                                              22.640670
```

This **group by** example illustrates a column and function in the **select** list and the repetition of the column again in the **group by** clause.

having

Just as you have used selection criteria to reduce the result set, you can apply the **having** clause to summarized data from a group by operation to restrict the groups returned. Using the previous example, suppose you only wanted to see the Product Subcategory groups that had an average amount sold greater than 300. The following is a **having** clause executed against the **avg**(amount_sold) aggregation example:

```
SQL> select prod_subcategory, avg(amount_sold)
  2  from    sales s, products p
  3  where   s.prod_id = p.prod_id
  4  and     prod_category = 'Electronics'
  5  group by prod_subcategory
  6  having avg(amount_sold) > 300;

PROD_SUBCATEGORY                                    AVG(AMOUNT_SOLD)
-------------------------------------------------- ----------------
Game Consoles                                            300.523928
Home Audio                                               582.175922
```

Project 2-3   Grouping Data in Your select Statements

One final example will demonstrate the grouping of multiple columns and more than one function being performed for each group. As we build on this example, we will introduce column aliases, a **round** function combined with an **avg** function and the use of a **substr** function, which will serve to select only a specified number of characters for the product subcategories and names results.

Step by Step

Let's start with the preceding **group by** example and build on it as we introduce some formatting and intermediate concepts. Look at the output each time and see how we are transforming it along the way. A final output listing has been provided at the end for you to compare against.

1. Start SQL*Plus and re-execute the preceding **group by** example:

```
select prod_subcategory, avg(amount_sold)
from    sales s, products p
where   s.prod_id = p.prod_id
and     prod_category = 'Electronics'
group by prod_subcategory;
```

2. Add the product name to the **select** list. Don't forget to add it to the **group by** also.

```
select prod_subcategory, prod_name, avg(amount_sold)
from    sales s, products p
where   s.prod_id = p.prod_id
and     prod_category = 'Electronics'
group by prod_subcategory, prod_name;
```

3. Rewrite the query to use a **natural join**, remove the table aliases and exclude the 'Home Audio' subcategory from the selection:

```
select prod_subcategory, prod_name, avg(amount_sold)
from    sales natural join products
where   prod_category = 'Electronics'
and     prod_subcategory != 'Home Audio'
group by prod_subcategory, prod_name;
```

4. Add a **max** function calculation on the **amount_sold** to the query:

```
select prod_subcategory, prod_name, max(amount_sold), avg(amount_sold)
from    sales natural join products
where   prod_category = 'Electronics'
and     prod_subcategory != 'Home Audio'
group by prod_subcategory, prod_name;
```

5. Add a **substr** function to both the **prod_subcategory** and **prod_name,** selecting the first 18 and 25 characters, respectively, to shorten the

(continued)

displayed results. Don't forget to change the **group by** at the same time.

```
select substr(prod_subcategory,1,18),
       substr(prod_name,1,25),
       max(amount_sold),
       avg(amount_sold)
from   sales natural join products
where  prod_category = 'Electronics'
and    prod_subcategory != 'Home Audio'
group by substr(prod_subcategory,1,18),
         substr(prod_name,1,25);
```

6. Add a **round** function to the **avg(amount_sold)** function. In this step, let's also give the column names aliases to make the results more readable:

```
select substr(prod_subcategory,1,18) Subcategory,
       substr(prod_name,1,25) Product_Name,
       max(amount_sold) Max_Amt_Sold,
       round(avg(amount_sold),2) Avg_Amt_Sold
from   sales natural join products
where  prod_category = 'Electronics'
and    prod_subcategory != 'Home Audio'
group by substr(prod_subcategory,1,18),
         substr(prod_name,1,25);
```

7. Add a **having** clause to return aggregated rows that have both a maximum amount sold and an average amount sold greater than 10. As one final measure, let's also add an **order by**:

```
select substr(prod_subcategory,1,18) Subcategory,
       substr(prod_name,1,25) Product_Name,
       max(amount_sold) Max_Amt_Sold,
       round(avg(amount_sold),2) Avg_Amt_Sold
from   sales natural join products
where  prod_category = 'Electronics'
and    prod_subcategory != 'Home Audio'
group by substr(prod_subcategory,1,18),
         substr(prod_name,1,25)
having max(amount_sold) > 10
and    avg(amount_sold) > 10
order by substr(prod_subcategory,1,18),
         substr(prod_name,1,25);
```

8. Your final output should look like this:

```
SUBCATEGORY          PRODUCT_NAME              MAX_AMT_SOLD AVG_AMT_SOLD
------------------   -------------------------  ------------ ------------
Game Consoles        Y Box                            326.39       300.52
Y Box Accessories    Xtend Memory                      29.8        24.15
Y Box Games          Adventures with Numbers          17.03        13.78
```

Y Box Games	Bounce		25.55	21.13
Y Box Games	Comic Book Heroes		25.76	22.14
Y Box Games	Endurance Racing		42.58	34.29
Y Box Games	Finding Fido		16.6	12.79
Y Box Games	Martial Arts Champions		25.76	22.14
Y Box Games	Smash up Boxing		38.64	33.2

```
9 rows selected.
```

Project Summary

While the final example, and a few transformations along the way, could be considered more along the lines of intermediate SQL, take some time to study each of the steps and the resulting changes to the output. Once you understand the different components of the SQL statement that evolved in this project, you'll be well on your way to unleashing the power of SQL.

Progress Check

1. Retrieve a list of all product categories, subcategories, names, and list prices where the list price is greater than $100. Order this query by product category, subcategory, and name.

2. List the aggregate total sales for every product category and subcategory group using the ANSI **natural join** syntax.

3. Retrieve a list of all customers IDs and last names where the customer only has one entry in the SALES table.

Progress Check Answers

1. An ordered list of all product categories, subcategories, names, and list prices greater than $100 are returned by the following query:

```
SQL> select prod_category, prod_subcategory, prod_name, prod_list_price
  2  from    products
  3  where   prod_list_price > 100
  4  order by prod_category, prod_subcategory, prod_name;
```

2. The SQL statement that will return the aggregate amount sold for every product category and subcategory using the ANSI SQL **natural join** is shown here:

```
SQL> select prod_category, prod_subcategory, sum(amount_sold)
  2  from    products natural join sales
  3  group by prod_category, prod_subcategory;
```

3. The list of all customer IDs and last names for customers that only had one sale is returned by the following SQL statement:

```
SQL> select c.cust_id, cust_last_name, count(*)
  2  from    customers c, sales s
  3  where   c.cust_id = s.cust_id
  4  group by c.cust_id, cust_last_name
  5  having count(*) = 1;
```

CRITICAL SKILL 2.10

Learn Subqueries: Simple and Correlated Comparison with Joins

Within SQL, functionality exists to create subqueries, which are essentially queries within queries. This power capability makes it possible to produce results based on another result or set of results. Let's explore this concept a little further.

Simple Subquery

Without the functionality of subqueries, it would take a couple SQL queries to retrieve product information for the product with the maximum list price. The first query would have to find the value of **max(prod_list_price)**. A subsequent query would have to use the value resolved for **max(prod_list_price)** to find the product details. Let's take a look at how we can resolve this with a subquery embedded in the **where** clause of the main query:

```
select prod_id, prod_name, prod_category
from    products
where   prod_list_price = (select max(prod_list_price)
                           from   products);
```

The subquery is enclosed in parentheses and is part of the **where** clause. The main query is resolved based on the results of the subquery, in this case, the maximum product list price. As you can see, the ability to have a query within a query is very powerful.

Running SQL queries with embedded subqueries can affect performance. As your experience with subqueries increases, you will find that you will need to work closely with your database administrator, more commonly referred to as a DBA, to optimize statements with subquery processing.

Ask the Expert

Q: What would happen if the subquery returned multiple values?

A: Since the subquery in the example could return only a single value, it was acceptable for it to be written with the equals (=) operand. If multiple values are expected from the subquery, the **in** list operand should be used.

Correlated Subqueries with Joins

A correlated subquery is a query that references a column from the main query. In our example that follows, it enables us to first retrieve the average list price for each product category and then join it back (correlate it) to the product category in the outer query. Let's take a look at the example and its output:

```
SQL> select  substr(prod_category,1,22) Category,
  2           substr(prod_name,1,39) Product,
  3           prod_list_price List
  4  from     products p
  5  where    prod_list_price > (select avg(prod_list_price)
  6                               from    products
  7                               where   p.prod_category = prod_category)
  8  order by substr(prod_category,1,22), prod_list_price desc;
```

```
CATEGORY                PRODUCT                                 LIST
----------------------  --------------------------------------  --------
Electronics             Home Theatre Package with DVD-Audio/Vid   599.99
Electronics             8.3 Minitower Speaker                     499.99
Electronics             Y Box                                     299.99
Hardware                Envoy Ambassador                         1299.99
Peripherals and Access  17" LCD w/built-in HDTV Tuner             999.99
Peripherals and Access  18" Flat Panel Graphics Monitor           899.99
Peripherals and Access  Model NM500X High Yield Toner Cartridge   192.99
Peripherals and Access  SIMM- 16MB PCMCIAII card                  149.99
Photo                   Mini DV Camcorder with 3.5" Swivel LCD   1099.99
Photo                   5MP Telephoto Digital Camera              899.99
Software/Other          Unix/Windows 1-user pack                  199.99
Software/Other          Laptop carrying case                       55.99
Software/Other          DVD-R Discs, 4.7GB, Pack of 5              49.99
Software/Other          O/S Documentation Set - English           44.99
Software/Other          O/S Documentation Set - German            44.99
Software/Other          O/S Documentation Set - French            44.99
Software/Other          O/S Documentation Set - Spanish           44.99
Software/Other          O/S Documentation Set - Italian           44.99
Software/Other          O/S Documentation Set - Kanji             44.99

19 rows selected.
```

The main query retrieves the Category, Product, and List Price details for each product that is greater than the average list price of all products within its category. This wouldn't otherwise be possible without the correlated join of the subqueries product category with the main queries product category, referenced by the main queries table alias.

Notice as well that the **order by** exists on the outer query. If it were placed in the subquery, it wouldn't work. The displayed results are what we want to order, not the subquery results.

CRITICAL SKILL 2.11

Use Set Operators: Union, Intersect, Minus

One of the nice things about a relational database is that SQL queries act upon sets of data versus a single row of data. Oracle provides us with a series of set functions that can be used to join sets together, for example. The set functions will be discussed in the next few sections using two single column tables: table x and table y. Before proceeding to the discussion on the set functions, let's first take a look at the contents of these tables.

Table x:

```
SQL> select * from x;

COL
---
1
2
3
4
5
6

6 rows selected.
```

Table y:

```
SQL> select * from y;

COL
---
5
6
7

3 rows selected.
```

union

When you use this operator in SQL*Plus, it returns all the rows in both tables without any duplicates. This is done by Oracle with a sort operation. In the preceding table listings, both tables have columns with values of 5 and 6. A closer look at the **union** query and resulting output is shown here:

```
SQL> select * from x
  2  union
  3  select * from y;
```

```
COL
---
1
2
3
4
5
6
7

7 rows selected.
```

union all

The **union all** set function is similar to the **union** query with the exception that it returns all rows from both tables with duplicates. The following example is a rewrite of the preceding **union** example using **union all**:

```
SQL> select * from x
  2  union all
  3  select * from y;

COL
---
1
2
3
4
5
6
5
6
7

9 rows selected.
```

intersect

The **intersect** operator will return all the rows in one table that also reside in the other. Column values 5 and 6 exist in both the tables. The following example demonstrates the **intersect** set function:

```
SQL> select * from x
  2  intersect
  3  select * from y;

COL
---
5
6
```

NOTE
*Please be aware that the **intersect** set operator can introduce major performance problems. If you are venturing down this path, weigh the alternatives first.*

minus

The **minus** set function returns all the rows in the first table minus the rows in the first table that are also in the second table. The order of the tables is important. Pay close attention to the order of the tables and the different results in these two query examples:

```
SQL> select * from x
  2  minus
  3  select * from y;

COL
---
1
2
3
4

SQL> select * from y
  2  minus
  3  select * from x;

COL
---
7
```

Project 2-4   Using the union Function in Your SQL

During our discussion of Oracle *outer joins* and the associated Project 2.1, we mentioned that a *full outer join* wasn't readily available using the Oracle syntax. We went on to mention that when we learned about the **union** set function, we'd take a moment to revisit creating an *outer join* without using ANSI SQL syntax.

Step by Step

Let's first recall the Oracle *right outer join* and *left outer join* examples we were working on in Project 2.1.

   1. Use the right outer join example from Project 2.1:

```
SQL> select a.id, a.desc1, b.id, b.desc2
  2  from   temp1 a, temp2  b
  3  where  a.id = b.id(+);

       ID DESC1          ID DESC2
---------- ----- ---------- -----
      123 ABCDE
      456 FGHIJ          456 ZZZZZ
```

2. Now, use the left outer join example from Project 2.1:

```
SQL> select a.id, a.desc1, b.id, b.desc2
  2  from   temp1 a, temp2  b
  3  where  a.id(+) = b.id;

       ID DESC1          ID DESC2
---------- ----- ---------- -----
      456 FGHIJ          456 ZZZZZ
                         789 MMMMM
```

3. Now, let's put the two together with a full outer join using **union.** ANSI
   SQL *outer join* syntax provided us with a **full outer join** option that wasn't
   available with Oracle's standard SQL. With the **union** set function in our
   Oracle tool belt, we have another way to solve this problem. So now, let's
   take the two queries from the recalled examples and **union** them together:

```
SQL> select a.id, a.desc1, b.id, b.desc2
  2  from temp1 a, temp2 b
  3  where a.id = b.id(+)
  4  union
  5  select a.id, a.desc1, b.id, b.desc2
  6  from temp1 a, temp2 b
  7  where a.id(+) = b.id;

       ID DESC1          ID DESC2
---------- ----- ---------- -----
      123 ABCDE
      456 FGHIJ          456 ZZZZZ
                         789 MMMMM
```

Project Summary

In this project, by combining the right and left outer join Oracle statements together
with a **union** set operator, we were able to mimic the ANSI SQL full outer join
functionality.

Use Views

Views are database objects that are based on one or more tables. They allow the user to create a pseudo-table that has no data. The view consists solely of an SQL query that retrieves specific columns and rows. The data that is retrieved by a view is presented like a table.

Views can provide a level of security, making only certain rows and columns from one or more tables available to the end user. We could hide the underlying tables, CUSTOMERS and SALES from all the users in our organization and only make available the data for states they are entitled to see. In the following example, we are creating a view to only show specific details about Utah-based customers sales:

```
SQL> create view utah_sales
  2  as
  3  select c.cust_id ID,
  4         substr(cust_last_name,1,20) Name,
  5         substr(cust_city,1,20) City,
  6         substr(cust_state_province,1,5) State,
  7         sum(amount_sold) Total
  8  from   customers c, sales s
  9  where  c.cust_id = s.cust_id
 10  and    cust_state_province = 'UT'
 11  group by c.cust_id,
 12         substr(cust_last_name,1,20),
 13         substr(cust_city,1,20),
 14         substr(cust_state_province,1,5);

View created.
```

The **create view** statement names the view and then uses keywords **as select** to define the select list, tables, and selection criteria that the view will be based upon. The following code listing issues a **desc** statement to demonstrate that the view looks just like a table. Notice that the column names have been changed from their original ones and were instead created using the column aliases from the select statement in the preceding view creation DDL.

```
SQL> desc utah_sales
 Name                                      Null?    Type
 ----------------------------------------- -------- --------------------
 ID                                        NOT NULL NUMBER
 NAME                                               VARCHAR2(20)
 CITY                                               VARCHAR2(20)
 STATE                                              VARCHAR2(5)
 TOTAL                                              NUMBER
```

The view looks like a table as demonstrated by the preceding code listing, so let's now issue a couple of queries against it. The first one that follows selects all rows and columns from this view. The second example selects only the name and total columns for customers whose sales are greater than 20,000. Keep in mind, this is still only for Utah customers.

```
SQL> select *
  2  from    utah_sales;

        ID NAME                     CITY                 STATE       TOTAL
---------- --------------------     -------------------- -----  ----------
       118 Kuehler                  Farmington           UT        23258.4
       392 Eubank                   Farmington           UT       21297.49
       411 Vankirk                  Farmington           UT       19279.94
       462 Nielley                  Farmington           UT       64509.91
       599 Robbinette               Farmington           UT       11167.65
      7003 Bane                     Farmington           UT       62605.42
    100207 Campbell                 Farmington           UT          11.99
    100267 Desai                    Farmington           UT         240.95
    100308 Wilbur                   Farmington           UT         190.96

9 rows selected.

SQL> select name, total
  2  from    utah_sales
  3  where   total > 20000;

NAME                      TOTAL
--------------------  ----------
Kuehler                  23258.4
Eubank                  21297.49
Nielley                 64509.91
Bane                    62605.42
```

It's easy to see how we could keep certain users in our company from accessing sales information from more than the states they are granted access to. If this sample database had sale representatives with assigned territories, one could imagine how the use of territory-based views could keep one salesperson from viewing the sales and commissions of another territory representative.

We have demonstrated here that views contain no data. All the data for our view example in this section resides in the underlying tables. In Chapter 9, we will introduce you to materialized views, which is a physical implementation of a view.

CRITICAL SKILL 2.13

Learn Sequences: Just Simple Stuff

Quite often, primary keys in tables are simply generated numeric values that are sequential. In the sample database that we've used throughout this chapter, cust_id and prod_id in the CUSTOMERS and PRODUCTS tables are likely candidates for creation using a sequence.

Sequences are objects in the database that can be used to provide sequentially generated integers. Without these valuable objects available to users, generating values sequentially would only be possible through the use of programs.

Sequences are generally created and named by a DBA. Among the attributes that can be defined when creating a sequence are a minimum value, a maximum value, a number to increment by and a number to start with. They are then made available to the systems applications and users that would need to generate them.

For the following example, we have established a **cust_id_seq** sequence, which increments by one each time it's called. When we created the sequence, we specified that 104501 should be the number to start with. For demonstration purposes, we'll use the DUAL table to select the next two sequence numbers. More often than not, an application will retrieve and assign the sequence numbers as records are inserted into the associated table.

```
SQL> select cust_id_seq.nextval
  2  from dual;

   NEXTVAL
----------
    104501

SQL> select cust_id_seq.nextval
  2  from dual;

   NEXTVAL
----------
    104502
```

CRITICAL SKILL 2.14

Employ Constraints: Linkage to Entity Models, Types, Deferred, Enforced, Gathering Exceptions

In our section on joins in this chapter, we introduced the concept of primary and foreign keys. These were, in fact, constraints on our tables. Constraints preserve the integrity of our database by enforcing business rules.

The primary key for the PROMOTIONS table in our sample schema is an integrity constraint. It requires that each value in **promo_id** be unique. Let's see what would happen if we tried to insert a row in this table with a **promo_id** value that already exists:

```
SQL> insert into promotions
  2    (promo_id,
  3      promo_name,
```

```
 4      promo_subcategory,
 5      promo_subcategory_id,
 6      promo_category,
 7      promo_category_id,
 8      promo_cost,
 9      promo_begin_date,
10      promo_end_date,
11      promo_total,
12      promo_total_id)
13   values
14      (36,
15       'Thanksgiving Sale',
16       'Newspaper',
17       28,
18       'ad news',
19       4,
20       250,
21       '23-NOV-03',
22       '27-NOV-03',
23       'Promotion Total',
24       5);
insert into promotions
*
ERROR at line 1:
ORA-00001: unique constraint (SH.PROMO_PK) violated
```

Since the value 36 already existed for **promo_id**, the unique constraint was violated when we tried to insert another row in the table with the same value. This constraint preserved the integrity of the data by enforcing the business rule that every promotion must be identified uniquely.

Linkage to Entity Models

Many organizations have complex databases and as a result, they use entity models to document each system's database objects and constraints. These models of the organizations database schemas graphically represent the relationships between objects.

The function of database design could be the responsibility of the developer, DBA or a database designer. Among other uses, entity-modeling software allows the database designer to graphically define and link tables to each other. The result is a data model with tables, columns, primary keys, and foreign keys. Throughout this chapter, we have issued DDL to create tables. Typically, entity-modeling software will generate the DDL in a script that can be executed against the database. This makes the job of defining and maintaining database objects and their associated constraints and relationships with each other a lot easier.

Types

There are a number of different types of integrity constraints. The following is a list of the integrity constraints that are available in the Oracle database:

- NULL constraints are defined on a single column and dictate whether or not the column must contain a value. If a column is defined as NOT NULL, it must contain values in each and every record.

- UNIQUE constraints allow a value in a column to be inserted or updated providing it contains a unique value.

- PRIMARY KEY constraints require that the key uniquely identifies each row in the table. The key may consist of one column or a combination of columns.

- FOREIGN KEY constraints define the relationships between tables. This is commonly referred to as referential integrity. These are rules that are based on a key in one table that assure that the values exist in the key of the referenced table.

- CHECK constraints enable users to define and enforce rules on columns. Acceptable values are defined for a column and **insert**, **update**, and **delete** commands are interrogated and are accepted or rejected based on whether or not the values are specifically allowed. A separate check constraint definition is required if the requirement exists to perform either similar or different checks on more than one column. The following example illustrates the creation of a table with a single check constraint, followed by an insert with an acceptable value and an attempted insert with a disallowed value:

```
SQL> create table check_constraint_example
  2       (col1 char(1)
  3           constraint check_col1
  4           check (col1 in ('B','G','N')));

Table created.

SQL> insert into check_constraint_example values ('B');

1 row created.

SQL> insert into check_constraint_example values ('C');
insert into check_constraint_example values ('C')
*
ERROR at line 1:
ORA-02290: check constraint (SH.CHECK_COL1) violated
```

Ask the Expert

Q: Is a single space an acceptable entry into a NOT NULL constrained column?

A: Yes. Oracle will allow you to enter a space as the sole character in a NOT NULL constrained column. Be careful though. The single space will look like a NULL value when a **select** statement retrieves and displays this row. The space is very different than a NULL.

Deferred

When constraints are created, they can be created either as **deferrable** or **not deferrable**. A constraint that is not deferred is checked immediately upon execution of each statement and if the constraint is violated, it is immediately rolled back. A constraint that is deferred will not be checked until a **commit** statement is issued. This is useful when inserting rows or updating values that reference other values that do not exist but are part of the overall batch of statements. By deferring the constraint checking until the **commit** is issued, we can complete the entire batch of entries before determining if there are any constraint violations.

CRITICAL SKILL 2.15

Format Your Output with SQL*Plus

Throughout this chapter, we've seen the results of many SQL queries. In some, we added functions like **substr** to reduce the size of the columns and keep the results confined within one line. In SQL*Plus, there are many parameters that can be set to control how the output is displayed. A list of all of the available settings is easily obtained by issuing the **show all** command within SQL*Plus. Alternatively, if you know the parameter and want to see its current value, the command **show parameter_name** will give you the answer. Before we close out this chapter, let's visit a number of the more useful SQL*Plus parameters.

Page and Line Size

The **set linesize** command tells Oracle how wide the line output is before wrapping the results to the next line. To set the line size to 100, enter the command **set linesize 100**. There is no semicolon required to end **set** commands.

Ask the Expert

Q: Once I set parameters, do I ever have to set them again?

A: Yes. Parameters are good only for the current setting. The parameters always reset to their default settings when you start up a new SQL*Plus session. However, the parameter defaults can be overwritten at the start of each SQL*Plus session by entering and saving them in the login.sql file.

The **set pagesize** command determines the length of the page. The default page size is 14 lines. If you don't want to repeat the result headings every 14 lines, use this command. If you want your page to be 50 lines long, issue the command **set pagesize 50**.

Page Titles

The **ttitle** command includes a number of options. The default settings return the date and page number on every page followed by the title text centered on the next line. Multiple headings can also be produced by separating the text with the vertical bar character. The command **ttitle 'Customer List | Utah'** centers the text "Customer List" on the first line followed by "Utah" on the second line.

Page Footers

The **btitle** command will center text at the bottom of the page. The command **btitle 'sample.sql'** places the text "sample.sql" at the bottom center of the output listing. The command **btitle left 'sample.sql'** results in the footer text "sample.sql" being placed at the left edge of the footer.

Formatting Columns

Quite often, you'll need to format the actual column data. The **column** command is used to accomplish this. Suppose we are going to select the last name from the CUSTOMERS table along with a number of other columns. We know that, by default, the last name data will take up more space than it needs. The command **column cust_last_name format a12 wrap heading 'Last | Name'** tells SQL*Plus that there should be only 12 characters of the last name displayed and that the column title 'Last Name' should be displayed on two separate lines.

Project 2-5   Formatting Your SQL Output

Let's put these SQL*Plus concepts together and format the output of a SQL query. The following step-by-step instructions will lead you through a few of these basic formatting commands.

Step by Step

In this project, we're going to select some customer and sales information for the customers from Utah. Let's first take a look at our sample SQL query and output before any formatting kicks in:

```
SQL> select cust_last_name, cust_city, sum(amount_sold)
  2  from    customers natural join sales
  3  where   cust_state_province = 'UT'
  4  group by cust_last_name, cust_city;

CUST_LAST_NAME                           CUST_CITY
---------------------------------------- ----------------------------
SUM(AMOUNT_SOLD)
----------------
Bane                                     Farmington
       62605.42

Desai                                    Farmington
         240.95

Eubank                                   Farmington
       21297.49


CUST_LAST_NAME                           CUST_CITY
---------------------------------------- ----------------------------
SUM(AMOUNT_SOLD)
----------------
Wilbur                                   Farmington
         190.96

Kuehler                                  Farmington
        23258.4

Nielley                                  Farmington
       64509.91


CUST_LAST_NAME                           CUST_CITY
---------------------------------------- ----------------------------
SUM(AMOUNT_SOLD)
----------------
Vankirk                                  Farmington
       19279.94

Campbell                                 Farmington
          11.99
```

(continued)

```
Robbinette                              Farmington
        11167.65


9 rows selected.
```

The following steps correspond to the **set** commands in the code listing that follows them. The original SQL query will also be executed a second time with much nicer formatting results.

1. Set the page size to 15. (You'll probably never have such a small page size, but we're doing this to illustrate multiple pages with this small result set.)

2. Set the line size to 70.

3. Add a title at the top of the page with "Customer Sales Report" and "Utah Region" in the first and second lines, respectively.

4. Add a footer with "CONFIDENTIAL REPORT" displayed.

5. Format the last name to be exactly 12 characters long and with a title "Last Name" listed on two separate lines.

6. Format the city with "City" as the title and the data fixed at 15 characters long.

7. Format the summed amount sold with a two-line title "Total Sales." Format the data to include a dollar sign, two digits following the decimal point, and a comma to denote thousands.

```
SQL> set pagesize 15
SQL> set linesize 70
SQL> ttitle 'Customer Sales Report | Utah Region'
SQL> btitle 'CONFIDENTIAL REPORT'
SQL> column cust_last_name format a12 wrap heading 'Last | Name'
SQL> column cust_city format a15 heading 'City'
SQL> column sum(amount_sold) format $999,999.99 wrap heading 'Total | Sales'
SQL> select cust_last_name, cust_city, sum(amount_sold)
  2  from    customers natural join sales
  3  where   cust_state_province = 'UT'
  4  group by cust_last_name, cust_city;

Mon Jan 12                                          page    1
                     Customer Sales Report
                        Utah Region


Last                           Total
    Name        City           Sales
------------ --------------- ------------
Bane         Farmington       $62,605.42
Desai        Farmington          $240.95
Eubank       Farmington       $21,297.49
Wilbur       Farmington          $190.96
Kuehler      Farmington       $23,258.40
```

```
Nielley      Farmington       $64,509.91
                       CONFIDENTIAL REPORT

Mon Jan 12                                             page    2
                      Customer Sales Report
                          Utah Region

Last                            Total
   Name        City             Sales
------------  ---------------  ------------
Vankirk       Farmington       $19,279.94
Campbell      Farmington          $11.99
Robbinette    Farmington       $11,167.65



                       CONFIDENTIAL REPORT

9 rows selected.
```

Project Summary

With some simple formatting commands available within SQL*Plus, we were able to transform the unformatted, difficult-to-read output into a simple and effective report. SQL*Plus has many formatting options available above and beyond the few we have demonstrated here. As you become more familiar with SQL and SQL*Plus, take the time to research and try more of the available formatting options. We think you'll agree that SQL*Plus is an effective query tool and report formatter.

Writing SQL*Plus Output to a File

The **spool** command will save the output to a datafile. If your database is on a Windows operating system, the command **spool c:\reports\output.dat** would capture the output of the query execution in the "output.dat" file.

☑ Chapter 2 Mastery Check

1. DDL and DML translate to _____ and _____, respectively.

2. Which of the following descriptions is true about **insert** statements?

    A. Insert statements must always have a **where** clause.

    B. Insert statements can never have a **where** clause.

    C. Insert statements can optionally include a **where** clause.

3. In addition to the two mandatory keywords required to retrieve data from the database, there are three optional keywords. Name them.

4. Write a SQL statement to select the customer last name, city, state, and amount sold for the customer represented by customer ID 100895.

5. Retrieve a list of all product categories, subcategories, names, and list prices where the list price is greater than $100 while displaying the results for the product category all in uppercase.

6. Rewrite the query from the previous question and round the amount sold so that there are no cents in the display of the list prices.

7. Retrieve a list of all customer IDs and last names where the customer has more than 200 entries in the SALES table.

8. Display the product name of all products that have the lowest list price.

9. Create a view that contains all products in the Electronics category.

10. Sequences provide _____ generated integers.

11. This referential integrity constraint defines the relationship between two tables. Name it.

12. Check constraints enable users to define and enforce rules for:

   A. One or more tables

   B. No more than one column

   C. One or more columns

   D. Only one table

13. Deferred constraints are not checked until this statement is issued.

CHAPTER
3

The Database Administrator

CRITICAL SKILLS

3.1 Learn the Job of the DBA

3.2 Understand the Oracle Database 10*g* DBA Skill Set

3.3 Perform Day-to-Day Operations

3.4 Understand the Oracle Database 10*g* Infrastructure

3.5 Operate Modes of an Oracle Database 10*g*

3.6 Get Started with Oracle Enterprise Manager

3.7 Manage Database Objects

3.8 Manage Space

3.9 Manage Users

3.10 Manage Privileges for Database Users

o, you've decided to be a *Database Administrator (DBA)*. Great choice! On top of that, you've chosen Oracle as the *Database Management System (DBMS)* that you want to work with. Even better! All you need to do now is figure out how to learn what you need to know to do the job. Reading this book is a great start. However, the job of a DBA cannot be learned entirely in a few short months. It is a work in progress that can take several years to become really good at. Don't get us wrong—you can learn the basics that will make you a productive DBA in a few short months, but there is a great deal to learn, and we don't become really good at this job until we've actually run the utility, executed the SQL, or performed the task. In other words, don't just read this book—try the examples and don't be afraid to make mistakes.

CRITICAL SKILL 3.1
Learn the Job of the DBA

The role of a DBA is more of a career than a job. Those of us who have been doing this for many years are always learning new things and just trying to keep up! That's the exciting thing about being a DBA: the job keeps changing. Databases are growing at a phenomenal pace, the number of users is increasing, availability requirements are striving for that magical 24/7 mark, and security has become a much greater concern. As you will see in this book, databases now include more than just data. They are also about the Internet and grid computing and XML and Java. So, how long will it take you to learn how to be a DBA? For as long as you're practicing this career.

There are some concrete steps that you can take to jump-start your learning process. Undertaking an Oracle Certification will provide you with a structured program that offers you clear steps to help learn the details of the job. Instructor-led courses as well as CD- and Internet-based classes can help you through the process. Also, read as much as you can and then get your hands on a test database and practice what you've learned.

Applications come and go, but data stays around. All of the information that makes your company valuable is (or should be) stored in a database. Customer, vendor, employee, and financial data, as well as every other corporate data is stored in a database, and your company would have great difficulty surviving if any of that data was lost. Learn your job well. People are depending on you.

CRITICAL SKILL 3.2
Understand the Oracle Database 10*g* DBA Skill Set

There is good news for DBAs: Oracle has tools to help you do your job and manage your databases. These tools have existed for many versions of Oracle and have improved with each release to the point where the Oracle Database 10*g* offerings are extensive. In many cases, you will have the option of doing your job using a *Graphical User Interface (GUI),* and you will also have the option of using a command-line interface. We recommend learning both. You will need to use the command-line interface in many cases to schedule work through scripts. The GUI can be used for performing day-to-day operations and can also be used as a great learning tool the first time you perform an operation. In many cases, you will be able to generate the low-level commands from the GUI and can copy them to a file to be used later on.

As we've mentioned, there is a great deal that you will need to know in order to be able to provide well-rounded coverage of your Oracle environment. We can categorize the specialized areas of database management so that you will be aware of the whole picture and can break your work into well-defined groupings.

CRITICAL SKILL 3.3

Perform Day-to-Day Operations

In order to properly perform the role of Database Administrator, you will need to develop and implement solutions that cover all areas of this discipline. The amazing part of this job is that you may be asked to do many, or perhaps all, aspects of your job on any given day. Your daily tasks will vary from doing high-level architecture and design to performing low-level tasks. Let's take a look at the things that you will be getting involved in.

Architecture and Design

DBAs should be involved with the architecture and design of new applications, databases, and even technical infrastructure changes. Decisions made here will have a large impact on database performance and scalability and database knowledge will help choose a better technical implementation. Data design tools such as Oracle Designer can assist the DBA.

Capacity Planning

Short and long range planning needs to be performed on your databases and applications. This will focus on performance and sizing characteristics of your systems that will help to determine upcoming storage, CPU, memory, and network needs. This is an area that is often neglected and can lead to big problems if it is not done properly.

Backup and Recovery

A backup and recovery plan is, of course, critical in order to protect your corporate data. You need to ensure that data can be recovered quickly to the nearest point in time as possible. There is also a performance aspect to this since backups must be performed using minimal resources while the database is up and running and recoveries need to be performed within a time limit predefined by Service Level Agreements (*sla*) that are developed to meet customers' requirements. A complete backup and recovery implementation should include local recovery and remote recovery that is also referred to as disaster recovery planning (*drp*). You will see more on backup and recovery later in Chapter 5.

Security

This is an area that has become very sensitive due to the number of users that can access our databases and the amount of external, web-based access. Database users need to be authenticated so that we know with certainty who is accessing our database. They must then be given authorization to use the resources that they need to do their job by granting access to the objects in Oracle. This can be managed with Oracle Enterprise Manager, and we will show examples of this later in this chapter. External users require extra web-based security that is beyond the scope of this book.

Performance and Tuning

Performance and tuning is arguably the most exciting area of database management. Changes here are noticed almost immediately and every experienced DBA has stories about small changes they've made that resulted in large performance gains. On the other hand, every performance glitch in the environment will be blamed on the database and you will need to learn how to deal with this. Statspack, OEM Performance Management, and third-party tools will assist you in this area. There is a lot to learn here, but the proper tools will simplify this considerably.

Managing Database Objects

We need to manage all schema objects such as tables, indexes, views, synonyms, sequences, clusters, and source types such as packages, procedures, functions, and triggers to ensure they are valid and organized in a fashion that will deliver adequate performance and have adequate space. The space requirements of schema objects are directly related to tablespaces and datafiles that are growing at incredible rates. Using OEM, this can be simplified, something we will see examples of later in this chapter.

Storage Management

Databases are growing at incredible rates. We need to carefully manage space and pay particular attention to the space used by datafiles and archive logs. Online utilities are supported to help reorg objects while they remain online. Reorgs use considerable resources, however, so do not perform these operations unless it is necessary. See the section "Managing Space" for more on this.

TIP
Do not reorg unless you absolutely need to.

Change Management

Being able to upgrade or change the database is a discipline that includes many areas. Upgrades to the database schema, procedural logic in the database, and database software must all be performed in a controlled manner. Change control procedures and tools such as Oracle's Change Manager and third-party offerings will assist you.

Schedule Jobs

Oracle Database 10g comes with a new scheduler that allows you to schedule a job for a specific date and time, and to categorize jobs into job classes that can be prioritized. So, resources can be controlled by job class. Of course, other native scheduling systems such as "at" in Windows and crontab in UNIX can be used as well as other third-party offerings.

Network Management

Oracle Networking is a fundamental component of the database that you will need to become comfortable with. Database connectivity options like Tnsnames, the Oracle Internet Directory (OID), and the Oracle Listener require planning to ensure that performance and security requirements are met in a way that is simple to manage. You will see more of this in the next chapter.

Troubleshooting

Though troubleshooting may not be what you'd consider a classic area of Database Management, it is one area that you will encounter daily. You will need tools to help you with this. Oracle MetaLink technical support, available to customers who purchase the service, is invaluable. Oracle alert logs and dump files will also help you greatly. Experience will be your biggest ally here and the sooner you dive into database support, the faster you will progress.

You've seen the areas of database management that need to be handled, now it's time to look at the Oracle schema and storage infrastructure.

CRITICAL SKILL 3.4

Understand the Oracle Database 10g Infrastructure

Oracle's memory and process infrastructure have already been discussed in Chapter 1. In this section, we will take a look at the Oracle schema and storage infrastructure since these are a large part of what you will be required to manage.

Schemas

An Oracle database has many schemas contained in it. The schema is a logical structure that contains objects like segments, views, procedures, functions, packages, triggers, user-defined objects, collection types, sequences, synonyms, and database links. A segment is a data structure that can be a table, index, or temporary or undo segment. The schema name is the user that controls the schema. Examples of schemas are the System, Sys, Scott, and SH schemas. Figure 3-1 shows the relationship between these schema objects.

Segments, Extents, and Blocks

As you can see in Figure 3-1, a schema can have many segments and many segment types. Each segment is a single instance of a table, partition, cluster, index, or temporary or undo segment. So, for example, a table with two indexes is implemented as three segments in the schema. A segment is broken down further into extents, which are a collection of contiguous data blocks. As data is added to Oracle, it will first fill the blocks in the allocated extents and once those extents are full, new extents can be added to the segment as long as space allows. Oracle segment types are listed here:

■ Tables are where the data is kept in rows and columns. This is the heart of your database and a table is implemented in one schema and one tablespace. The exception to this is a special type of table called a partitioned table where the table can be split into different ranges or sets of values called a partition and each partition can be implemented in a different tablespace.

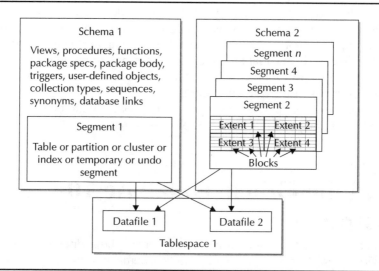

FIGURE 3-1. *The database and user schemas*

Remember, however, that each partition is itself a segment and each segment can only reside in one tablespace. Clustered tables are another special case where two tables with a close link between them can have their data stored together in a single block to improve join operations.

■ Indexes are optionally built on tables for performance reasons and to help implement integrity constraints such as primary keys and uniqueness.

■ Temporary segments are used as a temporary storage area by Oracle to run an SQL statement. For example, they may be used for sorting data and then discarded once a query or transaction is complete.

■ Undo segments are used to manage the before image of changes to allow data to roll back if needed and to help provide data consistency for users querying data that is being changed. There will be more on this in Chapter 5.

Segments can be thought of as physical structures since they actually are used to store data that is kept in a tablespace, although some of this is temporary in nature. There are other structures stored in the schema that are more logical in nature.

Logical Schema Structures

Not everything stored in a database and schema is data. Oracle also manages source modules as well as supporting structures such as sequences that are used to populate new unique and primary key values when inserting data into the database. These objects belong to a schema and are stored in the Oracle Catalog. These can all be easily managed through OEM, as shown in Figure 3-2. Take a look at the following for a brief description of these logical structures:

■ Views give you the capability of subsetting a table and combining multiple tables through a single named object. They can be thought of as a stored query. With the exception of a special type of view called a materialized view that is used for data warehousing, data is not stored in views. They are simply a new way of defining access to the underlying tables. These can be used for security, performance, and ease-of-use.

■ Synonyms are used to create a new name or alias for another database object such as a table, view, another synonym, and sources such as a procedure, package, function, java class, and so on. They can be used to simplify access. As with views, data is not stored in a synonym.

■ Sequences are used to generate new unique numbers that can be used by applications when inserting data into tables.

■ Source programs can be stored in the catalog and written in Oracle's proprietary PL/SQL or Java. PL/SQL source types include business logic that can be written as Packages, Procedures, and Functions. Triggers can also be used to implement business logic, but are often used to implement data integrity since they are not executed directly by a user or source program, but rather are automatically executed when an action is performed on the database. Java Sources and Java Classes are also implemented directly in Oracle. This server-side support of application logic improves performance since the logic resides with the data and it also improves performance.

- User types can be created by you to support object-oriented development. Array types, Object types, and Table types can all be created by you. As well, the Oracle XML Schema Processor supports XML processing by adding data types to XML documents that can be used to ensure the integrity of data in XML documents.

So now that you have seen all of our schema objects, it's time to tie these together to our storage architecture.

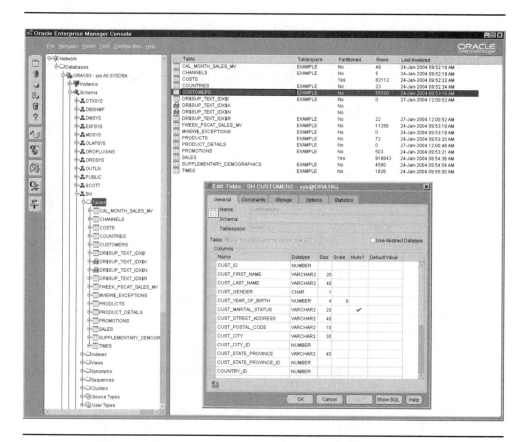

FIGURE 3-2. *Enterprise Manager table definition view*

Storage Structures

As shown in Figure 3-1, the physical schema objects are stored as segments in the database. Each segment can only be stored in a single tablespace and a tablespace can be made up of one or more datafiles. If a tablespace is running out of space, you can expand the datafiles it is made up of, or you can also add a new datafile to the tablespace. A datafile can only store data for a single tablespace.

A single tablespace can store data for multiple segments and in fact for several segment types. Segments from multiple schemas can also exist in the same tablespace. So, for example, table_a from schema1 and index_b from schema2 can both be implemented in the same tablespace. Oh and by the way, a tablespace can only store data for a single database.

The logical structures such as views and source code are stored in the Oracle catalog but are part of a schema. So, this means that the Oracle-supplied SH schema can contain all of the objects that it needs to run the entire application under its own schema name. This provides strong security and management benefits.

Progress Check

1. Name five areas that you will need to address as a DBA.

2. What is a schema and what does it contain?

3. Can a tablespace store more than one segment type?

4. Under which circumstances would you bother to start up the database in nomount mode?

CRITICAL SKILL 3.5

Operate Modes of an Oracle Database 10g

Oracle is a software package like many others that you may have used. However, when you run most programs, they run one and only one way. So when I open my accounting software, I run it the same way all the time. However, you have options

---

Progress Check Answers

1. As a DBA, you will need to address architecture, capacity planning, backup and recovery, and security and performance, among others.

2. A schema is a logical structure that contains objects like segments, views, procedures, functions, packages, triggers, user-defined objects, collection types, sequences, synonyms, and database links.

3. A single tablespace can store data for multiple segments and different segment types. Segments from multiple schemas can also exist in the same tablespace. So, for example, table_a from schema1 and index_b from schema2 can be implemented as two segments in the same tablespace.

4. When started in nomount mode, the parameter file is read and memory structures and processes are started for the instance. The database is not yet associated with the instance. You will use this in cases where you need to re-create the controlfile.

with Oracle. This section discusses the many ways that you can run Oracle. Some of these methods will be important to administrators, while others will allow for full use. This feature is important when you need to perform both critical and noncritical activities, and not interfere with your users or your data.

Modes of Operation

Oracle has several modes of operation. In most cases, when you start Oracle, you will simply issue the command:

```
> Startup;
```

This command actually takes Oracle through three distinct startup phases automatically, or you could also choose to explicitly step through these phases:

1. In the *nomount phase,* the database reads the spfile or the init.ora parameter file and starts up the Oracle memory structures as well as the background processes. The instance is started, but the database is not yet associated with the newly started instance. This is usually used in cases where you need to re-create the controlfile. The command to perform this is

   ```
   > startup nomount;
   ```

2. In order to associate a database with the instance, the instance "mounts" the database. This is done in the *mount phase.* The previously read parameter file is used to find those controlfiles, which contain the name of the data files and redo logs. The database is then mounted to allow some maintenance activities to be performed. Datafiles and redo logs are not opened when the database is in mount mode, so the database is not yet accessible by end users for normal tasks. Commands to mount a database are

   ```
   > startup mount;
   > alter database mount;
   ```

3. When Oracle opens the database in the *open phase,* it opens the data files and redo logs, making the database available for normal operations. Your redo logs must exist in order for the database to open. If they do not, the **resetlogs** command must be used to create new redo logs in the location specified in the control files.

   ```
   > Startup {open} {resetlogs};
   > alter database open;
   ```

Other Ways to Open the Database

There are some other options for opening a database. For example, you may want to open it in Read-Only mode so that no database changes (inserts, updates, or deletes) can be performed. There are also the upgrade/downgrade options that allow a database to be opened to perform a downgrade or upgrade to another version of Oracle.

```
> alter database open read only;
```

A common option you will use to perform maintenance will be to open the database in restricted mode. When you issue the command **startup restrict**, only users with both the **create session** and **restricted session** privileges will be able to use the database. So, as a DBA this is a helpful way to open the database that only you can use.

```
> startup restrict;
```

The database can be placed in a state where only the **sys** and **system** users can query the database without stopping the database and performing a subsequent **startup restrict**. The activities of other users continue until they become inactive. This can be performed using the **quiesce** option of alter session when the Database Resource Manager option has been set up.

```
> alter system quiesce restrict;
> alter system unquiesce;
```

Forcing a Startup

Over time, you will run into situations where Oracle has not shutdown properly and you are unable to restart it. In these rare instances, you will need to use the **force** option of the **startup** command. This will first perform a "shutdown abort" that forces the database to shutdown (see the next section for more information on this) followed by a database startup.

```
> startup force
```

Database and Instance Shutdown

When shutting down an instance, perform these steps, which are reverse from those you just saw when opening a database:

1. Close the database, including the data files and redo logs, so that it is no longer usable for normal tasks.

2. Unmount the database from the instance so that only the instance memory structures and background tasks are left running without a database associated with them.

3. Shut down the instance to close the control files.

In order to shut down a database, four different approaches can be used: Shutdown Normal, Immediate, Transactional, and Abort.

- *Normal* is, in a sense, the "perfect" way to shut down, since this approach will wait for all users to disconnect from the database and all transactions to complete before the shutdown occurs. Once this command has been issued, new users are not allowed into the system. This can be impractical in cases where users remain on the system for long periods of time.

```
> shutdown normal;
```

- *Immediate* is a practical shutdown approach that also leaves the database in a consistent state. When the database is put through a "shutdown immediate," all current transactions are rolled back and users are disconnected. No new transactions are allowed into the system. This will be relatively quick if the rollback operations are small, and is an excellent way to shut down the database before performing a database backup.

```
> shutdown immediate;
```

- A *transactional shutdown* is similar to the immediate variety except that running transactions are allowed to complete. So, once transactions have been committed, the user running it is disconnected. This is useful in cases where you do not want to shutdown until currently running transactions have finished or in cases where it will be quicker to complete existing transactions than it will be to roll them back.

```
> shutdown transactional
```

- *Abort* is the least graceful shutdown option of the four. When this is used, all transactions are ended immediately without waiting for a rollback or commit and all users are instantly disconnected while the database is brought down. Use this only if you are experiencing problems shutting down the database using one of the three options described previously or in cases where you need to shutdown the database immediately. The database needs to go through recovery procedures the next time it is restarted. After a shutdown abort has been performed, you should try to immediately start up the database so that you can then perform a shutdown (normal, immediate, or transactional) to bring the database down in the proper manner.

```
> shutdown abort;
```

OEM can help with instance and database startup and shutdown, as shown in Figure 3-3. Open OEM. In the left panel, choose the instance you want to work on and select "Instance" under the instance name (in this case, it's ora10g), then on the right side of the panel, choose View And Edit The Values Of Instance Parameters.

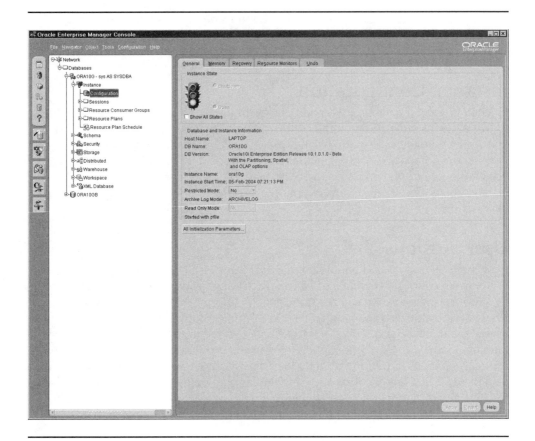

FIGURE 3-3. *Enterprise Manager instance configuration view*

CRITICAL SKILL 3.6
Get Started with Oracle Enterprise Manager

Oracle Enterprise Manager (OEM) is a great tool to assist the beginner DBA through to the experienced one. You should, however, also learn the low-level commands that will allow you to do your job through an interface like SQL*Plus. OEM can help you with this by showing you the SQL that it has generated when you select the Show Sql button that exists on many windows. Given how many options OEM has to help you do your job as a DBA, we will take a quick look at them here.

First off, OEM can be used to manage all of the databases in your network. As you can see in Figure 3-3, once you expand the network, you can select Databases and manage your databases from there. The right side of this OEM panel shows all of the objects that can be managed through OEM such as instances, schemas, security, distributed, warehouse, and workspace management features.

Instance Configuration

Once you select a database, which in our example is named ora10g, you can drill down to the instance and then the configuration of that instance. Figure 3-3 shows that we can see the state of an instance as well as all initialization parameters and whether the database is running in archive log mode and if it is in a restricted state. As you can see from the tabs on the right panel of this screen, we can see and manage memory settings, recovery options, resource monitors in effect, and undo information.

User Sessions

Now that we have a good handle on managing our instances and databases, we can drill down to our user sessions to see exactly what is going on inside the database. By choosing a session, we can see some general information such as the user session ID, when they logged in, and what the OS username and terminal name are for this user. As you can see from Figure 3-4, we can also see the SQL that is currently running, along with the explain plan being used. You can follow the order that each explain step is being performed in by the Step # column and can step through the plan or see it in a graphical layout using the far right column. You can also manage sessions and disconnect users by right-clicking the username and issuing the **kill session** command. I admit that the command name may be a bit harsh, but it does get the idea across.

Resource Consumer Groups

Next, we can select the Resource Consumer Groups item to see all of the groups that exist. A resource consumer group provides a way to group together users so that they can share similar processing requirements. The DATABASE_RESOURCE_ MANAGER package is used to allocate the maximum amount of CPU that a session can use or to set a limit for parallel execution for a session or to set the number of sessions that can be active for a consumer group as a few examples of this capability. OEM can assist in managing these groups by giving us an easy way to add new groups and edit those that exist. This panel allows us to enter a description of the group and attach users and database roles to a group. If you look at Figure 3-5, you will see all of the resource consumer groups listed. If you select one of these consumer groups, you will be presented with the capabilities to manage users, roles, and general information it.

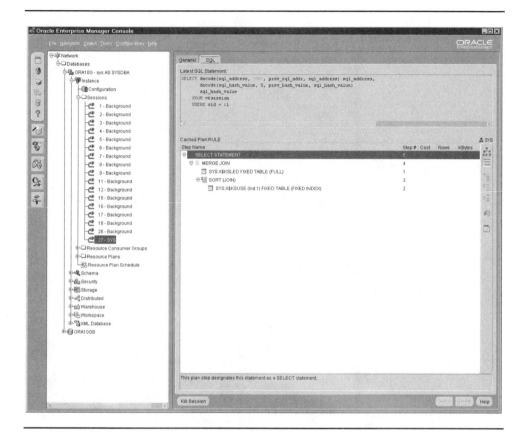

FIGURE 3-4. *SQL explain plan*

A resource plan builds on the resource consumer groups by providing a way to define how system resources will be allocated to the resource consumer groups that we just discussed. Figure 3-5 shows a list of the groups and subplans that can be set up here. We see tabs that allow us to define maximum parallelism, concurrently active sessions, undo pool space, and execution time limits for the group. Group switching allows for a session to change groups after a predefined amount of execution time has been reached. Presumably, you would move the user to a lower priority group to free resources to other sessions. The resource plan schedule can be used to set daily schedules to enable and disable resource plans.

Schema, Security, and Storage Management

The next items on the OEM console are schema, security, and storage management. We will visit these in sections 3.7, 3.8, and 3.9/3.10, respectively. It is worth mentioning now, however, that all three of these can be completely managed through OEM.

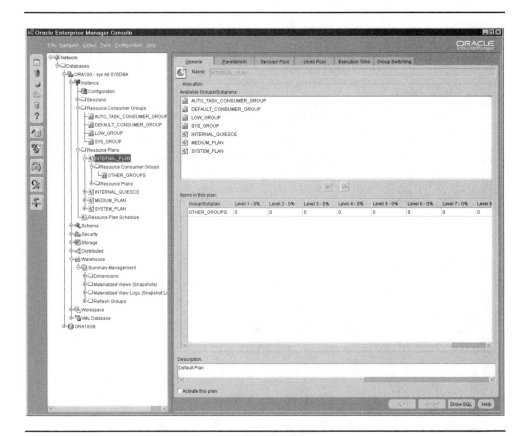

FIGURE 3-5. *Enterprise Manager resource group view*

Distributed Management

Some Oracle distributed capabilities are handled through the Distributed option. These include the ability to:

- Manage in-doubt transactions that can result from two-phase commit.

- Create, edit, and drop database links.

- Use streams to implement messaging.

- Use advanced queues and replication to pass messages and data to applications.

This can be a difficult area to manage and having a tool such as the OEM Console to help us out with this is a very welcome feature.

Warehouse Features

Warehouse options such as summary management, materialized views, and dimensions can all be dealt with through OEM, as shown in Figure 3-5.

Other Tools

You will notice that the toolbar has an option called Tools. This includes more advanced tools for managing our environment. Let's very quickly review the Tools that are included here. These tools can all be selected, as shown in Figure 3-6.

Database Tools to analyze data, perform backup management, and provide data management for utilities such as export, import, and load are included in the first option. Choose Tools and then Database Tools to get to these. Once Database Tools has been chosen, you will be presented with options to back up, recover, maintain, and configure your backup and recovery jobs. Backup management can be selected under Tools, as shown in Figure 3-6.

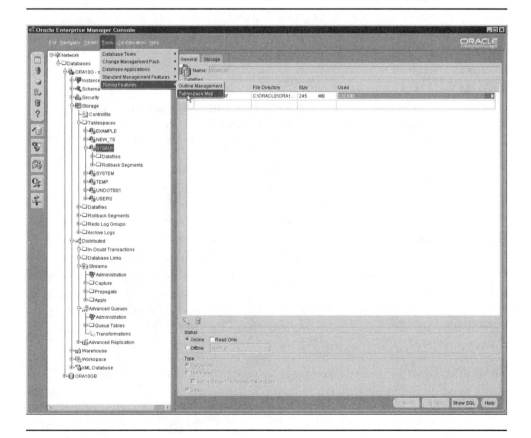

FIGURE 3-6. *Enterprise Manager tool options*

Database change management can be performed through the Change Management Pack. Under Tools, choose Change Management Pack or Standard Management Features and these will lead you to the Change Manager utility.

Database applications will provide support for the spatial index advisor, SQL*Plus Worksheet, and the Oracle Text Manager.

Tuning facilities such as performance manager, outline management, and tablespace maps are provided through Standard Management Features and Tuning Features, as shown in Figure 3-6.

As you can see from this overview of OEM console capabilities, many of the tools that we need to perform our day-to-day tasks can be found in this one console. Now that we have confidence that there's a toolset to support us, let's take a quick look at what you need to think about when managing database objects.

CRITICAL SKILL 3.7

Manage Database Objects

A large part of your job as a DBA will be to manage the objects that exist in a database. Let's look at the objects that you need to concern yourself with and discuss the main management issues that you will have in each of these areas.

Controlfiles

It is critical to the database that you have at least one valid control file for your database. These are small files and can be multiplexed by the Oracle instance. Ensuring that you have at least three copies of the controlfiles (remember, they are small), as well as text and binary backups whenever a data file, log file, or tablespace is changed and on a regularly scheduled basis (at least daily) will go a long way towards ensuring that your control files are in good shape. Controlfiles will be discussed in more detail in Chapter 5.

Redo Logs

Redo logs are necessary to ensure database integrity and should be duplexed in Oracle. Oracle mirroring helps even if your redo logs are mirrored by your storage subsystem since Oracle will use the alternate redo log if one should become corrupt. You will need to ensure that you have enough redo logs and that they are sized properly to support database performance. How large should your redo logs be? They should be large enough that a log switch does not usually occur more than once every 15 minutes due to the checkpointing that occurs during a log switch and the overhead that is incurred during this operation. How many redo logs should you have? You should have enough redo logs that the system will not wrap around to a log that has not yet completed a checkpoint or completed archiving (for systems in archivelog mode). Redo logs can be added, deleted, and switched through OEM.

Undo Management

The Undo segment is where the before images of changed rows are stored. Oracle will manage your undo segments for you, but you need to determine how large to make the tablespace that the Undo segment is stored in. The size that you make this depends on the length of time that you want the undo information to be available to you. If you look at Figure 3-7, you will see how OEM helps you determine the length of time that Undo can be retained based on the system activity and Undo tablespace. This is in the Configuration section for an instance. If the tablespace is not the correct size, it can be changed using the Storage feature of OEM, which you will see later in this chapter. Undo segments are covered further in Chapter 5.

If you choose to implement user-managed rollback segments, then these can be managed in the Storage section of OEM by choosing Rollback Segments and then selecting the segment name that you want to manage. If you look at Figure 3-7, you will see a Rollback Segment named System. By the way, the System rollback segment will always exist but should never be used as a rollback segment for user processes.

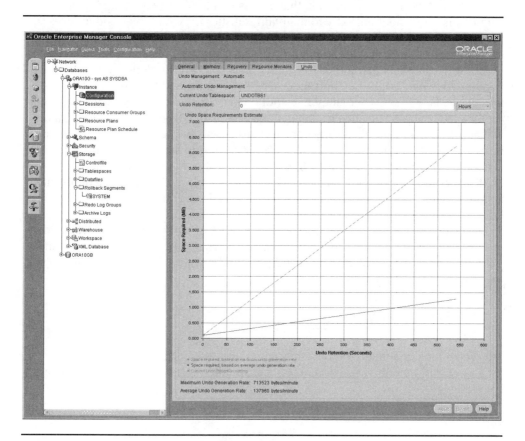

FIGURE 3-7. *Enterprise Manager Automatic Undo Management view*

Schema Objects

Schema objects were discussed earlier in this chapter, and you saw that we can manage schema objects through OEM. There are also some things that you may want to do with your own SQL scripts that run as scheduled jobs. When managing schemas, you need to ensure that those physical objects that take up a great deal of space, do in fact have enough space to grow. This includes tables, indexes, clusters, and partitioned tables. Manage this space through the tablespace that they are implemented in and ensure that there is enough room to grow in the tablespace. Ensuring that the extent sizes are large enough that you do not need to allocate too many extents is something that you need to monitor. But, do not become reorg-happy. You do not need to reorg a table if it is in hundreds of extents. You only need to reorg if there are a large number of chained or migrated rows. Indexes, on the other hand, will need to be reorged more frequently. We will find out more about managing space in the next section.

Figure 3-2 shows an example of how the SH.Customers table can be managed through OEM. Note the Storage tab that allows you to change the table's storage parameters. You should also try to maintain statistics on your tables and indexes so they are up-to-date. This will assist the optimizer make better decisions when choosing access paths for your queries and can be used to validate the structures. In Oracle Database 10g, a scheduler job called *gather_stats_job* will run during a maintenance window between 10:00 P.M. and 6:00 A.M., by default, and will run statistics for those objects in cases where they have not been collected yet or are stale. Setting the Oracle Database 10g initialization parameter **statistics_level** to typical (the default) will allow Oracle to automatically update statistics as a background task on a regular basis and is the recommended approach for gathering statistics. In pre–Oracle Database 10g releases, the DBMS_STATS package should be run manually or can use the *Monitoring* keyword in a CREATE or ALTER table. Monitoring is a deprecated feature in Oracle Database 10g and the keyword (along with "nomonitoring") will be ignored.

Logical schema objects that do not take up a lot of space need to be watched to ensure they are not invalid. Triggers, views, synonyms, procedures, functions, and packages are examples of the objects that should be valid. You can check this with the SQL statement that follows.

```
select owner, object_name, object_type
from dba_objects where status ^= 'VALID';
```

We've looked at many of the database objects that will require your attention. Let's now explore one area that requires special attention due to the size of today's databases.

Ask the Expert

Q: Why is it important for DBAs to get involved with the architecture and design of a new system?

A: Decisions made on the technical infrastructure as well as data and application designs here will have a large impact on database performance and scalability. Database knowledge will help choose a better technical implementation. Once chosen, these can be difficult to change.

Q: Which method do you normally use to shut down a database?

A: Although the **shutdown normal** operation is a recommended approach, it is often impractical since you need users to disconnect themselves. The approach that I prefer is to perform a checkpoint using the command **alter system checkpoint** which will write data out to data files and speed up the restart. I then perform a **shutdown abort**, immediately followed by a **startup restrict**, and **shutdown immediate**. This is a fast, guaranteed shutdown that leaves the database in a consistent state once all of the steps have been completed.

Q: What is the best way to become a good Oracle DBA quickly and then to keep improving?

A: There are many things that you will need to do and many skills that you'll need to develop to do this job. First, learning the basic DBA skills, which you can get from books such as this as well as from courses, will give you a head start. Practicing what you see is probably the quickest and most practical way to learn. Getting involved in supporting some databases in development and production will force you to learn very quickly. Then working on development systems for different types of applications will help to round out your skills. Keep reading and learning and never assume that you know it all and you will do very well.

CRITICAL SKILL 3.8

Manage Space

The challenge of managing data in your Oracle Database 10*g* is one that provides you with options. In this section, we will look at the methods that have been used in the many versions of the database to manage your information. Today's version of the database provides us with options. The first that we will discuss is managing your data and the files in which they reside in a manual way. Another option, automatic storage management, is discussed in Chapter 9.

Archive Logs

When you put the database in archive logging mode, the redo logs are written out to a directory that is named in your parameter or SPFILE. If that directory becomes full and the database attempts to write another archive log, the database activity will be suspended until sufficient space is made available for the new file. Create a large directory and schedule jobs to move the archive log files from online storage to tape before you encounter a space issue. RMAN does a nice job of helping you manage this. Please see Chapter 5 for more information on this.

Tablespaces and Datafiles

Space should be managed at the datafile and tablespace level rather than at a lower level such as a table or index. Using locally managed tablespaces with uniform extent sizes will simplify your management. Do not worry that you have some extents in a tablespace or for an object. This does not create a performance issue since the extents contain a number of blocks that must be contiguous. You can see the amount of space available in your datafiles by selecting Datafiles in OEM, as in Figure 3-8. This shows the amount of free space available in the currently allocated space. If you have used the autoextend feature to allow a datafile to extend in size when more space is needed, the extra space is not shown in this graph. Do not allow temporary tablespaces or undo tablespaces to autoextend since they will grow to use all of the space.

TIP

*Do not autoextend **temporary** and **undo** tablespaces, since they will quickly grow to use all of the space to which they can autoextend.*

What do you do if you run out of space in a datafile? Just enter **OEM**, click the datafile, and choose the Storage tab. Once there, you can change the autoextend feature and enter the size of the extensions that you would like. Do not forget to limit the size of the datafile so that it does not grow to use all of your space. After you've completed this, click Apply and you're done. If you select the Show SQL button, you can see the **alter database** syntax, which is also shown next.

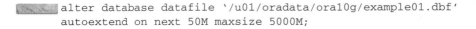

```
alter database datafile '/u01/oradata/ora10g/example01.dbf'
autoextend on next 50M maxsize 5000M;
```

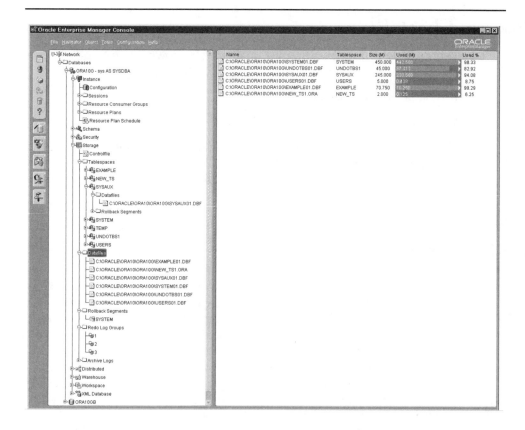

FIGURE 3-8. *Tablespace view in Enterprise Manager*

You can write your own scripts to compare the amount of allocated space for a datafile in view dba_data_files to the amount of free space, as shown in view dba_free_space.

OEM also provides you with a more detailed map of how space is used. In OEM, select a tablespace and then navigate from Tools to Tuning Features, finally choosing Tablespace Map. This opens a graphical layout showing each segment in the tablespace. From the tablespace map, you can choose the Tablespace Analysis Report tab for a written report on the space being used.

Managing the database objects discussed earlier will be a large part of your role as a DBA. In the next section, let's take a look at setting up and managing users. After all, without database users, there is no point in doing any of this!

Progress Check ⊖

1. What's better: "shutdown transactional" or "shutdown immediate"?

2. Do you only need to worry about logical schema objects that do not take up a large amount of space?

3. What happens if your archive log directory becomes full?

4. Why would you want to use a command-line interface rather than a GUI to perform your tasks as a DBA?

CRITICAL SKILL 3.9

Manage Users

Before you can do anything in Oracle, you need to have a user ID created to enable you to log in to Oracle. As a DBA, you will begin with the SYS or SYSTEM accounts since these accounts both have the DBA role and exist in all Oracle databases. They are often used to perform database administration tasks. The SYS account is also granted the **sysdba** privilege and is the schema that the Oracle catalog is stored in. You should only use the SYS account when you need to perform a task as SYS or need the **sysdba** privilege. If your database was created using the Database Configuration Assistant (dbca), then you will also automatically get the SYSMAN and DBSNMP accounts. SYSMAN is used to administer Oracle Enterprise Manager (OEM) and DBSNMP is used by the agent that OEM employs to monitor Oracle databases. Several other accounts will also be set up for the "example" schemas, such as the Sales History ('SH') user that we will utilize throughout this book. The OUTLN schema will be created to allow you to use plan stability through the stored outline feature. Depending on the options you choose when creating your database, other accounts may be set up for you. For example, if you install the OLAP option, the OLAPSYS account will be created.

Progress Check Answers

1. Both leave your database in a consistent state. It depends on how long your transactions will take to complete or roll back. If all things are equal and you think that it will take as long to commit the transactions that are already running, then you should use "shutdown transactional" since commits will be allowed to complete and no data will be lost.

2. Logical schema objects need to be watched to ensure they are in a valid state.

3. If database attempts to write an archive log after the directory has become full, the database activity will be suspended until sufficient space is made available for the new file.

4. You may want to place the command in a script that is scheduled or run as a repetitive task.

Create a User

When you create a user, you can either use the **create user** syntax or the OEM, which is an easier approach. In order to create a user, you will need to decide the following things:

- The default tablespace where segments created by this user will be placed unless a tablespace name is used in the DDL to override this.

- Whether to expire the password so that the user needs to change it the first time they log in to Oracle.

- A temporary tablespace to store internal data used by Oracle while queries are running. Sort operations make use of the temporary tablespace if there is not enough room in the SGA to perform the sort operation.

- Whether to employ user quotas on tablespaces, which put a limit on the amount of space that a user's objects can take up in that tablespace.

- The authentication type, which allows you to specify whether you want Oracle to force the user to specify a password when they log in, or you can trust the operating system to do this for you.

- The initial password that the user will log in with. The user must change this during the first log in if you chose to expire the password in advance of the user's first logon.

- Privileges to grant to the user. These can be direct privileges or roles. We will discuss them in the next section.

- A profile for the user, which can be employed to manage the user's session by limiting resources that sessions can use, and that help implement corporate password policies. We will also see this in the next section.

- Whether to lock or unlock the user.

The OEM console in Figure 3-9 shows the options available to you to create and edit a user. For each user, there are eight separate tabs that allow you to easily enter a user's information. You can see the SQL that will be generated by selecting the Show Sql button at the bottom of the panel. Another great option allows you to model a user and create another user like one that already exists. To do this, click the user that you want to model, select Object from the top of the panel, and then select the Create Like option.

Here is a sample **CREATE USER** statement:

```
CREATE USER "NEWUSER" PROFILE "DEFAULT" IDENTIFIED BY "newpassword"
PASSWORD EXPIRE DEFAULT TABLESPACE "USERS" TEMPORARY TABLESPACE "TEMP"
QUOTA UNLIMITED ON TEMP QUOTA UNLIMITED ON USERS
ACCOUNT UNLOCK;
GRANT "CONNECT" TO "NEWUSER";
```

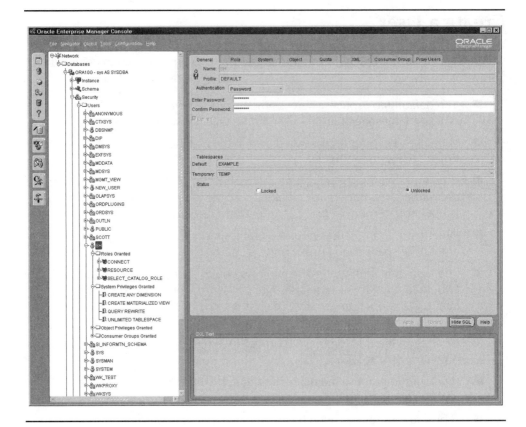

FIGURE 3-9. *User Management view*

Edit Users

Once a user has been created, you will be asked at different times to edit users to change quotas or reset passwords or unlock an account. This can be easily performed through OEM by selecting the User, choosing the option you want to change through the Gui, and then applying the change.

Editing users can also be performed using the **ALTER USER** statement, as shown next, where a user account is unlocked, the password is changed, and a tablespace quota is increased.

```
ALTER USER "username"  IDENTIFIED BY "newpwd " QUOTA UNLIMITED
ON TOOLS ACCOUNT UNLOCK;
```

We've now created a user and it's time to grant them some privileges. Let's see how we do this in the next section.

CRITICAL SKILL 3.10

Manage Privileges for Database Users

Creating a user in Oracle has accomplished the first part of user setup and that is authentication. We have a user ID and password and have authorized this user to use an Oracle database. Once the user logs in, however, they will not be able to do very much because they will not have privileges that allow them to access any objects. This leads us to the second step of setting up a user: authorization. In order to authorize a user to perform their tasks, we need to grant access.

Grant Authority

You now need to give permission to the user to do things in Oracle. Actions like accessing a table or executing a procedure or running a utility require you to "grant" the authority to that user. When you perform a grant, you can specify four things:

- The user that is being granted the authority.

- The object that is being granted. Examples of these are a table, procedure, or role.

- The type of access being granted, such as select, insert, update, or delete on a table, or execute on a procedure, function, or package.

- Whether this user has authority to then grant the same authority to other users. By default, they do not, but this can be added by using the With Grant option.

Here are two examples that grant a user "NEWUSER" access to a table and then to a package.

```
GRANT SELECT ON "TABLE_NAME" TO "NEWUSER" WITH GRANT OPTION;
GRANT INSERT ON "TABLE_NAME" TO "NEWUSER" WITH GRANT OPTION;
GRANT EXECUTE ON "PROCEDURE_NAME" TO "NEWUSER"
```

Types of Grants

There are two types of grants that can be given to a user: system privileges and object privileges.

- System privileges are predefined Oracle privileges granting authority to overall system objects rather than individual ones. The ability to perform a **create tablespace**, **alter system**, and **back up any table** are just a few examples of some system-level privileges that can be granted to a user.

- Object privileges are a lower-level authority where a named object is granted to a user. So, the ability to perform an operation on a particular table, or execute an individual function, package, or procedure are object privileges as opposed to the ability to **execute any procedure** or **select any table**, which are system-level privileges.

Take Away Authority

What is given can be taken away. In order to take privileges away from a user, we use the **REVOKE** command and the syntax is very similar to the syntax we use when issuing a grant. Here are two examples of a **REVOKE** operation:

```
REVOKE INSERT ON "TABLE_NAME" FROM "NEWUSER";
REVOKE EXECUTE ON "TABLE_NAME" FROM "NEWUSER";
```

Roles

When you think of the number of privileges that need to be managed in situations where you have thousands of database objects as well as thousands of users, you quickly realize that it would be nice to organize the privileges into groups that can be easily managed. This is where roles come into play.

A "role" is used to group privileges together into a predefined group that can be granted to users. So, rather than granting object and system privileges individually to every user in your system, you can grant them to a role, which in turn is granted to the user.

Oracle-Defined Roles

Some special roles are created by Oracle through the install process or by running Oracle-supplied scripts. The DBA, Connect, Resource, Imp_Full_Database, and Select_Catalog_Role are some examples of roles that are supplied by Oracle and should not be changed.

Create and Grant a Role

Roles are created using the **create** statement in the same manner as creating users. We can also revoke privileges from roles and drop roles when they are no longer needed. Roles can also be granted to other roles. You can see an example of this next where the Oracle role **CONNECT** is granted to the newly created role **TESTROLE**, along with a system and object privilege.

```
CREATE ROLE "TESTROLE";
GRANT CONNECT TO "TESTROLE"
GRANT EXECUTE ANY PROCEDURE TO "TESTROLE"
GRANT SELECT ON "table_name" TO "TESTROLE"
```

The new role can then be granted to a user as shown next, where "testrole" is granted to user "Testuser."

```
Grant "testrole" to "Testuser";
```

The "TESTROLE" is then dropped since it is no longer required.

```
DROP ROLE "TESTROLE";
```

Now that we've created users and roles, we can fine-tune our management of these by implementing some user policies through *profiles,* which we will explore next.

Profiles

A profile can be used to implement a password management policy, as well as limit resources for a user. When you created the user NEWUSER earlier, a password was supplied along with the DEFAULT profile. Using this DEFAULT profile, the user never needs to change their password and there are no limits placed on any system resources. You can create new profiles to implement your corporate password policies in Oracle. For example, you can specify the number of days after which a user must change their password. You can also establish a policy where a password cannot be reused within a certain period of time and must contain a certain number of changes. A function can be used to ensure that a complex password is created by the user. For example, you may require that a password be more than eight characters long, use alpha, numeric, and special characters, and that it does not repeat a character more than twice. This can all be implemented in a function. An account can be locked after a specified number of login attempts and can remain locked for the number of days defined in the profile.

System limits for a user can also be implemented by a profile. These include limiting system resources such as those for CPU, connect, and idle time as well as the number of sessions employed by the user, limits on reads, and the SGA used. You should note, however, that the Database Resource Manager is the preferred way to limit resources and that you should use profiles to manage passwords.

The following is an example of the creation of a new policy that will lock an account after three failed login attempts and will keep the account locked indefinitely. The password needs to be changed every 60 days and the new password will be verified by your custom function **COMPLEX_PASSWORD**. The old password cannot be reused for 120 days.

```
CREATE PROFILE "NEWPOLICY"
FAILED_LOGIN_ATTEMPTS 3
PASSWORD_LOCK_TIME UNLIMITED
PASSWORD_LIFE_TIME 60
PASSWORD_REUSE_TIME 120
PASSWORD_VERIFY_FUNCTION COMPLEX_PASSWORD
```

Now, let's grant this policy to user NEWUSER:

```
ALTER USER NEWUSER PROFILE NEWPOLICY;
```

In Conclusion

As you have seen in this chapter, there is a great deal that a DBA needs to be aware of to properly manage a database. The good news is that you will have tools such as OEM to help you. Do your best to keep your environment as simple as you possibly can! You will be glad that you did as your overall database environment continues to grow.

Project 3-1   Creating Essential Objects

This project will walk you through the creation of the essential storage and schema objects after a database has been created, which in this project will be called ora10g. You will create a new tablespace called **NEW_TS** and will than add a user **NEW_USER** who will be given the authority to this tablespace. You will then create a role called **NEW_ROLE** and grant privileges to it. Afterward, you'll grant this role to the new user. A table and index will be created on this tablespace by the new user. Lastly, you will resize the undo tablespace to make it larger. You will see how to do this in OEM and the generated SQL will also be shown to you so you can do this in SQL*Plus.

Step by Step

1. You have been asked to create a new used named **NEW_USER** who will need to create objects in a new tablespace called **NEW_TS** that should be sized at 5MB. Your first step will be to create the tablespace. In OEM, log in as user SYSTEM, go to database ora10g, choose storage, then choose tablespace and select an existing tablespace to model. Under Objects in the toolbar, select the Create Like option to model your new tablespace after the existing one. Enter the new tablespace name, datafile name, and all properties including the size. Make this a locally managed tablespace 5MB in size with uniform extents 96KB in size. If you choose the Show Sql button, you will see the generated SQL. It should look something like the following SQL. You can either apply the change in OEM or you can copy and paste the generated SQL and run it in SQL*Plus.

```
CREATE TABLESPACE "NEW_TS" LOGGING
DATAFILE 'C:\ORACLE\ORA10\ORA10G\NEW_TS1.ora' SIZE 2M REUSE AUTOEXTEND ON
NEXT  1280K MAXSIZE  32767M EXTENT MANAGEMENT LOCAL UNIFORM SIZE 96K SEGMENT
SPACE MANAGEMENT  AUTO;
```

2. Now you will create **NEW_USER**. As with the preceding tablespace creation, you can model an existing user. In OEM, go to Security and then to User, choose an existing user to model, and select Object from the toolbar. Once again, use the Create Like feature. The user should now have a password of **new_password**, which will be unlocked. Set the default tablespace to NEW_TS.

```
CREATE USER "NEW_USER"  PROFILE "DEFAULT" IDENTIFIED BY "new_password" PASSWORD
EXPIRE DEFAULT TABLESPACE "NEW_TS"
TEMPORARY TABLESPACE "TEMP" QUOTA UNLIMITED    ON "TEMP";
```

3. Create a role called NEW_ROLE. In OEM, go to security, and then choose Role. Under Object in the toolbar, select Create and enter the role name.

```
CREATE ROLE "NEW_ROLE"  NOT IDENTIFIED;
```

4. Grant the **CREATE TABLE** system privilege, the **OLAP_USER** role, and the object privilege **SELECT** on table **SQLPLUS_PRODUCT_PROFILE** to **NEW_ROLE**. In OEM, go to role and choose **NEW_ROLE**. Use the tabs System, Object, and Role to choose the objects listed here. Click the Apply button to make the changes. The generated SQL will look like the three grants listed next.

```
GRANT CREATE TABLE TO "NEW_ROLE";
GRANT SELECT ON  "SYSTEM"."SQLPLUS_PRODUCT_PROFILE" TO "NEW_ROLE";
GRANT "OLAP_USER" TO "NEW_ROLE";
```

5. Grant **NEW_ROLE** and connect to **NEW_USER**. Also, give **NEW_USER** an unlimited quota on **NEW_TS** to allow for objects to be created in the tablespace. In OEM, navigate to Users and choose **NEW_USER**. Once there, choose the Role tab and select **NEW_ROLE**, and then select the down arrow. Click the Apply button to make the change.

```
GRANT "NEW_ROLE" TO "NEW_USER";
ALTER USER "NEW_USER" DEFAULT ROLE  ALL;
ALTER USER "NEW_USER"  QUOTA UNLIMITED ON "NEW_TS";
```

6. You will now log into the database as **NEW_USER** and can use OEM with the **NEW_USER** account. Once in OEM, you will create a table called **NEW_TABLE** with columns col01 as number(15) and col02 as varchar2(30). In OEM, in the toolbar, select Object and under that choose Create, and then choose Table. Make sure the table is created in **NEW_TS**. Follow the screens to add col01 and col02. You will then create a primary key called **NEW_TABLE_PK** using col01. Follow the screens and choose the options you would like. We recommend you name any keys and constraints rather than relying on system defaults. Choose Finish and you have created a new table with a primary key!

```
CREATE TABLE "NEW_USER"."NEW_TABLE"
("COL01" NUMBER(15) NOT NULL,
 "COL02" VARCHAR2(30) NOT NULL,
CONSTRAINT "NEW_TABLE_PK" PRIMARY KEY("COL01"),
CONSTRAINT "NEW_TABLE_U1" UNIQUE("COL01"))
TABLESPACE "NEW_TS";
```

7. You now have one last task: resizing the undo tablespace to add 100MB to it. Log in to OEM as user System and choose the datafile under the **undo** tablespace. Enter the new size and click Apply. It's as easy as that. The SQL to increase this from 50MB to 150MB is shown here:

```
ALTER DATABASE DATAFILE '/u01/oradata/ORA10G/UNDOTBS01.DBF' RESIZE  150M;
```

(continued)

Project Summary

This project has taken you through the basic steps of creating an environment for a new user, including using roles and granting privileges. You've seen how to manage users as well as space and have even created objects. Armed with these capabilities, you are now on your way to being a productive DBA. Congratulations!

☑ Chapter 3 Mastery Check

1. What is the benefit of a role?

2. Should a table that is in tens or hundreds of extents be reorged?

3. What is the preferred method for collecting object statistics?

4. What is a segment?

5. What is an extent?

6. Name two reasons for implementing an index.

7. How can you place a database in maintenance mode without first shutting it down?

8. How can we limit the resources that a particular user can consume and how does this work?

9. When managing undo segments, what are the things that you need to think about?

10. What is likely to happen if you turn on the autoextend property for undo and temporary tablespaces with a maxsize set to unlimited?

11. What is special about the SYS user account and how does it differ from SYSTEM?

12. What are temporary tablespaces used for?

13. What are the two aspects of security that are covered in Oracle's implementation?

14. Name and describe the types of privileges that can be granted to a user.

15. How would you implement your corporate password policy in Oracle?

CHAPTER
4

Networking

CRITICAL SKILLS

4.1 Use Oracle Net Services

4.2 Learn the Difference Between Dedicated and Shared Server Architectures

4.3 Define Connections

4.4 Use the Oracle Net Listener

4.5 Learn Naming Methods

4.6 Use Oracle Configuration Files

4.7 Use Administration Tools

4.8 Use Profiles

4.9 Network in a Multitiered Environment

his chapter introduces Oracle Net Services, which allow database applications running on remote systems to access an Oracle database. It creates and maintains the network connection, and also exchanges data between the application and the database. Oracle networking plays a critical role in performance and availability. Each new version of Oracle is designed to support more data and users than the previous release. This increased amount of database activity and network traffic needs to be addressed from an availability and performance perspective and should be managed by the DBA. A DBA also has to be able to determine if a performance issue is due to networking, and if so, then they must be able to resolve any network performance issues from a database configuration perspective.

Throughout this chapter we will refer to DBAs, which in this context means anyone that is performing networking administration operations to make the database connectivity work. These days, more developers are managing their own development databases and performing operations traditionally reserved for DBAs.

NOTE
Oracle Net Services is a large topic. The emphasis in this chapter is to introduce DBAs to Oracle Net Services terminology and concepts, feature/functionality, and key components and tools. Once a beginning DBA reads this section, they should be able to understand the Oracle networking references and be capable of performing simple operations using the Oracle GUI tools and wizards for Oracle Net Services.

CRITICAL SKILL 4.1

Use Oracle Net Services

Oracle Net Services is the software component that allows enterprise connectivity across heterogeneous environments. Oracle Net is the part of Oracle Net Services that manages data communication between a remote application and the Oracle database, and runs on top of a network protocol like TCP/IP. The software used by Oracle Net software resides on the remote system and the Oracle database platform.

A listener process must be running on the database server to receive the network request. (A listener is a program that listens on a port for incoming network requests and then hands the request to another program for processing.) The listener then determines the appropriate type of process to handle the request.

The network protocol sends a request to the Oracle Protocol layer, which sends the information to the Oracle Net Foundation layer, which then communicates with the database server. The Oracle network communication stack, shown in Figure 4-1, is similar on both the client- and server-side.

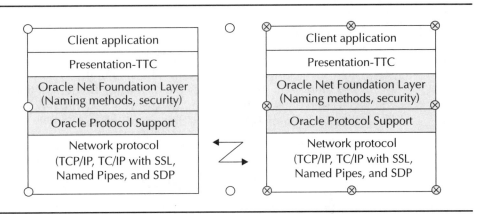

FIGURE 4-1. *The Oracle network communication stack*

Oracle Net (Oracle Net Foundation Layer and Oracle Protocol Support) fits into the session layer of the Open Systems Interconnect (OSI) model (visit www.ietf.org for more information about the OSI model).

Network Protocols

Oracle supports a number of industry standard protocols. These protocols transport the data between the remote platform and the database server platform. The protocols also display how users need to work with data differently than they did a few years ago. Oracle-supporting protocols like SDP, HTTP, FTP, and WebDAV show that Oracle Database 10*g* enhances network performance and offers increased flexibility for users working with data. In this section, the term application server will be used to address both web and application server services available in the middle tier. Table 4-1 lists the supported industry-standard protocols.

Protocol	Description
TCP/IP	The Transmission Control Protocol/Internet Protocol (TCP/IP) is the standard protocol used in client server environments.
TCP/IP with SSL	TCP/IP with Secure Sockets Layer (SSL) provides authentication (certificates and private keys) encryption. The Oracle Advanced Security option is required for this protocol.

TABLE 4-1. *Standard Industry Network Protocols*

Protocol	Description
SDP	The Sockets Directory Protocol (SDP) is an industry-standard high-speed protocol. SDP is used with an InfiniBand network. The InfiniBand network takes the messaging burden off the CPU and onto the network hardware. This network reduces the overhead of TCP/IP, providing increased bandwidth.
Named Pipes	Supports interprocess communication between remote platforms and the database server platform using pipes. A pipe is opened on one end and information is sent down the pipe to allow I/O between the platforms.
HTTP	The Hypertext Transport Protocol (HTTP) is an industry-standard protocol that is primarily used between clients and application servers. Oracle can also start up an HTTP listener to handle a request over HTTP directly.
FTP	File Transfer Protocol (FTP) is a standard method for transferring files across the Internet. It makes it easy to transfer files back and forth between different platforms. A server that can receive an FTP connection is referred to as an FTP server or FTP site. FTP addresses looks similar to HTTP; ftp://ftp.trubix.com is an example of an FTP server address.
WebDAV	The WWW Distributed Authoring Protocol (WebDAV) supports collaborative authoring over the Internet. The benefits of WebDAV include locking mechanisms, interoperable publishing with HTTP and XML support, writing over the Web with embedded devices, versioning, and Access Control Lists.

TABLE 4-1.   *Standard Industry Network Protocols* (continued)

Optimize Network Bandwidth

Multitiered architectures need to maximize the bandwidth between the application server and the database server platforms. Oracle Net Services supports the high-speed networks of InfiniBand, a channel-based, high-speed interconnect technology designed to optimize performance between different platforms. It's used for server clustering and network interfaces to storage area networks (SANs) and local area networks (LANs). Vendors such as Hewlett-Packard, IBM, Sun Microsystems, Dell, and Microsoft support InfiniBand technology, and the SDP protocol, an industry-standard wire protocol, is also used with the InfiniBand network. Highly active multitiered environments should consider using high-speed interconnects between the application server and the database server.

Character Sets

There can be character set differences between the application platforms and the database server. This is important because if the character sets are different between the database server and the application environment, data conversion will occur. If there are any conversion issues, the data will be malformed. If the character sets are not defined, the database default is the US7ASCII.

New Oracle Database 10*g*'s should strongly consider a Unicode character set such as AL32UTF8. The presentation layer manages character set and data type conversions between these two platforms. Two Task Common (TTC) is the presentation layer used by client/server environments.

The Oracle environmental variable, **NLS_LANG**, can be used to control locale behavior for the database and the application environment. (A locale is a linguistic and cultural environment where the application is running.) The database also contains **NLS_ initialization** parameters that can set language characteristics.

Two Oracle tools that can help with data conversion issues are the Database Character Set Scanner and the Database Character Set Scanner CSALTER script. The Database Character Set Scanner utility reports on conversion issues relating to migrating from one database character set to another. The Database Character Set Scanner generates a report on conversion issues concerning migration. Scans can be performed at the database, table, and user level. The Database Character Set Scanner CSALTER script should be used when migrating to a superset of the current database character set. A full database scan must be performed by the database character set scanner before running the CSALTER script, which performs the character set conversion. This is an alternative to using export/import to perform the conversion. However, the database should be backed up before running the CSALTER script. Look at the *Globalization Support Guide* for more detailed information.

The **NLS_LANG** parameter is defined with a language, territory, and character set component. The default is AMERICAN_AMERICA.US7ASCII. The following shows the format:

```
NLS_LANG = language_territory.charset
```

Connections

A connection is an Oracle communication path between a user process and the Oracle database server. If this communication path is dropped, a user must establish a new session. A transaction is rolled back if the connection for its session is lost. A session is a specific connection for a user between the user process and the Oracle database server.

Maintain Connections

The Oracle Net Foundation Layer establishes and maintains connections with the database server. Transparent Network Substrate (TNS) is the common interface between all the industry-standard protocols. Oracle Protocol Support maps the industry-standard protocols (TCP/IP, TCP/IP with SSL, SDP and Named Pipes) used in the connection.

Figure 4-2 shows us how Oracle Net works. Oracle Net software will reside on the database server platform and the platform that is running the Oracle applications. With an application server, HTTP runs on top of a network protocol between the browser platform and the application server platform. Oracle Net then runs on top of a network protocol between the application server and the database server. For a client/server configuration, Oracle Net will reside on the client platform and the database server platform, and will run on top of a network protocol between the client and the database server platforms.

If Java programs are running, a Java Database Connectivity (JDBC) OCI, or Thin driver, will communicate with Oracle Net to process the database request. A JDBC OCI driver requires Oracle Net on the remote platform and the database server. A JDBC Thin driver written entirely in Java uses JavaNet to communicate, and requires Oracle Net only on the server platform. Chapter 7 will discuss the Java drivers in more detail.

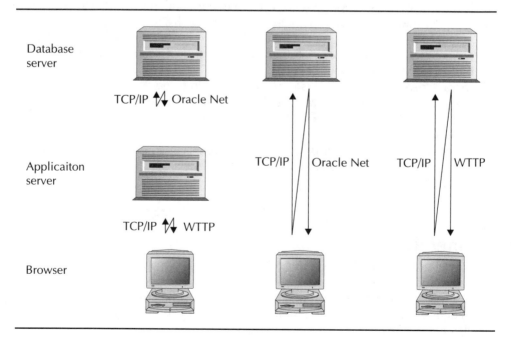

FIGURE 4-2. *An Oracle network overview*

Define a Location

Locations need to be defined so a remote application can find the correct Oracle database server on the network. A service name, such as **customer.us.trubix.com**, is used to define the unique location of each database server. In the preceding example, **customer** is the database name and **us.trubix.com** is the domain name. On the plus side, if the physical location of the database is changed, the service name can stay the same.

A database can support multiple services. The service name, defined with the initialization parameter **SERVICE_NAMES**, makes the physical location of the database transparent and will default to the global database name (the name of your database), which uses the format database_name.database_domain, as in customer.us.trubix.com.

The database domain name is the domain where the database is located, and is made up of the initialization parameters **DB_NAME** and **DB_DOMAIN**. The combination of the **DB_NAME** and **DB_DOMAIN** (customer.us.trubix.com) name distinguishes one database from another, as shown in the following examples:

```
DB_NAME=customer
DB_DOMAIN=us.trubix.com
```

CRITICAL SKILL 4.2

Learn the Difference Between Dedicated and Shared Server Architectures

An Oracle database server can be configured to run a dedicated or shared server architecture. This decision determines how the listener processes requests and how server processes work for an Oracle instance. Server processes are the interface between the Oracle database server and user processes, the latter of which must go through a server process that handles the database communication between the user process and the database. The following are a few facts about server processes:

- Processes database requests, accesses data, and returns the results.

- Performs data translations and conversions between the application and database server environments.

- Protects the database server from illegal operations by the user processes. A server process accesses Oracle database and memory structures on behalf of the user process. This separates user process activity from direct access to Oracle's internal memory.

Dedicated Server

A dedicated server environment uses a "dedicated" server process for each user process. The benefit is that each user process has a dedicated server process to handle all of its database requests. If there are a hundred separate sessions, there will be a hundred dedicated server processes running on the same platform as the database server.

The problem is that each dedicated server process is often idle a large percentage of the time. This takes up a lot of operating system resources for server processes that are sitting idle, and creates issues when large numbers of users are accessing a system. Oracle databases that allow access from the Internet can have tremendous spikes of activity that generate a large number of dedicated server processes. The dedicated server architecture also does not support FTP, HTTP, or WebDAV clients.

Figure 4-3 illustrates that dedicated server processes run on the database server platform. A dedicated server process will be run for each user session.

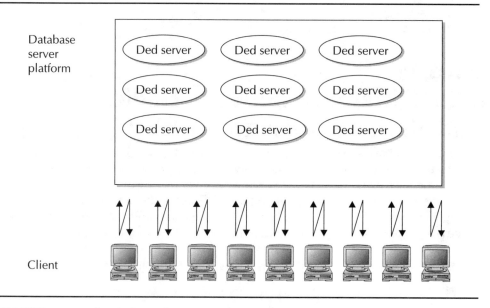

FIGURE 4-3. *The dedicated server architecture*

Shared Server

A shared server architecture offers increased scalability for a large number of users. This is possible because a single server process can be "shared" among a number of user processes, allowing a single server process to be able to support a large number of user processes. If there are 100 separate sessions, there may in turn be 20 shared server processes supporting them. Having a small pool of server processes that can support a large number of sessions increases scalability. This shared server architecture is much more scalable than a dedicated architecture as the number of users for a system increase. The shared server process can also handle large spikes of user activity much better than a dedicated server process configuration.

When a user request arrives, the listener will route the request to a dispatcher, which then processes and routes the request to a common queue. From a pool of shared server processes, an idle shared server will see if there is work in the common queue. Requests are processed on a first-in first-out basis. The shared server then processes the request and puts the results in a response queue (each dispatcher has one) that a dispatcher can return to the user process. Afterward, the dispatcher returns the results from its response queue to the appropriate user process.

A dispatcher supports multiple connections with virtual circuits, which are sections of shared memory that contain the information necessary for client communication. The dispatcher puts the virtual circuit on the common (request) queue accessed by the server process.

There are some administration operations that cannot be performed through a dispatcher, however. To perform these restricted administration operations in a shared server environment, the DBA needs to connect with a dedicated server process instead of a dispatcher process. The restricted operation needs a connect descriptor with a setting of **SERVER=DEDICATED**, defined in the **CONNECT_DATA** section. Restricted operations include the following:

- Starting up an instance
- Shutting down an instance
- Media recovery

As Figure 4-4 shows, a shared server process can support multiple user sessions.

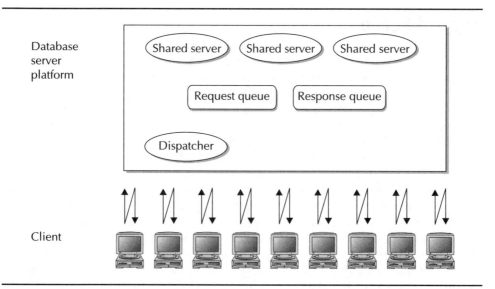

FIGURE 4-4. *The shared server architecture*

Table 4-2 illustrates the initialization parameters that are used to configure the shared server architecture. Possible values for these parameters are dependent on the level of user activity and the types of operations the server processes are executing.

Oracle Initialization Parameter	Definition
DISPATCHERS	Defines the number of dispatcher processes to start in a shared server architecture. The number of dispatchers can be dynamically added or reduced. There must be at least one dispatcher for each network protocol. Additional dispatchers can be defined based upon the workload.
MAX_DISPATCHERS	Defines the maximum number of dispatchers. This is not a fixed limit. In this release, this value can be dynamically exceeded at runtime.

TABLE 4-2. *Initialization Parameters Used by Shared Servers*

Oracle Initialization Parameter	Definition
SHARED_SERVERS	Defines the number of shared servers to invoke on database startup in a shared server architecture.
MAX_SHARED_SERVERS	Defines the maximum number of shared server processes.
SESSIONS	Defines the maximum number of sessions that can be active in a system.
SHARED_SERVER__SESSIONS	Defines the maximum number of shared server sessions that can be started in a system. Allows dedicated sessions to be reserved in a shared server environment. Sessions started above this limit will use dedicated server processes.
CIRCUITS	Defines the maximum number of virtual circuits.
LARGE_POOL_SIZE	Defines the size of the large pool area in the SGA. If a large pool exists, the session information will be stored in the large pool, not the shared pool area.

TABLE 4-2. *Initialization Parameters Used by Shared Servers* (continued)

Oracle recommends starting with one shared server process for every ten connections. It then automatically increases the number of shared servers based upon the workload up to the MAX_SHARED_SERVERS that are defined. The PMON process is responsible for adding and removing shared servers. The number of shared servers will never drop below the value contained in the SHARED_SERVERS parameter. You should also note that the parameters that control the minimum and maximum number of these shared can be set dynamically and therefore you can always ensure that you can react quickly to shared server issues.

Set Dispatchers

To set the number of dispatchers, determine the maximum number of concurrent sessions and divide this by the number of connections per dispatcher. Then, dependent upon the level of activity, the number of dispatchers may need to be increased or decreased. A single dispatcher can handle a large number of shared server processes, but the number of dispatchers per shared server is dependent upon the activity of the shared server processes.

One of the following attributes—**PROTOCOL**, **ADDRESS**, or **DESCRIPTION**—can be set with dispatchers. **PROTOCOL** defines the network protocol to use, **ADDRESS** defines the network protocol address on which the dispatchers listen, and **DESCRIPTION** is the network description. Default values are used if the attributes are not defined, and additional network options can be defined if the **ADDRESS** or **DESCRIPTION** attribute is set.

Additional attributes that can be set with ADDRESS or DESCRIPTION include the following:

- **SESSIONS**   Defines the maximum number of network sessions per dispatcher.

- **CONNECTIONS**   Defines the maximum number of network connections per dispatcher.

- **TICKS**   Defines the length of a network tick (seconds). A tick defines the length of time for a message to get from the client to the database server or from the database server to the client.

- **POOL**   Defines the timeout in ticks for incoming (IN=15) and outgoing (OUT=20) connections, and whether connection pooling is enabled. The number of ticks multiplied by the POOL value determines the total connection pool timeout.

- **MULTIPLEX**   Defines if multiplexing with the Connection Manager is set for incoming and outgoing connections. Multiplexing allows multiple sessions to transport over a single network connection. This is used to increase the network capacity for a large number of sessions.

- **LISTENER**   Defines the network name of an address for the listener.

- **SERVICE**   Defines the server names that dispatchers determine with the listeners.

- **INDEX**   Defines which dispatcher should be modified.

In your init.ora file, you will define the dispatchers. The following are examples of different types of entries that will typically be created to support shared servers:

Define the number of dispatchers to start:

```
DISPATCHERS='(PROTOCOL=TCP)(DISPATCHERS=5)'
```

Define a dispatcher to start on a specific port:

```
DISPATCHERS='(ADDRESS=(PROTOCOL=TCP)(DISPATCHERS=5))'
```

Define a dispatcher with more options:

```
DISPATCHERS="(DESCRIPTION=(ADDRESS=(PROTOCOL=TCP)
              (HOST=eclipse)(PORT=1521)(QUEUESIZE=20)))
              (DISPATCHERS=2)
              (SERVICE = customer.us.trubix.com)
              (SESSIONS=2000)
              (CONNECTIONS = 2000)
              (MULTIPLEX = ON)
              (POOL = ON)
              (TICK = 5)"
```

As you see, there are numerous options that may be used, depending on the configuration methods that you select when configuring the dispatcher.

Views to Monitor the Shared Server

The following views can be used to monitor the load on the dispatchers:

- V$DISPATCHER

- V$DISPATCHER_RATE

- V$QUEUE

- V$DISPATCHER_CONFIG

The following views can be used to monitor the load on the shared servers:

- V$SHARED_SERVER

- V$SHARED_SERVER_MONITOR

- V$QUEUE

The V$CIRCUIT view can be used to monitor virtual circuits.

The following views can be used to monitor the SGA memory associated with the shared server environment:

- V$SGA

- V$SGASTAT

- V$SHARED_POOL_RESERVED

These views provide you with the ability to monitor your database and the activity related to your shared servers and database. We encourage you to take a look at the data in these tables before and after you implement shared servers, to see how they change your database and how it functions.

Define Connections

This section will discuss the core components required to handle Oracle connections.

A Connect Descriptor

A connect descriptor is used to define the service name and the location of the database. The address component of a connect descriptor defines the protocol, host name, and port number. Though port numbers can be between 1 to 65535, those from 1 to 1024 are usually reserved for special processes. The connect data component of the description describes the service to which you want to connect. If you do not include the **instance_name** in your descriptor, it will default to the Oracle SID if not defined.

A sample connect descriptor for **customer.us.trubix.com** looks like the following:

```
(DESCRIPTION =
    (ADDRESS=(PROTOCOL=tcp)(HOST=eclipse)(PORT=1521))
    (CONNECT_DATA=
        (SERVICE_NAME=customer.us.trubix.com)))
```

A specific connect descriptor can be defined for a specific service handler. For example, in a shared server architecture, a dedicated service handler can be chosen, which can be set to dedicated **(SERVER=dedicated)** or shared **(SERVER=shared)**. If no dispatchers are available, a dedicated server will be used and the default service handler is shared.

```
(DESCRIPTION =
    (ADDRESS=(PROTOCOL=tcp)(HOST=eclipse)(PORT=1521))
    (CONNECT_DATA=
        (SERVICE_NAME=customer.us.trubix.com)
          (SERVER=dedicated)))
```

Define a Connect Descriptor

When establishing a connection, a detailed connect descriptor can be defined, or a manual name that maps to a connect descriptor can be used. The following example shows you how to define a manual connect descriptor or name a connection descriptor name.

```
-- Manual definition of a connection descriptor
CONNECT
```

```
username/password@(DESCRIPTION = (ADDRESS=(PROTOCOL=tcp) (HOST=eclipse)
(PORT=1521))  (CONNECT_DATA= (SERVICE_NAME=customer.us.trubix.com)))
-- Connect using a pre-defined descriptor
CONNECT username/password@cust
```

The Oracle Connection Manager

The Oracle Connection Manager processes and filters requests to the database
server. It can also optimize network performance for a large number of sessions.
Figure 4-5 illustrates the various layers between the users and the database that
need to be controlled by the manager.

The Oracle Connection Manager Control utility allows administration of the
Oracle Connection Manager. The syntax is

```
cmctl {command} [parameter1 … parameterN] {-c instance_name} {-p password}
```

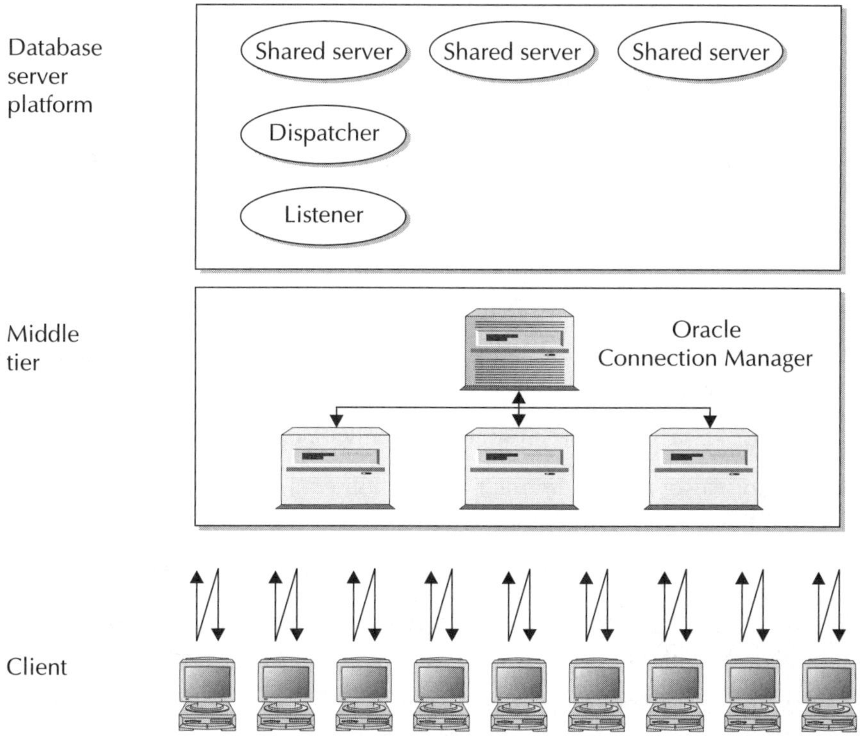

FIGURE 4-5.   *The Oracle Connection Manager architecture*

Connection Manager commands can be executed from within the utility, as shown here:

```
cmctl
CMCTL> startup -c cman0
```

The Oracle Connection Manager can offload network I/O from the application servers.

We will now move on and look at the Oracle Connection Manager options to include session multiplexing and firewall access control.

Session Multiplexing

The Oracle Connection Manager allows a number of different client network sessions to be shared (multiplexed) through a single network connection to the database server. Multiplexing sessions increases the number of network sessions that can be supported. Similarly, multiple Connection Managers can be used to handle hundreds or thousands of concurrent users; they run on the application server platform in order to multiplex sessions to the Oracle database server.

Firewall Access Control

The Oracle Connection Manager can define filtering rules to grant or deny access to the database server; this is done via the Oracle Net Firewall Proxy. The Oracle Net Firewall Proxy is software that provides Oracle Connection Manager features through different firewall vendors.

Progress Check ⊕

1. The protocol _____ supports collaborative authoring over the Internet.

2. True or False: The SDP protocol adds advanced network security features.

3. True or False: A virtual circuit is a section of shared memory that contains information for client communication.

4. True or False: Port numbers from 1 to 1024 are usually reserved for SSL.

5. The _____ server architecture does not support FTP, HTTP, or WebDAV clients.

6. True or False: The Oracle Connection Manager supports multiplexing sessions.

CRITICAL SKILL 4.4

Use the Oracle Net Listener

The Oracle Net Listener (listener) listens on a network port (listening endpoints) for incoming database requests. A listening endpoint defines the protocol addresses the listener is defined to listen on. Listening endpoints include HTTP, FTP, WebDAV, and Oracle XML. Look at the *ORACLE XML DB Developer's Guide* for more detail on registering FTP, HTTP, and WebDAV listening points.

The process is fairly simple. The listener receives a request and hands the request to a service handler, which is a server process that runs on the same platform as the Oracle database server. The service handler can be a dedicated server or a dispatcher, the latter of which works with shared servers.

The PMON background process registers the service information to the listener. During registration, PMON gives the listener information on the database services and instance information. PMON then tries to register with the listener once the listener has been started. Dynamic registration is supported with the **alter system register** command. If PMON has not registered with the listener, a TNS listener error will occur. View the *Oracle Database 10g Error Messages* reference manual for more details.

The listener will receive the database request and spawn a dedicated server process if the environment is configured for the dedicated server architecture. The dispatcher will hand the request over to a dispatcher if running a shared server architecture. A client application can bypass the listener if it is running on the same platform as the database server. Once the listener hands off the request it will resume listening for additional network requests.

A default listener (named listener) is configured at installation with the Oracle Net Configuration Assistant making it easy to start up the default listener when a system is first built. An additional ICP protocol address is defined for external routes during installation.

Progress Check Answers

1. The protocol *WebDAV* supports collaborative authoring over the Internet.

2. False. The SDP protocol is used with high-speed networks.

3. True. A virtual circuit is a section of shared memory that contains information for client communication.

4. False. Ports 1 to 1024 are used for special processes. They are not reserved for SSL.

5. The *dedicated* server architecture does not support FTP, HTTP, or WebDAV clients.

6. True. Yes, this is one of the advantages of using the Oracle Connection Manager.

The following is a sample listener.ora file:

```
LISTENER =
  (DESCRIPTION_LIST =
    (DESCRIPTION =
      (ADDRESS_LIST =
        (ADDRESS = (PROTOCOL = IPC)(KEY = EXTPROC0))
      )
      (ADDRESS_LIST =
        (ADDRESS = (PROTOCOL = TCP)(HOST = eclipse)(PORT = 1521))
      )
    )
  )
```

Table 4-3 illustrates the contents of the listener.ora file.

In the following, **host** defines the server name, **PORT** defines the port number, **SERVER** defines the host server name, **PIPE** defines the pipe name, and **KEY** defines a unique name for the service. It is recommended to use the Oracle SID value for the key.

Table 4-4 defines the components of the protocol definition.

After installation, the Oracle Net Manager can be used to modify the listener configuration. Some of the values that can be configured for the listener include:

■ If the default port of 1521 is not specified, the **LOCAL_LISTENER** initialization parameter needs to be defined through a naming method. The **LOCAL_LISTENER** parameter is dynamic and can be set with the **alter system** command.

Parameter	Description
DESCRIPTION	Defines a connect descriptor for a net service name.
DESCRIPTION_LIST	Defines a list of connect descriptors.
LISTENER	Defines the listener alias.
ADDRESS	Defines the listener protocol address.
ADDRESS_LIST	Defines a list of protocol addresses that contain common behavior.

TABLE 4-3. *Listener.ora File Formats*

- Be careful, because the **LISTENER** parameter overrides the **LOCAL_LISTENER** parameter. A host system can have multiple IP addresses, and a listener can be configured to listen on them.

- The I/O buffer size for send and receive operations can be defined.

- Heterogeneous services can be set to support additional services such as external routines.

- The **QUEUESIZE** parameter can be defined for environments that may have a large number of concurrent connection requests for a listener on a listening endpoint.

Password Authentication

A password needs to be set for the listener. The **change_password** command can be used to change a password or set a new password. If a password is not set, someone can accidentally impact the availability of the database—for example, accidentally shutting down the listener. If you don't have a listener, new sessions cannot be established. It is important that a DBA protect access to listener management.

The following example sets the listener password:

```
lsnrctl> change_password
Old password: <enter>
New password: newpassword
Reenter new password: newpassword
lsnrctl> save_config
```

Protocol	Example
TCP	(PROTOCOL=tcp)(host=eclipse)(PORT=1521)
TCP/IP with SSL	(PROTOCOL=tcps)(host=eclipse)(PORT=2484)
IPC	(PROTOCOL=ipc)(KEY=cust)
Named pipes	(PROTOCOL=nmp)(SERVER=eclipse)(PIPE=pipe01)
SDP	(PROTOCOL=sdp)(host=eclipse)(PORT=1521)

TABLE 4-4.   *Protocol Examples for the listener.ora File*

Multiple Listeners

Multiple listeners can be defined for a service, and offer a number of advantages for more complex environments. These advantages include the following:

- Failover
- Transparent application failover
- Load balancing

The following is a sample connect descriptor for a listener:

```
(DESCRIPTION =
  (ADDRESS_LIST=
    (ADDRESS=(PROTOCOL=tcp)(HOST=eclipse)(PORT=1521))
  (CONNECT_DATA=
    (SERVICE_NAME=customer.us.trubix.com)))
```

Connection Pooling

A shared server architecture is used to improve user scalability. So it is assumed that if this architecture is being used there is a potential for a large number of users. As mentioned previously, at any point in time there can be a large percentage of idle processes. Connection pooling allows the database server to timeout sessions that are idle and then use the connection to support an active session. These sessions remain open but in an idle state. When they become active again, a connection is reestablished.

CRITICAL SKILL 4.5

Learn Naming Methods

A naming method defines the type of repository used to configure Oracle network information. This repository is accessed to define where the Oracle database server is located.

Oracle supports various types of naming methods, such as:

- Directory naming (centralized configuration)
- Local naming (client configuration)
- External naming (external configuration)
- Easy naming (manual configuration)

Directory Naming Method

For centralized network management, Oracle Net Services uses a Lightweight Directory Access Protocol (LDAP) directory server as the repository. LDAP uses hierarchical structures (directories) that contain different components of a communication path. The LDAP directory stores all database network information, policies, security, and authentication information in this centralized repository. Remote applications will go to the centralized repository to find network configuration information. The results are then returned containing the communication path to the Oracle database server.

Different vendors provide their own LDAP directory server. The Oracle LDAP directory, for instance, is named the Oracle Internet Directory (OID). While the Microsoft version of this is named Microsoft Active Directory.

You should note that there are some restrictions when using the Microsoft Active Directory. The Oracle Net Configuration Assistant may be used with the Microsoft Active Directory, however the Oracle Internet Directory Configuration tool cannot be used with the Microsoft Active Directory.

Storing network information in a centralized location is much more efficient from an administration perspective. Make a change in one place and it is reflected everywhere. It's also better from a security perspective because the database location is stored in a centralized repository instead of a file on a local machine.

Directory Information Trees

LDAP directory servers store information in a hierarchical tree structure called a Directory Information Tree (DIT). DITs are typically organized in a Domain Name Space (DNS) structure (usually along corporate or geographical lines), and are defined by the Oracle Internet Directory Configuration Assistant. Every node in the tree is referred to as an entry, each of which can be modified with the Oracle Enterprise Manager or the Oracle Net Manager. The following example shows how a connect descriptor maps to a DIT:

```
(DESCRIPTION =
    (ADDRESS=(PROTOCOL=tcp)(HOST=eclipse)(PORT=1521))
  (CONNECT_DATA=
        (SERVICE_NAME=customer.us.trubix.com)))
```

Figure 4-6 illustrates how the directories are organized and may be navigated when using the Oracle Internet Directory Configuration Assistant. It is important to know your directory trees to ensure that you correctly move through your hierarchy.

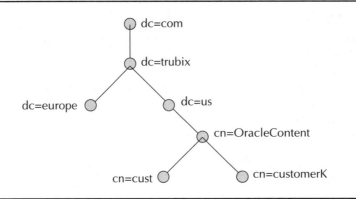

FIGURE 4-6. *A Directory Information Tree (DIT)*

Distinguished Names

A distinguished name (DN) defines where an entry resides in the directory path, and begins at the lowest entry. The DN for the customer distinguished name is dn:cn=customer, cn=OracleContext, dc=us, dc=trubix, and dc=com. Relative distinguished names (RDNs), on the other hand, define the sequences within the path. An RDN contains an attribute that defines the RDN. An important RDN is the Oracle Context, which defines the default location for connect identifiers. An identity management realm, meanwhile, defines a set of identities that share the same administration policies.

How to Find the Directory Naming Information

With this naming method, a client needs to find the centralized information that is stored in the LDAP repository to be able to connect to the database server. There are two ways to find the centralized directory naming information stored on a separate system.

■ The Static Method, which works via a local ldap.ora file.

■ The Dynamic Method, which works via a domain name server (DNS).

A ldap.ora file is a statically configured file containing the location of the LDAP server. DNS uses name servers to map names and IP addresses for systems. If the latter changes, the next time the name is looked for on the domain name server, it will map to the new IP address.

Net Service Alias Entries

A net service alias entry is another name for a net service name. A net service alias references the directory location. The name **cust** in the directory information tree is a net service alias. Aliases simplify management by using a short alias instead of having to specify the full path.

The Local Naming Method

The local naming method uses a local configuration file called *tnsnames.ora*. The tnsnames.ora file stores net service names and connect descriptors, and resides on the platform running the database application. It contains the information required to find and connect to the Oracle database server. The following definition defines the address (protocol, host, port number) along with the dedicated server environment and which service to connect to.

```
CUST =
  (DESCRIPTION =
    (ADDRESS_LIST =
      (ADDRESS = (PROTOCOL = TCP)(HOST = eclipse)(PORT = 1521))
    )
    (CONNECT_DATA =
      (SERVER = DEDICATED)
      (SERVICE_NAME = CUST)
    )
  )
```

This is a simple file to configure. The problem is if you have 1000 users, you need to make sure the tnsnames.ora file has been updated for all of the client machines. From a security perspective, it is not ideal to allow clients access to a server location and the connection information.

The Easy Naming Method

The easy naming method explicitly defines the connect information. The connect information contains the host, port, service name, and instance name. This allows someone to connect in a specific way without going through the configuration effort. The format is

```
CONNECT username/password@eclipse:1521/customer.us.trubix.com/cust
```

An advantage of the easy naming method is that it is easy to configure. The user need only provide minimal information to get a connection. As a result, no other naming methods need to be configured. This method cannot be used if more advanced features are required.

The External Naming Method

The external naming method uses net service names that are defined in a non-Oracle environment. This naming method works well for administrators that want to use their native naming service, and allows them to use native tools and utilities with which they have experience. The disadvantage of this approach is that Oracle Net tools cannot be used for these native naming methods. Supported non-Oracle services include the Network Information Service (NIS) or Cell Directory Services (CDS). CDS is part of a Distributed Computing Environment (DCE) environment. DCE is an integrated distributed environment designed to resolve interoperability issues with heterogeneous environments. DCE is maintained by the Open Systems Foundation (OSF).

Which Naming Method to Use

The local naming method (tnsnames.ora) has traditionally been the most popular method. However, there are a number of administration and security issues in stored local configuration with a tnsnames.ora file. The directory (centralized) naming method is more scalable and has less administration than the local naming method. For large systems, the directory method is becoming more popular. Oracle Names is an Oracle proprietary centralized naming method and is no longer supported in Oracle Database 10g. Oracle Name environments should migrate to the directory naming method. The easy naming method and external naming method are not used as often.

CRITICAL SKILL 4.6

Use Oracle Configuration Files

Remote applications will look for Oracle Net configuration files to determine how to access the Oracle database server. Configuration files can be found in the ORACLE_HOME/network/admin directory location. Table 4-5 defines the primary configuration files.

Syntax for Configuration Files

DBAs can use the management tools to modify Oracle Net Services configurations. However, since the configuration files have a simple syntax, it is easy to modify the configuration files directly. The following is an example of the listener.ora file.

```
# LISTENER.ORA Date: 04/25/2004
LISTENER =
  (DESCRIPTION_LIST =
    (DESCRIPTION =
      (ADDRESS_LIST =
        (ADDRESS = (PROTOCOL = IPC)(KEY = EXTPROC0))
      )
      (ADDRESS_LIST =
        (ADDRESS = (PROTOCOL = TCP)(HOST = eclipse)(PORT = 1521))
      )
    )
  )
```

Network Configuration Filename	Description
listener.ora	The listener.ora file defines how the listeners are configured on the database server.
sqlnet.ora	The sqlnet.ora file resides on the database server and the local platform. Profile information is stored in the sqlnet.ora file. This file defines information on service names, naming methods, external naming information, Advanced Security parameters, and database access information. The TNS_ADMIN environmental variable can override the default location.
tnsnames.ora	Resides on the local system and is used with the local naming method. Defines net service names and connect descriptor information.
cman.ora	The configuration file for the Oracle Connection Manager. This file resides on the same platform where the Oracle Connection Manager runs.
ldap.ora	The directory usage file is created by the Oracle Internet Directory Configuration Assistant.

TABLE 4-5.   *Primary Configuration Files for Oracle Net Services*

Should a DBA want to modify the files directly, the following syntax rules must be followed:

- Comments must begin with a pound sign (#). Anything following the pound sign is treated as a comment.

- Keywords are not case sensitive and cannot contain spaces.

- Spaces are optional around equal (=) signs.

- Values can only contain spaces if they are surrounded by quotes. The values may be case sensitive depending on the operating system and protocol.

- A connect descriptor can be no more than 4KB in length.

- All characters must be part of the network set.

CRITICAL SKILL 4.7

Use Administration Tools

Oracle Net Services contains a number of user interfaces and tools that simplify the management of the Oracle network, including the following:

- Oracle Enterprise Manager (OEM)
- The OEM console
- Oracle Net Manager
- Oracle Net Configuration Assistant
- Oracle Connection Manager
- Oracle Internet Directory Configuration Assistant
- Command-line utilities
- Oracle Advanced Security

The Oracle Enterprise Manager

Along with database administration, OEM allows configuration of Oracle Net Services. OEM can be used to perform the following administration features:

- The configuration of listeners
- The configuration of naming definitions such as connect descriptors

The Oracle Net Manager

The Oracle Net Manager allows the configuration of Oracle Net Services and can be started from the OEM console, by choosing Tools | Service Management | Oracle Net Manager.

The Oracle Net Manager provides the following administration support:

- **Listeners** Supports creating and configuring listeners.

- **Naming** Supports defining simple names. Simple names specify information for connect descriptors and service location information.

- **Naming methods** Supports the definition of naming methods.

Some of the functionality in OEM is also available in the Oracle Net Manager. Table 4-6 shows the overlapping functionality and the differences between the two tools.

The following can be used to start Oracle Net Manager manually through UNIX:

```
$  $ORACLE_HOME/bin/netmgr
```

Oracle Net Manager can also be started manually through Windows by selecting Start | Programs | Oracle—OraHome10 | Configuration and Migration Tools | Net Manager.

Oracle Enterprise Manager	Oracle Net Manager
Local naming (tnsnames.ora)	Local naming (tnsnames.ora)
Directory naming	Directory naming
Listeners	Listeners
Oracle home support for multiple hosts	Oracle home support for a single host
Search capability on local and directory names	Profiles
Export directory entries to tnsnames.ora file	
Changing tracing and logging settings	

TABLE 4-6. *Common Features and Differences Between OEM and Oracle Net Manager*

The OEM Console

The Oracle Enterprise Manager Central Console is a web-based interface for managing the entire enterprise from the console. It offers a lot more functionality than the standard Oracle Enterprise Manager that comes with a typical database install. The default ports for running in a non-secure mode are 7777-7877; default ports for running in a secure mode are 4443-4533.

You can access the OEM Central Console from the following URLs: http://<oms hostname>.<domain>.<port>/em and https://<oms hostname>.<domain>.<port>/em. The OEM Central Console requires the Oracle Management Service unless the Oracle Management Agent is installed separately.

The OEM Components

The OEM console uses the following components, which are installed with the Oracle application server:

- **The Oracle Management Service**   A web-based application that runs on the Oracle application server. It provides the user interface for the OEM console, and interfaces with the management agents to process and monitor information.

- **The Oracle Management Agent**   Monitors information from sites that need to be managed and which are loaded into the management service.

- **The Oracle Management Repository**   Contains all the information managed by the Oracle Enterprise Manager.

Before installing the Complete Enterprise Manager, make sure to read the requirements for the complete installation that includes the Oracle Application Server 10*g*, Web Cache, and the Management Service application.

The Oracle Net Configuration Assistant

The Oracle Net Configuration Assistant is used during installation to configure the basic network components. The Oracle Net Configuration Assistant can also be run standalone to modify the same values configured during installation. Configurable components include the following:

- Naming methods
- Net service names (tnsnames.ora)
- Listener names and protocol addresses
- Directory server usage

The following can be used to start the Oracle Net Configuration Assistant manually through UNIX:

```
$   $ORACLE_HOME/bin/netca
```

The Oracle Net Configuration Assistant can also be started manually through Windows by selecting Start | Programs | Oracle—OraHome10 | Configuration and Migration Tools | Net Configuration Assistant.

The Oracle Internet Directory Configuration Assistant

The Oracle Internet Directory Configuration Assistant can be used to configure the Oracle Internet Directory. The directory configuration file ldap.ora can be configured with the Oracle Internet Directory Configuration Assistant or the Oracle Net Configuration Assistant. The ldap.ora file can reside in different locations depending on which tool created the ldap.ora file.

- If created by the OID Configuration Assistant, the ldap.ora file is stored in the ORACLE_HOME/ldap/admin directory.

- If created by the Oracle Net Configuration Assistant, the ldap.ora file is stored in the ORACLE_HOME/network/admin directory.

- The ldap.ora file location can be manually specified with the LDAP_ADMIN or TNS_ADMIN environmental variables.

Command-Line Utilities

The Listener Control utility can be used to start and stop listeners, check their status, and perform tracing and other management operations. The syntax is

```
lsnrctl  command [listener_name]
```

Listener commands can also be executed from within the Listener Control utility. The listener name is the one defined in the listener.ora file, but a default listener named LISTENER can be used instead. If LISTENER is used, a listener name does not need to be specified.

The following shows how to stop the listener. Here, executing the **lsnrctl** command generates an LSNRCTL prompt:

```
$ lsnrctl
LSNRCTL> stop
Connecting to (DESCRIPTION=(ADDRESS=(PROTOCOL=IPC)(KEY=EXTPROC0)))
The command completed successfully
```

The next example shows a sample of the type of information displayed when starting the listener:

```
LSNRCTL> start

starting tnslsnr: please wait...
 TNSLSNR for 32-bit Windows: Version 10.1.0.2.0 -
System parameter file is C:\oracle\ora10\network\admin\listener.ora
Log messages written to C:\oracle\ora10\network\log\listener.log
Listening on: (DESCRIPTION=(ADDRESS=(PROTOCOL=tcp)(HOST=eclipse)(PORT=1521)))
Connecting to (DESCRIPTION=(ADDRESS=(PROTOCOL=IPC)(KEY=EXTPROC0)))
STATUS of the LISTENER
------------------------
Alias                    LISTENER
Version                  TNSLSNR for 32-bit Windows: Version 10.1.0.2.0
Start Date               03-FEB-2004 21:26:56
Uptime                   0 days 0 hr. 0 min. 2 sec
Trace Level              off
Security                 OFF
SNMP                     OFF
Listener Parameter File  C:\oracle\ora10\network\admin\listener.ora
Listener Log File        C:\oracle\ora10\network\log\listener.log
Listening Endpoints Summary...
   (DESCRIPTION=(ADDRESS=(PROTOCOL=tcp)(HOST=eclipse)(PORT=1521)))
Services Summary...
Service "cust" has 1 instance(s).
  Instance "cust", status UNKNOWN, has 1 handler(s) for this service...
The command completed successfully
```

The **status** command displays detailed information on the status of the listener. Information includes the start time of the listener, the location of log and configuration files, and so on.

```
LSNRCTL> status
```

The **services** command lists dispatchers in a shared server environment and dedicated servers in a dedicated server environment.

```
LSNRCTL> services
```

Here is a list of listener commands:

- **change_password**
- **exit**
- **help**
- **quit**
- **reload**
- **save_config**

- **services**
- **set**
- **show**
- **spawn**
- **start**
- **status**
- **stop**
- **trace**
- **version**

The **set** command can be used to modify different parameter values for a listener. The **set** command, by itself, will display the parameter values that can be modified.

```
LSNRCTL> set
password                        rawmode
displaymode                     trc_file
trc_directory                   trc_level
log_file                        log_directory
log_status                      current_listener
inbound_connect_timeout         startup_waittime
save_config_on_stop
```

The Oracle Advanced Security Option

The Oracle Advanced Security option supports data encryption, enhanced authentication, integrity checking, single sign-on, and the Distributed Computing Environment (DCE). The Oracle Net Manager is used to configure Oracle Advanced Security options.

Dispatchers

The **DISPATCHERS** parameter can be set to define how dispatchers will work with the shared server architecture. Dispatchers must be defined to work with different protocols, as shown in the following:

```
DISPATCHERS="(PROTOCOL=tcp)(DISPATCHERS=6)(CONNECTIONS=1000)"
DISPATCHERS="(PROTOCOL=tcps)(DISPATCHERS=6)(CONNECTIONS=1000)"
```

Connection pooling can also be defined as shown next:

```
DISPATCHERS="(PROTOCOL=tcp)(DISPATCHERS=6)(POOL=on)
(TICK=1)(CONNECTIONS=1000)(SESSIONS=5000)"
DISPATCHERS="(PROTOCOL=tcps)(DISPATCHERS=6)(POOL=on)
(TICK=1)(CONNECTIONS=1000)(SESSIONS=5000)"
```

Project 4-1 Testing a Connection

The following project will walk you through the steps of testing a connection to an Oracle database server.

Step by Step

The first step is to test the network connectivity between the remote system and the Oracle database server. The **ping** command will verify network access. If ping is successful, the remote system can resolve the name of the host server name. The host server name should be defined in the hosts file for the operating system.

The hosts file in UNIX is in the /etc directory; the hosts files in Windows is in the \winnt directory. The following is an example hosts file entry.

```
eclipse        customer.us.trubix.com
```

1. Ping the host server name.

   ```
   ping eclipse
   ```

   If the ping is not successful using the host server name then use the IP address to verify that the remote system can access the host server through the network.

   ```
   ping 122.23.20.24
   ```

2. Start the listener. If the listener does not start, check the listener.ora file for the proper entries. The listener.ora file can be found in ORACLE_HOME/network/admin directory.

   ```
   lsnrctl start listener_name
   ```

3. Verify that the service registration has been completed and that the listener is ready to handle requests.

   ```
   lsnrctl services listener_name
   ```

   Service registration is impacted by a number of initialization parameters. They include **SERVICE_NAMES** (cust.us.acme.com) and **INSTANCE_NAME** (cust). The **SERVICE_NAMES** parameter defaults to the global database name. The global database name is made up of the **DB_NAME** and **DB_DOMAIN** parameters.

4. The remote system now needs to be configured. The Oracle Net Configuration Assistant can be used for configuration. Start the Oracle Net Configuration Assistant.

5. Of the four configuration options on the Welcome page, select the Local Net Service Name configuration.

6. Select Add, and then click Next.

7. Enter the service name (**cust**) and click Next.

8. Select the protocol (TCP/IP) and click Next.

9. Select the host name and port number, and then select Next.

10. Select Yes, perform a test, and then click Next. If the test fails, check whether the instance and listener are running. If they are, check the protocol information, and if it still fails, double-check the username and password used for the test.

11. Enter the net service name and click Next.

12. Select No when asked if would you like to configure another net service name, and then click Next.

13. At the Congratulations screen, select Next and click Finish.

14. The local naming method will create a connect descriptor in the tnsnames.ora file similar to this one:

```
cust=
(DESCRIPTION =
   (ADDRESS=(PROTOCOL=tcp)(HOST=eclipse)(PORT=1521))
   (CONNECT_DATA=
        (SERVICE_NAME=customer.us.trubix.com)))
```

15. For the final test, log into Oracle and see if you can connect using the new net service name:

```
SQL> CONNECT username/password@cust
```

The tnsping utility can also be used to test a service. If unsuccessful, it will return the error that occurred. tnsping requires the net service name found in the tnsnames.ora file. The count parameter defines how many attempts are made to reach the server.

```
tnsping net_service_name  [count]
```

If unable to connect, the trcroute utility can be used to get more detailed error information. The trcroute utility tracks the TNS address of every node it accesses in the path.

```
trcroute net_service_name
```

Project Summary

This project walked you through the steps a DBA will go through to test a simple connection for an Oracle database server using the local naming method.

Use Profiles

A profile contains a set of parameters that define Oracle Net options on the remote or database server. Profiles are stored in the sqlnet.ora file and can be used to

- Route connections to specific processes

- Control access through protocol-specific parameters

- Prioritize naming methods

- Control logging and tracing features

- Configure for external naming

- Define how the client domain should append to unqualified names

During installation, the priority order for the naming methods will be defined. If the first naming method cannot resolve the connect identifier, the next naming method will be checked. The results will then be stored in the sqlnet.ora file, as shown in the following example:

```
NAMES.DIRECTORY_PATH=(ezconnect, tnsnames)
```

After installation, Oracle Net Manager can be used to modify the sqlnet.ora configuration file.

Control Access

The sqlnet.ora file can be used to grant or deny access to the Oracle database server. Table 4-7 displays sqlnet.ora parameters that control access.

sqlnet.ora Parameter Name	Description
TCP.VALIDNODE_CHECKING	Determines where to control access to the database. If this parameter is set, the following parameters will be used to define the access.
TCP.EXCLUDED_NODES	Defines which systems are denied access to the database.
TCP.INVITED_NODES	Defines which systems are granted access to the database.

TABLE 4-7. *sqlnet.ora Parameters*

The Oracle Net Manager is used to define database access control. To define database access control, perform the following steps using Oracle Net Manager:

1. After starting Net Manager, select Local | Profile.

2. Choose General.

3. Select Access Rights.

4. Choose Check TCP/IP Client Access Rights.

5. In the Clients Excluded From Access and the Clients Allowed To Access fields access control can now be defined.

CRITICAL SKILL 4.9

Network in a Multitiered Environment

Although the Oracle Database 10g has new features that simplify database administration, the environment the database server runs in is becoming more complex. The following areas continue to increase the complexity of Oracle networking environments:

■ Oracle Database 10g–supporting HTTP, FTP, and WebDAV protocols are changing how data is used and accessed.

■ The OEM Central Console is changing how Oracle DBAs perform administration across multiple databases.

■ Multitiered architectures are placing increasing demands on network performance and security.

Traditionally, most Oracle networks have been set with the local naming method. In the future, more Oracle networking environments will work with multitiered architectures, the Oracle OEM Central Console, encryption, and the directory naming method. Companies are going to need people with skills to manage these complex environments. This chapter introduced you to the main components of Oracle Net Services. To begin working with Oracle Net Services, you may want to look at the following areas in the following order in terms of developing your skills:

■ Strengthen your understanding of the Oracle Net Services architecture.

■ Obtain a solid understanding of configuring dedicated and shared server environments.

■ Become comfortable working with listeners and the local naming method.

- Get comfortable working with the directory naming method.

- Be able to work with the OEM Central Console and the environment required to support it.

This list should be able to keep you busy for a few days. After that, developing skill in tuning and troubleshooting the Oracle Net Services environment will be important. Not included in these discussions, but also very important, is the ability to troubleshoot and tune the network from an operating system perspective.

☑ Chapter 4 Mastery Check

1. The _____ background process registers the service information to the listener.

2. True or False: The **LOCAL_LISTENER** parameter should be set to work with port 1521.

3. The _____ is used during installation to configure Oracle Net Services.

4. The _____file can be used to define, grant, or deny access to the Oracle database server.

5. The _____utility can also be used to test a service.

6. A _____ contains a set of parameters that define Oracle Net options on the remote or database server.

7. The ldap.ora file location can be manually specified with the _____ or **TNS_ADMIN** environmental variables.

8. True or False: The easy naming method is a valid naming method.

9. The Oracle LDAP directory is called the _____.

10. True or False: The Oracle Management Service is a repository of information generated by the Management Agent.

CHAPTER
5

Backup and Recovery

CRITICAL SKILLS

5.1 Oracle Backup and Recovery Fundamentals

5.2 Learn about Oracle User-Managed Backup and Recovery

5.3 Write a Database Backup

5.4 Back Up Archived Redo Logs

5.5 Get Started with Oracle Data Pump

5.6 Use Oracle Data Pump Export

5.7 Work with Oracle Data Pump Import

5.8 Use Traditional Export and Import

5.9 Get Started with Recovery Manager

his chapter discusses many concepts that are very important to Oracle DBAs and users. Backing up your data is crucial, and this chapter discusses how to do so as well as how to recover when things go wrong. As we have said before, the best way to learn is to do, and backup and recovery are tasks that every DBA must learn and, more important, practice. Just remember that if you do plan to perform the exercises and examples in this chapter, do it on a database that is not being used, or create one just for this purpose…just in case.

Oracle Backup and Recovery Fundamentals

As you should already know, data is a valuable asset. To ensure that you can protect your investment, it is important to insure your valuable property. To support this important data need, Oracle Database 10*g* provides numerous features to enable you to protect your investment. The ability to back up your data in case of a failure is an invaluable capability. Now you have the chance to back up your data without interruption to your business processes. Just as important as it is to back up your data is the ability to quickly recovery from a failure. Whether you lose data due to hardware, software, or human failures, the time to recover costs businesses opportunity and money. This chapter introduces you to how Oracle supports the need to back up and recover data.

Where Do I Start?

Oracle's implementation of backup and recovery is an extensive one that provides you with the advantage of having many options that you can use. This is a good thing, but can leave you wondering, "Where should I start and which options are best for me?" This chapter will take you on a quick tour of backup and recovery and should leave you with a good understanding of how this is implemented in Oracle. As you review the backup and recovery utilities presented in this chapter, keep in mind that we strongly recommend using *Recovery Manager* (*RMAN*) for performing backup and recovery and will explain why later. But for now, just know that we're off to a good start since we've answered our first question already!

One of the most important elements of an advanced database management system (DBMS) is the capability to perform backup and recovery in a manner that guarantees data will not be lost. Oracle provides you with many options that can be used, from basic backup and recovery through advanced facilities to keep the database up in a high-availability environment. As a DBA, when you need to deal with a situation where the database is corrupted and needs to be recovered, there is nothing more comforting than knowing that you have valid backups for recovery and that you know how to use them!

In this chapter, you will see basic approaches and sound practices for performing backup and recovery. We will cover some examples and provide you with scripts you can use to start implementing your own backup and recovery procedures.

Three fundamental types of backups and recoveries can be performed in Oracle:

- **Physical backup and recovery**   This is performed on the entire database without regard for the underlying logical data structures. All of the database files are backed up together so they may be recovered simultaneously. These are often referred to as hot or cold backups.

- **Logical backup and recovery**   This is performed by choosing specific logical database structures such as named tables, indexes, and perhaps even schemas. They allow you to restore the database in a more granular fashion than is possible with a physical backup. Logical backups are implemented by tools such as Oracle's Data Pump Export and Data Pump Import facilities. You should note that you cannot use a logical backup for a recovery. You can only use it for a restore.

- **Recovery Manager (RMAN)**   This Oracle tool allows you to perform physical database backups in a more controlled manner. With RMAN, the backups and recoveries are managed for you through the RMAN toolset as well as with a GUI interface using Enterprise Management. Syntax is simplified and the scripting is powerful and consistent across platforms. This is the toolset that Oracle has been investing in and moving toward since Oracle 8 and is the recovery toolset we recommend you use.

TIP
Which types of backups should you use: physical or logical? That's easy! Both, whenever possible. Always try to have more than one way to restore or recover data when faced with this task. Having a logical and physical backup on hand provides you, the DBA, with more options when presented with a recovery scenario.

Backup Architecture

There are many types of failures and corruptions that can occur and impact the database, including server, network, and media failures that may render the database inoperable. They can come in the form of data corruptions caused by software failures in the OS, in Oracle, or in the application. Human error can also create problems with the database, but these errors are never the result of the DBA, of course!

In order to understand the type of backup and recovery needed for a given situation, it's important to understand Oracle's database architecture fundamentals.

The database architecture, as it relates to backup and recovery principles, includes many components. Let's examine those structures critical to performing Oracle backup and recovery.

Oracle Binaries

Oracle binaries are the programs that make up the actual installed Oracle software, and which perform the logic of the Oracle database. This should be backed up after the install of every release and product patch. A patch is software containing fixes for known problems and, in some cases, enhancements to major versions or releases of the database. Patches are installed over the top of a release and in some cases after other patches have already been applied.

Though you can always reinstall the software, you should back up your Oracle binaries for the following reasons:

- Installs of software are slower than file restores.

- CDs and web sites that contain the software for download may not be available.

- You may not remember the exact patch level applied to a particular server.

So, the Oracle binaries should be backed up after every software change and on a regularly scheduled basis. At a minimum, there should be a weekly backup.

The Parameter Files

The text-based init.ora parameter file and executable *Server Parameter file* (*spfile*) contain a list of directives of how the instance will operate once it has been started. All parameters that define the database are either stored in these files, derived from parameters that are stored here, or are set to system defaults. These files are not volatile, but should be backed up so that the current state of the database can be re-created from a consistent set of backups. Not having a backed-up parameter file forces you to guess which parameters the database is using.

TIP
Back up the init.ora file and spfile on a nightly basis.

Control Files

Introduced in Chapter 1, the control file contains information that assists the recovery process. The history of archive logs, the name of the current online redo log file, and datafile header checkpoint data are some of the information maintained by the control file. This is a small but critical piece of the database without which Oracle cannot run! Because of this, control files should be multiplexed so that at least three copies are used. A text version of this file and a binary version should both be backed up.

TIP
*Back up a text and binary version of the control files
with your regular database backups, and every time
you alter a data file, tablespace, or redo logs.*

```
alter database backup controlfile to trace;          -- text backup
alter database backup controlfile to '/directory/file';   -- binary backup
```

Redo Logs

When data is changed in Oracle, data buffers are changed to reflect the change to
tables and indexes. For performance purposes, these are usually not written out
to physical disk immediately. In order to protect the data, change records are written
out to allow changes to be undone (*undo records*) when a transaction is rolled back,
or redone (*redo records*) for the purpose of forward recovery. At transaction commit
time, all redo records that make up the transaction have been written to the redo log
files along with a unique system change number (*scn*) and the time of the change. Once
redo logs have been written, data protection is guaranteed. The changes to the data
files are in the buffer and can be written out at a later time. Multiple log files in a
database are used in a round-robin format. So, once one redo log file fills up, the next
redo log will then be used until it is full, followed by the next one and so on until
finally the first redo log will be used again. This is a continuous cycle. Redo logs
should be multiplexed so each redo log can be a group of two or more identical
members. In this manner, if there is a problem with one file being corrupted, the
database can still operate as long as the other file(s) remain intact. The redo logs
are absolutely required by Oracle to ensure that changes to data aren't lost!

Undo Segments

When data is changed, as mentioned earlier, "before images" of the data are created
to allow a transaction to roll back. This is accomplished through undo records being
written to undo segments (also called rollback segments) and tablespaces. These
tablespaces are managed in the same way as any other tablespace and the data in
undo tablespaces are subsequently logged as redo logs. Rollback segments allow
changes to be undone either for system reasons, perhaps due to a transaction that has
failed, or because the application explicitly has requested that a rollback be performed.
Undo or rollback tablespaces need to be included as part of your backup strategy.

Checkpoints

As you've seen, the redo logs and database data are not written out at the same time.
The redo logs are guaranteed to be written out at commit time, but the data is not
changed simultaneously. If that's the case, just when then is the data written from
the buffers to the data files? This is determined by one type of Oracle process called
Database Writer Process (DBWn); this process manages the writing of information to

the database. DBWn writes changes to the data files to free up dirty buffers (buffers that have changed data in them) to allow more changes to occur at system checkpoint time. A checkpoint is a background event that ensures all of the changed data has been written to the data files.

Archive Logs

Archive logs are the mechanism used to provide continuous availability to an Oracle database by allowing you to back up the database while it is running. This is known as a *hot backup.* They also allow you to recover databases by performing a "roll-forward" of changes using redo logs up to either the current point in time or to a time that we specify the database should be rolled forward to. This cannot be done with online redo logs because they are written to sequentially and eventually wrap-around. When that occurs, the previous records that existed in the wrapped redo file are overwritten. By placing the database in archivelog mode, online redo logs can be written out to files to be kept indefinitely. The files can be named with sequential incrementing names so that we know the order they should be applied in. As with redo logs, archive logs can be multiplexed. In other words, more than one copy of each archive log can be written to different locations.

Datafiles, Tablespaces, Segments, Extents, and Blocks

Datafiles are the low level structures that make up what you probably think of as a database. To put it simply, the tables and indexes that make up your applications are stored in tablespaces and each tablespace is created on one or more datafiles. A particular datafile will store data for one tablespace and a tablespace can contain many tables and indexes. Tables and indexes are a subset of a type of database object called a *segment.* Examples of segments are indexes, tables, rollback/undos, clusters, lobindexes, and lobsegments. A segment is made up of extents that are a collection of contiguous blocks. So, to put this into a single sentence, a tablespace is created on one or more datafiles and consists of one or more segments made up of one or more extents that are a contiguous collection of blocks. Got it? Good. It's an important set of relationships to understand.

From a backup and recovery point-of-view, it's important to be aware of the relationship between tables, tablespaces, and datafiles. Whenever you perform a backup where you are not backing up the entire database at the same time, it is important to consider any referential integrity constraints enforced by the backup or application that must be honored. You should employ a naming standard that makes it easy to determine the tablespace that a data file supports.

Trace Files

There are three types of dump files that contain information about errors that occur in the database. Background dumps are written out by Oracle background processes when an error occurs. User dumps are files written for user processes for the purpose of debugging. Core dumps are a place where Oracle dumps core files in a UNIX environment. These may be worth backing up as a history of problems that have occurred to help you troubleshoot future issues. One particular file that should be backed up regularly is a special trace file called an *alert log.* This file reports on a great deal of activity such as when the database is stopped and started, when checkpoints occurred and the system change number (*scn*—a unique number given to every change in the database) where the current *incarnation* or version of the database began. This is all valuable information that can be of great assistance when it comes time to recover your database.

TIP

Back up your alert log with your regular database backups.

You have now seen the structures that are critical to your backup and recovery operations. Armed with this knowledge, you are ready to learn about *User-Manager Backup and Recovery.*

Progress Check ⏱

1. Name some files that should be backed up as part of your strategy.

2. What does multiplexing mean and which objects should be multiplexed?

3. Why would you want to use archive logging?

Progress Check Answers

1. Some files that should be backed up include parameter, control, undo, archive log, data, online redo, dump, and trace files.

2. Multiplexing is a term to describe data that's written to more than one location or file at the same time. Redo logs, archive logs, and control files should be multiplexed and each copy should go to a different disk to protect against the loss of one disk.

3. Archive logging allows you to perform full recovery of the database. Without archive logs, no recovery is possible (only restores can be performed). Also, the database can be backed up while it is up and running. It is needed to deliver high availability.

Learn about Oracle User-Managed Backup and Recovery

Oracle supports backing up data in a number of ways. This section discusses how and why to use user-managed backups. These backups are by nature handled more mechanically than other methods and are just as effective. Also presented here is the information needed to recover your first database. Please remember that you should try this on test databases before trying your first backup and ultimate recovery on a business database.

Types of User-Managed Backups

User-managed database backups can be performed as either cold or hot physical backups. A *cold backup* means that all users are disconnected from the database and it is shut down in order to perform the backup. A *hot backup* is performed while the database is up and end users can remain connected to the database. In fact, they can be changing the very data that is being backed up! Let's examine these in more detail.

Cold Backups

Cold backups are the simplest type of backup operation you can perform. Cold backups are performed with the database completely shut down in a consistent manner. Once that is done, all database files should be backed up to disk or tape. Once the file copies are complete, the database can be started and users can resume their activity. The database does not need to be in archivelog mode in order to perform a cold backup but without archive logging, the database can only be recovered to the point in time that the cold backup was done. Cold backups are a simple option and limited in the way they must be run, but once you have a cold backup, it can be easier to work with and can provide a fair degree of functionality.

In order to perform a cold backup, the database must be shut down in a consistent manner. In other words, the database should be shut down by issuing one of the following commands:

- **shutdown normal**
- **shutdown immediate**
- **shutdown transactional**

Do not perform a cold backup of the database immediately after a **shutdown abort**. If you must shut down the database in this manner, follow it up with a **startup restrict** and **shutdown [immediate, transactional, normal]**. In this way, you can be confident that you have a database in which all of the transactions have completed or rolled back and the data is in a consistent state. When the database has been shut down, copy the files to another location on disk or to tape. The files that you should back up include

- All database datafiles and tablespaces including system, temp, and rollback/undo

- Control files, backup binary control files, and text control files

- Archive logs if they are being used

- Alert logs

- Oracle password files if they exist

- Parameter files init<SID>.ora and spfile

- Redo logs—BUT you should be careful whenever restoring redo logs since the restore of a redo log could overwrite existing current redo logs that contain the final entries in the redo stream needed to complete the recovery. Because of this, Oracle recommends not backing up redo logs.

Once the backups have been completed, the database can be restarted. If the backups were made to disk, these files can later be backed up to tape after the database is restarted.

You should be careful whenever restoring redo logs since the restore of a redo log could overwrite existing redo logs that contain the final entries in the redo stream needed to complete the recovery. Because of this (to repeat ourselves), Oracle recommends not backing up redo logs.

Hot Backups

A hot backup is a backup done while the database is up and running. The entire database can be backed up, or a subset of the tablespaces or data files can be backed up at one time, and while this is happening, end users can continue to perform all of their normal operations against it. In order to do this, the database must be running in archivelog mode. This is done by setting the parameter **log_archive_start = true** (for pre–Oracle Database 10*g* databases only) and then running the sql statement **alter database archivelog** (this is needed for Oracle Database 10*g* and earlier versions) while the database is mounted. The tablespaces to be backed up are put in backup mode with the **alter tablespace *tablespace_name* begin backup** command. The data files are then copied using OS copies, and the backup is completed with the **alter tablespace *tablespace_name* end backup** command. This looks like the following:

```
alter tablespace <tablespace_name> begin backup;
[os file copy command such as cp in unix or ocopy in Windows]
alter tablespace <tablespace_name> end backup;
```

Once the backup is complete, you will need to ensure that all of the log records created during the backup operation have been subsequently archived. Do this with the sql statement **archive log current**. This command ensures that all redo logs have been archived and it will wait for the archive to complete. You should note that the ocopy utility is required in Windows environments to allow a file to be shared between the copy utility and Oracle. It is not needed in UNIX environments.

After a hot backup has been successfully completed, the database can be recovered to a particular point in time by restoring the data files from the hot backup and rolling forward archive logs to the time required. Online redo logs should never be backed up during a hot backup. Rather, archive the current redo logs and back those up. As a result, you will create the redo logs at the end of recovery when an **alter database open resetlogs** is performed (resetlogs is discussed later in this chapter in the section "Recovery Using Backup Control Files").

In order to recover from a hot or cold backup it is important to remember that all of the files that make up the database must be recovered to the same point in time in order to keep the entire database consistent. The exception to this rule is that read-only tablespaces can be restored to the point that they were made read-only. This makes sense since the tablespace cannot be changed once it has been made read-only. In order to recover a tablespace that is open for read-write operations to a point in time that is different from the rest of the database, a special operation called Tablespace Point In Time Recovery (TSPITR) must be performed which requires a clone database and is beyond the scope of this chapter.

Whenever a tablespace status changes to read-only or read-write, it should be backed up. You will need to keep track of these backups so that you know where they are when it comes time to use them in a recovery situation. Consider backing up "read only" tablespaces periodically to deal with potential expiry dates on tape as well as other tape management problems that could result from older tapes.

TIP
Run hot backups when the system is not busy. Also, only put one tablespace between the begin and end backup operations to reduce the amount of system overhead associated with this activity since system logging is increased on tablespaces that are in backup mode. You can group multiple tablespaces together in cases where change activity will not be high on them during the backup.

Hot backups and archivelogs will be a requirement of every system that has true high-availability requirements.

Recovery from a Cold Backup

Database recovery can be broken into two distinct steps. The first step involves file restores where files are copied from tape or a disk backup to a location on disk where the actual database resides. This is the location of files pointed to by the control files. The second step is forward recovery where the archive logs can be processed and applied to the database making the data as current as possible. In the case of the database in noarchivelog mode (which is often the case where cold backups are concerned), there are no logs with which to recover, so all data files, control files, and redo logs are simply restored to their proper location. Other files such as the init.ora and spfile parameter files, as well as password files, must also be in the proper place.

Ask the Expert

Q: Why would I ever want to use cold backups if hot backups are so powerful?

A: There are situations where you only need to restore a database from a cold backup and where high availability is not a concern. In these cases, you can consider using a cold backup.

Q: How often should I back up read-only tablespaces?

A: Back up read-only tablespaces periodically to deal with potential expiry dates on tape, as well as other tape management problems that could result from older tapes. When using RMAN, back these up once previous backups become "obsolete." We will cover obsolete backups in the RMAN section.

Q: What is the downside to performing hot backups and running in archivelog mode, if any?

A: You will need to manage the archive log files, but RMAN can help you with this (more information can be had in the upcoming RMAN section). There is also extra logging that occurs when a tablespace is placed in backup mode. This can be overcome by backing up when the database is not busy or by using RMAN, which does not place tablespaces in backup mode. Restores from hot backups require more care and practice but the benefits to hot backups outweigh the disadvantages by a great deal.

Restoring a database from a cold backup is one of the simpler things you can do as a DBA, and this simplicity is perhaps the biggest benefit of performing a cold backup. A cold backup of a database that is in archivelog mode can be recovered, but there is no recovery from a cold backup that is not in archivelog mode (note that a hot backup is only performed on databases in archivelog mode). There are only file restores. Once these files have been restored, the database can be started. That's it!

Recovery from a Hot Backup

This is one of the places where you will earn your stripes as a DBA since you will always need to perform recovery from a hot backup. To clarify this point, recovery can be performed on any database that is in archivelog mode, whether the backup was a hot or cold one, but hot backups always require that recovery be performed. There are two fundamental types of recovery: *complete recovery* and *incomplete recovery*.

Complete recovery describes a recovery where the database is restored and then recovered forward using all available archive logs. You are performing as complete a recovery as you can, with no data loss. Complete recovery can be performed at the database, tablespace, datafile, or block level.

Incomplete or point-in-time recovery is one where the database is restored and then optionally rolled forward to a predetermined point in time or *system change number (scn)* by applying only some, but not all, of the logs. This produces a version of the database that is not current and is often done to bring the database back to a time before a problem occurred. There are three fundamental types of incomplete recovery:

- Cancel-based is a recovery that runs until you issue a **cancel** command.

- Timestamp recovery applies to all of the logs until a timestamp you enter is reached.

- Change-based recovery applies to all of the logs until an scn you enter is reached.

Examples of these are shown next:

```
SQL> recover database until cancel;
SQL> recover database until change 1234567;
SQL> recover database until time '2004-04-15:14:33:00';
```

TIP
When performing a recovery, always try to recover as much data as possible by running a complete recovery or applying archive logs to the latest timestamp or scn that you possibly can.

Seven Steps to Recovery

The fundamental steps to perform when doing a recovery are summed up here:

1. Restore data files from tape or a backup location on disk to the location where the database file should reside.

2. Startup nomount. This step reads the parameter file, allocates the memory structure of the SGA and starts the background Oracle processes. Also, the alert log and trace files are opened. Note that the data files are not open during a Startup nomount. This step has to be performed if the control file needs to be rebuilt.

3. Create the control file. This step is optional and only needed if the control file is unavailable. A text version of the control file should be used to create a new binary version of the control file.

4. Ensure that all the data files to recover are online. Read-only data files once restored do not need to be recovered since no data will have changed in these files.

5. Mount the database. This step associates a database with the instance that was started in step 2. The database, however, is not opened at this time. The control file listed in the parameter file is opened and all database files are located.

6. Recover the database by locating and applying the archive logs.

7. Open the database. The database, including the redo logs and data files, is opened with the **Startup Open** command.

In some cases, you only need to recover a single tablespace or data file without touching the rest of the database. These must be complete recoveries and the tablespace or data file must be taken offline to perform this. A block level recovery can also be performed, but only by RMAN and can be done with the datafile online. This feature allows you to recover a small number of corrupt blocks of a datafile and is one of the great reasons to use RMAN!

Recovery Using Backup Control Files

You can create both a text version of the control file and a binary version of the control file as backups. When recovering the database, you should try to use the current control file. If that is not possible, then your next option should be to try to use a backup control file since it contains useful information that assists recovery that is not included in the text-based control file. With a backup control file, you will need to perform media recovery and use the **using backup control file** syntax when performing the **recover database** command. A **resetlogs** command will then

Ask the Expert

Q: What would happen if I restored the redo logs before I performed a point-in-time recovery? It seems like this is the best approach to use.

A: There is an end-of-redo marker on the online redo logs that will stop the recovery immediately. Oracle will think the forward recovery is complete and archive logs will not be applied.

Q: How can I find out the state of a file when a backup control file was taken? I need to know which files are read-write, read-only, or offline, but how can I do that?

A: Whenever you back up a control file, run an sql script that queries **dba_data_files** and writes the status of all of your data files to a file that is kept with the backup control file. We will show you an example of this in the following section.

need to be performed when the database is opened and this will create new redo logs as well as a new version, or *incarnation,* of the database. You also need to know the status of data files when the backup control file was created. If a data file had a status of read-write when the backup control file was created, but should be opened as a read-only file, then it should be taken offline before recovery begins. Backup control files are a useful and sometimes required feature, but can complicate your database recovery.

TIP
Always back up the database after performing an incomplete recovery and opening the database with the Resetlogs option.

CRITICAL SKILL 5.3

Write a Database Backup

When you decide to use a user-managed backup strategy rather than RMAN, you will need to develop scripts to perform hot or cold backups. One of the most important things you should do to simplify your maintenance requirements is to develop scripts that are generated from the Oracle catalog. If done properly, you won't need to change your backup scripts every time you add a new file or change the location of a file.

TIP
*Automate your backups with scripts that
are generated from the Oracle Catalog.*

Whenever you perform a backup, it is extremely useful to know the status of your
database including the data files and parameters in effect. Information such as which
data files are open in read-only mode at backup time is invaluable, as is a listing of
the file locations and sizes. Shown next is a simple example of some SQL queries
that provides information about the state of a database when you need to restore:

```
select * from dba_tablespaces;    -- Tablespace Information
select * from dba_data_files;     -- Data file Information
select * from v$datafile;         -- More data file information
select * from v$logfile;          -- log file information
select * from v$log;              -- more log file information
select * from v$controlfile;      -- control file information
select * from v$parameter;        -- database parameters in effect
select * from v$nls_parameters;   -- language characters in effect
-- Get the log history information for the past 3 days
select * from v$log_history where first_time > sysdate - 3;
```

The preceding should be spooled to the backup directory and kept with your
backups. You can list the specific columns you want to see in the previous queries,
but when it comes to needing information during a high-pressure recovery, we would
rather err on the side of having a little too much information rather than risk missing
a piece of information that would be useful. Once you have this information, your
backup can be performed. The following is an example of a hot backup SQL script.
This script must be executed on a database running in archivelog mode.

```
set echo on;
spool /u02/backup/ora10g/hotBackup1.lst;
alter system archive log current;
alter tablespace INDX begin backup;
! cp /u01/oradata/ora10g/indx01.dbf /u02/backup/ora10g
alter tablespace INDX end backup;
alter tablespace TABLESPACE_n begin backup;
! cp /u01/oradata/ora10g/tablespace_n01.dbf /u02/backup/ora10g
! cp /u01/oradata/ora10g/tablespace_n02.dbf /u02/backup/ora10g
alter tablespace TABLESPACE_n end backup;
… more tablespaces …
alter tablespace SYSTEM begin backup;
! cp /u01/oradata/ora10g/system01.dbf /u02/backup/ora10g
alter tablespace SYSTEM end backup;
-- Backup the log file
alter system archive log current;
--  Create 3 copies of a binary controlfile backup.
alter database backup controlfile to /u02/backup/ora10g/CONTROL01.CTL' reuse;
alter database backup controlfile to /u02/backup/ora10g/CONTROL02.CTL' reuse;
alter database backup controlfile to /u02/backup/ora10g/CONTROL03.CTL' reuse;
```

```
-- Create a text version of a controlfile backup
alter database backup controlfile to trace;
spool off;
exit;
```

This is a SQL script that can be run from a UNIX shell script or a Windows command file. To run this in Windows environments, the file copies are performed using the **host start /wait c:\oracle\ora81\bin\ocopy.exe** command rather than with the UNIX **! cp** command, which hosts out and runs the UNIX version of copy. *ocopy* is an Oracle copy utility that must be run under Windows to allow file sharing to occur during hot backups. The standard DOS **copy** command does not allow this.

Cold backups are similar to the preceding except that the **begin backup** and **end backup** commands are not needed. The copy commands are surrounded by a consistent database shutdown before the copies have started, and a startup after the copies have completed. Note that in Windows environments, you should use the standard "copy" utility for cold backups.

You should also add your parameter files, dump files, and alert logs to your backups. Once you've added those, you'll have everything backed up except for your archive logs. Let's see how to manage those next.

Back Up Archived Redo Logs

Managing archive logs is one of the more difficult tasks on a busy Oracle database. You will want to have archive logs available to you in case they are needed for a database recovery. At the same time, the archive logs must be written to disk and if disk space fills up, the instance will stop processing requests until more space becomes available. Trying to balance both of these competing requirements can be tricky, especially if your system writes a large number of log records.

To meet the first requirement of trying to keep the archive logs available to your online system in the event of a recovery, try to keep archive logs since the last backup (or, even better, the last two backups) on disk. Compress the archive files if you need to. If you are unable to keep archive logs online due to space issues, then you will need to write a script that regularly backs up the archive logs to tape and deletes them from disk. An example of a space management script that backs up archive logs once the archive directory is over 50 percent full is shown here:

```
#Pseudo-shell-code for free archive log space
# Check used and free space: this is a very simple script
# df -k   (on linux: location of fields varies by platform)
# Filesystem    1k-blocks Used      Available Use%    Mounted on
# /dev/hda3     3763404   102676    3469556   3%       /
Log_arch_dest='/u01/oradata/db01/arch'
arch_dir_mountPoint=`df -k ${log_arch_dest}|grep -v blocks|awk '{print $6}'`
arch_dir_freeSpace=`df -k ${log_arch_dest}|grep -v blocks|awk '{print $4}'`
```

```
arch_dir_used=`df -k ${LOG_ARCH_DEST}|grep -v blocks|awk '{print $3}'`
if [${arch_dir_freeSpace} -le  ${arch_dir_Used}]; then
 echo "Place archiving logic here"
fi
```

All of this is unnecessary when you use RMAN since it will back up archive logs to tape, delete the files on disk, and manage the tape files in the RMAN repository. We will see more of this later in the "Get Started with Recovery Manager" section.

CRITICAL SKILL 5.5

Get Started with Oracle Data Pump

Oracle Data Pump is a new utility available with Oracle Database 10*g* that can be used to move data and *metadata* (metadata is the "data about the data," or in Oracle terms is the catalog information) from one database to another. If you are used to the pre–Oracle Database 10*g* versions of Export and Import, you will be familiar with the functionality of Data Pump Export and Data Pump Import and will recognize a similar interface with these new utilities. However, these are completely separate utilities. The performance of Oracle's new utilities Data Pump Export and Data Pump Import will increase greatly over the old Export and Import utilities and can also take advantage of parallelism to accomplish this. The Data Pump Export and Import utilities use the **expdp** and **impdp** commands, respectively. You are encouraged to use these rather than the pre–Oracle Database 10*g* exp and imp utilities since those do not support all Oracle Database 10*g* features, while the Data Pump utilities do.

Data Pump will allow a subset of data and metadata to be moved through filters implemented in the Export and Import parameters. The Data Pump Export utility unloads data, metadata, and control information from the database into one or more operating system files that are called dump files. These are written in a proprietary format that can only be read by the Data Pump Import utility. These can be imported into a target database that resides on another server and a totally different operating system.

The Data Pump Import utility can read these dump files and load a target database with metadata, data, and all objects that have been previously exported. For example, table DDL, security in the form of grants, objects such as triggers, stored procedures, and views can also be imported, among other things. In fact an entire target database can be created from a Data Pump Full Export using the Import utility. Some useful options provided through Data Pump are

- The ability to view object DDL without running it using the SQLFILE parameter

- The network import which allows a Data Pump Import to occur using a source database rather than a dump file set

- The ability to restart Data Pump jobs using parameter **start_job** to restart import jobs

■ Using the Parallel parameter to define the maximum number of threads and degrees of parallelism for export and import jobs

■ The ability to now monitor jobs by detaching and reattaching to running jobs

■ The ability to estimate the amount of space an export file will occupy by using the **estimate_only** clause

The Data Pump Export and Import for data and metadata are performed using the Data Pump *application programming interface (API)* and uses procedures in the DBMS_DATAPUMP PL/SQL Package. The metadata API is implemented through the DBMS_METADATA package. This package retrieves metadata in XML format that can be used in many ways. For example, XML can be transformed into DDL or *XSLT (Extensible Stylesheet Language Transformation)* and the XML itself can be used to create an object. There is a new Remap attribute that allows the attributes of an object to be changed. For example, schema names can be changed using this feature. The Data Pump API supports all objects needed to perform a full export.

There are three ways to perform Data Pump Export and Import utilities. There is the command-line interface where export and import parameters are listed on a command line or in a script. A variation of the command-line interface is to add a parameter file using the **parfile** parameter, which points to a different file where all of the import or export parameters are listed. An interactive-command interface can also be used by entering CTRL-C during an import or export run which will then allow you to enter commands when prompted.

Let's now explore some details about actual running Data Pump exports and imports.

Use Oracle Data Pump Export

There are five mutually exclusive modes for performing the Oracle Data Pump Export:

■ Full Export is where the entire database is exported using the **full** parameter. This can be used to completely rebuild the database if needed.

■ Schema Export is the default mode and allows you to export one or more schemas in the database. The **schemas** parameter is used to run this. Please note that objects in other schemas related or dependent on objects in this schema are not exported unless the other schema is also mentioned in the schema list.

■ Table Export allows for the export of tables or partitions and their dependent objects using the **tables** parameter.

■ Tablespace Export can be used to unload all of the tables that have been created in the given tablespace set using the **tablespaces** parameter.

■ Transportable Tablespace mode differs from the preceding bullet in that only the metadata is exported from the database for a given tablespace set. This uses the **transport_tablespaces** parameter.

The **exp_full_database** role must be granted to a user performing a full or tablespace export or an export of a schema or table that is outside of the user's schema.

A useful feature of the Data Pump Export is the use of filters that can be used on both data and metadata to restrict the rows to be exported. For data, this places restrictions on the rows to be exported. The data filters are applied with the query parameter and the filter is executed once per table per job. For metadata, either the **exclude** or **include** parameters can be used and these are mutually exclusive commands. When filters are applied to metadata, the objects that are included will also have their dependent objects included. For example, included tables will also have indexes, triggers, grants, and constraints included with them. You can use the **datapump_paths** view to see which objects can be filtered on. When multiple filters are applied to an object, they are processed with an **and** condition between them. When using filters, we recommend using the **parfile** parameter and placing all parameters in the **parfile** including the filter operators.

The parameters for the Data Pump Export command can be seen using the command **expdp help=y**. A subset of the output from this, which contains the parameters along with a brief description, is shown next.

Export parameters extracted from the command: **expdt help=y**

```
>expdp help=y
Keyword                 Description (Default)
------------------------------------------------------------------------
ATTACH                  Attach to existing job, e.g. ATTACH, [=job name].
CONTENT                 Specifies data to unload where the valid keywords are:
                        (ALL), DATA_ONLY, and METADATA_ONLY.
DIRECTORY               Directory object to be used for dumpfiles and logfiles.
DUMPFILE                List of destination dump files (expdat.dmp),
                        e.g., DUMPFILE=scott1.dmp, scott2.dmp, dmpdir:scott3.dmp.
ESTIMATE                Calculate job estimates where the valid keywords are
                        (BLOCKS), SAMPLING, and STATISTICS.
ESTIMATE_ONLY           Calculate job estimates without performing the export.
EXCLUDE                 Exclude specific object types, e.g., EXCLUDE=TABLE:EMP.
FILESIZE                Specify the size of each dumpfile in units of bytes.
FLASHBACK_SCN           SCN used to reset session snapshot.
FLASHBACK_TIME          Time used to get the SCN closest to the specified time.
FULL                    Export entire database (N).
HELP                    Display Help messages (N).
INCLUDE                 Include specific object types, e.g., INCLUDE=TABLE_DATA.
JOB_NAME                Name of export job to create.
LOGFILE                 Log file name (export.log).
NETWORK_LINK            Name of remote database link to the source system.
NOLOGFILE               Do not write logfile (N).
PARALLEL                Change the number of active workers for current job.
PARFILE                 Specify parameter file.
QUERY                   Predicate clause used to export a subset of a table.
```

```
SCHEMAS                    List of schemas to export (login schema).
STATUS                     Frequency (secs) job status is to be monitored where
                           the default (0) will show new status when available.
TABLES                     Identifies a list of tables to export - one schema only.
TABLESPACES                Identifies a list of tablespaces to export.
TRANSPORT_FULL_CHECK       Verify storage segments of all tables (N).
TRANSPORT_TABLESPACES      Export transportable tablespace metadata (N).
VERSION                    Version of objects to export where valid keywords are
                           (COMPATIBLE), LATEST, or any valid database version.
The following commands are valid while in interactive mode.
Command                    Description
--------------------------------------------------------------------------
ADD_FILE                   Add dumpfile to dumpfile set.
                           ADD_FILE=<dirobj:>dumpfile-name
CONTINUE_CLIENT            Return to logging mode. Job will be re-started if idle.
EXIT_CLIENT                Quit client session and leave job running.
HELP                       Summarize interactive commands.
KILL_JOB                   Detach and delete job.
PARALLEL                   Change the number of active workers for current job.
                           PARALLEL=<number of workers>.
START_JOB                  Start/resume current job.
STATUS                     Frequency (secs) job status is to be monitored where
                           the default (0) will show new status when available.
                           STATUS=[interval]
STOP_JOB                   Stops job execution and exits the client.
```

The values in brackets in the preceding list are the default values in use for the parameter. Some parameters worth noting are explored further in the following bullet points.

■ DIRECTORY is the directory that is created using the sql **create directory** syntax in Oracle and is the location that the dump file is written to. The default name is **DPUMP_DIR**. For example, set this as follows:

```
create or replace directory DPUMP_DIR as '\u01\';
grant read, write on dpump_dir to export_user;
```

■ ESTIMATE allows you to specify whether to estimate the space in blocks (the default), by sampling data, a number of rows, or using table statistics. Estimates are performed for the data only and not for the metadata.

■ EXCLUDE can be used to exclude metadata, dependent objects, and data to be exported. To exclude data, you must use data filtering through a **query** and **where** clause. Once an object has been excluded, all of its dependent objects will also be excluded.

■ FLASHBACK_SCN and _TIME directs the export to unload data that is consistent with the time or scn listed.

■ INCLUDE is used to list metadata objects and dependent data that will be exported. This can include object types and object names. Only objects explicitly listed in the INCLUDE statement will be exported.

■ NETWORK_LINK allows an import into a target database directly from a source database rather than from a dump file.

■ PARALLEL is a performance option that can be used to specify the maximum number of threads that can be used to speed up an export by running it in parallel.

■ PARFILE can be included to point to another file that includes export parameters. Use this when filtering data and metadata using the **exclude**, **include**, or **query** parameters.

■ QUERY can be used to apply syntax similar to qualifiers that you would use in a **select...where** clause to filter the rows to be exported.

■ TRANSPORT_TABLESPACES (*TTS*) is the parameter used to specify the tablespaces that will have their metadata exported during a transportable tablespace operation. When this is done, the tablespaces in the source database should be placed in read-only mode and their underlying datafiles copied to a new location. The datafile copies are performed at the OS level. The only "export" is that of the metadata. The datafile copies and exported metadata can be used to plug in the tablespaces to a target database. The tablespaces must be a self-contained set and the **transport_full_check** parameter can be used to ensure this is the case.

■ ADD_FILE is valuable if an export operation fills the current dump file. When this occurs, you will be prompted to add a new dump file and you are able to do so.

■ START_JOB allows you to start a job to which you are attached. This allows you to restart an export after a previous failure and is valuable for long-running jobs.

Examples that use some of these appear in the next section.

Some Export Examples

To perform a full database export using data pump, run the following:

```
expdp system/manager DUMPFILE=expdat.dmp FULL=y LOGFILE=export.log
```

A Schema Level Export of the Sales History (SH) schema can be performed as follows:

```
expdp system/manager DUMPFILE=expdat.dmp SCHEMAS=sh LOGFILE=export.log
```

A single table can be exported, as shown next with the sh.customers table:

```
expdp system/manager DUMPFILE=expdat.dmp TABLES=sh.customers LOGFILE=export.log
```

Here is an example of data filtering where the tables in the SH schema are exported except for the PROMOTIONS table and CUSTOMERS table which has one row exported.

```
expdp sh/sh parfile=exp.par
```

The contents of the exp.par file are shown here:

```
DIRECTORY=DPUMP_DIR
DUMPFILE=testsh.dmp
CONTENT=DATA_ONLY
EXCLUDE=TABLE:"in ('PROMOTIONS')"
QUERY=customers:"where cust_id=1"
```

The Data Pump Export utility is valuable for performing backups of a database or objects in a database, as well as for moving data from one database to another. Experiment with the different parameters and test your exports by performing imports to another database to ensure that the entire export and import stream is working properly.

CRITICAL SKILL 5.7

Work with Oracle Data Pump Import

You've successfully performed exports and they seem to have worked, but that's only half of the job. You now need to perform the ultimate test of whether those exports worked by performing Data Pump Imports.

Imports are performed using the **impdp** command that is new with Oracle Database 10*g*. As with Data Pump Export, this utility has similar functionality with the import utility found in pre–Oracle Database 10*g* versions, but this is a brand new utility. There are five modes for performing the Oracle Data Pump Import. The modes correspond to the export modes, but an import can be run using an export of the exact same mode or an export mode that is a higher level in the hierarchy. For example, a table-mode import can be performed using a source that is a Full, Schema, Tablespace, or Table mode export dump file as well as a Network-Link. These modes are mutually exclusive and are described next.

- **Full Import**   The entire database is imported using the FULL parameter. This can be used to completely rebuild the database if needed. This can be run using a source dump file or a source database using a Network_Link.

- **Schema Import**   The default mode allows you to import one or more schemas in the database using the SCHEMAS parameter. Objects in other schemas that are dependent on objects in this schema are not imported unless the other schema is also mentioned in the schema list. The source for this can be a Full export dump file or a Schema level export dump file or another database using a Network_Link.

- **Table Import**   Allows for the import of tables or partitions and their dependent objects using the **tables** parameter. To import tables that are not in your schema, the **imp_full_database** role must be granted to you. The source for this can be a Full, Schema, Table, or Tablespace level dump file, or another database using a Network_Link.

- **Tablespace Import**   Can be used to load all of the tables that have been created in the given tablespace set using the **tablespaces** parameter. The source for this can be a Full, Schema, Table, or Tablespace level dump file, or another database using a Network_Link.

- **Transportable Tablespace (TTS)**   Differs from its siblings in that only the metadata is imported to the database for a given tablespace set. This uses the **transport_tablespaces** parameter. The metadata that was exported using a TTS export are imported into the target database and the datafiles need to be copied into the correct location as specified by the metadata (note that the paths can be changed). The source for this can be a transportable tablespace export dump file or a source database.

As with imports, filters can be used on both data and metadata to restrict the rows to be imported. For data, restrictions on the rows to be imported are implemented with the **query** parameter and the filter is executed once per table, per job. For metadata, either the **exclude** or **include** parameters can be used and these are mutually exclusive commands. When filters are applied to metadata, the objects that are included will also have their dependent objects included.

The parameters available with Data Pump Import can be seen using the command **impdp help=y**. A subset of the output from this, which contains the parameters along with a brief description, is shown next.

Import parameters extracted from the command: **impdp help=y**

```
>impdp help=y
Keyword                  Description (Default)
-----------------------------------------------------------------------------
ATTACH                   Attach to existing job, e.g., ATTACH [=job name].
CONTENT                  Specifies data to load where the valid keywords are
                         (ALL), DATA_ONLY, and METADATA_ONLY.
DIRECTORY                Directory object to be used for dump, log, and sql files.
DUMPFILE                 List of dumpfiles to import from (expdat.dmp),
                         e.g., DUMPFILE=scott1.dmp, scott2.dmp, dmpdir:scott3.dmp.
ESTIMATE                 Calculate job estimates where the valid keywords are
                         (BLOCKS), SAMPLING, and STATISTICS.
EXCLUDE                  Exclude specific object types, e.g., EXCLUDE=TABLE:EMP.
FLASHBACK_SCN            SCN used to reset the session snapshot.
FLASHBACK_TIME           Time used to get the SCN closest to the specified time.
FULL                     Import everything from source (Y).
HELP                     Display help messages (N).
INCLUDE                  Include specific object types, e.g., INCLUDE=TABLE_DATA.
JOB_NAME                 Name of import job to create.
LOGFILE                  Log file name (import.log).
```

```
NETWORK_LINK            Name of remote database link to the source system.
NOLOGFILE               Do not write logfile.
PARALLEL                Change the number of active workers for current job.
PARFILE                 Specify parameter file.
QUERY                   Predicate clause used to import a subset of a table.
REMAP_DATAFILE          Redefine datafile references in all DDL statements.
REMAP_SCHEMA            Objects from one schema are loaded into another schema.
REMAP_TABLESPACE        Tablespace object is remapped to another tablespace.
REUSE_DATAFILES         Tablespace will be initialized if it already exists (N).
SCHEMAS                 List of schemas to import.
SKIP_UNUSABLE_INDEXES   Skip indexes that were set to the Index Unusable state.
SQLFILE                 Write all the SQL DDL to a specified file.
STATUS                  Frequency (secs) job status is to be monitored where
                        the default (0) will show new status when available.
TABLE_EXISTS_ACTION     Action to take if imported object already exists.
                        Valid keywords: (SKIP), APPEND, REPLACE, and TRUNCATE.
TABLES                  Identifies a list of tables to import.
TABLESPACES             Identifies a list of tablespaces to import.
TRANSFORM               Metadata transform to apply (Y/N) to specific objects.
                        Valid transform keywords: SEGMENT_ATTRIBUTES and STORAGE.
                        e.g., TRANSFORM=SEGMENT_ATTRIBUTES:N:TABLE.
TRANSPORT_DATAFILES     List of datafiles to be imported by transportable mode.
TRANSPORT_FULL_CHECK    Verify storage segments of all tables (N).
TRANSPORT_TABLESPACES   List of tablespaces from which metadata will be loaded.
                        Only valid in NETWORK_LINK mode import operations.
VERSION                 Version of objects to export where valid keywords are
                        (COMPATIBLE), LATEST, or any valid database version.
                        Only valid for NETWORK_LINK and SQLFILE.
The following commands are valid while in interactive mode.
Command                 Description (Default)
------------------------------------------------------------------------
CONTINUE_CLIENT         Return to logging mode. Job will be re-started if idle.
EXIT_CLIENT             Quit client session and leave job running.
HELP                    Summarize interactive commands.
KILL_JOB                Detach and delete job.
PARALLEL                Change the number of active workers for current job.
                        PARALLEL=<number of workers>.
START_JOB               Start/resume current job.
STATUS                  Frequency (secs) job status is to be monitored where
                        the default (0) will show new status when available.
                        STATUS=[interval]
STOP_JOB                Stops job execution and exits the client.
```

The values in brackets in the preceding list are the default values in use for the parameter. Some parameters worth noting are as follows:

- EXCLUDE can be used to exclude metadata and dependent objects and data to be imported. To exclude data only, you must use data filtering through a query. Once an object has been excluded, all of its dependent objects will also be excluded.

- FLASHBACK_SCN and _TIME specify the system change number (scn) or time that the import will use as a point of consistency. In other words, the import will be performed in a manner in which the data is consistent with the time or scn listed. This is only used with a Network_Link, and specifies the scn or time from the source database.

■ INCLUDE is used to include metadata objects and dependent data during an import. This can include object types as well as object names. Only objects explicitly listed in the **include** statement will be imported. Employ a **parfile** when using this option.

■ NETWORK_LINK allows for an import into a target database directly from a source database rather than from a dump file that was previously exported.

■ PARALLEL is a performance option that specifies the maximum number of threads that can be used to speed up an import by running it in parallel.

■ PARFILE can be included to point to another file that includes import parameters. Use this when filtering data and metadata using the **exclude**, **include**, or **query** parameters.

■ QUERY is used to apply syntax similar to qualifiers that you would use in a **select...where** clause to filter rows to be imported. Use a **parfile** with this parameter.

■ Remap parameters: **remap_datafile**, **remap_schema**, **remap_tablespace**, **remap_datafiles**. These allow you to change the names of datafiles, schemas, tablespaces, and datafiles when moving objects from one database to another.

■ **reuse_datafiles** should be used with extreme caution. When set to Y, existing datafiles will be used and data will be overwritten when a Create Tablespace operation is performed. The default is N and a **create tablespace** command will fail when a dependent datafile exists.

■ SQLFILE names a file where all of the DDL that would be executed will be written. So, rather than executing the DDL, it writes the statements to the SQLFILE named here.

■ TRANSPORT_TABLESPACES (TTS) specifies tablespaces that will have their metadata imported during a TTS operation. The datafile copies and previously exported metadata can be used to plug in the tablespaces to a target database.

A Data Pump Export and Import Example

Let's look at an example of data filtering where all data from all tables in the SH schema are exported except for the SALES table. We will then use the dump file created by this export in a separate import job that renames the schema and only imports one table. Here are the export script and parameter files:

```
expdp system/manager parfile=exp.par
```

Contents of the exp.par parameter file are shown here:

```
DIRECTORY=DPUMP_DIR
DUMPFILE=testsh.dmp
SCHEMAS=SH
EXCLUDE=TABLE:"in ('SALES')"
```

An import that uses the preceding dump file is shown next. Notice that we are importing a single table into a different schema **SHNEW** as specified by the **REMAP_SCHEMA** command. If the table already exists, then this will be skipped and the import will continue through the **TABLE_EXISTS_ACTION** parameter. Note that the **SHNEW** schema must already exist in the database with the proper authority to create all of the objects in it since this was a schema level export. In order to create the **SHNEW** schema with Data Pump Import, a full export would need to be run.

```
impdp system/manager parfile=imp.par
```

Contents of the imp.par file are shown here:

```
DIRECTORY=DPUMP_DIR
DUMPFILE=testsh.dmp
REMAP_SCHEMA=SH:SHNEW
TABLES=SH.PRODUCTS
TABLE_EXISTS_ACTION=SKIP
```

Progress Check ⏱

1. Describe the data and metadata that is exported with the following command:

   ```
   expdb system/manager dumpfile=testsh.dmp schemas=sh
   logfile=testsh.txt
   ```

2. What is the result of the following export?

   ```
   expdb system/manager dumpfile=testsh.dmp full=Y
   EXCLUDE=TABLE:"LIKE'%'"
   ```

3. Why would you run a Data Pump export or import rather than an original Oracle export?

4. How does a transportable tablespace export and import differ from the others?

5. What makes the metadata export and import so useful and flexible?

CRITICAL SKILL 5.8

Use Traditional Export and Import

The original (non–Data Pump) Export and Import utilities that were used in pre–Oracle10g versions can be found in Oracle Database 10g. However, we strongly recommend you use the new Data Pump utilities since they support all Oracle Database 10g features and will increase performance. Here, we'll review the original Export and Import utilities since you'll be using them with earlier versions of Oracle.

How to Run the Original Utilities

Before running the original export and import, the catexp.sql catalog script needs to be run to prepare Oracle for these utilities, and it is invoked from the catalog.sql script. These scripts can be found in the ORACLE_HOME/rdbms/admin directory.

Once the catalog has been set up for export and import, you are ready to run the utilities. As with Data Pump, these utilities can be run as a command-line interface, by using parameter files or interactive commands.

To run an original export, issue the **exp** executable in a manner similar to using Data Pump. Use the following syntax to run a command-line export or an export using a parameter file or an interactive export, respectively:

```
exp user/password@SID parameter_list
exp PARFILE
exp   (and respond interactively to the export requests)
```

To find all of the export and import syntax, issue the following command:

```
exp help=y
```

Progress Check Answers

1. The entire schema, including metadata and all table data, is exported to file testsh.dmp.

2. Although the FULL=Y option is used, all tables were excluded through the wildcard LIKE '%'. No tables were exported, nor were any table dependencies and metadata.

3. The Data Pump export provides considerable performance enhancements such as parallelism and it supports all Oracle Database 10g features.

4. Data is not exported and imported using Transportable Tablespaces (TTS). Rather, all of the metadata associated with the objects are exported from the source database and imported into the target. The datafiles in the source database are placed in read-only mode and the files are copied to the target location before the TTS Import step begins.

5. The metadata is retrieved in XML format that can be used in many different ways. The **remap_schema** parameter facilitates object renames.

To run an original import, issue the **imp** executable in a manner similar to using Data Pump. Use the same syntax as for export in the previous example, except that the utility to be run is imp. The three types of import can be run as shown next:

```
imp user/password@SID parameter_list
imp PARFILE
imp   (and respond interactively to the export requests)
```

To find all of the export syntax, issue the following command:

```
imp help=y
```

The parameters for export and import are a little different than the Data Pump ones, but as with Data Pump, these can be run in different, mutually exclusive, modes. They are

- Full export and import

- User export and import

- Table export and import

- **transportable_tablespace** export and import

These utilities can also be run in Direct-Path or Conventional-Path mode. Conventional Path performs the utilities as SQL statements that are more versatile than Direct-Path exports. These can be used to move data across different server platform types or different Oracle versions. Direct path exports and imports are much faster than conventional ones but are less versatile. A direct path export and import needs to be run on the same Oracle version and the same server platform. Conventional is the default and Direct is run with the DIRECT=Y parameter.

Examples Using Original Export and Import

Let's look at a few examples using the original export and import. The first example is a full export with all grants, rows, constraints, and triggers being exported. This is a conventional export rather than Direct-Path and is being run in consistent mode. This **consistent** parameter is important and means that all data exported will be consistent as of the beginning scn of the export run. Undo/rollback segments will be used to ensure that this consistency is met. The buffer parameter is used to increase the performance of conventional exports and imports. A log file of the export will be created and the compress option will be used to combine all of the extents of an object into a single extent.

```
exp system/manager full=y grants=y rows=y triggers=y buffer=10000000 direct=n
consistent=Y constraints=Y compress=Y file=shexp.dmp log=shexp.log
```

This can be transformed to a *user* export by replacing **full=y** with the **owner** parameter:

```
exp system/manager OWNER=SH grants=y rows=y triggers=y buffer=10000000 direct=n
consistent=Y constraints=Y compress=Y file=shexp.dmp log=shexp.log
```

Now let's look at a Table level direct export using a parameter file as specified by the **parfile** parameter. Notice that we have removed the **full=y** parameter used in the preceding example and the buffer parameter which only is used for conventional exports.

```
exp SYSTEM/manager parfile=exp.par
```

The parameter file named **exp.par** contains the following parameters:

```
TABLES=(SH.PRODUCTS) grants=y rows=y triggers=y direct=Y consistent=Y
constraints=Y compress=Y file=shexp.dmp log=shexp.log
```

An example of a user import employing the user export file from the previous example is shown next. Notice that the schema name has been changed to import all of the data into a new schema and the ignore parameter is used to have the import continue if objects already exist. For example, a table may already exist, so the **create table** will fail, but the rows can still be loaded into the table if **ignore=Y** is used. The compile parameter is used to compile all functions, procedures, and packages, and tablespaces will not be overwritten due to the **Destroy=N** parameter. The user **SHNEW** must already exist in order for this user-mode import to run successfully.

```
imp system/manager FROMUSER=SH TOUSER=SHNEW ignore=y compile=y
destroy=n grants=y rows=y buffer=10000000 constraints=y file=shexp.dmp
log=shimp.log
```

CRITICAL SKILL 5.9
Get Started with Recovery Manager

We have seen different ways to provide backup and recovery in this section as a matter of background and completeness. We will now look into the method that Oracle recommends you should be using or at least migrating to. This is *Recovery Manager (RMAN)*. The RMAN utility has been available since Oracle8*i* and has been improving steadily with each new release. RMAN is an Oracle tool that manages all backup and recovery activities, including backup, copy, restore and recovery of datafiles, control files, and archived redo logs. It is included with the Oracle server at no extra charge, and Enterprise Manager's backup and recovery is based on RMAN. RMAN provides many benefits over other types of Oracle backup and recovery:

- Can perform full and incremental backups.

- Creates backup scripting and automation.

- Has powerful reporting capabilities.

- You can use either a GUI or command-line mode.

- Compresses backups so that only blocks that have been written to are included.

- Tablespaces are not put into backup mode, so no extra redo is generated.

- Verifies backups and detects corrupt blocks.

- Parallels and verifies backups.

- Backs up data files, control files, archive redo logs, backup pieces, and spfiles (Oracle9*i*).

- Allows online restores of corrupt blocks.

RMAN Architecture

The RMAN architecture includes a target database, repository, and Media Management Layer, as well as Server Processes, Channels, Backup Sets, and Backup Pieces. The target database is the database that is either being backed up or restored. RMAN connects to the target database using server sessions.

The repository is a separate database or schema that contains the metadata about your target database and all of the backup and recovery information for that database for maintenance purposes. It can keep track of all of the information about every backup that you perform, including all of the file information, the time of the backup, and the database *incarnation* (the database version) at the time of the backup. This information can all be used to restore files and recover the database by issuing very simple restore and recovery commands. All of the information needed to complete these operations is stored in the repository. This repository can be implemented in one of two ways:

- By using control files

- As a recovery catalog database

Control files are the default option for implementing a repository since backup information is written to control files making the recovery catalog optional. Using a control file, however, limits the functionality of RMAN, while a recovery catalog provides you with the use of all RMAN features (this option is strongly recommended by the authors). Some of the advantages that a recovery catalog gives include the following:

- The catalog will store the physical structure of the target database and a log of backups of datafiles, control files, and archive logs.

- You can store scripts of common tasks.

- Multiple databases can be managed from one location.

- Offers complete reporting capabilities.

- Provides access to a longer history of backups and metadata.

- Enables you to perform recovery when control files are lost.

- Gives a complete set of options when you try to restore from previous backup sets.

- Has more recovery flexibility and options.

One disadvantage of using an RMAN recovery is that it needs to be managed itself. However, this is a small database or schema, so maintenance is minimal. Backups can be performed easily through a hot backup or database export. You also need to keep the recovery catalog in sync with the control files and this is performed with the RMAN-provided **resync** command.

TIP
When using RMAN, use the recovery catalog rather than the control file if it provides you with specific needed features that are above and beyond those provided by the control file.

The Media Management Layer (*MML*) is the third-party software that manages the reading, writing, loading, and labeling of backups to tape. This can be integrated with RMAN to streamline the process of backup, restore, and recovery from the database through to the tape library and keeps track of where files are cataloged on tape.

Oracle publishes a media management API that third-party vendors use to build software that works with RMAN. Tapes will, over time, become unavailable to the system after backups have been performed, and the RMAN MML option will perform crosschecks to determine if backup pieces are still available to the system and missing backups will be marked as "Expired". This can be run simply as follows:

```
RMAN> crosscheck backup;
```

The preceding code checks that the RMAN catalog is in sync with the backup files on disk or the media management catalog.

Channels are server processes that are used to read and write backup files, connect to your target database, to the catalog, and to allocate and open an I/O channel for backup or recovery using tape (called *sbt* in RMAN) or disk. Many configuration options can be set up through channels such as implementing a degree of parallelism for a backup operation or configuring default settings to be used for a specific channel. Allocating a channel starts a server process at the target server and establishes a connection between the RMAN and the target. A channel can do things such as determine the maximum size of files, the maximum rate files are read, the max number of files open at one time, the number of processes accessing a device simultaneously, or the type of I/O device disk or sbt_tape. A channel will be allocated for you automatically using default options unless you explicitly allocate a channel and specify overriding options for the channel in effect.

Backup sets are a complete set of backup pieces that constitute a full or incremental backup of the objects specified in the "Backup" command. Each backup creates a backup set that is composed of one or more backup pieces (that is, files) that are in an RMAN proprietary format.

Set Up a Recovery Catalog and Target Database

Setting up a recovery catalog is a very simple process. This can be done through the Enterprise Manager GUI or through some simple commands in SQL*Plus and the RMAN command-line interface. In SQL*Plus, all you need to do is to create a tablespace to store the catalog data in, create an RMAN user and grant the **recovery_catalog_owner** role to the RMAN user. In RMAN, run the **create catalog** statement.

```
SQL>create tablespace rcatts datafile '/u01/oradata/rcatts.dbf' size 10M;
SQL>create user rcat identified by rcat temporary tablespace temp default
tablespace rcatts quota unlimited on rcatts;
SQL>grant connect, resource, recovery_catalog_owner to rcat;
```

In the RMAN command-line interface, log in and create the catalog:

```
$ rman catalog=rmancat/rmancat
RMAN> create catalog
```

Now you need to register the target database in the catalog. To do this, connect to the target and the catalog database and register the target database in the catalog. This can be done from either location. The target connection must have a user ID with sysdba privileges, so an oracle password file must be created using the orapwd utility. You also need to create the Oracle networking configuration using tnsnames or an equivalent for both the target and recovery catalog instances.

```
$ rman
RMAN> connect catalog rmancat/rmancat@sid
RMAN> connect target sys/pwd@sid
RMAN> register database;
```

You are now ready to start using RMAN, but before going too far, let's take a quick tour of some RMAN features.

Key RMAN Features

Stored Scripts

A stored script is a set of RMAN commands that are stored in the recovery catalog. These can be used to perform tasks such as backup restore, recovery, or reporting. This option allows you to develop, test, and save commands, as well as minimize the potential for operator errors. Each script relates to one target database only. The following is a sample stored script that allocates a channel and performs an incremental level 0 full database backup. The current log is archived and all archive logs are then backed up and deleted.

```
RMAN> create script b_whole_l0 {
allocate channel c1 type disk;
backup
      incremental level 0
      format /u01/backup/b_t%t_s%s_p%p'
      (database);
sql 'ALTER SYSTEM ARCHIVE LOG CURRENT';
backup (archivelog all delete input);              }
```

Archive Log Management

As shown in the preceding script, RMAN can back up archive logs to tape and then delete the online versions once they have been successfully backed up. This is a great space saver!

Multiplexing Backups

Oracle multiplexes datafile blocks from different data files into the same backup set to control backup and overall system performance. In Oracle Database 10g, this is set by the lesser of the number of files in each backup set and the default number of files that RMAN reads in a single channel (which is eight). There are three performance benefits of multiplexed backups:

1. Keeps a high-performance sequential output device streaming by including a sufficient number of datafiles in the backup.

2. Prevents saturating a single datafile with too many read requests.

3. The read rate can be limited with the set limit channel command.

The following example sets the read rate to 50K blocks per second for a named channel:

```
run { allocate channel c1 type disk;
set limit channel c1 readrate=50; …}
```

Backup and Restore Optimization

RMAN can optimize backups so files that have not changed are not backed up. This will save you from performing repeated backups of read-only files. In the same manner, restores are optimized so that online files that have not been changed since the last backup will not be restored. This also allows restores to be restartable.

```
configure backup optimization {ON | OFF | CLEAR}
```

Corruption and Verification Checks

When RMAN moves a backup piece to another location, it verifies that the backup piece is not corrupt. A multiplexed copy will be used if a corruption is found. Archive logs are also checked in the same manner, and another archive log location will be used if a corruption is found. As part of backup, RMAN checks every datafile block, performs verification checks and logs the corrupted blocks. These can be viewed in the views **v$backup_corruption** and **v$copy_corruption**. Each corrupt block encountered is also recorded in the control file and alert log. RMAN will not allow an unusable backup or corrupt restore to be performed.

Configuration and Default Settings

RMAN allows you to set defaults once using the **configure** command to use with all of your backup and recovery jobs. These can be overridden when needed. The configure settings are stored in the control file and recovery catalog once synched. These configuration commands can all be displayed with the **show all** command in RMAN. An example of an extremely valuable setting is the one that follows which directs RMAN to automatically back up the control file after every backup, or every copy in RMAN prompt, or in a Run block.

```
configure controlfile autobackup;
```

Channels can be allocated automatically by RMAN and when configuration defaults are applied to a channel these can also be applied automatically. To configure a channel to have a default file format, a configure command such as the one listed next can be issued:

```
Configure channel 1 device type disk format
  '/orarecover/backup/db01/tp_%U';
```

Redundancy vs. Recovery Windows

An important backup management consideration is to determine how long backups should be kept and then to automate the implementation of your policy. RMAN helps you with this through the mutually exclusive commands **redundancy** and **recovery window**. Redundancy specifies the number of backups to be kept before RMAN will start to delete backup files. This is very good for controlling disk space. For example, to start deleting backups after four backups have been taken, issue the following command:

```
configure retention policy to redundancy 4;
```

A recovery window specifies the amount of time that point-in-time recovery should be able to go back to, which is specified in days. To make point-in-time recovery possible up to the last 15 days and make backups taken more than 14 days ago obsolete, issue the following command:

```
configure retention policy to recovery window of 15 days;
```

Block Media Recovery

Individual blocks can now be recovered from backups and this option is only available with RMAN. The database stays up while the blocks are being recovered but the blocks being recovered remain unavailable until the recovery is complete. This speeds up recovery if only a small number of blocks need to be recovered. The DBA specifies which block to recover by entering a corrupt block address that can be found in the v$backup_corruption or v$copy_corruption views, or in the alert log.

Trial Recovery

A trial recovery can be performed which lets you find all of the corrupt blocks in a database. You perform a trial recovery by adding the parameter **test** to the end of a **recover** command.

Reporting

A major advantage of RMAN is that it gives you the ability to run lists and reports on the repository. Lists allow you to display the contents of the RMAN repository such as image copies, incarnations of the database, and backups of data files or archive logs, among other things. Reports provide a more detailed analysis and can help you determine what should be done. These help report on objects that have not been backed up lately, or backups that are obsolete and can be deleted, or data files that are not recoverable, to mention a few. Such reports and lists are valuable in managing your backup and recovery environment.

To list backup sets and their detailed files and pieces, run the following:

```
List backup by file
```

To report on backups that are no longer needed because they exceed the retention policy:

```
Report obsolete
```

Backups

Oracle RMAN backups can be performed as either image copies or as backups. image copies are a complete copy of the binary data files used in the database. These files can be used by both RMAN or user-managed backup and recovery. Backup sets, on the other hand, are in a proprietary RMAN format and each set consists of one or more files called backup pieces. These backups can only be used by RMAN but have the advantage of performing unused block compression and incremental backups. Image copies can only be made to disk, while backup sets can be made to disk or tape.

When performing database backups, RMAN supports both *full* and *incremental* backups. A full backup will copy all used blocks in the data files specified. An incremental backup, on the other hand, only backs up those blocks that have changed since the previous incremental backup. Incrementals require a *level 0* backup, which is similar to a full backup except that it serves as a baseline to allow future incremental backups. Incremental backups can save recovery time when compared to the time that may be needed to apply archive logs and they take up less disk space and network resources than full backups do. There are two types of incremental backups. *differential* incrementals back up all blocks that have changed since the last backup at this level or lower, and *cumulative* incrementals only back up blocks that have changed since the last backup at a level lower than this. So, a differential incremental level 2 backup will back up all blocks changed since the last level 2, 1, or 0 backup where a cumulative incremental level 2 backs up all blocks since the last level 1 or 0. Differential backups have less data to back up while cumulative backups have less data to restore and can result in quicker restores.

Believe it or not, before Oracle Database 10*g*, incremental backups ran as slow or slower than full backups because table scans needed to be performed to find the blocks that had changed. This has changed with Oracle Database 10*g* since a block-change tracking file consisting of bitmaps is used rather than performing full table scans to discover changed blocks.

In order to back up a database, the target database must be either open or mounted so that RMAN can access the control file before performing a backup. If the database is mounted, it needs to have a consistent backup (that is, it must NOT have been abnormally terminated), and the control file must be current. Backups can be performed as either offline or online, and the target database must be placed in archivelog mode to allow you to perform online backups.

- **Offline Backup**   Performs an immediate or normal shutdown and then a startup mount. This does not require archivelog mode.

- **Online Backup**   For this to be done, the database must be open and in archivelog mode.

To help manage your backup and recovery space, a *Flash Recovery Area* should be created as the storage area for most of your backup and recovery files. Archive logs can be placed here and, if possible, the Flash Recovery Area should be large enough to handle two complete backup cycles for your database, including the archive logs. The backup retention policy of either recovery window or redundancy are used to manage space in the Flash Recovery Area. The Flash Recovery Area is an Oracle-managed area that can be used to store all of the files required for backup and recovery, including RMAN backups.

Now that you're familiar with the options available through RMAN, you're ready to back up a database.

Performing Backups

There are a number of ways that RMAN backups can be performed. In this section, we will cover examples of the basic set of backups. Namely, you will see an example of a database, data file, tablespace, and incremental backup, as well as an image copy.

Database Backup

An RMAN database backup can be as simple or as complex as you want to make it. In its simplest form, you can preconfigure channel defaults as discussed previously, connect to the catalog and the target, and then run the **backup** command:

```
RMAN > connect catalog rmancat/rmancat@test2
RMAN > connect target sys/lexus4me@TEST1
rman> backup database;
```

Datafile Backup

It doesn't get any easier than that! Let's now look at a backup that allocates one channel and backs up three datafiles using multiplexing. The archive logs are then backed up.

```
RMAN > run {
RMAN > allocate channel c1 type disk;
RMAN > allocate channel c2 type disk;
RMAN > allocate channel c3 type disk;
RMAN > backup (datafile 1,2,3 filesperset =3 channel c1)
RMAN > (archivelog all channel c3);}
```

Tablespace Backup

A tablespace backup is performed along with a backup of the control file and archivelog. Of course, the tablespace backup is implemented by RMAN as a series of data file backups.

```
RMAN > backup tablespace EXAMPLE include controlfile plus archivelog;
```

Incremental Backup

We can configure default settings for a channel and then perform an incremental level 1 backup. You need to perform an incremental level 0 backup first to provide a baseline for this incremental to be compared to. If an incremental level 0 does not exist, then this level 1 backup will be changed to level 0. Check the output of your backup run to make sure that the backup ran exactly as you expected it to. Backup optimization will be used to ignore any data files that have not changed since the last backup was performed. A backup script will be used in this example.

```
replace script BackupTEST1 {
configure backup optimization on;
configure channel device type disk;
sql 'alter system archive log current';
backup database incremental 2 cumulative database;
release channel d1;
}
run {execute script BackupTEST1;}
```

Image Copy

An Image Copy can be performed using the RMAN **copy** command. Here is a copy of a System data file to a named location. As you can see, there are no **begin backup** and **end backup** statements. The syntax is simple and RMAN performs the copy without incurring extra logging overhead.

```
RMAN > run { allocate channel c1 type disk;
RMAN > copy datafile 1 to '/u01/back/system.dbf';}
```

We've only done the first part of the job, but as you can see, the commands are relatively simple. We now need to think about how to use these backups in a recovery situation. Fortunately, the RMAN toolset also simplifies our restores and recoveries a great deal! Let's take a look at an example of how we can recover a database with RMAN.

Restore and Recovery

RMAN can automate file restores and can be used to restore data files, control files, and archived redo logs. In this example, you will see a full restore and recovery where the control file is restored from backup and the archive logs that we need are also restored. We have changed the archive log directory destination to write the archive log restores to. Notice that there is no mention of file names in this script. The recovery catalog has kept track of all of the files for us and if files were stored on tape, the Media Management Layer software may have also assisted with this.

```
RMAN> connect catalog rmancat/rmancat@ora10g
RMAN> connect target sys/change_on_install@ora10g

MAN> replace script fullRestoreTEST1 {
allocate channel ch1 type disk;
# Set a new location for logs
set archivelog destination to '/TD70/sandbox/TEST1/arch';
startup nomount;
restore archivelog from logseq 2123 until logseq 2145;
restore controlfile;
alter database mount;
restore database;
recover database;
alter database open resetlogs;
release channel ch1;
}
host 'echo "start `date`"';
run {execute script fullRestoreTEST1;}
host 'echo "stop `date`"';
exit
```

That's it! This script is simple and very powerful. We've now covered some basic RMAN backup options to give you an overview of how you can use RMAN on your databases. You should now test out various backup and recovery options to see how they function and how well the different options work in your environment. The settings that you use on one set of servers may not be the ones you will use on another, so testing your RMAN backup and recovery setup is essential!

Project 5-1   RMAN End-to-End

This project will take you from start to finish using RMAN. We will first assume that you have two Oracle databases to work with. The target database will be called ora10g in this project and the catalog database will be called oracat. You will first set up the RMAN catalog and then connect to the target database and register that database in the catalog. A full database backup will be performed and once that has been successfully completed, we will use that backup to perform a full database restore using RMAN. Look carefully at the output that RMAN produces to help better understand what is going on behind the scenes. Once you've completed this project, you will have used RMAN from end to end and will be comfortable with basic RMAN functionality.

(continued)

Step by Step

1. In SQL*Plus, create the RMAN tablespace, catalog, and user named **rcat**. Grant the authority that user rcat needs to perform all RMAN operations.

```
> export ORACLE_SID=oracat
SQL> sqlplus /nolog
SQL> connect sys/change_on_install as sysdba
SQL> create tablespace rcatts datafile '/u01/oradata/oracat/rcatts.dbf' size 50M;
SQL> create user rcat identified by rcat temporary tablespace temp default
SQL> tablespace rcatts quota unlimited on rcat;
SQL> grant connect, resource, recovery_catalog_owner to rcat;
SQL> exit
```

2. Your RMAN environment and user have now been created, so you need to go into RMAN to create the recovery catalog. Note that we are using a recovery catalog here rather than the control file and strongly encourage using this approach. We first log in to the catalog, then connect with the rcat user, and run the **create catalog** command.

```
> rman catalog=rcat/rcat@oracat
RMAN> catalog rcat/rcat@oracat
RMAN> create catalog;
RMAN> exit;
```

3. Register the target database ora10g with the RMAN catalog. Once you've completed this, you will be connected to both the target database and a fully functional catalog and will be ready to begin issuing RMAN commands.

```
RMAN> connect catalog rcat/rcat@oracat
RMAN> connect target sys/manager@ora10g
RMAN> register database;
```

4. It's now time to back up your entire database. We'll start by applying a couple of configuration settings to set the default backup device to disk and to state that we always want to back up the control file and spfile with every backup. The spfile is automatically included with control file backups. Once these are configured, we can back up the database, archivelogs, control file, and spfile. This sounds like a lot of work, but just look at how easy this is to do with RMAN!

```
RMAN> configure default device type to disk;
RMAN> configure controlfile autobackup on;
RMAN> backup database plus archivelog;
RMAN> exit;
```

5. Once the backup has completed successfully, we want to set up the environment for a restore. To do this, shut down the database and delete all of the data files, archive logs, control files, and the spfile SPFILEORA10G.ora of the target database.

6. Now for the big test! The database restore and recovery is the one thing that absolutely tests how well we've done everything so far. Once again in RMAN, connect to the catalog and target and then put the database in nomount mode. Once that's done, restore the archive logs and control files, and then mount the database. You should now see these files in their proper location. Restore the database and watch the files being created in another window. Once that's complete, recover the database and open it up.

```
RMAN> connect catalog rcat/rcat@oracat
RMAN> connect target sys/manager@ora10g
RMAN> startup nomount;
RMAN> restore archivelog all;
RMAN> restore controlfile;
RMAN> alter database mount;
RMAN> restore database;
RMAN> recover database;
RMAN> alter database open resetlogs;
```

The resetlogs step at the end, is needed to create new log files. This creates a new incarnation (that is, version) of the database and it should be backed up immediately.

Project Summary

This project has taken you from the very first step of setting up RMAN through a full backup, restore, and recovery. Congratulations! You have successfully completed the RMAN fundamentals and are now ready to explore it further and exploit this powerful tool in your own environment.

☑ Chapter 5 Mastery Check

1. What are some advantages of cold backups, and when would you use them?

2. What are disadvantages of cold backups?

3. Describe the difference between a logical and a physical backup.

4. Name three different types of backups.

5. What is the difference between an RMAN backup and an RMAN image copy?

6. Under what situations should redo logs be restored in a recovery situation?

7. Name three interfaces that can be used to perform a Data Pump Export and Import.

8. List some advantages of using RMAN.

9. Why would RMAN's recovery catalog be used rather than a control file to implement the repository?

10. Are there any disadvantages to an RMAN recovery catalog?

11. How can default settings be set up by you for future runs of RMAN?

12. What is an RMAN backup-set and how does it relate to a backup-piece?

13. Describe the ways in which corrupt blocks can be recovered.

14. What are some advantages to incremental image copies?

15. When performing a recovery from a hot backup, do all files and tablespaces need to be brought forward to the same point in time?

CHAPTER 6

PL/SQL

CRITICAL SKILLS

6.1 Define PL/SQL and Why We Use It

6.2 Describe the Basic PL/SQL Program Structure

6.3 Define PL/SQL Data Types

6.4 Write PL/SQL Programs in SQL*Plus

6.5 Handle Error Conditions in PL/SQL

6.6 Include Conditions in Your Programs

6.7 Create Stored Procedures—How and Why

6.8 Create and Use Functions

6.9 Call PL/SQL Programs

he basic way we access data with Oracle is via SQL. It provides us with the ability to manage both the database and the information. However, you generally will find that SQL cannot do everything that the programmer needs to do. SQL has an inherent lack of procedural control of the output. (It has no array handling, looping constructs, and other programming language features.) PL/SQL can be regarded as an extension to SQL for fine control of database data processing. To address this need, Oracle developed PL/SQL Oracle's proprietary programming language.

To this end, Oracle provides us with a built-in programming language called Procedural Language for Structured Query Language (PL/SQL). PL/SQL, Oracle's contribution to the programming world, is a programming environment that resides directly in the database. We will discuss its architecture later in this chapter. First though, some background about this powerful programming environment.

PL/SQL first appeared in Oracle Version 6 in 1985. It was primarily used within Oracle's user interface product SQL*Forms to allow for the inclusion of complex logic within the forms; it replaced an odd step-method for logical control. It also provided a reasonably simple block-structured programming language that resembles ADA and C. We can use PL/SQL to read our data, perform logical tasks, populate our database, create stored objects, and even to display web pages. PL/SQL has certainly developed into a mature product, and Oracle has shown a very strong dedication to the language, as illustrated by its use of PL/SQL in many of its products (such as Oracle Applications). Oracle also uses the web extensions of PL/SQL quite extensively in many other applications and products.

In this chapter, we will discuss the basic concepts and constructs of PL/SQL so you'll understand how to create your own PL/SQL programs. There is a lot to cover, but, as important as it is to learn SQL, you need to know PL/SQL as well, because if you're looking to become a DBA or an Oracle developer, you must have knowledge of PL/SQL in your database toolkit.

CRITICAL SKILL 6.1
Define PL/SQL and Why We Use It

The Oracle Database 10g is more than just a database. It is also an engine for many programming languages. Not only does it serve as a Java engine with the built-in Java Virtual Machine (JVM), it's a PL/SQL engine as well. This means that the code you write may be stored in the database and then run as required.

The PL/SQL engine is bundled together with the database, and is an integral part of Oracle's database, providing you with a powerful language to empower your logic and data. Let's look at how PL/SQL fits into the Oracle database. Figure 6-1 shows you how PL/SQL works from within, and from outside, the database.

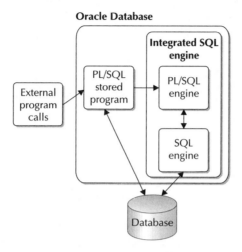

FIGURE 6-1.   *The PL/SQL architecture*

At the center of the Oracle Database 10*g* server in Figure 6-1 is the primary engine for the database. It serves as the coordinator for all calls to and from the database. So when a call is made from a program to the server to run a PL/SQL program, the Oracle database loads the compiled program into memory and then the PL/SQL engine and SQL engine execute the program. The PL/SQL engine will handle the program's memory structures and logical program flow, and then the SQL engine issues data requests to the database. It is a closed system and one that allows for very efficient programming.

PL/SQL is used in numerous Oracle products, including the following:

- The Oracle Server
- Oracle Forms
- Oracle Reports
- Oracle Warehouse Builder
- Oracle Applications
- Oracle Portal

All of these programs use PL/SQL to some extent. If we look at the internals of Oracle applications, there may be as many as five million lines of PL/SQL code contained within it. The following PL/SQL programs can be called from these Oracle development environments:

- SQL*Plus

- Oracle Grid Control/Oracle Enterprise Manager

- Oracle Precompilers (such as Pro*C, Pro*COBOL, and so on)

- Oracle Call Interface (OCI)

- Server Manager

- Oracle Application Server 10*g*

- Java Virtual Machine (JVM)

As you can see, PL/SQL is well established within Oracle's line of products.

The reasons for using PL/SQL are primarily its tight integration with the database server and its ease of use. You will find that there are few tasks that PL/SQL cannot handle.

TIP
Use PL/SQL to program tasks that are complex or for program elements that may be used many times over and over again.

CRITICAL SKILL 6.2

Describe the Basic PL/SQL Program Structure

The structure we use in PL/SQL is the foundation for all of the language. Once you've mastered it, you will then be able to move forward; however, if you do not take the time to get this first step right, your journey will be difficult. Thankfully, it's quite simple.

The structure is quite basic. You will have areas for your program parameters (these are used to pass values from outside a program to the program itself), your internal variables, the main program code and logic, and various ways to deal with problem situations. Let's look at the basic form of a PL/SQL block:

```
[DECLARE]
    -- Put Variables Here
BEGIN
    -- Put Program Here
[EXCEPTION]
    -- Put exception handlers here
END;
/
```

That's it. This is the basic structure of every PL/SQL program. When we talk about PL/SQL programs, they are referred to as PL/SQL blocks. *PL/SQL blocks* are simply programs that are complete and which contain the programming required to be run successfully. A PL/SQL program is comprised of one or more of these blocks. As you consider writing a program, you will find that each block addresses a particular task or subtask. It is these structures that you will use in all of your PL/SQL programs. The PL/SQL block structures form the basis for any program you shall be writing in PL/SQL. This chapter builds upon that fundamental form, each section helping you move toward more complex programs.

In its basic form, you will usually need to declare variables in your PL/SQL program. It is these variables that are used in the PL/SQL that hold the declarative or working storage area (constants, variables, select statements, data arrays, and such) within your program. These variables are then available for use in your program. So if you need a counter, or a data array, or data variables or even Boolean variables, you will declare them here.

NOTE
PL/SQL variables defined in the declaration section of a PL/SQL block are local to the block in which they are defined.

Next is the program body or executable section. It is the only section you really need to include in your PL/SQL block since you could write a program without variables or exception handling. It is in this section that you build your program logic and database access. That is why you must always remember **BEGIN** and **END**; these are your PL/SQL bookends. It is between these two lines that your program logic is contained.

The final section is the exception section. It is within this section that you will find all the error handling needed for your program. This section is an optional portion of the PL/SQL block. However, it is recommended that all programs include the use of exception handling to ensure a controlled run of your programs.

Ask the Expert

Q: What are the only lines of the PL/SQL block that are required to create a functional program?

A: The only lines of the basic PL/SQL block that are required to create a functioning program are **BEGIN** and **END**.

Define PL/SQL Data Types

The use of local variables within a PL/SQL program is an important knowledge point for everyone using the language. It is a basic component of each program and as such it is invaluable to gain the knowledge of what is available and how best to use it. We can now look at how we use and define variables and working storage within our PL/SQL programs.

The PL/SQL Character Set

As with all programming languages, there are characters that you use to write your programs. Each language has its own rules and restrictions when it comes to the valid characters. In the following sections, we will show you the following:

- Valid characters when programming in PL/SQL

- Arithmetic operators

- Relational operators

Supported Characters

When programming in PL/SQL, you may use only characters as defined here:

- Characters can be typed in either upper- or lowercase. PL/SQL is case insensitive.

- All digits between 0 and 9.

- The following symbols: ( ) + - * / < > = ! ~ ; : . ' @ % , " ' # ^ & _ | { } ? [ ]

Some of these characters are for program commands; others serve as relational or arithmetic operators. Together they form a program.

Arithmetic Operators

Table 6-1 shows the common arithmetic operators used in PL/SQL. They are listed in the order of precedence in which they are executed (that is, by priority). When the functions appear in the same line, this means they are executed with the same level of precedence, so the position of the expression determines which goes first.

Table 6-2 shows the common relational operators used in PL/SQL. These are the logical variables that are used to compare data.

The use of variables in a PL/SQL program is usually something that is required to truly leverage the power of the language. It is here that we define how our data is to be held while we work it through our program. These variables can be the same types as we have already learned about in the SQL language. However, in addition to these standard data types, we have some special ones that have been created specifically for the PL/SQL language.

Operator	Meaning
**	Exponent
*,/	Multiplication, Division
+,-, ||	Addition, Subtraction, Concatenation

TABLE 6-1. *Common Mathematical Operators*

NOTE
All SQL within Oracle is supported directly with PL/SQL.

One of the important features of Oracle Database 10g is the tight integration of the SQL and PL/SQL engines into one system. This means that from Oracle9i forward you can run the same commands in PL/SQL that you use in SQL. This was not true in earlier versions of PL/SQL, so take care if using these versions.

Now we can move on to the most common data types that you will use when writing PL/SQL programs:

- varchar2
- number
- date
- boolean

Operator	Meaning
=	Equal
<> or !=	Not equal
>	Greater than
<	Less than
>=	Greater than or equal to
<=	Less than or equal to

TABLE 6-2. *Common Logical Operators*

Assigning values to variables is very important when programming in PL/SQL or any other programming language. You are able to assign values to variables in any section of your program code, and may assign values to variables in the declare section. By defining your variable in the declare section is done to initialize values in advance of their use in the program or to define values that will be used as constants in your program. To assign a value to a variable in the declaration section, you would use the following format:

```
Variable_name      variable_type      := value;
```

NOTE
The important item that you should notice here is that we use the := to assign a value. This is the standard that will be used in PL/SQL.

You may also define variable values in the execution and exception sections of your PL/SQL program. Within the program, you would use the following format to assign a value to a variable:

```
Variable_name      := value;
```

To assign values to variables you use, let's look at a small program that assigns values in each section of a program:

```
-- declaration section of the program
declare
        l_counter      number := 0; -- initiate value to 0
        l_today        date   := sysdate; -- assign system date to variable
        l_name varchar2(50);           -- variable is defined but has no value
-- execution section of the program
begin
        l_counter := l_counter + 1; -- add one to current value of counter
        l_name := 'YOGI THE CAT'; -- set a value to name variable
-- Error handling section of the program
exception
        -- Generic error handling to handle any type of error
        when others then
-- print out an error message
raise_application_error (-20100, 'error#' || sqlcode || ' desc: ' sqlerrm)
end;
```

NOTE
*Oracle has some special variables that may be used in a PL/SQL program. In the example, we used the **sqlcode** and **sqlerrm** variables. These variables respectively represent the Oracle error number and the Oracle error message. You may use these to capture Oracle errors in your program.*

The varchar2 Data Type

varchar2 is a variable-length alphanumeric data type. In PL/SQL, it may have a length up to 32,767 bytes. When you define the **varchar2** variable in the declare section, remember to terminate the line with a semicolon (;). The following is the form of varchar2 variable declarations:

```
Variable_name      varchar2(max_length);
```

where the **max_length** is a positive integer, as in

```
l_name      varchar2(30);
```

You may also set an initial or default value for the variable. This is done on the same line as the variable declaration in the declare section of your program. So you can do this by using the syntax:

```
L_name      varchar2(30) := 'ABRAMSON';
```

The preceding statement will set that value of the variable **L_name** to the value of **ABRAMSON**.

The number Data Type

The number data type is used to represent all numeric data. The format of the declaration is

```
Number_field number(length, decimal_places);
```

where the length can be from 1 to 38 numerical positions, and decimal_places represents the positions for numerical precision of the decimal place for the variable. Keep this in mind when you define your numerical variable, as in

```
L_average_amount      number(12,2);
```

This describes a variable that may hold up to ten digits (Length(12) - decimal_places(2)) and up to two decimal places. This means the variable may hold a number up to a value of 9,999,999,999.99.

The date Data Type

The date data type variable is used to store date and datetime values. The following is the format of the date declaration:

```
Date_variable      date;
```

By default, Oracle displays values using the format *DD-MON-YY*. So a value of 14-JAN-03 would be the equivalent of saying January 14, 2003. When programming in PL/SQL, you should always use this data type when performing date manipulation. It is possible when combining this data type with some built-in Oracle functions to extend the flexibility of your date manipulations. For example, let's say that we create a variable for a start date and we want to place values into this variable, let's see how this may be done.

```
Declare
      L_start_date       date;
Begin
      L_start_date := '29-SEP-05';    -- Sets variable
                                 -- to September 29, 2005.
      L_start_date := to_date('29-SEP-2083 ', 'DD-MON-YYYY');
                -- Sets variable to September 29, 2083
      L_start_date := to_date('09-JUN-91:13:01 ', 'DD-MON-YY:HH24:MI');
                -- Sets variable to June 9, 1991, 1:01p.m.
End;
```

So here we have set the date variable in three different forms. The first is the simplest, while the second is more complex (since it uses the to_date function), but it does allow for more flexible data declarations, since we can use a four-digit year definition. The final example shows you how you may put a datetime into the variable. Again we use the to_date function, but include the time in the value and then define it with the date mask definition.

NOTE
For more information on other Oracle built-in functions, see the "Oracle Database SQL Reference," on the documentation CD.

You should also familiarize yourself with the variations of the date data type. These include the timestamp data type, which provides additional date support that may not be available with the simple date data type.

The boolean Data Type
The final basic data type we will discuss is the boolean data type. Simply put, this variable will hold either a value of *true* or *false*. When you use this data type, you must test its status and then do one thing if it is true or another if it is false. You can use a Boolean expression to compare arithmetic expressions or character expressions. So, if you have the following arithmetic values:

```
L_record_goals := 91;
L_season_goals := 77;
```

```
-- Therefore the following expression will be true
L_record_goals > l_season_goals
-- However the next is false
l_record_goals <= l_season_goals
```

If you wish to compare character strings, the same may be done. Here's an example:

```
l_Cognos_developer := 'Falcon';
l_Oracle_dba := 'Ruxpinnah';
-- The following expression will be true in a true Boolean value
l_Cognos_developer != l_oracle_dba
```

It is important to understand that comparisons provide Boolean results that may then be used during conditional program control, so take the time to know the difference between *true* and *false*. There are numerous other data types, but by mastering these simple ones you may already build some complex programs. In C++ and other languages, Booleans can be represented as either *true/false* or *1/0*. In PL/SQL, the value is assigned only *true* or *false*.

Ask the Expert

Q: How do you let Oracle set the definition of a variable within PL/SQL programs based on a table's column definition?

A: The use of dynamic variable definitions based on column definitions is a very important feature that you should always utilize within PL/SQL. This ties the variable definition to a table within the database. When defining your variable, use the name of the table, the column, and the special string of **%TYPE**. The following is an example of using the product table's prod_id as a variable data definition:

```
v_product_id        products.prod_id%TYPE
```

By using the %TYPE variable type, we have freed our program of the need to ever redefine this field. So if the column's definition changes, so will the variable within your program.

Progress Check ⏲

1. Name four programs or facilities where you can use PL/SQL.

2. Name three sections that may be contained in a PL/SQL block.

3. What is the only required section in a PL/SQL block?

4. What data type would you use to store each of the following?

   A. 12344.50

   B. True

   C. April 11, 1963

   D. PINK FLOYD

CRITICAL SKILL 6.4

Write PL/SQL Programs in SQL*Plus

When we write PL/SQL programs, we have a couple of options on how to run a program. A program may be run directly in SQL*Plus (or some other SQL environment), or it can be stored in the database and then run from a SQL environment or a program. When you store a program in the database, we call this a stored program or stored object. We'll cover this later in the chapter. For now let's discuss how to write a program using SQL*Plus.

Progress Check Answers

1. Any four from among the following would be acceptable answers: Oracle Forms, Reports, Warehouse Builder, Oracle Applications, Oracle Portal, SQL*Plus, Oracle Grid Control, Oracle Pre-compilers, and Oracle Application Server.

2. The three sections that may be contained in a PL/SQL block are the Declaration, Execution, and Exception sections.

3. The Execution section is the only required section in a PL/SQL block.

4. The data types used to store each of the variables would be

   A. Number or number(8,2). The storage of a number should always be done in a number data type. You can specify the precision or simply define it as a number with no precision, when you do not know the exact nature of your data.

   B. boolean. The boolean data type is used to store true and false information.

   C. Date. The date data type stores date and time information.

   D. varchar2(10). Character values should be stored in the varchar2 data type. This is more effective for storing the data, yet it has a limit of 4000 bytes. If you need more than 4000 bytes, you should then use the LONG data type, which allows you to store up to 2GB of data.

When first writing a program, you can create and modify it using the command line in SQL*Plus. To do this:

1. Log into SQL*Plus.

2. Type in your program via the command line.

3. For each line you write, press ENTER to get to the next line.

4. When you finish typing in your program, remember to terminate it with a "/" character. This tells Oracle to run the program that you just finished entering.

5. Monitor Oracle to see if your program ran successfully. If your program does run without errors (syntax errors), you will see the message "PL/SQL procedure successfully completed." If you see anything else, this is an indication that an error occurred.

6. To see the errors that were created by your program, type in **Show errors**, and SQL*Plus will display the errors it encountered during the current run of your program.

7. Should you receive an error, you will need to edit your program. If your SQL*Plus and Oracle environment is set up correctly, you should be able to simply enter **edit** on the command line and your program will be loaded into an editor where you can then fix it. Once you exit the editor, the program will be reloaded into the SQL buffer and may be run again.

Let's move on and look at an example of this process.

Ask the Expert

Q: How can I get feedback/output from my PL/SQL programs?

A: Oracle provides a built-in package named dbms_output for this purpose. Oracle supplies many of these packages that provide users with additional functionality, such as outputting data to the screen. By placing the dbms_output.put_line command into your programs, Oracle PL/SQL can then provide information to the user as shown in this chapter's examples.

To actually see this information, you must enable screen output by entering **SET SERVEROUTPUT ON** at the SQL> prompt before executing your PL/SQL routine.

Now let's move on to illustrate how to construct a PL/SQL program and get some output of our results.

Project 6-1 Creating a PL/SQL Program

This will be the first PL/SQL program that you will create. The concept is straightforward. We will declare some variables, place some values into them, and then output the data to the screen with SQL*Plus.

Step by Step

1. Log into SQL*Plus.

2. At the SQL> prompt, enter the serveroutput command: **set serveroutput on;**.

3. Enter the following PL/SQL program:

```
Declare
      L_start_date    date;
Begin
        L_start_date := '29-SEP-2005';
        dbms_output.putline (l_start_date); --show date
End;
/
```

4. You should now see the following output on your screen:

```
SQL> /
29-SEP-05
PL/SQL procedure successfully completed.
```

5. You have now completed your first PL/SQL program.

6. Take the time to add to the program and add lines that use other date formats or perform some date addition. For example, you may wish to add the following code and see the results that they provide:

```
L_start_date := to_date('14-JAN-2063', 'DD-MON-YYYY');
dbms_output.put_line (l_start_date);
L_start_date := to_date('09-JUN-91:13:01', 'DD-MON-YY:HH24:MI');
dbms_output.put_line (l_start_date);
```

Next, we need to discuss how to include database data within your PL/SQL programs.

Project Summary

This project enables you to see how to construct a PL/SQL program. You now have seen how to create, run, and then re-run it, allowing you to see the output. This is a simple example, presented to show you the basis of all PL/SQL programs.

SQL in Your PL/SQL Programs

We have looked at a lot of structure up until now. You should know that a PL/SQL program will always have a **BEGIN** and **END** statement. It may have variables, loops, or logic control, but now we need to get real database data into our programs. What gives PL/SQL its power is its tight integration with SQL. You may want the information so that you can create a report, update data, create new data, delete old data, or perform just about any other function you can think of. It is very important for you to see how you can integrate data into PL/SQL code. Without data, PL/SQL is just PL.

Cursors

How do you get data to your programs? Simple—select it from the database. This is the easiest way to use SQL in your program. Thus, inserting a line like the following will provide you with the ability to access data in the database:

```
select prod_name
into     v_prod_name
from products
```

Let's break down the statement and look at what it means to the program. As you look at the **select** statement, you see that it looks very similar to a standard **select** statement. However, you should also have noticed the *into* word in the statement. You must be wondering: What's it for? This is how you put a value into a variable using a **select** statement.

The following example illustrates how we include a SQL statement in our PL/SQL program:

```
 1  declare
 2    v_prod_name varchar2(80);
 3  begin
 4        select prod_name
 5        into    v_prod_name
 6        from products
 7        where rownum = 1;
 8     dbms_output.put_line(v_prod_name);
 9* end;
10  /
```

In addition to selecting one value from the database, you also have the ability to select more than one value as well as add conditions that you want to include. To do this, use the following cursor format:

```
select prod_name, prod_list_price, prod_min_price from products
where rownum < 10
```

Ask the Expert

Q: Why did we include rownum = 1 in our select statement?

A: The reason we include rownum = 1 when using an implicit cursor is that in this particular case the select statement will return more than 1 row. This will result in an Oracle error that terminates the processing of this PL/SQL block. To avoid this situation, we include the rownum = 1 condition.

You can use any SQL statement you want within your program. It can be a *select, insert, update,* or a *delete* statement. All of these will be supported. When you use a *select* statement like we did in the preceding example, this is called an implicit cursor. An *implicit cursor* is a SQL statement that is contained within the executable section of the program and has an *into* statement, as in the case of a *select* statement. With an implicit cursor, Oracle will handle everything for you, but there is a cost to doing this: the program will run slower. You need to understand what you can do; it may not be the best way to perform a *select* statement, but you must use an implicit cursor when you want to run a *delete, update,* or *insert* statement. So, let's move on to see a better way of doing the same thing. We will revisit our previous example so you can compare the two.

The better way is by creating an explicit cursor. An *explicit cursor* is a *select* statement that is declared in the declare section of a program. You do this so that Oracle will then prepare your SQL statement in advance of running your program. This makes for very efficient use of memory by the program. Let's look at what the program would look like with an explicit cursor:

```
 1  declare
 2    v_prod_name varchar2(80);
 3    cursor get_data is
 4      select prod_name
 5      from products;
 6  begin
 7      open get_data;
 8      fetch get_data into v_prod_name;
 9      dbms_output.put_line(v_prod_name);
10      close get_data;
11* end;
```

We converted the initial example into one that uses an explicit cursor. Notice that the **select** statement is now contained in the declaration section. There is also no longer an **into** clause. This functionality is moved into the execution section, where it is used in the **fetch** command.

You will also note that we introduced three new PL/SQL commands: **open**, **fetch**, and **close**. With these three simple commands, you can get data from your database using SQL cursors. The **open** command tells Oracle to reserve memory that will need to be used by the select statement. The **fetch** command, meanwhile, pulls the data from the first row of the result set, and the **close** command returns the memory back to Oracle for other uses.

NOTE
In this example, Oracle Database 10g will retrieve only one row from the database. However, a similar method may be used in conjunction with a loop to retrieve more than one row. We will discuss this in the next section.

NOTE
Always remember to close your cursors when you are done with them. If you don't, you may start getting memory problems, or you could get results that you don't expect.

The Cursor FOR Loop

You get a better sense of the power of the cursor by combining it with a loop. The cursor FOR loop is the result of combining the *select* cursor with a FOR loop (we go into additional detail about this loop in the next section). This allows you to retrieve multiple rows from the database if your result set should do this. It also is simpler to program, and you don't have to worry about opening or closing your cursor; Oracle handles all that within the loop. Let's look at an example of the cursor FOR loop. The important lines have been highlighted for you.

```
SQL> set serveroutput on
SQL>  declare
  2     v_prod_name varchar2(80);
  3     cursor get_data is
  4       select prod_name
  5       from products;
  6  begin
  7     for i in get_data
  8     LOOP
  9             dbms_output.put_line(i.prod_name);
 10     END LOOP;
```

```
11 end;
12 /
5MP Telephoto Digital Camera
17" LCD w/built-in HDTV Tuner
Envoy 256MB - 40GB
Y Box
Mini DV Camcorder with 3.5" Swivel LCD
Envoy Ambassador
Laptop carrying case
Home Theatre Package with DVD-Audio/Video Play …
```

NOTE
*To reference columns during a FOR loop, use the name of the loop and concatenate it with the name of the column as defined within the cursor declaration. Thus, your result will be a variable named **cursorname.fieldname** (in our example, we did this using the variable **i.prod_name**).*

The cursor FOR loop is truly PL/SQL power in action. It provides you with the ability to easily move through the result set of a select statement and perform the logic and manipulations you need to be successful.

We have just touched the surface of getting information from PL/SQL. One concept that you will need to get comfortable with is the debugging of PL/SQL programs. The task of debugging can be very complex. Experience has taught us that finding our errors is never a task to be taken lightly, or one that can be ignored. Using a simple facility like *dbms_output,* you have a way of tracking the progress of your program.

NOTE
*Another facility that is available is **dbms_profiler**. This package analyzes how your program is running and collects statistics on how long each line takes to execute. This helps you find code that runs slowly or inefficiently. When you need to access more advanced statistics about your programs, take the time to investigate this package and how to integrate it into your PL/SQL code. Since this is a beginner's guide, we'll only direct you to an important feature when you need its functionality.*

Having seen how to write and debug programs, we can now make those programs more complex.

CRITICAL SKILL 6.5
Handle Error Conditions in PL/SQL

As we have seen in the previous section, bad things happen to good programs. However, you also have to deal with bad or problematic data as well. To deal with problems during the processing of data, PL/SQL provides us with the robust ability to handle these types of errors. We call this type of program code *exception handling*.

To raise an error from within a PL/SQL program, use the built-in function named **raise_application_error**. The function requires two arguments. One is for the error number. This number must be between –20000 and –20999. The second argument is the error that you want the user to see.

As with all exception handling, this program code is placed into the **EXCEPTION** section of your PL/SQL program. Thus, our program structure will now be

```
BEGIN
    -- Put Program Here
EXCEPTION
-- Put exception handlers here
END;
/
```

Table 6-3 looks at some of the most common errors that Oracle helps you handle.

NOTE
You must always make the "Others" error handle the last one in your program, since Oracle will not process any exception handles after this one.

Exception Name	Explanation	Oracle Error
No_data_found	When a select statement returns no rows, this error may be raised. It usually occurs when you use an implicit cursor and perform a SELECT INTO.	ORA-01403
Too_many_rows	When a case that should only return a single row returns multiple rows, this exception is raised.	ORA-01422
Dup_val_on_index	This exception is raised when you try to insert a record into a table that has a primary key on it and the record that you are inserting is a duplicate of one that already exists in the table.	ORA-00001

TABLE 6-3.   *Common Exceptions in PL/SQL*

Exception Name	Explanation	Oracle Error
Value_error	This error occurs when you attempt to put a value into a variable, but the value is either incompatible (for example, inserting a value of 'REDSKYDATA' into a numerical field) or you input a value that is too big (for instance, inputting 'JILLIANABRAMSON' into a variable that is only six characters long).	ORA-06502
ZERO_DIVIDE	This error is encountered when you attempt to divide by zero.	ORA-01476
Others	This exception is used to catch any errors not handled by specific error handles.	Non-specific

TABLE 6-3.   *Common Exceptions in PL/SQL* (continued)

The following is the line that your program may contain to provide feedback to the user:

```
raise_application_error (-20123, 'This is an error, you have done a bad thing');
```

So let's see how these all come together in a single program:

```
SQL> run
  1  declare
  2        l_emp_count number;
  3        i            number;  -- We will use this as our counter
  4        l_row        employee%rowtype;
  5  begin
  6          select *
  7          into l_row
  8          from   employee
  9          order by emp_name;
 10  EXCEPTION
 11  WHEN no_data_found then
 12   raise_application_error (-20052,'Sorry no data in this table. TRY AGAIN!');
 13  WHEN others then
 14    raise_application_error (-20999,'Something has gone really wrong...you better
guess');
 15* end;
declare
*
ERROR at line 1:
ORA-20052: Sorry no data in this table. TRY AGAIN!
ORA-06512: at line 12
```

This program will handle instances where no data is found, as well as anything else that happens that is not a result of lack of data. So, with these simple techniques you may now handle problems that might occur in your programs.

You may also extend the functionality of the Oracle exception handling facility with your own *user-defined exceptions.*

User-defined exceptions are defined within your program code. There are three components to defining and using this exception type. They include

- Declaring the exception

- Raising the exception during program execution

- The exception handle itself

These three items must all be in place for an exception to be valid and to be used within the program. This differs from the Oracle-defined exceptions, which may be used within a program without declaring them or even raising an error condition. So let's see how this all comes together in a program:

```
Declare
        L_counter    number := 0;
        L_name employee.employee_name%type;
        Cursor get_employee_name is
        Select employee_name
        From employee;
excep_old_friend    Exception;
never_met_them                Exception;
Begin
        Open    get_employee_name;
        Fetch   get_employee_name into l_name;
        If l_name = 'CARL DUDLEY' then
              Raise excep_old_friend;
Else
        Raise excep_never_met_them;
        End if;
        Close get_employee_name;
Exception
        When excep_old_friend then
              Dbms_output.put_line('I know this person');
When     excep_old_friend then
              Dbms_output.put_line('I do not know this person');
End;
```

As you can see in this program, the definition and use of a user-defined exception is really driven by your needs. In this case, we select data from the employee table. Should the name of the person I retrieve be *Carl Dudley,* then I raise the exception that I defined called excep_old_friend. In any other case, I would raise excep_never_met_them. Based on this decision, I *raise* the exception that I want to handle for the situation.

So, let's look at the three components we need to allow us to use this exception we've created specially. First, there is the declaration of the exceptions. These go into the Declaration section. You simply name the exception and tell Oracle that they are of the type exception, just as we have done in the following lines of program code:

```
excep_old_friend    Exception;
never_met_them          Exception;
```

Next, we need to call the appropriate exception within the program code. We want to call the exception when something occurs—in this case, when we obtain the name of a friend or the name of a stranger.

> **NOTE**
> *User-defined exceptions may be raised to handle an error or to handle a condition that may not be seen by Oracle as an error.*

In our case, we are not concerned with an error. We just want to deal with a situation. Therefore, in your program code all that is needed to call a user-defined exception is to simply use the *raise* command followed by the name of the exception, as in the following code snippet:

```
        Raise excep_old_friend;
```

You have taken the first two steps toward defining and calling your own exception (Declaration and Execution sections), all that's left is to define what the exception is going to do. This is done in the Exception section of your program. To do this, simply include the exception in the Exception section:

```
Exception
    When excep_old_friend then
        Dbms_output.put_line('I know this person');
```

In our case, we simply will output that we know this person.

This example has shown you how to set up user-defined exceptions and how to use them. The way in which you implement exceptions is limited only by your imagination.

Error Handling Oracle-Supplied Variables

As well as being able to define your own exceptions within your PL/SQL program, Oracle also provides some standard variables that may be used in your PL/SQL programs. These variables are available to you in many different forms depending on where you use them in your program. These variables are known as *pseudo-columns.* A *pseudo-column* is a column that may be used in a select statement or may be used during the processing of data. Some examples of the pseudo-columns include

- Current system date (sysdate)
- Row number (rownum)
- Oracle error number (sqlcode)
- Oracle error message (sqlerrm)

In this section, we will only look at the last two, which in exception handling are two that are often used. They provide us access to the Oracle error number and message and will therefore allow us to write programs that may always end successfully. Even though they may still encounter an error, it's handled in a manner that is quite robust and manageable. Let's look at the same program, except we will add another exception handle for when any error occurs. We do this by adding the **when others** exception.

```
Declare
        L_counter       number := 0;
        L_name employee.employee_name%type;
        Cursor get_employee_name is
        Select employee_name
        From employee;
excep_old_friend    Exception;
never_met_them              Exception;
Begin
        Open    get_employee_name;
        Fetch  get_employee_name into l_name;
        If l_name = 'JACQUI DEBIQUE' then
                Raise excep_old_friend;
Else
        Raise excep_never_met_them;
End if;
        Close get_employee_name;
Exception
        When excep_old_friend then
                Dbms_output.put_line('I know this person');
When excep_never_met_them then
                Dbms_output.put_line('I do not know this person');
    When others then
                Dbms_output.put_line('Oracle Error: ' || sqlcode);
                Dbms_output.put_line('Oracle error message is: '|| sqlerrm);
End;
```

As you can see, we have now added an extra error handling condition. The one we added is the infamous *when others* exception. This exception may be used to handle any error that occurs for which no other exception has been defined. It must also be the last exception in your exception section, since Oracle stops processing when it encounters an exception that meets the criteria. Therefore, if this exception is first, Oracle will stop once it hits the when others condition.

In our example, we have now used the pseudo-columns, sqlcode and sqlerrm. You should always consider using these variables in your program code to ensure all your PL/SQL program completes in a manageable manner and provides the necessary feedback to diagnose potential problems and errors.

Progress Check ⟳

1. What facility do you use to get output from within a PL/SQL program?

2. What is wrong with the following cursor declaration?

```
Cursor get_data is;
Select cust_id, cust_last_name
From customers;
```

3. What are the two basic types of exception handles within PL/SQL?

4. To call an exception, what PL/SQL command should you use?

5. Name two pseudo-columns that help with exception feedback?

CRITICAL SKILL 6.6

Include Conditions in Your Programs

The inclusion of conditions in your programs is the heart of all advanced programming languages. In the previous section, we actually included some statements to perform these types of tasks. You may have noticed IF statements and loops. It is in this section that we now illustrate how to construct them by providing you with a step-by-step guide. Since programs are written to handle a number of different situations, the manner in which different conditions are detected and dealt with is the biggest part of program control. This section will provide you with details on the following topics:

■ Program control

■ Various types of IF logic structures

Progress Check Answers

1. The dbms_output package can be used to get output from within a PL/SQL program.

2. The extra ";" on line 1 of the cursor should not be there.

3. Built-in exceptions like **when others** and **when no_data_found** are the two basic types of exception handles within PL/SQL.

4. The **raise** command is used.

5. Two pseudo-columns that help with exception feedback are sqlcode and sqlerrm.

- CASE expressions
- Various types of looping structures

Program Control

Program control is governed by the status of variables that it uses and the data it reads and writes from the database. As an example, picture yourself going to the Department of Motor Vehicles to renew your driver's license. Upon entering the office, you are presented with a number of directional signs. One sign is "Drivers Testing;" for this you go to the 2nd floor. Another sign tells you that "License Renewals" are on the 3rd floor. So, since you are here for a renewal, you proceed to the 3rd floor. Once you arrive in the renewal office, you are once again faced with some new choices—after all, this is a government office; it's not going to be a simple exercise. So, now you have to decide if you are going to pay by cash or credit card. Cash payments are being accepted to the right and credit cards are to the left. Noting that you have enough cash, you head to the payment wicket on the right. Let's look at Table 6-4 and see how our program control influenced our choices.

IF Logic Structures

When you are writing computer programs, situations present themselves in which you must test a condition. So, when you ask a question in your program, you are usually presented with one of two answers. First, it may be true or it may be false. Computer programs are quite black and white. So, in computer logic there can only be true or false answers to our questions, no maybes here. PL/SQL provides you with three distinctive IF logic structures that allow you to test for true and false conditions. In everyday life, we are presented with decisions that we need to make. The following sections show you how to do so using PL/SQL.

IF/THEN The IF/THEN construct tests the simplest type of condition. If the condition evaluates to TRUE, then one or more lines of program code will be executed. If the condition evaluates as FALSE, then no action is taken. The following code snippet illustrates how this is performed with a PL/SQL program:

```
IF l_date > '11-APR-63' then
     l_salary :=  l_salary * 1.15; -- Increase salary by 15%
END IF;
```

Step #	Process or Decision to Make	Next Steps	
1	Here for a driver's license transaction	Yes = 2	No = 4
2	Here for a driving test	Yes = 5	No = 3
3	Here for a license renewal	Yes = 6	No = 4
4	Ask for help	Right place = 1	Wrong place = 13
5	Go to 2nd floor	7	
6	Go to 3rd floor	9	
7	Line up for driver's test	8	
8	Pass test (we hope)	6	
9	Payment method	Cash = 10	Credit = 11
10	Cash payment wicket	12	
11	Credit-card payment wicket	12	
12	Receive new license	13	
13	Leave building, head home		

TABLE 6-4.   *Program Control Decision Matrix*

In this case, we are asking that if the value of the variable l_date is greater than (>) April 11, 1963, then we will increase the salary by 15 percent. This statement may also be restated using the following:

```
IF not(l_date <= '11-APR-63') then
     l_salary :=  l_salary * 1.15; -- Increase salary by 15%
END IF;
```

You may nest IF/THEN statements to increase the power of your statements. So, let's add an additional condition to limit who gets the raise:

```
IF l_date > '11-APR-63' then
IF l_last_name = 'PAKMAN' then
l_salary :=  l_salary * 1.15; -- Increase salary by 15%
END IF;
END IF;
```

So, not only must the date be greater than April 11th, 1963, but your last name must be equal to 'PAKMAN' in order to get the raise. This is a method we use to make sure that human resource programs ensure that programmers get a raise every year.

What you should also notice in this code is that there are now two END IF statements. This is a required construct, since you must always pair up an IF statement with an END IF. So, if you are going to have nested IF statements, you must ensure that each is paired with a matching END IF.

NOTE
*Each IF statement is followed by its own THEN.
There is also no semicolon (;) terminator on a line
that begins with an IF. The END IF; clause will
always terminate your IF statements and include
a semicolon (;).*

NOTE
*Each IF statement block must have at least one line
of program code. If you wish to do nothing within
your program code, then simply use the NULL;
command.*

IF/THEN/ELSE   The IF/THEN/ELSE construct is similar to the simple IF/THEN construct. The difference here is that if the condition executes as FALSE, you perform the program statements that follow the ELSE statement. The following code illustrates this logic within PL/SQL:

```
IF l_date > '11-APR-63' then
           l_salary :=  l_salary * 1.15; -- Increase salary by 15%
ELSE
l_salary := l_salary * 1.05;  -- Increase salary by 5%
END IF;
```

In this code listing, you see the condition that if the date is greater than April 11, 1963, you will get a 15 percent salary increase. However, when the date is less than or equal to this date, you only receive a 5 percent increase.

As with the simple for of the IF/THEN construct, you may nest the IF/THEN/ELSE construct. Let's look at how this might appear in your PL/SQL program:

```
IF l_date > '11-APR-63' then
If l_last_name = 'PAKMAN' then
l_salary :=  l_salary * 1.15; -- Increase salary by 15%
ELSE
l_salary :=  l_salary * 1.10; -- Increase salary by 10%
END IF;
ELSE
l_salary := l_salary * 1.05;  -- Increase salary by 5%
END IF;
```

This leads us to another two points on using the IF statement within PL/SQL:

- There may only be one ELSE statement within every IF statement construct.

- There is no semicolon (;) on the line starting with ELSE.

IF/THEN/ELSIF   The final IF construct that we will show you is the IF-THEN-ELSIF one. In this case, you provide yourself with the option to test another condition where the condition is evaluated as FALSE. So, should you want to test for more than one condition without using nested IF statements, this is the type of statement you might use:

```
IF l_last_name = 'PAKMAN' then
                  l_salary :=  l_salary * 1.15; -- Increase salary by 15%
ELSIF l_last_name = 'ASTROFF' then
                  l_salary :=  l_salary * 1.10; -- Increase salary by 10%
ELSE
                  l_salary :=  l_salary * 1.05; -- Increase salary by 5%
END IF;
```

In this statement, if your last name is Pakman, you get a 15 percent raise. If it is Astroff, you get 10 percent, and the rest of us get only a 5 percent raise.

Note that there is no limit to the number of ELSIF conditions you may use within this construct. The following shows an example of using multiple ELSIF statements within the construct.

```
IF l_city = 'OTTAWA' then
      L_team_name := 'SENATORS';
ELSIF l_city = 'BOSTON' then
      L_team_name := 'BRUINS';
ELSIF l_city = 'NEW YORK' then
      L_team_name := 'RANGERS'
ELSIF l_city = 'TORONTO' then
      L_team_name := 'MAPLE LEAFS';
END IF;
```

NOTE
There is no matching END IF statement for each ELSIF. Only a single END IF is required within this construct.

When writing your PL/SQL program, you should use indentation to simplify the reading of the program. Notice in our code segments that we use indentation to make it easier for you to read the code statements. As a rule, you should line up each IF/THEN/ELSE statement and indent the program code that lies between each of these words.

CASE Statements

The next logical step from the IF statement is the CASE statement. The CASE statement was introduced with Oracle9*i*, and is an evolution in logical control. It differs from the IF/THEN/ELSE constructs in that we now can use a simple structure to logically select from a list of values. More important, it may be used to set the value of a variable. Let's explore how this is done.

First, let's look at the format we will need to follow:

```
CASE variable
    WHEN expression1 then value1
    WHEN expression2 then value2
    WHEN expression3 then value3
    WHEN expression4 then value4
    ELSE value5
END;
```

There is no limit to the number of expressions that may be defined in a CASE statement. The following is an example of the use of the CASE expression:

```
        SQL> run
          1   declare
          2      val      varchar2(100);
  3     city    varchar2(20) := 'TORONTO';
          4   begin
          5      val := CASE city
          6              WHEN 'TORONTO' then 'RAPTORS'
          7              WHEN 'LOS ANGELES' then 'LAKERS'
          8              WHEN 'BOSTON' then 'CELTICS'
          9              WHEN 'CHICAGO' then 'BULLS'
         10              ELSE 'NO TEAM'
         11          END;
         12
         13   dbms_output.put_line(val); -- output to the screen
         14* end;
        RAPTORS
        PL/SQL procedure successfully completed.
```

Ask the Expert

Q: How do I add comments to my PL/SQL programs?

A: To add comments to your code, simply start a comment with a /* and end it with a */ or use the -- (as we have done previously). If you use the --, you need to make sure you put it on its own line, or after your program code if you place it on the same line. The following is an example of valid comments:

```
/* This is a comment */
-- This is also a comment
```

Although we may have been able to use the IF/ELSIF/THEN/ELSE construct to achieve the same purpose, the CASE statement is easier to read and is more efficient with the database.

Loops

When was the last time that you visited an amusement park? Well, if you have been to one in recent years, you will surely have seen a roller coaster. That roller coaster, if it's a really good roller coaster, probably had one or more loops. PL/SQL is that kind of ride. It is a ride that includes loops. Loops are control structures that allow you to repeat a set of commands until you decide that it is time to stop the looping.

Generally, the format that all loops take is the following:

```
LOOP
      Executable statements;
END LOOP;
```

Each time the loop is executed, the statements within the loop are executed, and the program returns to the top of the LOOP structure to do it all over again. However, if you ever want this processing to stop, you need to learn about the EXIT statement.

The EXIT statement allows you to stop executing within a loop without a condition. It then passes control back to the program and continues on after the LOOP statements.

The following is how to get out of a tight LOOP:

```
LOOP
      IF l_bank_balance >= 0 then EXIT;
      ELSE
            L_decision := 'ACCOUNT OVERDRAWN';
      END IF;
END LOOP;
```

NOTE
*Without an EXIT statement in a simple LOOP,
the loop will be infinite.*

There are many other kinds of loops, some of which provide more control over
your looping. Each has its use in PL/SQL programming and each should be learned
in order to give your programming the greatest flexibility.

The WHILE Loop

The WHILE loop will continue to execute as long as the condition that you have
defined continues to be true. If the condition becomes false, then you exit your
loop. Let's look at an example:

```
WHILE l_sales_total < 100000 LOOP
        Select sales_amount into l_sale_amount from daily_sales;
        l_sales_total := l_sales_total + l_sale_amount;

END LOOP;
```

Although you may have used the EXIT command to do the same thing, it is
better form to use the WHILE expression.

The FOR Loop

The FOR loop is one of the most common loops you will encounter in your PL/SQL
programming, and allows you to control the number of times a loop executes. In the
case of the WHILE loop, we are never quite sure how many times a loop is executed,
since it will continue to loop until a condition is met. However, in the case of the
FOR loop, this is not the case.

The FOR loop allows you to define the number of times to loop when you
program the loop itself. You will define the value that starts your loop, as well
as the value that terminates it. Let's look at some syntax:

```
FOR l_counter IN 1 .. 10
LOOP
        Statements;
END LOOP;
```

So, what is important to note in the preceding statement? First, you need to know
that the variable l_counter will hold the value between 1 and 10. How do we know
it will be between 1 and 10? Well, after the IN word, we place the counter's range.
In our case, we would like the counter to start at 1, the low bound, and continue to
10. You should also note that between the two integer values (1 and 10) we place
two dots (..). This is done to tell Oracle that you would like it to count between

these two numbers. You also have the ability to count backwards using the REVERSE clause. This listing shows you how the REVERSE clause may be used:

```
declare
    l_counter number;
begin
    FOR l_counter IN REVERSE 1..5
    LOOP
            dbms_output.put_line(l_counter);
    END LOOP;
end;
/
5
4
3
2
1

PL/SQL procedure successfully completed.
```

Now you can see how simple it is to use simple loops. But don't be fooled—loops have a lot of power, some of which we will see later. When you use loops like the WHILE loop or the FOR loop, you have the ability to use variables instead of hard-coded values. This allows you to have the greatest possible flexibility since you can have the database or external data provide you with the limits within your loop. Let's look at how this might work. The example below illustrates the simplest form of the FOR loop. In this case, we select the number of employees we have in our employee table and then simply show how the counter counts from 1 to the number of employees in our small company:

```
SQL> run
  1  declare
  2      l_emp_count number;
  3      i               number;  -- We will use this as our counter
  4  begin
  5   -- Select the number of employees in the l_emp_count variable
  6      select count(*) into l_emp_count from employee;
  7
  8      FOR i IN 1 .. l_emp_count  LOOP

  9              dbms_output.put_line('Employee ' || i);
 10      END LOOP;
 11* end;
Employee 1
Employee 2
Employee 3
Employee 4
Employee 5
Employee 6
PL/SQL procedure successfully completed.
```

So, as you might have guessed, we have six employees in our company. It may be small, but it's very good. However, the important thing to know is that you may use variables in your loops. The other line you may have noticed was the SELECT statement contained in the PL/SQL block.

Project 6-2 Using Conditions and Loops in PL/SQL

In this project, we will create a PL/SQL program that will read the data in the products table and then print out the products that have a price above $50.

Step by Step

1. Log into SQL*Plus.

2. At the SQL> prompt, enter the serveroutput command: **set serveroutput on;**.

3. Enter the following PL/SQL program:

```
 1  declare
 2    cursor get_data is
 3      select prod_name, prod_list_price
 4      from products;
 5  begin
 6      for i in get_data
 7      LOOP
 8        if i.prod_list_price > 50 then
 9          dbms_output.put_line(i.prod_name||' Price: '|| i.prod_list_price);
10        end if;
11      END LOOP;
12* end;
```

4. You should now see the following output on your screen:

```
SQL> /
5MP Telephoto Digital Camera Price: 899.99
17" LCD w/built-in HDTV Tuner Price: 999.99
Envoy 256MB - 40GB Price: 999.99
Y Box Price: 299.99
Mini DV Camcorder with 3.5" Swivel LCD Price: 1099.99
Envoy Ambassador Price: 1299.99
Laptop carrying case Price: 55.99
Home Theatre Package with DVD-Audio/Video Play Price: 599.99
18" Flat Panel Graphics Monitor Price: 899.99
SIMM- 8MB PCMCIAII card Price: 112.99
SIMM- 16MB PCMCIAII card Price: 149.99
Unix/Windows 1-user pack Price: 199.99
8.3 Minitower Speaker Price: 499.99
Multimedia speakers- 5" cones Price: 67.99
Envoy External 8X CD-ROM Price: 54.99
Model NM500X High Yield Toner Cartridge Price: 192.99
Model A3827H Black Image Cartridge Price: 89.99
```

(continued)

```
128MB Memory Card Price: 52.99
256MB Memory Card Price: 69.99

PL/SQL procedure successfully completed.
```

5. You may now change the criteria we have used so that we print out messages for products under $50. This is done by adding the following text in the right place in the code:

```
else
    dbms_output.put_line(i.prod_name || ' Product under 50');
```

6. More output will appear, including that of all the products.

Project Summary

This project illustrates how to use loops and conditional clauses and how you can easily select data and use it within a PL/SQL program.

Create Stored Procedures—How and Why

PL/SQL is a very powerful language, and one of its most important features is the ability to store programs in the database and share them with others. We generally refer to these as stored objects or stored programs. There are four distinct types: procedures, functions, triggers, and packages. Up until now in this chapter, we have looked at anonymous PL/SQL blocks. Stored PL/SQL programs differ from these since they are named objects that are stored inside the database. Anonymous blocks are not stored in the database and must be loaded each time you want to run them.

We create stored programs for a number of reasons. The most important reason to create programs that are stored instead of anonymous is that it provides you with the ability to share programs and optimize performance. By storing programs, you can grant many different users the privilege of running your program. You can also simplify them and have different programs perform specific functions. These programs can then be called from a central program, which can optimize performance and programming time. This concept is very familiar to object-oriented programmers and is known as modularity.

If you are to truly take advantage of PL/SQL within the confines of your Oracle database, you will need to understand how to create and maintain PL/SQL stored objects. Let's look at the various types of PL/SQL stored programs.

The first stored object is called a stored procedure. A stored procedure is a PL/SQL program-adding construct that tells the database you want to store an object. Just as we do when we create a table, a procedure is created or updated with the **create procedure** command. By adding this at the beginning of a PL/SQL block, you create an object in the database known as a **procedure**. Another feature of stored procedures, provided to you at no extra cost, is the ability to pass values in and out of a procedure.

NOTE
*You should put **create or replace procedure** in your **create procedure** commands. If you do not use the **replace** portion of the command, you will need to drop your procedure before trying to re-create it. By including **replace**, the procedure will be created if it does not exist or will be replaced if it does.*

Let's look at one of the programs we have already created and convert it to a stored procedure:

```
 1  create or replace procedure print_products
 2  as
 3  declare
 4    cursor get_data is
 5      select prod_name, prod_list_price
 6      from products;
 7  begin
 8  for i in get_data
 9    LOOP
10     if i.prod_list_price > 50 then
11       dbms_output.put_line(i.prod_name || ' Price: ' || i.prod_MIN_price);
12     else
13       dbms_output.put_line(i.prod_name || ' Product under 50');
14     end if;
15   END LOOP;
16* end;
```

Warning: Procedure created with compilation errors.

Now it looks like we have a couple of errors. Even authors get errors when we write PL/SQL. To see what errors you have received from your program, simply enter **show errors**. Oracle will then show you the errors that have occurred during the compiling of your program. Let's see what we did wrong:

```
SQL> show errors

Errors for PROCEDURE PRINT_PRODUCTS:

LINE/COL ERROR
-------- --------------------------------------------------------------
3/1      PLS-00103: Encountered the symbol "DECLARE" when expecting one of
         the following:
         begin function package pragma procedure subtype type use
         <an identifier> <a double-quoted delimited-identifier> form
         current cursor external language
         The symbol "begin" was substituted for "DECLARE" to continue.

16/4     PLS-00103: Encountered the symbol "end-of-file" when expecting
         one of the following:
         begin case declare end exception exit for goto if loop mod
```

```
null pragma raise return select update while with
<an identifier> <a double-quoted delimited-identifier>
<a bind variable> << close current delete fetch lock insert
open rollback savepoint set sql execute commit forall merge
<a single-quoted SQL string> pipe
<an alternatively-quoted SQL string>
```

It looks like we have errors on lines 3 and 16. When creating a stored object, you do not always need to include the **declare** statement since PL/SQL understands that, based on the way the program is structured, after a **create** statement it expects to see the reserved word **as**, which will be followed by the Declaration section. So you can think of it this way: **as** replaces **declare** when creating a stored object. Let's now look at the repaired PL/SQL code. The lines we changed are highlighted in bold:

```
  1   create or replace procedure print_products
  2   as
3     cursor get_data is
  4      select prod_name, prod_list_price
  5      from products;
  6   begin
  7      for i in get_data
  8      LOOP
  9      if i.prod_list_price > 50 then
 10        dbms_output.put_line(i.prod_name ||' Price: '|| i.prod_LIST_price);
 11      else
 12         dbms_output.put_line(i.prod_name || ' Product under 50');
 13       end if;
 14      END LOOP;
 15* end;
SQL> /

Procedure created.
```

That's good news. The program has compiled and will now run when we call it. Let's look at how to call a procedure from SQL*Plus. Using the **execute** command, you may run a stored program:

```
SQL>> execute print_products
PL/SQL procedure successfully completed.t
```

We have added a parameter to our program to show you how to get information into it. We use parameters within the program when we supply data to the procedure, and we can then return a value to the program that calls it through another output parameter. It is also possible to define parameters as both input and output. However, to simplify our parameters, we usually define them for only one of the two purposes. In this case, we will use SQL*Plus to call our procedure since it works. Our example will input a character that will be used to find only products that begin with the input string:

```
  1   create or replace procedure print_products
  2   (FIRST_CHARACTER IN VARCHAR)
```

Ask the Expert

Q: I get an error "ORA-20000: ORU-10027: buffer overflow, limit of 2000 bytes" when running my PL/SQL programs that use dbms_output. How can I fix this problem?

A: The default buffer size for the DBMS__OUTPUT package is defaulted to 2000 bytes. This is usually sufficient for most testing purposes. However, if you need to increase this, you can do it through the serveroutput command. One parameter it has is **size**, whose value may be set to between 2000 and 1,000,000 bytes. You perform this by issuing the following command:

```
SQL> set serveroutput on size 100000
```

```
3  as
  4     cursor get_data is
  5       select prod_name, prod_list_price
  6       from products
  7       where prod_name like FIRST_CHARACTER || '%';
  8  begin
  9  for i in get_data
 10    LOOP
 11     if i.prod_list_price > 50 then
 12       dbms_output.put_line(i.prod_name ||' Price: '||
i.prod_LiST_price);
 13     else
 14       dbms_output.put_line(i.prod_name || ' Product under 50');
 15     end if;
 16    END LOOP;
 17* end print_products;
```

Now, let's see how to describe our procedure, as indicated by the bold text in the next listing. Here, we learn the name of the program and get a list of any parameters we may need to pass:

```
SQL> describe print_products
PROCEDURE print_products
 Argument Name                  Type                    In/Out Default?
 ------------------------------ ----------------------- ------ --------
 FIRST_CHARACTER                VARCHAR2                 IN
```

Next, we need to run the procedure. In our case, we are running it in SQL*Plus. When in this facility, if you want to receive data from a program, you need to declare a variable. This is done in the first line of the following listing. We will then run the program with the **execute** command.

```
SQL> exec print_products ('A');
Adventures with Numbers Product under 50

PL/SQL procedure successfully completed.
```

As you can tell, we called the program print_products. We want to print the products that begin with an "A". The results show us that we only have one product that begins with the character "A". As you may have gleaned from the results, the program has functioned as expected.

Now that we have learned to create stored objects in Oracle Database 10*g*, let's look at a specialized program, called a function, that can extend the functionality of the database.

Progress Check

1. What type of IF structure should be used if you had a single test and only one alternate choice?

2. What is wrong with the following IF structure? What other way may this type of logic be implemented with Oracle Database 10*g*?

```
IF surname = 'ABRAMSON' then
     Salary = salary * 1.12;
IF surname = 'ABBEY' then
     Salary = salary * 1.22;
IF surname = 'COREY' then
     Salary = salary * 2.5;
END IF;
```

3. True or False: When naming your stored programs, you must follow the same rules as naming a table.

4. What are the three types of procedure parameters you can have?

5. What SQL*Plus command do you use to run your stored programs?

Progress Check Answers

1. You would use the IF/THEN/ELSE structure.

2. We should not use chained IF statements, but instead use ELSIF in the secondary IF statements. The best way to implement this type of logic is to employ a CASE statement.

3. True. When naming your stored programs you must follow the same rules as naming a table.

4. You can have any or all of the following: INPUT, OUTPUT, or INPUT&OUTPUT.

5. Use the **execute** command to run your stored programs.

CRITICAL SKILL 6.8

Create and Use Functions

We may also create stored objects that can be used within a **select** command. Oracle provides us with functions. There are functions to trim spaces from a field, or replace one character with another. All of these provide us with an ability to extend the capabilities of Oracle itself.

Functions are very much like stored procedures. The main difference is that functions may be used within a select statement in the column list or may also be used in the where clause.

When creating a function, you perform a **create or replace function** command. You can have variables input to the function, as well as return a value to the calling statement. A function must return a value. The data type of the returned value must be defined when creating the function. This is how a function differs from a procedure. The function will then perform its task during regular processing, allowing you to utilize the results along with your regular data, thus extending the value of your data and your database.

Project 6-3 Creating and Using a Function

The following project will walk you through the process of defining a function. Then we use the function in two select statements. The first will use the function in the returned columns and the next will use it as a data constraint. The function that we will create will perform the simple task of adding a 15-percent tax to the list price to give the price with taxes included.

Step by Step

1. Log into SQL*Plus.

2. At the SQL> prompt, type in the following command:

```
create or replace function GetProductTaxIn
(in_product_id number)
return number
is
    v_price number;
    cursor get_price_tax  is
    select nvl(round(prod_list_price * 1.15,2),0)
    from   products
    where  prod_id = in_product_id;
begin
    open get_price_tax;
    fetch get_price_tax into v_price;
    return v_price;
```

(continued)

```
exception
    when others then v_price := 0;
    return v_price;
end;
```

```
Function created.
```

3. If you receive any errors, you will need to fix them before you move on.

4. Create a **select** statement that uses the function in the columns specification. The following is an example:

```
select prod_id, prod_list_price, GetProductTaxIn(Prod_id)
from products
```

5. Your results may look similar to this:

```
PROD_ID PROD_LIST_PRICE GETPRODUCTTAXIN(PROD_ID)
---------- --------------- ------------------------
       13          899.99                  1034.99
       14          999.99                  1149.99
       15          999.99                  1149.99
       16          299.99                   344.99
       17         1099.99                  1264.99
       18         1299.99                  1494.99
       19           55.99                    64.39
       20          599.99                   689.99
       21          899.99                  1034.99
       22           24.99                    28.74
       23           21.99                    25.29
...
```

6. Now use the function in the where clause of a SQL statement. The following is an example of using the function within a where clause:

```
select prod_id, prod_list_price, GetProductTaxIn(Prod_id)
  from products
 where GetProductTaxIn(Prod_id)>= 500
```

Project Summary

This project illustrates how you can extend the functionality of your database as well as add value to your organization by building standard rules that can be utilized by everyone using your database.

Functions provide us all with the ability to define standard rules and derivations for our user community and ensure that programs perform predictably and optimally.

CRITICAL SKILL 6.9

Call PL/SQL Programs

Up to this point in the chapter, we have done the following:

- Defined a PL/SQL block

- Defined a PL/SQL program

- Created a stored program

- Debugged our code

This is fine if we simply want to write every program and have it run as a simple standalone program. However, as with many programming languages it is important to write a number of separate programs that perform specific tasks, rather than a single program that performs all of your tasks. So, when writing PL/SQL programs, you should think the same way. Have programs that perform table maintenance, that perform complex logic, or simply read data from tables or files. This leads us to how to call programs from other programs, a process similar to calling subroutines within C programs. Procedures may be called from programs ranging from Oracle Forms to perl scripts, but for this section we will simply show you how to call procedures from each other.

To call a procedure from another, we can use our previous procedure, named *print_products.* Let's create another procedure that calls this procedure.

```
create or replace procedure call_print_prods
as
begin
  for l_alpha IN 65 .. 90
  LOOP
   print_products(chr(l_alpha));
  END LOOP;
end;
/
```

We have created a new procedure. It loops through the values of 65 to 90, the ASCII values for A to Z. Using the CHR function, we can convert the value to an ASCII character. We need to do this since we cannot loop through character values. So, the procedure will loop through the values calling the print_products procedure each time. This calling of programs can be looped extensively and can be organized into efficient and simple program units. This is similar to modularization seen in object-oriented programming language.

As you can tell, Oracle's PL/SQL is a powerful and deep language. In this chapter, we've helped provide you with the ability to start writing programs and to incorporate some complex logic using the basic features of the language. As with any language, you can achieve a significant amount of productivity with only a limited number of commands. We encourage you to use this as a starting point and build upon it to ultimately create the programs you and your organization will need.

☑ Chapter 6 Mastery Check

1. Where is PL/SQL executed?

2. Which type of PL/SQL statement would you use to increase the price values by 15 percent for items with more than 1500 in stock and by 20 percent for items with fewer than 500 in stock?

    A. A cursor FOR loop

    B. An IF-THEN-ELSE command

    C. An **insert** statement

    D. An **update** statement

3. What is the **fetch** command used for?

4. What will the following command perform?

    ```
    V_PRICE_TOLERANCE := 500;
    ```

5. What is wrong with this function definition?

    ```
    CREATE OR REPLACE FUNCTION raise_price
        (original_price IN NUMBER)
    RETURN number
    IS
    BEGIN
        RETURN (original_price * 1.25);
    END lower_price;
    ```

6. What is the advantage of using the %TYPE attribute when defining PL/SQL variables?

7. What Oracle Database 10*g* facility besides PL/SQL supports exception handling based on error numbers?

8. A commit that is issued in a PL/SQL program will commit what?

CHAPTER
7

Java

CRITICAL SKILLS

7.1 What Does Java Mean to an Oracle DBA?

7.2 Overview of Java

7.3 Configure Java for Oracle

7.4 Java in Oracle

7.5 JDBC Drivers

7.6 Use JDBC

7.7 Use SQLJ

7.8 Java-Stored Procedures

7.9 Create Java Objects in Oracle

7.10 Understand Oracle Java Products

his chapter introduces the key features of Java that an Oracle DBA needs to understand when managing Oracle Database 10*g*. Topics include Java features and terminology, configuring Java in the database, connecting to Oracle using Java, JDBC, and SQLJ, Java-stored procedures, and the direction of Java in Oracle. This chapter may give some traditional Oracle DBAs a headache but the information in this chapter describes a popular application environment that Oracle Database 10*g* will run in, and which some DBAs need to be able to support.

Java Server Fundamentals

Mention Java to an Oracle DBA and you will often see a look of curiosity, disdain, disinterest, or fear. It has been a subject that most production DBAs have ignored for years. Although a core language since Oracle 8.1.5, most production DBAs have not placed a lot of emphasis on learning Java. A primary reason is that Java has not impacted most Oracle DBAs' job responsibilities in older releases of Oracle. However, changes in the industry, markets and Oracle technology directions no longer provide DBAs with that luxury. Java technology is integrated tightly with the Oracle Database 10*g*, Oracle Application Server 10*g*, Oracle JDeveloper 10*g*, Oracle Application Server Web Services, Oracle XML DB, and the Oracle Developer Suite 10*g*, including Oracle Forms and Reports.

NOTE
Many of the topics discussed in this chapter could, each on their own, take an entire book to cover completely. Since this is an introductory book, specifics for some topics have been omitted. Real-world experiences and additional reading will build on this material.

CRITICAL SKILL 7.1

What Does Java Mean to an Oracle DBA?

Java is one of the core languages (SQL, PL/SQL, Java, XML, and HTML) that are tightly integrated in the Oracle Database 10*g* suite of products. The Extensible Markup Language (XML) is a hierarchical data structure that describes data by embedding the metadata with the data structure. Java has become the primary language for new applications that are written for Oracle databases. Why does an Oracle DBA care about Java? Java in an Oracle environment impacts architectural decisions, performance, leveraging new technologies, security, and application development. Java-stored procedures can run in the Oracle database server. So, if Java code can run in the Oracle database server, then DBAs are going to have to deal with related Java issues. Also, DBAs that can support the middle tier (application server, Web Services, J2EE, Oracle Net Services, and so on) in n-tiered environments as well as application development (Java, XML, HTML, and others) will increase their value to an organization. Java knowledge is important in all tiers of an Oracle Database 10g architectural environment. However, with Java playing such a key role in so many technology areas in Oracle Database 10g, the key features and functionality introduced in this section are important for DBAs to understand.

Java as a core language in Oracle environments should be known to an Oracle Database 10g DBA, with the understanding that they are not likely to be writing Java-stored procedures, servlets, or Enterprise JavaBeans. However, a DBA does need to understand the feature/functionality of the database, how Java applications impact the Oracle database server, and they should be able to support the developers. If developers are having problems running Java-stored procedures, a DBA needs to understand whether it is a configuration or an application issue. Inefficient Java programs that access a database have a negative impact on performance. Such things will impact the DBA.

In previous releases of Oracle, production DBAs focused on the Oracle Database 10g server and the environment the server ran in. This usually involved understanding the operating system, the Oracle server, networking, and storage management. Oracle Database 10g environments are involving application servers, Web Services, XML, Internet protocols, and n-tiered architectures. Java is integral to all of these areas. The first time a DBA has to tune a query using XML in the database or get asked to help figure out how an XML structure in the database got corrupted, they will care. The reason is that the DBA is responsible for tuning and data integrity. Highly valuable and marketable DBAs will understand the various Oracle Database 10g server environments.

The technology environment is more competitive than ever before. DBAs that can support the application environment are extremely valuable. Java is a key technology with Web Services and n-tiered architectures. DBAs that have a solid understanding of Java will be able to do a much better job of supporting the application environment for Oracle Database 10g.

Java applications can run in the Oracle database server as well as PL/SQL. It's not just an issue of running an industry-standard language (Java) versus a proprietary database (PL/SQL) language. Java is a systems language that offers a lot of functionality beyond the capabilities of PL/SQL. Java is also tightly integrated into new technologies such as Web Services. *Web Services* is a technology that allows different types of applications to communicate over the Web. Technologies integrated into Web Services include the following:

- **Simple Object Access Protocol (SOAP)** SOAP is a lightweight protocol used to exchange structured data (XML) in a heterogeneous, distributed environment.

■ **Extensible Markup Language (XML)**   This is an industry-standard language for documents containing structured information. Included in the XML data structures is the metadata associated with the data. XML is an extremely popular method of transferring data across the Internet. XML can handle complex data, but it often needs to be displayed or converted to another form. This can be done with XSL (Extensible Stylesheet Language), which converts data from one format to another—for instance, it will convert XML to HTML for displaying on a web browser. This is why XSLT is an important part of XSL.

■ **Web Services Description Language (WSDL)**   WSDL uses XML for describing network services as a set of network endpoints (ports) operating on messages with documents or procedural information.

Web Services is expected to be the next business model to leverage the capability of the Internet. Oracle Database 10*g* adds a significant amount of functionality supporting Web Services and related technology in the Oracle database. Most large organizations are likely to be implementing Web Services at some level in the next few years. Here are some reasons why organizations are moving to Web Services:

■ Companies need to have a simple way of integrating applications and resources in a heterogeneous environment.

■ It's based upon open standards that are being adopted by Oracle, IBM, Microsoft, Sun, HP, and other countries.

■ Leverages other open standards such as XML and Web Services Description Language (WSDL).

■ Web Services can be run on Windows, Linux, Macintosh, Solaris, AIX, HP-UX, WAP, and other systems.

■ Web Services can significantly reduce software development, maintenance, and integration costs for web applications.

■ An application can have a Web Services interface generated and it can then be executed by another program anywhere in the world in a matter of minutes. PL/SQL and Java applications in Oracle Database 10*g* can have Web Services interfaces generated.

There are three important reasons why Oracle Database 10*g* DBAs should care about Java and Java-related technologies such as XML, Web Services, SOAP, WSDL, and others:

■ A critical part of managing database systems involves moving information from one place to another and getting different environments (hardware, software, applications, networks) to work together.

- Oracle Database 10*g* supports technologies such as Java, XML, HTTP, and Web Services directly in the database server.

- Successful and marketable DBAs in Oracle Database 10*g* environments need to be able to do more than just performance tuning, backup/recovery, and storage management.

These technologies provide open standard solutions for integration and communication across heterogeneous, distributed environments. What's more important is that the industry is supporting these new standards and leveraging them. These standards, however, are still evolving and changing. Nevertheless, the strong advantages of these technologies cannot be ignored and large organizations are seriously looking at them.

Traditionally, Web Services has been deployed in the middle-tier. The middle-tier is the level between the client-tier (presentation-tier) and the information-tier (data-tier or database server-tier) that contains the business logic. The middle-tier usually contains an application or web server. In Oracle Database 10*g*, the database server can be a Web Services provider. Supporting Web Services in the database offers Enterprise Information Integration. With the proliferation of web-based applications, the integration and connectivity is critical. Web Services can provide the glue that leverages different technologies and environments. In disconnected environments (Internet), accessing stored procedures (Java), data, and metadata (XML) through Web Services offers additional options and flexibility.

So what does Java mean to an Oracle DBA? Java is a core language that is integrated in the Oracle Database 10*g* server and primary Oracle products such as the application server, Oracle development products, and applications. Second, Java is a key technology that is integral to technologies that are playing larger roles in database applications such as Web Services, application servers, XML, and the development of standards-based environments.

CRITICAL SKILL 7.2
Overview of Java

This section will introduce DBAs to the Java programming language from a DBA perspective. After reading this section, DBAs will also understand enough terms and acronyms to speak with confidence at any barbeque party where Java developers are in attendance. The emphasis in this section will be on terminology and concepts important for a new Oracle Database 10*g* DBA. Here are some of the reasons why Java has become a mainstream language:

- **Object-Oriented**   Java is an object-oriented programming (OOP) language that has become quite mainstream. An object-oriented language uses individual software components (objects) that can be connected together to build an application.

■ **Portable** Java allows Oracle programmers to write portable applications using an industry-standard language.

■ **Robust** Java offers the powerful system features of C and C++ but without a lot of the negative features (things like pointers, memory leaks, detailed low level code, inefficient language constructs) that impacted programming projects in C/C++.

■ **Flexible** Java is a high-performance language that supports dynamic applications.

■ **Mature** Design of Java began in 1991, but the Java craze didn't hit until 1995. It has matured significantly (versions 1.0, 1.1, 1.2 (Java 2), 1.3, 1.4, 1.5) adding large libraries and significant feature/functionality.

■ **Distributed** Java contains enormous libraries that support distributed applications.

■ **Standards** Using the Java features in the Oracle 10*g* suite of products allows enterprise applications to be written using industry standards. Oracle extensions do exist but it is up to the developers to determine if they wish to use them.

■ **Easy to Use** Java is a rich, powerful language that takes time to learn. Complex features such as networking, multithreading are much easier to perform in Java than older traditional languages such as C, C++, and Fortran.

So if all of this is true, why doesn't everybody have a Java book in their back pockets? Reasons include the following:

■ Java and the surrounding technologies that leverage Java take time to learn.

■ These technologies have completely different ways of doings things.

■ Although Java is extremely powerful, it's not necessary to use Java to solve all problems. PL/SQL is still an extremely powerful database programming language that can solve a lot of day-to-day problems.

■ Companies often find that the power of Java is not necessary. Client/server applications and .NET are simpler solutions to learn and implement.

- There are tremendous costs, time, and resources involved in switching to these new technologies.

Platform Independence

Java is a platform-independent language. A Java source program is compiled in bytecodes that do not contain any machine specific instructions. This allows a compiled Java program to run on different hardware platforms without being recompiled. A Java Virtual Machine (JVM) is the runtime environment that interprets the Java bytecodes (machine-independent compiled code) and is an application that is customized for specific platforms. The Java instructions are processed by the JVM to perform specific platform actions. A hardware or software vendor will build a JVM that conforms to an industry specification ensuring portability. Historically, interpreted code has provided portability at the cost of execution speed. Since the first Java release, Java has improved performance significantly with just-in-time (JIT) and native compilers. A JIT compiler will compile interpreted (bytecode) at runtime. A native compiler compiles interpreted code into machine specific instructions. So the first time the Java code runs, it is executed as native code.

Java in All Three Tiers

Oracle supports Java in all three tiers of the enterprise: the client-, middle-, and server-side tiers (see Figure 7-1). Oracle provides development tools on the client side (Oracle Developer Suite 10*g* and JDeveloper 10*g*), the application server in the middle-tier, and the database on the server side. Wherever Java runs, a JVM is required. Java contains a large set of libraries. The JVM executes Java code by accessing the Java libraries. The Java core set of libraries are organized into logical units called packages (different from PL/SQL packages). The Oracle database and application servers both contain JVMs. Internet browsers and tools like JDeveloper contain JVMs to execute Java code.

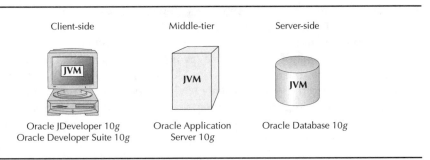

Client-side	Middle-tier	Server-side
JVM	JVM	JVM
Oracle JDeveloper 10*g* Oracle Developer Suite 10*g*	Oracle Application Server 10*g*	Oracle Database 10*g*

FIGURE 7-1.   *Java in the Oracle architecture*

Java 2 Platform, Standard Edition

Java 2 Platform, Standard Edition (J2SE) contains the functionality necessary to develop and run Java applications on desktops and servers. The J2SE also contains the foundation for the Java 2 Platform, Enterprise Edition (J2EE), and Java Web Services. The J2SE is broken into two conceptual groups:

- **Core Java addresses**   Database connectivity, security, and so on
- **Desktop Java addresses**   The graphical interface components

The current release of Oracle Database 10*g* supports a J2SE 1.4–compatible JVM. Oracle Database 10*g* supports the J2SE 1.4 release except for the GUI components. It does not make sense to generate a text field, a check box, or push button in the Oracle database kernel. However, The Oracle JVM supports Headless Abstract Windowing Toolkit (AWT). The J2SE allows database developers the ability to write Java database procedures.

The J2SE contains a Java 2 Runtime Environment, Standard Edition (JRE) and a Java 2 Software Development Kit, Standard Edition (SDK). The JRE contains the Java APIs, JVM and other Java components, for running Java applications. The Java 2 SDK contains the JRE and the tools necessary to develop Java applications. These tools include the compiler and debugger.

Java 2 Platform, Enterprise Edition

The Java 2 Platform, Enterprise Edition (J2EE), is the standard for developing and running component-based multitiered enterprise Java applications. The J2EE platform contains a large set of Java APIs for writing multitiered enterprise web-based applications. A J2EE component is a server-side self-contained software object that communicates with other software components. DBAs have always thought of the server as being the platform that runs the Oracle instance. With J2EE, the server is a non-client platform (such as the web server, application server, and so on) that contains the J2EE server. Containers are the interface between a software component and those platform-specific features necessary to use the software component. At this point, DBAs can think of an Enterprise JavaBean (EJB) as a portable software object that implements the business logic. The EJB container for the Oracle Application Server is Oracle Components For Java (OC4J). Before a web, enterprise bean, or application client component can be executed, it must be assembled into a J2EE application and deployed into its container. The Enterprise Information System is the tier that contains the database. J2EE components include

- **Application clients and applets**   These run on the client.

- **Java Servlet and JavaServer Pages (JSP)**   Server-side components that provide dynamic web content.

- **EJBs**   Server-side components containing the business logic.

- **Web Services**   Enterprise applications that use industry standards to allow different environments to exchange data. XML is used with Java to provide interoperability between Java and non-Java environments. Oracle Database 10g contains Database Web Services, HTML DB, and XML DB to support Web Services in the database.

The J2EE Server

The J2EE server (see Figure 7-2) runs the code (JSPs and servlets) that generates the graphical user interface and the business logic (EJBs). If an organization is going to use Java and they need a scalable enterprise solution, they are going to work with J2EE applications. If someone is writing J2EE applications, it is very important to use a framework. A Java framework provides a programming model for properly implementing J2EE solutions. Oracle uses the Business Components For Java (BC4J) and the Oracle Application Development Framework (ADF). These frameworks are way beyond the scope of this book. Visit otn.oracle.com for more information on these frameworks. The J2EE server also supports Web Services that allow interoperability with different platforms.

Different Types of Java Programs

There are different types of Java programs, most of which are designed to run on a specific tier. Usually by specifying a particular type of Java application someone can understand which tier the application is running on. The flexibility of running Java applications in the appropriate tier for a particular application derives from the ability to run Java in multiple tiers.

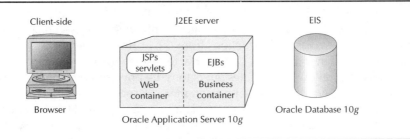

FIGURE 7-2.   *The J2EE server within Oracle*

Standalone Applications

Standalone applications can be written in Java similar to C, C++, Fortran, and so on. All Java source programs contain a .java extension. Then the source code is compiled into bytecodes, the compiled program having a .class extension. The Java compiler is javac. The Java interpreter is Java. The Java interpreter looks for a class file name by default, the extension does not need to be specified.

Compile a Java application from a UNIX prompt. This generates a HelloWorld.class file:

```
$  javac  HelloWorld.java
```

Execute a standalone Java program (HelloWorld.class) from a UNIX prompt:

```
$  java  HelloWorld
```

Applets

Applets are Java client applications designed to run inside the JVM of a browser, which can leverage the graphical capabilities of a browser. An HTML file can contain an instruction to load an applet locally or from an application server. Applets work best for applications that run on an intranet inside a firewall. When developers are writing applets, they are writing GUI applications that will run in a browser and which are loaded locally or from an application server. A Java plug-in and a security policy file may be required for the applet to run successfully.

JavaBeans

A JavaBean is a reusable software component written in Java that conforms to a particular specification. This makes it easy to plug and play a JavaBean into another Java component. JavaBeans can be visible or nonvisible, the latter of which are used in GUI applications.

JavaServer Pages and Servlets

JavaServer Pages (JSP) is an approach for generating dynamic web pages. JSPs contain the content display instructions from the business logic, as well as XML tags and scriplets written in Java that define how to display the web content. Compiled into servlets, they allow graphic designers to write powerful dynamic web pages.

A *servlet* is a Java program that runs in the J2EE server versus the browser on the client (applets). A servlet will get the data, convert it to an HTML format and download the HTML instructions to a browser. Though they can be written to provide the dynamic web content, JSPs are much easier to write, since servlets need to be written by a Java programmer. A JSP, on the other hand, can be written by a web designer.

The JSPs and servlets run on the platform containing the J2EE server and not the client. Servlets work based upon the request and response paradigm, while the J2EE server contains a servlet engine that provides a runtime container for executing servlets. When developers are writing JSPs and servlets, they are writing GUI components for the presentation layer.

Enterprise JavaBeans

Enterprise JavaBeans (EJBs) are portable reusable server-side components that are deployable across different platforms. The EJB component model provides support for transaction control, security, networking, database connectivity, and more. These features are configurable so an EJB can be deployed in different environments. This allows developers to focus on business logic and not the environment and infrastructure required to run the EJB. When developers are writing EJBs, they are focusing on the business logic layer.

Advantages of N-Tiered Architectures

Java environments and the n-tiered architectures in which they run are more complex than the traditional Oracle client-server architectures. So why are organizations moving to n-tiered architectures? N-tiered architectures offer the following advantages:

- It is easy to switch from one database to another.

- Costs of migrating business logic are greatly reduced.

- Reduced deployment costs.

- Better security. The business logic can reside inside of a firewall.

- Java code can be written conforming to industry standards versus a vendor's proprietary language.

- Each tier can be changed independent of the other tiers.

- Increased flexibility and scalability.

- Better reliability across multiple application services that provide load balancing and fault tolerance.

- Performance bottlenecks can be isolated to a specific tier.

- Oracle Database 10*g* can use Real Application Clusters (RAC) or grid computing to provide fault tolerance for the back-end database server platforms.

Java, XML, Web Services, and Oracle Database 10*g*

Web Services continue to play a larger and larger role in n-tiered architectures by allowing different types of platforms to communicate with each other. XML is an industry-standard markup language that makes data portable across platforms. This is very important to companies and people who are responsible for transporting data from one environment to another. Java, with its portability, is a natural choice for Web Services and XML. It has added a large number of APIs to support XML and Web Services. The Oracle Database 10*g* server contains support for Web Services, XML, and Java. Java will continue to play an integral role in the implementation of Web Services and XML with Oracle databases. Since XML, Java, and Web Services run in the Oracle Database 10*g* server, someone on the DBA team needs to understand them.

Opportunities for Oracle DBAs

Oracle Database 10*g* environments are going to open up new opportunities for those DBAs who can understand the n-tiered architectures that Oracle Database 10*g* runs in. While the database management for Oracle Database 10*g* is getting easier, the Oracle database server environments are going to increase significantly in their complexity. In the future, there is likely to be a much stronger demand for Data Infrastructure Administrators (DIAs) than Database Administrators (DBAs). A DIA is going to need to understand application servers, Internet security, XML, SOAP, Java, networking, and have a solid comprehension of n-tiered architectures. SOAP (Simple Object Access Protocol) is an XML-based lightweight protocol for exchanging data in a distributed environment. Someone in an Oracle Database 10*g* environment is going to need to understand Oracle Database 10*g* features such as Database Web Services, XML DB, and HTML DB. Figure 7-3 illustrates the many options that are available to the Oracle DBA and Java user.

We have covered a number of new topics in this section so far. Before we move on to the next section, let's do a quick progress check to make sure it all sank in. These topics and terms will allow you to join in on conversations with developers at social events.

Progress Check ⏱

1. Does the J2SE include a compiler or debugger?

2. Is the primary purpose of JSPs to implement business logic?

3. _____ is a technology that allows different types of applications to communicate over the Web.

4. True or False: Java is an industry-standard language that makes data portable across platforms.

5. True or False: One of the advantages of Oracle Database 10*g* is its capability to run J2EE applications in the server.

6. Applets run in the _____ tier.

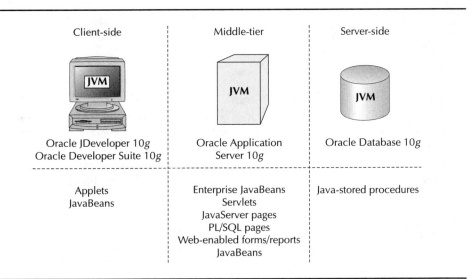

FIGURE 7-3. *The Java landscape in Oracle*

Progress Check Answers

1. True. The J2SE provides a full development environment.

2. False. The primary purpose of JSPs is to display content.

3. Web Services.

4. False. Java is a programming language that executes code. Technologies like XML, SOAP, and WSDL are involved in data transportation.

5. False. J2EE applications are not supported by the Oracle Database 10*g* server.

6. Client. Applets run in the browsers on client platforms.

CRITICAL SKILL 7.3

Configure Java for Oracle

The Oracle JVM must be configured and installed to run Java in Oracle Database 10*g*. The core Java classes, including the JDBC (Java Database Connectivity APIs) and SQLJ (embedded SQL for Java) classes are all natively compiled for performance. Once the Oracle JVM is installed, Java-stored procedures can be executed in the Oracle database, but they must be configured separately on the middle and client tiers. During the database installation, a large number of Java classes are loaded into Oracle Database 10*g*.

```
SQL>  CONNECT / AS SYSDBA
SQL> SELECT count(*)  FROM dba_objects WHERE object_type = 'JAVA CLASS';
  COUNT (*)
 ----------
      15681
```

The Oracle Database Configuration Assistant can also be used for installing the Oracle JVM option. The Oracle Net Assistant may also be needed to configure the Oracle environment based upon the network requirements.

Java classes may not load properly for multiple reasons. It is important to check for invalid classes that cannot be executed. The following code can check for invalid classes:

```
SQL> SELECT dbms_java.longname(object_name), status
     FROM   dba_objects
     WHERE  object_type = 'JAVA CLASS'
     AND    status = 'INVALID';
```

Java Initialization Parameters

The two primary initialization parameters for the Oracle JVM are **shared_pool_size** and **the java_pool_size** (default is 24MB rounded to nearest granule). **ORACLE_HOME/ javavm/initjvm.sql** is the script that must be run to configure Java in the Oracle Database 10*g*. The **initjvm.sql** script requires the **shared_pool_size** bet set to 50MB and the **java_pool_size** set to 20MB. The shared pool area uses memory during Java call specifications and tracking dynamically loaded Java classes. Java compilation takes a lot of memory. If a lot of compilation could occur due to complex Java applications, set the **java_pool_size** to 70MB and tune accordingly. Make sure the compatibility parameter is at least set to 8.1.0.

Java session space is the memory used to hold the Java state from one database call to another. The **java_max_sessionspace_size** (default is 0) initialization parameter sets the maximum amount of session space memory a Java program can hold. The range is 0 to 4GB. A user's session will be terminated if the session exceeds this memory amount. The **java_soft_sessionspace_limit** (default is 0) defines a soft limit on session space memory. If a session exceeds the soft space limit, a warning message is sent to the Oracle trace files. The range is 0 to 4GB.

Environmental Variables

The **CREATE JAVA** command exists for creating Java objects in the Oracle database. However, this is not efficient. A Java class is made up of a data structure and the interfaces that need to access and manipulate that data structure. This is an over simplification but it is similar to combining a table definition and a PL/SQL package made up of multiple functions and procedures into a single entity. These Java classes need to be created with a development tool versus being created manually in the database. It is much more efficient to use a Java client development tool to create the Java code and then load the Java classes into the Oracle database or into application servers.

The Java Development Toolkit (JDK) needs to be configured in order to create Java code on the client. SSL is the Secure Sockets Layer and provides encryption, authentication, and message integrity. It is included with all major browsers and web servers. Table 7-1 illustrates environmental variables that need to be defined.

init.ora Parameter	Description
JAVA_HOME	Primary directory for the JDK
PATH	The O.S. search path needs to include JAVA_HOME/bin
CLASS_PATH	Includes JAVA_HOME/lib/dt.jar for a Java 2 server ORACLE_HOME/jdbc/lib/classes12.zip for JDBC ORACLE_HOME/sqlj/lib/translator.zip for SQLJ ORACLE_HOME/sqlj/lib/runtime12.zip for SQLJ using a Java client ORACLE_HOME/sqlj/lib/runtime12ee.zip for SQLJ using J2EE ORACLE_HOME/jlib/jssl-1_2.jar for SSL on the client ORACLE_HOME/jlib/javax-ssl-1_2.jar for SSL on the client ORACLE_HOME/jlib/jta.jar for Java Transaction API ORACLE_HOME/jlib/jndi.jar for Java Naming and Directory Interface (JNDI) JAVA_HOME/lib/tools.jar for native compilation ORACLE_HOME/lib/aurora.zip if writing Java database server code on the client
LD_LIBRARY_PATH	ORACLE_HOME/lib to access shared libraries for the OCI driver

TABLE 7-1. *Oracle's Java Environment Variables*

Java in Oracle

The Java runtime environment contains the JVM, the Java runtime class libraries, JDBC, SQLJ, and a Java application launcher. Oracle Database 10*g* is a deployment environment, not a development environment. Java code should be created in a Java development tool such as Oracle JDeveloper 10*g*. The appropriate Java files should then be loaded into the Oracle database.

Once the Oracle JVM option is configured, Java-stored procedures can be executed using JDBC and SQLJ. The Oracle JVM also uses a PL/SQL package DBMS_JAVA. Be aware that Java names can exceed the SQL identifier length. The database allows a Java name to be up to 4000 characters in length. If a Java name (long name) exceeds the maximum SQL identifier name length, then Oracle will also create an alias (short name). The following query will display long and short names. The long names are abbreviated for display purposes.

Format the query, and display long and short names:

```
SQL> SET linesize 140
SQL> COLUMN longname FORMAT A80
SQL> SELECT * FROM javasnm;
```

The DBMS_JAVA package contains two functions that can be used to access the Java long name and the SQL short name:

- FUNCTION longname (shortname VARCHAR2) RETURN VARCHAR2

- FUNCTION shortname (longname VARCHAR2) RETURN VARCHAR2

Native Compilation

The Oracle Database 10*g* JVM enhances performance with a native Java compiler. A native Java compiler (Ahead-of-Time-Compilation) converts Java bytecodes to C code before runtime. This significantly improves the performance of Java code and allows it to achieve the performance benefits of C compilers. The core Java class libraries and JDBC code are natively compiled in Oracle Database 10*g*.

The Oracle JVM is integrated into the shared memory of the database. Java programs will run in the Oracle kernel for maximum performance, and may require access to multiple Java classes. Each of these classes must be loaded at runtime. Since they use the shared memory architecture, once they are loaded they can be executed by other sessions. Each session runs as if it had its own JVM, but each loaded Java class can be shared by other sessions.

Garbage Collection

The Oracle JVM will clean up Java memory automatically. This is called garbage collection. Java is a systems language and can access operating system resources if permissions are granted. Garbage collection will clean up Java objects automatically but not operating system resources. Java programmers have to make sure to clean up operating system resources themselves.

Things to Watch Out For

Java supports multithreading in the JVM. For a number of reasons, try to avoid multithreading in Java in the Oracle database server. The Oracle database has a higher degree of scalability and efficiency if multithreading is required to use the Oracle database versus the Oracle JVM. Be careful when using the shared server architecture and Java inside of the database. A session may not use the same process for following database calls. This can create issues if a Java program inside of Oracle is hanging onto operating system resources across different server processes with the shared server architecture (the shared server is defined in Chapter 4). There can also be performance issues in some situations. For example, static object information is migrated into session space at the end of a call. This migration can impact performance. Minimize this by cleaning up resources at the end of a call whenever possible.

Main Components of the JVM

The Oracle JVM contains a number of components, including the following:

- **Compiler**   Java 2 compiler.
- **Interpreter**   Interprets Java code. Java code in the Oracle JVM can also be natively compiled.
- **Library Manager**   Loads Java source, class, and resource files into the database.
- **Class Loader**   During runtime, finds the Java class, and loads and initializes Java classes for the Oracle JVM.
- **Verifier**   Works with Oracle and Java security to validate Java classes.
- **Server-Side JDBC Internal Driver**   Java driver in the Oracle database supporting Java database calls.
- **Server-Side SQLJ Translator**   Translates SQLJ code into JDBC code.

JDBC Drivers

Java DataBase Connectivity (JDBC) is a set of APIs that provide SQL capability for Java. JDBC is an industry-standard set of APIs for database access. There is one industry standard of APIs for JDBC. Each database vendor provides additional vendor-specific JDBC drivers that support database specific functionality. Oracle supports three different types of JDBC drivers.

JDBC Thin Driver

A JDBC thin driver is a driver written completely in Java. It is referred to as a thin driver because it does not require additional vendor-specific networking code. A JDBC thin driver is dynamically loaded at runtime. A thin driver, which uses TCP/IP, works well with standalone applications and firewalls within an intranet. Oracle networking software is not required on the client with a thin driver.

JDBC Thick Driver

A JDBC thick (OCI) driver requires additional vendor networking software. Oracle Net Services must be installed on the client or middle tier to use the JDBC thick driver. Oracle Net Services software uses the JDBC Oracle Call Interface (OCI) to access the Oracle database. Do not use the thick driver with applets. Java code using the JDBC thick driver can leverage the feature/functionality of Oracle Net Services such as connection pooling. The thick driver requires additional resources but performs better than the thin driver.

JDBC Server-Side Driver

A Java program that runs in the Oracle database server uses a server-side (KPRB) driver. This allows these server-side Java programs to access Oracle data directly without having to go through the network. With these programs running in the Oracle kernel space, this can offer a significant performance gain for data-intensive algorithms.

Use the Proper JDBC Driver

The type of JDBC driver to use is defined during database connection. Java applications that are running on a client can use a thin or thick driver. Thick drivers are used on the middle tier for application servers. Server-side drivers can only be used inside of the Oracle database. When a Java program tries to connect to the Oracle server, the JDBC driver needs to be specified. The following examples use a thin and OCI driver, respectively:

```
Oracle.connect("jdbc:oracle:thin:@hostname:portnumber:sid","username","password");
Oracle.connect("jdbc:oracle:oci:@hostname:portnumber:sid","username","password");
```

Java-stored procedures run inside of the Oracle kernel memory. To run a Java-stored procedure, a session must already be established. The connection inside a Java-stored procedure specifies to use the existing session similar to how a PL/SQL program runs inside of a current session. The following example tells the Java program to use the current session. A connection cannot be closed inside of a Java-stored procedure.

```
DriverManager.getConnection("jdbc:default:connection:").
```

A **getProperty** method exists to determine if the Java program is running in the Oracle database server. A method in a Java class is an interface to the data in the class. The method will return a string that contains the Oracle Database 10g release, or it will return a null value.

```
System.getProperty("oracle.jserver.version");
```

CRITICAL SKILL 7.6

Use JDBC

JDBC is based upon an industry standard. Java packages are a method of organizing related Java classes. They are different than PL/SQL packages. JDBC contains two types of packages. The standard JDBC packages work with different database vendors. Vendor-specific packages address vendor-specific functionality. Oracle provides an additional set of packages for JDBC that support Oracle specific features. To use JDBC, at least the standard JDBC packages need to be accessible within your program. An import statement defines where Java can find packages. Additional Oracle packages can be used to leverage Oracle data types (oracle.sql) and Oracle specific (oracle.jdbc) database features.

```
import java.sql.*;
import oracle.sql.*;
import oracle.jdbc.*;
```

How to Write Database Programs

When writing PL/SQL programs to access the database, there is a standard set of steps a PL/SQL programmer takes:

1. Defining a cursor.

2. Opening a cursor.

3. Fetching from the cursor.

4. Checking for end of data.

5. Closing the cursor.

When writing Java database programs, a similar set of steps need to be performed:

1. Registering a driver.

2. Connecting to a database.

3. Executing a statement.

4. Fetching data. (The check for end of data is done during the fetch.)

5. Closing the resources.

Project 7-1   Accessing the Database with Java

JDBC is required for accessing databases from within Java. In this project, you will walk through the necessary JDBC steps for performing a simple query.

Step by Step

1. The first step in connecting to a database requires registering a driver. Oracle offers two different ways of registering a driver:

```
Class.forName("oracle.jdbc.OracleDriver");
DriverManager.registerDriver(new oracle.jdbc.OracleDriver());
```

2. Once a driver is registered, a connection needs to be made. Oracle data sources can be used to connect to a database, but data sources are more appropriately covered in a Java programming course. When connecting from outside, the database connection information is required.

```
Connection conn = DriverManager.getConnection(
    "jdbc:oracle:thin:@hostname:portnumber:sid",
    "username", "password");
```

3. Now it's time to create the statement that will be run. This step takes you through the definition and execution of the SQL statement using Java. We include additional JDBC statements to execute statements. Statements that return records use result sets to process those records. You also need to keep in mind that variables that you have defined are compatible with your Oracle data. Now let's type in the commands that will define your

statement variable and use your previous connection. Then we will send the results of our SQL query into a result set variable, ready for use.

```
Statement   s = conn.createStatement();
ResultSet rs = s.executeQuery("SELECT empno, ename FROM scott.emp");
int   empno = 0;
String name = null;
```

4. Once the data is stored in a result set, it needs to be fetched in a fashion similar to a PL/SQL program. The next () method fetches a single record. A Boolean value of true is returned if a record is fetched.

```
while (rs.next()) {
   empno = rs.getInt("empno");
   name  = rs.getString("ename");
   System.out.println("The employee number is " + empno);
   System.out.println("The employee name  is   " +  name);
}
```

5. In PL/SQL, the programmer needs to eventually close a cursor and terminate the resources acquired to access the data. Java is no different.

```
rs.close();
s.close();
conn.close();
```

Project Summary

The steps in this project reinforce the standard steps necessary to perform a **select** operation from within Java.

CRITICAL SKILL **7.7**

Use SQLJ

SQLJ allows programmers to embed SQL statements directly into Java programs. Experienced Oracle programmers have worked with other embedded SQL environments like Pro*C, Pro*Fortran, and Pro*Cobol. Embedded SQL in Java is named SQLJ, not Pro*Java, because SQLJ is an industry standard and not an Oracle-specific product.

SQLJ Translator

Embedding SQL statements directly into a programming language reduces maintenance and makes it much easier to write Java database programs. A SQLJ translator (precompiler) is used to convert a .sqlj file containing embedded SQL statements into a .java file containing JDBC statements. The translated .java file is then compiled. SQLJ statements can contain queries, DML, transaction control, and DDL statements. The SQLJ translator in the database will automatically convert .sqlj files into compiled Java code.

Sample SQLJ Code

SQLJ makes it easier for traditional Oracle developers to write Java database code. Oracle developers can embed the SQL statements without having to work with all of the JDBC interfaces. SQLJ performs compile time checking of SQL statements while JDBC performs runtime checking of SQL statements. The following code snippets are some examples of using SQLJ.

```
String name;
int  empid = 7788;
…
  #sql {SELECT ename INTO :name FROM emp  WHERE empno=:empid};
  #sql {INSERT INTO emp (empno, ename, sal, deptno)
     VALUES (8888, 'TRUJILLO', 2400, 10);
  #sql {CREATE TABLE mytemp (id NUMBER, name VARCHAR2(20)) };
  #sql { UPDATE emp SET salary = salary * 1.10  WHERE id = :empid };
  #sql { DELETE FROM customer  WHERE id = :custid };
…
```

SQLJ Directions

SQLJ offers a number of advantages over JDBC. However, there are a number of performance benefits of writing the lower-level JDBC statements directly. SQLJ has been deprecated in the Oracle Database 10*g* server. SQLJ applications running in the database server will continue to work in Oracle Database 10*g*. In a future release, Oracle will provide a migration tool and options with existing Oracle tools to ease the migration to pure JDBC.

CRITICAL SKILL 7.8

Java-Stored Procedures

With the inclusion of Java within the database, Oracle wanted to have Java-similar support features that current Oracle users were used to, and one such area is stored procedures. As discussed in Chapter 6, storing objects with PL/SQL or Java has numerous advantages. The ability to call shared programs whether written in PL/SQL or Java is a strength of Oracle Database 10*g*.

Java Utilities for DBAs

Three Java utilities are available in Oracle Database 10*g*:

- loadjava is used to load Java classes and resources into the schemas of an Oracle database.

- dropjava is used to drop Java classes and resources that were installed with loadjava.

- ojvmjava provides an interface to an Oracle instance. It allows an interface similar to a UNIX shell program. Ojvmjava supports the direct execution of Java applications inside of Oracle from a UNIX-like shell prompt.

loadjava and dropjava Examples

Load a Java-compiled program from a Windows prompt:

```
C:\> loadjava -user scott/tiger@orcl MyFirstProgram.class
```

Drop the Java file loaded with the loadjava utility:

```
C:\> dropjava -user scott/tiger@orcl MyFirstProgram.class
```

ojvmjava Examples

Compile a Java application from a UNIX prompt. This generates a HelloWorld.class file:

```
$ javac  HelloWorld.java
```

Load a Java program (HelloWorld.class) from a UNIX prompt. ORCL is a database connect string:

```
$ loadjava -r -user scott/tiger@orcl
```

Start up a command-line interface to an Oracle instance from a UNIX prompt:

```
$ ojvmjava -user scott -password tiger - database orcl
```

Run the Java program from within the ojvmjava interface. This runs the Java code inside of the Oracle database server.

```
$ java   HelloWorld
  MyFirstProgram  yea
```

Privileges

To load Java classes, the **create procedure** and **create table** minimum privileges are required. Java classes are schema objects just like PL/SQL procedures or tables. Java files are stored in Java ARchive (JAR) files. A JAR file is a specialized type of Zip file. The following related Java files can be found in a JAR file: .java, .class, .properties, .sqlj, or .ser files.

Java classes can be loaded or created individually, or the loadjava tool can be used. The loadjava utility is similar to the SQL*Loader tool. loadjava loads Java files while SQL*Loader loads data. By default, Java-stored procedures run under invoker's rights.

Resolver Specifications

Programs often need to access additional programs. Typically, a search path is defined where the programs should look for additional files. Operating systems organize files in directories, while Oracle organizes database objects in schema. A Java class, on the other hand, is loaded into a schema. If a Java class needs additional classes, a search path needs to be defined. To do this, a resolver specification (spec) can be used, which defines where additional classes can be found. In other words, a resolver spec is a search path in Oracle of schemas to find Java classes.

The default resolver will automatically look in the current schema and then in PUBLIC, which is where the core Java class libraries are located. Resolvers can also be defined to specify additional schemas.

Project 7-2   Creating a Java-Stored Procedure

This project will take a DBA through the basic steps of creating a Java-stored procedure. Java programs can have a main () method. This is an entry point for a Java application. Java-stored procedures will be initiated from another application so they do not need a main () method.

Step by Step

1. Create a simple class named **MyFirstProgram.java**:

```
public class MyFirstProgram


    public static  String returnString()
    {
        return  "MyFirstProgram  yea";
    }
}
```

2. A Java JDK can be downloaded for compiling (www.javasoft.com). In this example, the Oracle environment was used to perform the simple compilation. Include the Java tools in the search path and verify the Java version.

```
C:\> SET PATH=%PATH%;C:\oracle\ora10\jdk\bin
C:\> java -version
C:\>
```

3. Compile the Java program. After compiling, verify that there is a class file.

```
C:\> javac MyFirstProgram.java
```

4. If using a default account, make sure it is not locked. Use the loadjava utility to load the Java class into the database. Then verify the class was properly loaded. To drop a Java program that is loaded, use the dropjava utility.

```
C:\> loadjava -user scott/tiger MyFirstProgram.class
C:\> dropjava -user scott/tiger MyFirstProgram.class
```

5. Publish a Java-stored procedure using a call specification:

```
SQL> connect scott/tiger
SQL> CREATE OR REPLACE FUNCTION displaystring RETURN varchar2 AS
       LANGUAGE  JAVA NAME
        'MyFirstProgram.returnString () return java.lang.String';
```

6. Test the Java-stored procedure:

```
SQL> VARIABLE myvalue VARCHAR2(50)
SQL> EXECUTE :myvalue := displaystring;
SQL> SET SERVEROUTPUT ON
SQL> PRINT myvalue
MYVALUE
-----------------------------------------------------------------
My First Program  Yea!
SQL>
```

7. View the status of the new database objects:

```
SQL> SELECT object_name, object_type, status
     FROM user_objects
     WHERE object_type = 'JAVA%' OR object_name = 'DISPLAYSTRING';

OBJECT_NAME                          OBJECT_TYPE       STATUS
-----------------------------------  ----------------  -------
MyFirstProgram                       JAVA CLASS        VALID
DISPLAYSTRING                        FUNCTION          VALID
SQL>
```

(continued)

Project Summary

This project walked you through the steps a DBA will take to create and test a Java-stored procedure.

Create Java Objects in Oracle

loadjava is one way of creating Java classes in the database. It is a preferred method since it can leverage Java development environments and then load the generated Java class and JAR files. The DDL statements described in the following sections can also be used to create Java classes or related files.

create java class

The **create java class** command can be used to load a Java class file from the operating system. An Oracle directory object must be created so the class file can be found on the operating system. The following statement can be used to load an individual Java class into Oracle:

```
SQL> CREATE JAVA CLASS
        USING BFILE (java_dir, 'MyFirstProgram.class');
```

create java source

The **create java source** command can be used to create a Java class file from within Oracle. Although this simple example works, Java classes can be hundreds of lines long. The following statement will create a Java class:

```
SQL> CREATE JAVA SOURCE NAMED "MyFirstProgram" AS
public class MyFirstProgram
{
    public static  String returnString()
    {
        return  "MyFirstProgram  yea";
    }
};
/
```

create java resource

The **create java resource** command can be used to create Java resource files needed by Java classes. The following statement will create a Java resource file:

```
SQL> CREATE JAVA RESOURCE NAMED  "myData"
        USING BFILE (java_dir, 'MyData.dat');
      }
```

CRITICAL SKILL 7.10

Understand Oracle Java Products

Oracle Database 10*g* expands the Oracle database server to provide stronger support for industry standards, J2EE applications, Web Services, XML, and multitiered architectures. All of these technical areas are leveraged by the Java programming language. The following list includes the primary Oracle products that use or support Java features:

- Oracle Database 10*g*

- Oracle Application Server 10*g*

- Oracle JDeveloper 10*g*

- Oracle Developer Suite 10*g*

- JPublisher

- loadjava, dropjava, and ojvmjava

As Java increases its role in Oracle environments, there is going to be a stronger need for DBAs that can support these products. Oracle has had a very strong presence with its database server. In Oracle Database 10*g*, Oracle also offers a strong solution in the middle tier and database development environment with the Oracle Application Server 10*g* and Oracle JDeveloper 10*g*.

Oracle Application Server 10*g*

Oracle Application Server 10*g* has evolved to become a powerful enterprise application server in this release and will play a large role in Oracle Database 10*g* environments. Organizations looking at implementing multitiered architectures and grid computing are going to need to strongly consider the Oracle Application Server 10*g*.

Oracle JDeveloper 10*g*

Oracle JDeveloper 10*g* is a robust enterprise development tool supporting the full development life cycle. Most of the people who will need to learn Java for Oracle JDeveloper 10*g* are DBAs and developers who understand PL/SQL and client/server development tools like Oracle Forms, PowerBuilder, and Visual Basic. Oracle JDeveloper 10*g* contains numerous wizards and simple interfaces that allow people new to Java to be able to quickly write Java applications. Just as important is the understanding that Oracle JDeveloper 10*g* can be a database development tool for SQL, PL/SQL, and XML as well as Java. This tool has evolved into a database development tool, not just a Java development tool. The features of Oracle JDeveloper 10*g* include the following:

- SQL, PL/SQL, XML, Web Services, HTML, and Java development
- Schema modeling
- SQL tuning
- PL/SQL and Java debugging
- OO modeling
- Oracle Application Development Framework (ADF)
- J2EE framework
- Open Source Integration with Apache Ant, JUnit, CVS, Struts, Tomcat, and Linux
- Code analysis

Ask the Expert

Q: This chapter highlights the importance of Java, but how does a DBA get up to speed in Java? Also, as a DBA I want to be able to support Java but not write detailed Java code.

A: Java is a very powerful and in-depth language whose details can take quite a while to understand. Therefore, DBAs need a tool that can allow them to bridge the gap between DBA administration and being able to build basic Java applications to test configurations, and so on. Oracle JDeveloper 10*g* is a tool designed to support the development of complex Java applications with simple point-and-click operations. For example, DBAs can publish a PL/SQL package with a Web Service interface through simple point-and-click operations. Manually, this would be very complex and require a lot of knowledge and experience in Java. With Oracle JDeveloper 10*g*, a DBA can build a Web Service interface in a few minutes. This makes it easier for DBAs to support Java without having to write detailed low-level code.

☑ Chapter 7 Mastery Check

1. True or False: One of the benefits of EJBs is that they combine business and user interface logic.

2. True or False: A benefit of the Oracle JVM is Java's multithreading capability in the database.

3. The _____ JDBC driver is used inside of the database.

4. A _____ can define where additional classes can be found.

5. The _____ command is used to create a Java class file from within Oracle.

6. True or False: SQLJ is the direction Oracle is going in when it comes to writing Java-stored procedures since it's easier to maintain than JDBC.

7. The _____ loads Java source, class, and resource files into the database.

8. When writing JDBC, _____ is the first step to be performed.

9. True or False: The SQLJ translator converts embedded SQL statements into JDBC code.

10. The _____ script is used to configure the Oracle JVM.

CHAPTER
8
XML

CRITICAL SKILLS

8.1 Understand XML

8.2 Oracle XML DB: Use XML
in the Database

8.3 SQLX: Create XML from Data
Stored in Oracle

8.4 Store XML in Oracle XML DB

8.5 Use Simple Queries

8.6 Create a Relational View from XML

8.7 Learn Programmatic Access
Using XSLT

efore we begin to see how Extensible Markup Language (XML) and Oracle Database 10*g* work together, we need to look at why XML is important for us and why Oracle has included significant support for XML in the Oracle XML DB. This chapter will discuss what XML is and why it is important to our computer futures. Additionally, we will show you how Oracle can become an integral part of all of your solutions that need to use XML.

Understand XML

Most of you have visited countless web sites, have navigated to the menu bar at the top of a browser screen, and then selected View | Source. At this point, guess what you are looking at—html or *hypertext markup language.* As html became more and more popular, the most brilliant minds decided to extend the power of the language. They were specifically interested in designing a way to enhance HTML's functionality with a set of user-defined tags. A *tag* is simply a keyword bound by greater-than signs, less-than signs, and a specially placed forward slash. The following listing shows a few sample tags in html; the tags themselves are bolded.

```
<h1>Welcome to my level one header</h1>
<b>I like to bold text too, do you</b>
<font color=green size=+2>I am big and green</font>
```

That's all fine and dandy, but in a nutshell, XML allows you to extend the functionality of tags. Suppose you were coding a page for a real estate application and you wanted to custom-define your own tags to resemble the following:

```
<ground_floor>Family room . . .
. . . with wood-burning . . .
. . .
</ground_floor>
```

No big deal when you look at these primitive examples, but take our word for it—XML is a big deal. A markup language, of which HTML and XML are two, is a mechanism to identify structures in a document. Markup is also a term for metadata—that is, information about information. In short, an XML document can be defined as a document that can describe itself. Mature database products, of which Oracle Database 10*g* is the subject at hand, have the capability to store XML data types.

> **NOTE**
> *As you may have noticed, we have glossed over the discussion of XML—it is a very big topic demanding its own phone book–sized volume. We will attend to Oracle XML DB specifics in the rest of this chapter, and leave you to discover the big picture of XML on your own.*

CRITICAL SKILL 8.2

Oracle XML DB: Use XML in the Database

XML is quickly being adopted as the data transport mechanism on the information highway—it is a W3C-endorsed standard markup language for documents. *W3C* stands for World Wide Web Consortium, an organization of approximately 400 members. They represent both public and private sectors, whose goal is to develop interoperable technologies (specifications, guidelines, software, and tools) for the World Wide Web. The following is an example XML document, leveraging the power of custom tags:

```
<?xml version="1.0"?>
<book isbn="0078822424" >
  <publisher>"OsborneMcGraw-Hill"</publisher>
  <title>Oracle Data Warehousing: The Practical Guide to Building a Data Warehouse</title>
  <author>Michael Abbey</author>
  <author>Michael Corey</author>
  <book_image href="0078822424.gif"/>
  <print>paperback</print>
  <instock>yes</instock>
  <price>55.95</price>
</book>
```

The first line in the preceding code specifies that it is an XML document. The rest of the document is a text format whose hierarchical structure and metadata is specified by tags between brackets and its data enclosed within the tags. There are three primary uses of XML:

- **Exchanges information** As stated earlier, XML is widely used as a mechanism for the transport of information, and is generated from a database, document, or from web content in a file system.

- **Offers a storage format** XML's format meets the requirements for long-lived or structurally rigorous document-centric information. It is the introduction of XML Schema, another W3C standard that expanded the scope of XML from interchange to modeling and storage. The purpose of an XML Schema is to define the legal building blocks of an XML document. It includes the valid tag-sets, the constraints placed on XML elements, and some specifications for the characteristics of the data.

■ **Enables styling and presentation**   XML has the capability to output the same information on multiple output devices and/or for different purposes and audiences.

As stated earlier, XML is mostly used as a transport mechanism for the information highway and is generated normally from a database or file system. It is this application that has caused the volume of XML documents to grow exponentially. However, ask different developers about how to work with a large collection of XML documents and you will get different answers. Storing, retrieving, and managing large collections of XML documents has typically been an art rather than a science.

Enter Oracle XML DB, an integrated set of information management capabilities within Oracle Database 10*g* for managing XML documents. It provides storage for two main document types:

■ **Data-centric documents**   These use XML as a data transport. Examples of data-centric documents are sales orders, flight schedules, and stock quotes. These documents are characterized by fairly regular structure, fine-grained data, and little or no mixed content.

■ **Document-centric documents**   This type is characterized by an irregular structure, larger-grained data, and lots of mixed content. Document-centric is meant to be human readable. Examples are books, e-mail, and web pages.

The distinction between data-centric and document-centric documents is not always clear, however. For example, an otherwise data-centric document, such as an invoice, might contain large-grained, irregularly structured data, such as a sales item description. An otherwise document-centric document, such as a technical manual, might contain fine-grained, regularly structured data such as an author's name and a revision date. In spite of this, characterizing your documents as data-centric or document-centric will help you decide where within Oracle Database 10*g* you want to manage XML documents.

Oracle XML DB also provides complete transparency and interchangeability between XML and SQL, allowing you to perform both XML operations and SQL operations on XML documents. This means that XML-savvy developers work using all their natural conventions and tools, yet transparently store and retrieve their XML documents in an Oracle Database 10*g*. Conversely, from a database perspective, DBAs can work with XML using the same performance and manageability characteristics that they already enjoy with relational data. With Oracle XML DB, you get all the advantages of both relational database technology and XML technology simultaneously.

Of course, before Oracle Database 10*g* looked to resolve the storage and management of XML documents, it too had to find a way to transport relational data stored along the information highway. Again, this data needed to be in a nonpersistent, self-describing, and nonproprietary way—Oracle Database 10*g* had to create XML documents from relational data.

Ask the Expert

Q: What is the major difference between an HTML document and an XML document?

A: An HTML document has predefined tags used mostly for presentation of text, while XML clearly addresses the structure of the data stored within, defining its own tag set.

Q: What is document-centric data?

A: Document-centric data is data that is considered readable by humans. An example would be a web page or e-mail.

Q: What is data-centric data?

A: Data-centric data is data that is structured, fine-grained (defined to its data type), with little or no mixed content.

Q: What are the primary uses of XML?

A: XML's primary uses are as follows:

- It exchanges information regardless of platform.

- It's used as a storage format.

- It separates content from the presentation and styling of the same information on multiple platforms.

SQLX: Create XML from Data Stored in Oracle

For years, organizations have been pouring their data into relational databases. If you're trading data with another organization, however, it's likely that you'll need to pull data out of your relational database and format that data as XML before transmitting it.

Let's first point out that generating XML from a relational source is a not a trivial task. It involves understanding how to map relational data into a hierarchal structure. On the other hand, creating the XML once you understand the mapping you want has been made easy.

The SQL/XML Standard

Oracle Database 10*g* implements a number of standards-based functions enabling you to query relational data and return XML documents. These functions collectively fall under the heading of SQL/XML, sometimes referred to as SQLX. SQL/XML is part of the ANSI/ISO SQL standard.

The international standard for SQL/XML defines the following elements:

- **XML**   A data type to hold XML data

- **XMLAgg**   A function to group, or aggregate, XML data in **group by** queries

- **XMLAttributes**   A function used to place attributes in XML elements returned by SQL queries

- **XMLConcat**   A function to concatenate two or more XML values

- **XMLElement**   A function to transform a relational value into an XML element, in the form: *<elementName>value</elementName>*

- **XMLForest**   A function to generate a list, called a "forest," of XML elements from a list of relational values

- **XMLNamespaces**   A function to declare namespaces in an XML element

- **XMLSerialize**   A function to serialize an XML value as a character string

Oracle Database 10*g* has implemented the following XML data type (as XMLType), XMLAgg, XMLConcat, XMLElement, and XMLForest. Support for the other functions is planned in future releases. In addition to the functions and the data type, the SQL/XML standard defines rules for transforming column names into XML element names and for transforming SQL data types into XML data types. These rules are applied automatically by XMLElement and the other SQL/XML functions. Let's look at four of many SQLX functions that are commonly used to produce XML from the relational database.

xmlelement()

The **xmlelement()** function is one of the most important SQLX functions to understand, because creating XML elements is the fundamental reason for SQLX's existence. Since every XML document starts with a root element, this function is always called first. It takes as parameters the element name, an optional **xmlattributes()** call, and other **xmlelement()** or SQLX functions calls, which make up the children of the element. It's important to understand that the **xmlelement()** function returns an XMLType value, not a character string value.

xmlattributes()

Within every XML element there may be defined an attribute. **xmlattibutes()** is used to create attributes inside an **xmlelement()**.

xmlforest()

The word *forest* means "a collection of trees," or in the case of XML, nodes. A fitting name—since the **xmlforest()** function allows you to pass 1 to *n* values making up a collection of child elements under an **xmlelement()** call. **xmlforest()** uses the name of the column as the name of the XML element, unless otherwise specified in an optional **as** clause, and uses the value of the SQL value expression as the content of the XML element.

NOTE
*The disadvantage of using **xmlforest()** is that you cannot specify element attributes. If you need to specify attributes for an element, you must use **xmlelement()** in conjunction with **xmlattibutes()**.*

Now, let's take a look at these SQLX functions in action by generating an XMLType that has a list of products belonging to the electronics product category and their list price. The following listing shows the PRODUCTS table currently in our database. Following it, in Figure 8-1, is a proposed hierarchy we want to produce for our XML.

```
SQL> desc products
 Name                          Null?    Type
 ----------------------------- -------- ----------------------------
 PROD_ID                       NOT NULL NUMBER(6)
 PROD_NAME                     NOT NULL VARCHAR2(50)
 PROD_DESC                     NOT NULL VARCHAR2(4000)
 PROD_SUBCATEGORY              NOT NULL VARCHAR2(50)
 PROD_SUBCATEGORY_ID           NOT NULL NUMBER
```

```
PROD_SUBCATEGORY_DESC       NOT NULL VARCHAR2(2000)
PROD_CATEGORY               NOT NULL VARCHAR2(50)
PROD_CATEGORY_ID            NOT NULL NUMBER
PROD_CATEGORY_DESC          NOT NULL VARCHAR2(2000)
PROD_WEIGHT_CLASS           NOT NULL NUMBER(3)
PROD_UNIT_OF_MEASURE                 VARCHAR2(20)
PROD_PACK_SIZE              NOT NULL VARCHAR2(30)
SUPPLIER_ID                 NOT NULL NUMBER(6)
PROD_STATUS                 NOT NULL VARCHAR2(20)
PROD_LIST_PRICE             NOT NULL NUMBER(8,2)
PROD_MIN_PRICE              NOT NULL NUMBER(8,2)
PROD_TOTAL                  NOT NULL VARCHAR2(13)
PROD_TOTAL_ID               NOT NULL NUMBER
PROD_SRC_ID                          NUMBER
PROD_EFF_FROM                        DATE
PROD_EFF_TO                          DATE
PROD_VALID                           VARCHAR2(1)
```

The following listing shows the SQLX functions: **xmlelement()**, **xmlattibutes()**, and **xmlforest()** that we will use to create our XML document to reflect the hierarchy shown in Figure 8-1.

```
1- select xmlelement( "Product",
2-          xmlattributes(p.prod_id,p.prod_name as "Name"),
3-          xmlforest(p.prod_category as "Category",
4-          p.prod_list_price as "List_price"))
5-    from products p
6-    where p.prod_category_id =  201;
```

Table 8-1 highlights the important points of this simple query.
The following is the expected result (partial) of our SQLX query:

```
<Product PROD_ID="16" name="Y Box">
 <category>Electronics</category>
 <list_price>299.99</list_price>
</Product>
```

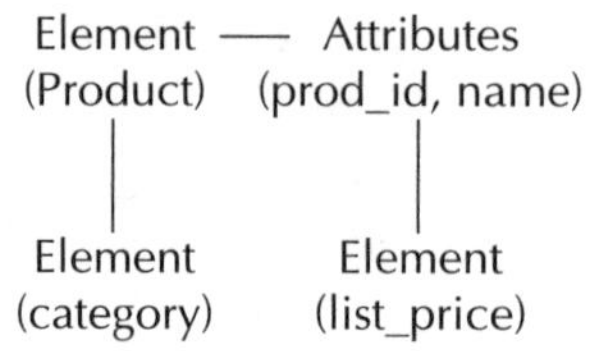

FIGURE 8-1.   *Product list hierarchy*

```
<Product PROD_ID="20" name="Home Theatre Package with DVD-Audio/Video Play">
 <category>Electronics</category>
 <list_price>599.99</list_price>
</Product>

<Product PROD_ID="29" name="8.3 Minitower Speaker">
 <category>Electronics</category>
 <list_price>499.99</list_price>
</Product>
  .   .   .
  .   .   .
```

This listing is a snippet of the full results, giving you a flavor of what the code looks like. Now let's look at **xmlagg()**.

xmlagg()

The previous query produces a separate XML document for each product. In many cases, there is a requirement such as to collect all the products for a product category together and transmit them in one document. You can do that by using the **xmlagg()** function in conjunction with a **group by** construct. **xmlagg()** is an aggregate function,

Line	Important Points
1	As stated earlier, the first **xmlelement()** function call creates the root element. In this case, the name of the root element is called "Product".
2	**xmlattibutes()** may be used only as an argument of **xmlelement()**. In this query, there are two attributes defined: **prod_id** and **name**. The first attribute name defaults with the column name **p.prod_id** (when the column name is used as the default, it will be defined in uppercase). The second attribute includes an **as** clause, which is used to name the attribute **"NAME"**.
3	**xmlforest()** produces a forest of XML elements from the given list of arguments. The arguments may be string expressions with optional aliases. Again if the **as** clause is omitted, the column name is used to name the XML element. The element names defined here are **category** and **price_list**.
4	The selection of data is being made against the PRODUCTS table.
5	We are constraining the query to obtain only the PRODUCTS rows whose **prod_category_id** = 201 (Electronics).

TABLE 8-1.   *Important Points about the SQLX Query*

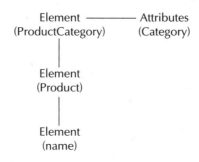

FIGURE 8-2. *Enhanced product category hierarchy*

just like **min**, **max**, and **avg**. The key to using it is to group your data on some common value. Figure 8-2 shows an enhanced product hierarchy.

The following listing demonstrates the use of **xmlagg()**:

```
1- select xmlelement( "Prodcategory",
2-              xmlattributes(p.prod_category as "Category"),
3-              xmlagg(xmlelement("Product",
4-                     xmlforest(p.prod_name as "Name"))))
5-  from products p
6-  group by p.prod_category
```

Table 8-2 discusses this listing.

Line	Important Points
1	**xmlelement()** takes an element name for identifier, in this case **"ProdCategory"**.
2	In this query, there is one attribute defined: **"Category"**.
3	The query groups data by **product_category**. The **xmlagg()** function then takes all the individual *<product>* elements for a given **product_category** from the list produced by **xmlforest()**, concatenates them together, and returns them as a single **xmltype()** value. That value then feeds into a new, enclosing **xmlelement()** function call that generates the *<category>* element.
4	The selection of data is being made against the PRODUCTS table.
5	Data is grouped by **product_category**.

TABLE 8-2. *More Points about the SQLX Query*

The following is the expected result (partial) of our SQL query:

```
<ProdCategory category="Electronics">
 <product>
  <name>Y Box</name>
 </product>
 <product>
  <name>Home Theatre Package with DVD-Audio/Video Play</name>
 </product>
...
</ProdCategory>
<ProdCategory category="Hardware">
 <product>
   <name>Envoy 256MB - 40GB</name>
 </product>
 <product>
  <name>Envoy Ambassador</name>
 </product>
</product>
```

Now, wasn't that fun? The best way to see how SQLX works is to try it yourself—meaning it's time for our first project!

Project 8-1   Creating an XML Listing

In this project, we will be creating an XML listing using a SQL query.

Step by Step

1. Log into SQL*Plus with the username/password **sh/sh**.

2. At the SQL> prompt, enter the long command, **set long 10000**, and then press ENTER.

3. At the SQL> prompt, enter the long command, **set pagesize 80**, and then press ENTER.

4. Enter the following SQL query (when you press ENTER at the end of the first line, Oracle Database 10g places the number **2>** there, and so on, each time you start a new line):

```
SQL> select xmlelement( "Country",
  2         xmlattributes(c.country_region as "Region"),
  3         xmlagg(xmlelement("Country",
  4                  xmlforest(c.country_name as "Name"))))
  5  from countries c
  6  where c.country_region_id = 52801
  7  group by c.country_region
```

(continued)

5. After entering the **c.country.region** text, you would have pressed ENTER by itself, bringing back the SQL prompt shown next. When you see the following on your screen, key the forward slash (/) character as shown in the next listing, to produce the output listed thereafter:

```
SQL> /
XMLELEMENT("COUNTRY",XMLATTRIBUTES(C.COUNTRY_REGIONAS"REGION"),XMLAGG(XMLELEMENT
--------------------------------------------------------------------------------
<Country region="Americas"><country><name>United States of America</name></count
ry><country><name>Brazil</name></country><country><name>Argentina</name></countr
y><country><name>Canada</name></country></Country>
```

6. Let's improve the appearance by making it easier to read, as shown here:

```
<Country region="Americas">
 <country>
    <name>United States of America</name>
 </country>
 <country>
    <name>Brazil</name>
 </country>
 <country>
    <name>Argentina</name>
 </country>
 <country>
    <name>Canada</name>
 </country>
</Country>
```

Project Summary

This project has in no way shown the reader the full power of the SQLX operations Oracle Database 10*g* has implemented for XML document creation. Another point to make is that to become fluent in the creation of XML using the relational information stored within the Oracle Database 10*g*, one must have a firm understanding of XML, specifically the nature of the hierarchical structure it is based upon. To be able to plainly go from relational to hierarchical will take some time.

With the generation of XML under our belt, we are ready to continue. Next, we will look at moving XML itself into the database.

Progress Check

1. XML is said to represent the data within the document in a hierarchical data structure. What is the definition of a hierarchical data structure?

2. Which SQLX function creates the **root** element within an XML type?

3. When can the **xmlattributes()** function be called?

4. What corresponding SQL clause must accompany an **xmlagg()** function?

CRITICAL SKILL 8.4

Store XML in Oracle XML DB

Databases are relational and XML is hierarchical, so prior to the introduction of Oracle XML DB there had been no simple, elegant way to integrate the two. Traditionally, developers have had two choices: either use a parser to deconstruct the document data into relational data and store it as such in the database, or store the entire document as a text file, preserving its text-based structure. Oracle XML DB starts it all off by first solving the problem of representing an XML document in its native format—the XMLType.

The Native XMLType

The XMLType was created to be able to preserve the XML paradigm while getting the benefits of relational performance and scalability. It is a native server data type that allows the database to understand that a column or table contains XML—in the same way that the DATE data type allows the database to understand that a column contains a date. The twist is that the XMLType also provides methods that allow common operations such as schema validation and XSL transformations to be performed on XML content.

The XMLType data type can be used just like any other data type, such as when creating a column in a relational table, when declaring PL/SQL variables, and when defining and calling PL/SQL procedures and functions. Since XMLType is an object type, it is also possible to create a table of XMLType. The following listing shows how to create a simple table with an XMLType column:

```
SQL> create table purchase_order
  2  (
  3  po_no number(9),
  4  po_file xmltype
  5  )
```

Progress Check Answers

1. The hierarchical data structure is a data structure that has several levels arranged in a tree-like structure.

2. xmlelement() is used to define all elements with the XML type. All XML types start with a root element.

3. The **xmlattributes()** function can only be called within an **xmlelement()** function call. The **xmlattributes()** function builds attributes for an element.

4. xmlagg() must be accompanied by a **group by** clause.

The XML DB Repository

The powerful table-row-column of the relational model is widely accepted as the most effective mechanism for managing structured data. The relational metaphor is not so effective when it comes to managing unstructured data that can be represented as XML documents.

With Oracle XML DB, it *is* possible to have your cake and eat it too, at least to an extent: You can store your document as an XMLType in Oracle's XML DB repository, which will preserve byte-by-byte document fidelity and also shred it into a SQL table, allowing the use of DML (Data Manipulation Language) against the document. The XML DB repository represents XML content as documents in a folder hierarchy, and allows use of hierarchical metaphors, such as paths and URLs, for access to these documents. It should be noted that Oracle XML DB repository is an integrated part of the Oracle Database 10*g*.

XML documents can be stored in the database by simply inserting the XML document file using SQL, PL/SQL, Java, or through one of the three popular protocols FTP, HTTP, or WebDAV that Oracle XML DB has native support for. Getting XML data out of your database can be as simple as executing a SQL query or reading a file using one of those Internet-standard protocols. *WebDAV* stands for web-based distributed authoring and versioning. It is a set of extensions to the HTTP protocol that allows users to collaboratively edit and manage files on remote web servers. Figure 8-3 shows a listing of directories containing XML files. This type of index is familiar to many readers, except that Oracle XML DB displays this one.

NOTE
Windows Explorer can connect directly to the Oracle XML DB repository using one's own database login username and password. No additional Oracle- or Microsoft-specific software has to be installed in order to make this work. This means that end users can work with the Oracle XML DB repository using the tools and interfaces with which they are already familiar.

Registering an XML Schema

The introduction of XML Schema expanded the scope of XML from interchange to modeling and storage. XML Schema is another W3C standard that specifies the structure, content, and certain semantics for a set of XML documents. Its purpose is to define the legal building blocks of an XML document. An XML Schema includes the valid tag-sets, the constraints placed on XML elements, and the specifications for data types, derivation, and inheritance. The following code is a partial listing of an

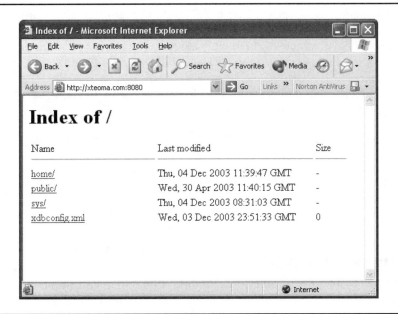

FIGURE 8-3. *Accessing an Oracle XML DB listing via a web browser*

XML document that is tied to an XML Schema. Defined at the root element is the attribute **xsi:schemaLocation** that allows you to tie a document to its XML Schema located at its URL (uniform resource locator; commonly referred to as a web address). In this case, the URL is http://xteoma.com/xsd/purchaseorder.xsd.

```
<PurchaseOrder
    xmlns=" http://xteoma.com/xsd/"
    xmlns:xsi="http://www.w3.org/2001/XMLSchema-instance"
    xsi:SchemaLocation="http://xteoma.com/xsd/purchaseorder.xsd">
....
</PurchaseOrder>
```

With XMLType, we have the ability to store XML documents that are *well formed,* but this was just half of the equation since we also need to store *valid* XML documents. Oracle XML DB incorporates the XML Schema standard into the Oracle Database 10*g*, making available a mechanism to validate XML documents stored within. To achieve this, the XML Schema must be "registered" in Oracle Database 10*g*. It is after this registration that the XML Schema is available to constrain XML documents we store within our XMLType.

An XML Schema is registered by the PL/SQL procedure called **dbms_xmlschema.register_schema()**. The XML Schema is registered under a URL, which is used internally as a unique key to identify the XML Schema. At no point does Oracle XML DB require direct access to the URL specified when registering the XML Schema.

The following listing demonstrates the use of **dbms_xmlschema.registerSchema()**, which is called within a PL/SQL procedure:

```
SQL> begin
  2  dbms_xmlschema.registerSchema (
  3  'http://xteoma.com/xsd/purchaseorder.xsd',
  4  xdbURIType('/xsd/purchaseorder.xsd').getClob(),
  5  True,True,False,True);
  6  end;
  7  /
```

Loading XML Data

As mentioned in the previous sections, loading XML documents into the Oracle XML DB repository database can be done by a simple insert statement from SQL or PL/SQL. Data being stored within an XMLType defined column is actually converted into an XMLType instance or object. Like all objects, when an instance XMLType is defined, it must use one of a number of variant constructors to instantiate itself. XMLType has defined constructors that can provide options for reducing the amount of processing associated with creating the XMLType. For instance, if the source XML document is known to be both well-formed and valid, the constructor allows flags to be passed that disable the default checking that is typically performed when instantiating the XMLType.

In the listing that follows, we are using the default constructor that has the XML document as its only argument. Using this provides for the validation of data by default.

```
SQL> insert into PURCHASE_ORDER
  2  values (67, XMLTYPE('
  3  <PurchaseOrder xmlns:xsi="http://www.w3.org/2001/XMLSchema-instance"
  4      xsi:noNamespaceSchemaLocation="http://xteoma.com/xsd/purchaseorder.xsd">
  5      <Reference>MALLIA-20040109123337403PDT</Reference>
  6      <Requestor>Sean Mallia</Requestor>
  7      <User>SHAUNA</User>
  8      <ShippingInstructions>
  9         <name>Paddy Mallia</name>
 10             <address>249 Kracqueric Ave.
 11  Ottawa
 12  ON
 13  K1A 1A1
 14  Canada</address>
 15             <telephone>613 555-2620</telephone>
```

```
16     </ShippingInstructions>
17     <SpecialInstructions>Air Mail</SpecialInstructions>
18     <LineItems>
19          <LineItem ItemNumber="1">
20               <Description>XML Done Easy</Description>
21               <Part Id="37429155721" UnitPrice="29.95" Quantity="3"/>
22          </LineItem>
23          <LineItem ItemNumber="2">
24               <Description>YATFG - A detailed explanation</Description>
25               <Part Id="37429158920" UnitPrice="39.95" Quantity="3"/>
26          </LineItem>
27     </LineItems>
28* </PurchaseOrder>'))
SQL> /
```

Notice that line 4 in the preceding code defines the XML Schema associated to the XML document. If the XML schema **http://xteoma.com/xsd/purchaseorder.xsd** were not registered, did not exist on the path specified, or if the XML document did not match the constraints found, Oracle Database 10g would throw ORA-19007, described in the next listing:

```
ORA-19007: Schema and element do not match
```

Project 8-2   Storing XML

In this project, we will be creating a table of type XMLType and storing an XML document using a SQL query in the Oracle Database 10g.

Step by Step

1. Log into SQL*Plus using the username/password **sh/sh**.

2. At the SQL> prompt, enter the long command, **set long 10000**, and then press ENTER.

3. At the SQL> prompt, enter the long command, **set pagesize 80**, and then press ENTER.

4. Enter the following SQL statement:

   ```
   SQL> create table xcustomer of xmltype
   ```

5. You should now see the following output on your screen:

   ```
   SQL> /
   Table created.
   ```

6. Enter the following SQL Query to load XML data:

(continued)

```
SQL> insert into XCUSTOMER values(XMLTYPE('
  2  <customer>
  3    <name>Chris Smith</name>
  4    <address>116 Main Street
  5  Big City
  6  U.S.A.</address>
  7    <telephone>123 555-1234</telephone>
  8  </customer>'))
  9  /
```

7. Let's see our data. Enter the following SQL statement:

```
SQL> select * from xcustomer;
```

8. You should now see output resembling the following on your screen:

```
SYS_NC_ROWINFO$
-----------------------------------------------------------------
<customer>
    <name>Chris Smith</name>
    <address>116 Main Street
Big City
U.S.A.</address>
    <telephone>123 555-1234</telephone>
</customer>
```

Project Summary

This project illustrated how you can define tables that will store XML documents natively, as well as how to insert XML documents using a simple **insert** statement.

Use the RESOURCE_VIEW

Now that we have been creating and loading XML documents into Oracle XML DB, let's take a look at what we have. An important view that you should be aware of is the view named **resource_view**. **resource_view** returns one row for each document or folder in the repository to which you have access. For example, we can get a list of all XML documents under the home/xteoma/xmldata/ folder by executing this query:

```
SQL> select any_path
  2  from resource_view
  3  where under_path(res,'/home/xteoma/xmldata/')=1
  4  and extractValue(res,'/Resource/ContentType')='text/xml';
ANY_PATH
------------------------------
/home/xteoma/xmldata/inv20040067.xml
/home/xteoma/xmldata/products.xml
```

Path-Based Access

As previously stated, path-based access to content stored within the Oracle XML DB repository is available from SQL. The function **xdburitype()** makes it possible to use a path-based metaphor to access content stored in the Oracle XML DB repository. Figure 8-4 shows the products sheet as stored in Oracle XML DB.

The following listing demonstrates the use of **xdburitype()** to access the document displayed in Figure 8-4, with its result set:

```
SQL> select xdburitype('/home/xteoma/xmldata/Products.xml')
  2    from dual;
XDBURITYPE('/HOME/XTEOMA/XMLDATA/PRODUCTS.XML')
-----------------------------------------------------------------
<?xml version="1.0"?>
<Products>
 <ProdCategory category="Electronics">
  <product><name>Y Box</name></product>
  <product><name>Home Theatre Package with DVD-Audio/Video Play</name></product>
  <product><name>8.3 Minitower Speaker</name></product>
  <product><name>Smash up Boxing</name></product>
  <product><name>Martial Arts Champions</name></product>
  <product><name>Endurance Racing</name></product>
  <product><name>Bounce</name></product>
```

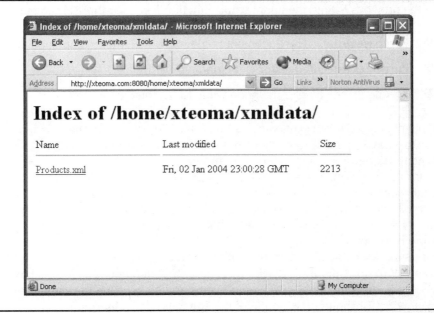

FIGURE 8-4. *Products.xml stored on Oracle XML DB*

```
<product><name>Comic Book Heroes</name></product>
<product><name>Finding Fido</name></product>
<product><name>Xtend Memory</name></product>
<product><name>Extension Cable</name></product>
<product><name>Adventures with Numbers</name></product>
<product><name>Fly Fishing</name></product>
</ProdCategory>
 . . .
 . . .
</Products>
```

Update the XML Document

Now that we have our XML documents loaded into the Oracle Database 10*g*, we will need a way to update them. The **updatexml()** function updates an attribute value, node, text node, or node tree for any XML document. The target for the update operation is identified using an XPath expression. The following listing shows how to update the XML document stored in a column defined as an XMLType:

```
update purchase_order
       set po_file = updateXML (PurchaseOrder,
         '/ PurchaseOrder/Requestor/text()', 'Speedo')
where po_no = 67
```

In the previous listing, the **updatexml()** function is passed three arguments:

- **PurchaseOrder**   The document name (or root element) being updated

- **PurchaseOrder/Requestor**   The node to be updated

- **Speedo**   The value of the node value to be changed

Note the use of XPath syntax in this function. The path '**/ PurchaseOrder/ Requestor/text()**' specifies that we want to update the text in the PurchaseOrder document's Requestor field. The third argument to update XML specifies the new value for that text. This is an in-place update, making it a very efficient operation. XML DB Repository does not need to reconstruct the entire XML document being changed. Because the schema is registered, XML DB Repository is able to rewrite this query in such a way that only the web site attribute in the underlying object structure is touched.

Updating XML documents stored within a table defined by XMLType is a little different. With no column to set within our **update** statement, Oracle Database 10*g* allows us to define the object we would like to update by using the **value()** function. The following list shows an example of the SQL with the **value()** function.

```
update xcustomer c
set value(c) = updateXML(value(c), '/customer/name/text()','Pat Jones')
/
```

CAUTION
*The previous statement will update all XML documents
stored within the XCUSTOMER table. To avoid this
global update, we must constrain our SQL query to
select only the XML document we want. To define the
constraint, we will need to identify the node within
the XML document we want and return its value, a
problem that will be addressed in the next section.*

NOTE
updatexml() *can be used to update, replace
elements, attributes, and other nodes with new
values. This function cannot be directly used to
insert new nodes or delete existing ones.*

As we have just defined, XMLType tables and columns are able to store XML
data within them. Let's continue on to see how we can retrieve the data.

CRITICAL SKILL 8.5
Use Simple Queries

The first thing you might do as a relational developer after finding out that XML
data can be loaded into an Oracle Database 10*g* is some querying. Is querying
different with this XML data? Are the queries ordinary SQL? Because Oracle XML DB
is fundamentally based on the Oracle Database 10*g* relational architecture, the
familiar SQL paradigm continues to work well in this new world.

The first thing to realize is that, to query documents in Oracle XML DB, you
use SQL with some functional extensions. Here are a handful of SQL functions
that use XPath notations and are part of a set of extensions to SQL that Oracle has
implemented in Oracle Database 10*g*:

■   The **existsnode()** function is used in the **where** clause of a SQL query to
    restrict the set of documents to be returned. The **existsnode()** function
    applies an XPath expression to an XML document and returns true (1)
    or false (0) depending on whether or not the document contains a node
    which matches the XPath expression.

- The **extract()** function is similar to the **existsnode()** function. The **extract()** function extracts the node or a set of nodes from the document identified by the XPath expression and returns an XMLType instance containing an XML fragment. The extracted nodes can be elements, attributes, or text nodes. When extracted out, all text nodes are collapsed into a single text node value.

- The **extractvalue()** function takes as arguments an XMLType instance and an XPath expression. It returns a scalar value corresponding to the result of the XPath evaluation on the XMLType instance. The **extractvalue()** tries to infer the proper return type from the XML schema of the document. If the XMLType is non-schema-based or the proper return type cannot be determined, Oracle XML DB returns a **varchar2**.

Let's have a look now at our SQL query, and then pick apart the text in Table 8-3.

```
1- select
extractvalue(p.PO_FILE,'PurchaseOrder/ShippingInstructions/address')
2- from PURCHASE_ORDER p
3- where existsnode(p.PO_FILE,'/PurchaseOrder/User = "SHAUNA"') = 1
```

The following is the expected result of our preceding SQL query:

```
EXTRACTVALUE(P.PO_FILE,'PURCHASEORDER/SHIPPINGINSTRUCTIONS/ADDRESS')
--------------------------------------------------------------------------
249 Kracqueric Ave.
Ottawa
ON
K1A 1A1
Canada
```

Line	Important Points
1	The **extractvalue()** first argument is **p.PO_FILE**, the second is the XPath expression **'PurchaseOrder/ShippingInstructions/address'**. The value at the defined location is returned, and its type will be inferred either by the associated XML Schema. In this case, it is **varchar2**.
2	The selection of data is being made against the PURCHASE_ORDER table.
3	The **existsnode()** first argument is **p.PO_FILE**, the second is the XPath expression **'/PurchaseOrder/User = "SHAUNA"'**. If the value is found at the defined location, then 1 is returned, signifying that the constraint is met.

TABLE 8-3. *The Address XML SQL Query Definition*

Project 8-3 Using Simple Queries

In this project, we will be querying for a specific XML document and then updating it.

Step by Step

1. Log into SQL*Plus.

2. At the SQL> prompt, enter the long command, **set long 10000**, and then press ENTER.

3. At the SQL> prompt, enter the long command, **set pagesize 80**, and then press ENTER.

4. Enter the following SQL query:

```
SQL> select extractvalue(value(c),'/customer/telephone')
  2  from xcustomer c
  3  where existsnode(value(c),'/customer/name = "Chris Smith"') = 1
```

5. Again, when you see the SQL prompt, enter the forward slash (/) to execute it:

```
SQL> /
EXTRACTVALUE(VALUE(C),'/CUSTOMER/TELEPHONE')
------------------------------------------------
123 555-1234
```

6. Enter the following SQL query to change the telephone number to 888 555-1234:

```
update xcustomer c
set value(c) = updateXML(value(c), '/customer/telephone/text()','888 555-1234')
where existsnode(value(c),'/customer/name = "Chris Smith"') = 1
/
```

7. See if your data has changed by entering the following query.

```
SQL> select extract(value(c), 'customer')
  2  from XCUSTOMER c
  3 where existsnode(value(c),'/customer/name = " Chris Smith "') = 1
  4 /
```

You should now see output similar to the following on your screen:

```
EXTRACT(VALUE(C),'CUSTOMER')
--------------------------------------
<customer>
  <name>Chris Smith</name>
  <address>116 Main street
Big City
U.S.A.</address>
  <telephone>888 555-1234</telephone>
</customer>
```

(continued)

Project Summary

This project illustrated the use of **existsnode()**, **extract()**, and **extractvalue()** when identifying an XML document stored in the Oracle Database 10g.

In the future, Oracle is looking at adding several new capabilities to this list, including additional database and XML functionalities, such as XQuery, which will be a language specifically designed to query XML data from a document perspective rather than the rows-and-tables perspective of SQL. We have had fun finding and returning XML documents. Let's proceed and look at how we can take XML documents and represent them relationally.

Progress Check

1. Is the Oracle XML DB repository separate from the Oracle Database 10g?

2. Why must we "register" the URL of XML Schemas into the Oracle XML DB repository?

3. How do we load an XML document into the Oracle XML DB repository?

4. What is the difference between the **existsnode()** function and the **extract()** function?

CRITICAL SKILL 8.6

Create a Relational View from XML

Oracle XML DB makes it possible to expose XML content, stored in the database through conventional relational views. This means that tools, applications, and programmers who have no understanding of XML, but understand the Oracle Database 10g, can now work with XML content. To accomplish this, the view

---

Progress Check Answers

1. No, the Oracle XML DB is integrated with Oracle Database 10g.

2. The XML Schema defines the legal structure for an XML document. To confirm that the XML stored within the XMLType is "valid," the URL for the XML Schema it is associated with must be registered.

3. XML documents can be loaded into the Oracle XML DB via programs using SQL, PL/SQL, and Java or by going through the protocols FTP, HTTP, and WebDAV.

4. The **existsnode()** function identifies the existence of a node returning a Boolean value, while the **extract()** function extracts the node or set of nodes identified, returning a single text node.

definitions use the SQL/XML functions and XPath expressions to map between the nodes in the XML document and the columns in the view.

Relational views can be used to expose the contents of an XML document as a row. Views created this way look and behave like a normal relational view.

This following SQL example creates a view called **purchaseorder_master_view**. Each row in the view will contain information from one document in the PURCHASEORDER table.

The view defines a set of columns as well as the XPath expressions required to map between the nodes in the document and the columns in the view:

```
SQL> create or replace view po_master_view
  2     (reference,requestor,userid,costcentre,
  3       shipto,shiptoaddress,instructions)
  4  as select extractvalue(value(x), '/PurchaseOrder/Reference'),
  5        extractvalue(value(x), '/PurchaseOrder/Requestor'),
  6        extractvalue(value(x), '/PurchaseOrder/User'),
  7        extractvalue(value(x), '/PurchaseOrder/ShippingInstructions/name'),
  8        extractvalue(value(x), '/PurchaseOrder/ShippingInstructions/address'),
  9           extractvalue(value(x), '/PurchaseOrder/SpecialInstructions')
 10  from PURCHASE_ORDER x
 11  /
```

When describing the view, we can see that we have defined a relational prospective to our XML document:

```
SQL> describe PO_MASTER_VIEW;
 Name                            Null?    Type
 ------------------------------- -------- ---------------------------
 REFERENCE                                VARCHAR2(4000)
 REQUESTOR                                VARCHAR2(4000)
 USERID                                   VARCHAR2(4000)
 SHIPTO                                   VARCHAR2(4000)
 SHIPTOADDRESS                            VARCHAR2(4000)
 INSTRUCTIONS                             VARCHAR2(4000)
```

When we select this view, we see the data stored within it:

```
SQL> select * from PO_MASTER_VIEW where userid = 'MALLIA';
MALLIA-20031009123337403PDT
Sean Mallia
SHAUNA
Paddy Mallia
249 Kracqueric Ave.
Ottawa
ON
K1A 1A1
Canada
Air Mail
```

Learn Programmatic Access Using XSLT

Data encapsulated in XML can be used in a number of ways. One common means of manipulating it is through the use of Extensible Stylesheet Language Transformations (XSLT), which enable developers to define operations that must be performed on an XML document to produce a specific result. This ability to transform information on the fly makes it possible to use a single source for multiple outputs such as HTML, whether those outputs lead to different databases or to different browsers. XML documents have structure but no format.

Oracle XML DB uses the template rules and other formatting elements that appear within the XSLT style sheets. It includes an XSLT-based transformation engine to automatically transform XML-tagged documents into multiple display formats, store the transformed renditions generated by the XSLT style sheets, and deliver content in the appropriate formats to various devices.

The following example shows how **transform()** can apply XSLT to an XSL style sheet, PurchaseOrder.xsl, to transform the PurchaseOrder.xml document:

```
SQL> select value(t).transform(xmltype(getDocument('purchaseOrder.xsl')))
  2    from xmltable t
  3    where existsnode(value(t),
  4          '/PurchaseOrder[Reference="MALLIA-2002033112000000000PST"]'
  5    ) = 1;
VALUE(T).TRANSFORM(XMLTYPE(GETDOCUMENT('PURCHASEORDER.XSL')))
-------------------------------------------------------------------------
<html>
  <head/>
  <body bgcolor="#003333" text="#FFFFCC" link="#FFCC00" vlink="#66CC99" alink="#
669999">
    <FONT FACE="Arial, Helvetica, sans-serif">
      <center>
...
    </FONT>
  </body>
</html>
```

And now we are at the end of this chapter. Unfortunately, we have only been able to lightly understand some of the functionality implemented with Oracle XML DB. As XML grows in popularity within the information management community, so too will Oracle's attention to this data type. If there are any detractors out there who want to complain that perhaps Oracle Database 10g's journey into XML is too little too late—watch out. Even if there is any substance to complaints about Oracle's technology direction and implementations, it won't be long before they are setting the trend in new areas yet again.

☑ Chapter 8 Mastery Check

1. XML stands for Extensible _____ Language.

2. XML documents are in what type of data structure?

    A. Relational

    B. Hierarchy

    C. Free format text

3. What is the notation used when querying XML documents, which is implemented with Oracle Database 10*g?*

4. What is a well-formed XML document?

5. Using the **existsnode()** function within a SQL query should return what value if the node exists?

    A. 0

    B. 2

    C. 99

    D. 1

6. Of the following four methods listed, which is used to store XML documents in Oracle XML DB?

    A. PL/SQL

    B. FTP

    C. Java

    D. All the above

7. What is used to ensure that an XML document is valid?

8. What is the defined data type that is used to store XML documents in Oracle Database 10*g?*

9. When using **xmlagg()** function to build an XML type, what SQL clause must it be accompanied by?

10. What does the acronym XSLT stand for?

    A. XML Structured Language Transformations

    B. XML Stylesheet Longform Transaction

    C. Extensible Stylesheet Language Transformations

11. What does the acronym SQLX stand for?

    A. Structured Query Language for XML

    B. Simple Query Language Extension

    C. Straightforward Question-based Learning Exam

CHAPTER
9

Large Database Features

CRITICAL SKILLS

9.1 What Is a Large Database?

9.2 Why and How to Use Data Partitioning

9.3 Compress Your Data

9.4 Use Parallel Processing to Improve Performance

9.5 Use Materialized Views

9.6 Real Application Clusters: A Primer

9.7 Automatic Storage Management: Another Primer

9.8 Grid Computing: The "*g*" in Oracle Database 10g

9.9 Use SQL Aggregate and Analysis Functions

9.10 Create SQL Models

n this chapter, we will be covering topics and features available in Oracle Database 10*g* with which you will need to be familiar when working with large databases. These features are among the more advanced that you will encounter, but they're necessary, as databases are growing larger and larger. When you start working with Oracle, you will find yourself facing the trials and tribulations associated with large databases sooner rather than later. The quicker you understand the features and know where and when to use them, the more effective you will be.

CRITICAL SKILL 9.1

What Is a Large Database?

Let's start by describing what we mean by a large database. "Large" is a relative term that changes over time. What was large five or ten years ago is small by today's standards, and what is large today will be peanuts a few years from now. Each release of Oracle has included new features and enhancements to address the need to store more and more data. For example, Oracle8*i* was released in 1999 and could handle databases with *terabytes* (1024 gigabytes) of data. In 2001, Oracle9*i* was released and could deal with up to 500 *petabytes* (1024 terabytes). Oracle Database 10*g* now offers support for *exabyte* (1024 petabytes) databases. You won't come across too many databases with exabytes of data right now, but in the future at least we know Oracle will support them.

The most obvious examples of large database implementations are data warehouses and decision support systems. These environments usually have tables with millions or billions of rows, or wide tables with large numbers of columns and many rows. There are also many OLTP systems that are very large and can benefit from the features we are about to cover. Since we've got many topics to get through, let's jump right in and start with data partitioning.

NOTE
Many of the topics discussed in this chapter could, each on their own, take an entire book to cover completely. Since this is an introductory book, specifics for some topics have been omitted. Real-world experiences and additional reading will build on this material.

CRITICAL SKILL 9.2

Why and How to Use Data Partitioning

As our user communities require more and more detailed information in order to remain competitive, it has fallen to us as database designers and administrators to help ensure that the information is managed efficiently and can be retrieved for analysis effectively. In this section, we will discuss partitioning data, and why it is so important when working with large databases. Afterward, we'll follow the steps required to make it all work.

Why Use Data Partitioning

Let's start by defining what we mean by *data partitioning*. In its simplest form, it is a way of breaking up or subsetting data into smaller units that can be managed and accessed separately. It has been around for a long time both as a design technique and as a technology. Let's look at some of the issues that gave rise to the need for partitioning and the solutions to these issues.

Tables containing very large numbers of rows have always posed problems and challenges for DBAs, application developers, and end-users alike. For the DBA, the problems centered on the maintenance and manageability of the underlying data files that contain the data for these tables. For the application developers and end users, the issues were query performance and data availability.

To mitigate these issues, the standard database design technique was to create physically separate tables, identical in structure (for example, columns), but with each containing a subset of the total data (we will refer to this design technique as *nonpartitioned*). These tables could be referred to directly or through a series of views. This technique solved some of the problems, but still meant maintenance for the DBA to create new tables and/or views as new subsets of data were acquired. In addition, if access to the entire dataset was required, a view was needed to join all subsets together.

Figure 9-1 illustrates this design technique. In this sample, separate tables with identical structures have been created to hold monthly sales information for 2005. Views have also been defined to group the monthly information into quarters using a **union** query. The quarterly views themselves are then grouped together into a view that represents the entire year. The same structures would be created for each year of data. In order to obtain data for a particular month or quarter, an end user would have to know which table or view to use.

Similar to the technique illustrated in Figure 9-1, the partitioning technology offered by Oracle Database 10g is a method of breaking up large amounts of data into smaller, more manageable chunks. But, unlike the nonpartitioned technique, it is transparent to

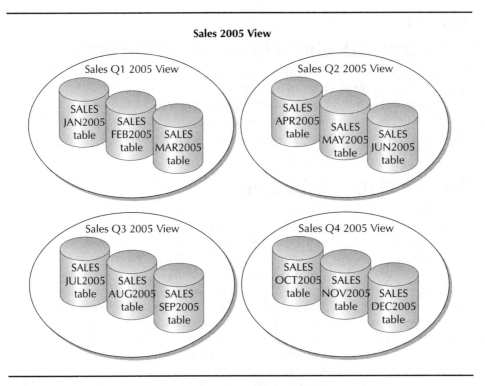

FIGURE 9-1. *Partitioning using separate physical tables*

the end user, offering improved performance and reduced maintenance. Figure 9-2 illustrates the same SALES table, but implemented using Oracle Database 10*g*'s partitioning option. From the end user's perspective, there is only one table called SALES and all that is required to access data from the correct partition is a date (or a month and year).

Oracle partitioning was first introduced in Oracle8 and is only available with the Enterprise Edition. Many improvements have been made since then and Oracle Database 10*g* contains all the latest features. The remainder of this section discusses these features in more detail.

Manageability
When administering large databases, DBAs are required to determine the most efficient and effective way to configure the underlying data files that support the tables in the database. The decisions made will affect data accessibility and availability as well as backup and recovery.

Some of the benefits to database manageability when using partitioned tables include the following:

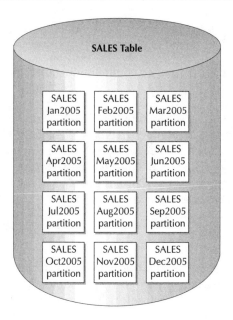

FIGURE 9-2.   *Partitioning using Oracle Database 10g partitioning*

- The size of each underlying data file is generally smaller for partitioned tables than nonpartitioned tables. This allows for easier and quicker backups.

- Historical partitions can be made read-only and will not need to be backed up more than once. This also means faster backups.

- The structure of a partitioned table needs to be defined only once. As new subsets of data are acquired, they will be assigned to the correct partition, based on the partition option chosen.

- Individual tablespaces and/or their data files can be taken offline for maintenance or archiving without affecting access to other subsets of data. For example, assuming data for a table is partitioned by month (later in this chapter, we will discuss the different types of partitioning) and only 13 months of data is to be kept online at any one time, when a new month is acquired, the earliest month is archived and dropped from the table. This is accomplished using the command **alter table abc drop partition xyz** and does not affect access to the remaining 12 months of data.

Ask the Expert

Q: Can you use the analyze table **command to gather statistics on partitioned tables?**

A: No; at least not correctly. The supplied DBMS_STATS package should be used instead to gather statistics on partitioned tables. The **analyze table** command does not gather all required statistics for partitioned tables, in particular global statistics. In addition, the **analyze** command will eventually be phased out (for all types of table and indexes) and only those statistics gathered by the DBMS_STATS package will be used by the cost-based optimizer.

■   Other commands that would normally apply at the table level can also be applied to a particular partition of the table. These include, but are not limited to: **delete**, **insert, select, truncate**, and **update**.

Performance

One of the main reasons for partitioning a table is to improve I/O response time when selecting data from the table. Having a table's data partitioned into subsets can yield much faster query results when you are looking for data that is limited to one subset of the total. Let's look at an example to illustrate.

Assume the SALES table contains 100 million records representing daily sales revenue for the three years 2005 to 2007 inclusive. We want to know what the total revenue is for February 2006. The query might look something like this:

```
select sum(amount_sold)
from sales
where time_id between to_date('2006-02-01', 'YYYY-MM-DD') and
to_date('2006-02-28', 'YYYY-MM-DD');
```

Using a nonpartitioned table design, all 100 million rows would need to be scanned to determine if they belong to the date criteria. Using a partitioned table design based on monthly partitions with about 2.8 million rows for each month, only those rows in the February 2006 partition (and therefore only about 2.8 million rows) would be scanned. The process of eliminating data not belonging to the subset defined by the query criteria is referred to as *partition pruning*.

With the basic concepts of partitioning and why we use it under our belts, we can now discuss the finer details of how to implement partitioning.

Implement Data Partitioning

Implementing data partitioning in Oracle Database 10*g* is a process that requires careful planning to ensure success. You will need to understand your database environment, hardware, structures, and data before you can make the appropriate decisions. In the next few sections, we will outline the steps you will take when partitioning. Let's start by looking at the characteristics of the candidate table.

Analyze the Candidate Table

The first step in the partitioning process is to analyze and understand the candidate table, its environment and its uses. Following are some criteria to consider.

Table Structure and Data Contents You will need to look at what attributes are available and what is the distribution of the data within each attribute. You must consider currently available data as well as projected future data. The distribution of data over each attribute is important because you want to ensure that the resulting data subsets are evenly distributed across the defined partitions.

Consider a table called PHONE_USAGE that contains detailed mobile phone call records with over 300 million records per month. It has many attributes including the toll type (**toll_type_cd**) and the date of call (**call_date**). Table 9-1 shows a sample row count for a month by **toll_type_cd**. As you can see, using this attribute would probably not be an ideal choice by which to create subsets since the distribution is heavily skewed toward LOCAL calls.

Table 9-2 looks at the distribution of the same data by the day of the week (for example, Sunday to Saturday based on **call_date**).

We can see that the day of the week provides a relatively even distribution that is more suitable for partitioning.

How the Data Will Be Accessed To access the data, you will need to know what the commonest data selection criteria are. This is perhaps the most important part of the analysis because, as we stated earlier, query performance is the most noticeable

toll_type_cd	Record Count (Sample Month)
INTNL	27,296,802
CONTNL US	52,227,998
LOCAL	189,554,584
NRTH AMRCA	36,367,841

TABLE 9-1. *Row Distribution by toll_type_cd Attribute*

Day of the Week (Based on call_date)	Record Count (Sample Month)
SUN	41,635,356
MON	44,235,019
TUE	42,875,502
WED	43,235,721
THU	43,922,997
FRI	45,005,293
SAT	44,537,337

TABLE 9-2. *Row Distribution by Day of the Week*

gain of data partitioning. In order for this to be realized, your data subsets need to be defined according to the commonest selection criteria so that unnecessary partitions can be pruned from the result set. The selection criteria will be determined largely by your user community and can be determined using historical query patterns (if available) or consulting business requirements.

Referring to our example using the SALES table, our analysis of query patterns for a three-month period (averaging 400 queries per month) yields the results shown in Table 9-3.

Attribute	Times Used in Query Selection Criteria (Average/Month)
prod_id	33
cust_id	40
time_id	355
channel_id	55
promo_id	298
quantity_sold	25
amount_sold	20

TABLE 9-3. *Query Frequency of SALES Table Attributes*

The analysis tells us that **time_id** and **promo_id** are both frequently used as query predicates. We would use this information along with the corresponding row distribution to determine which attribute would result in the better partitioning strategy.

Hardware Configuration   Factors such as the number of physical disks and disk controllers will contribute to the effectiveness of your partitioning strategy. Generally, the greater the number of disks and/or controllers, the better—you can spread the partitions over more hardware to improve I/O performance.

Identify the Partition Key

Once you understand the characteristics of your candidate table, the next step in the partitioning process is to select the attribute(s) of the candidate table that will define the partition subsets and how the subsets will be defined. The selected attributes will form the *partition key*. Only one set of attributes can be chosen to partition the data. This is an important decision, since it will affect the manageability and usability of the table.

The results of your analysis of the candidate table should provide you with a good idea of which attributes to use. The best attributes will be those that satisfy the most criteria. Keep in mind though, that the adage "you can satisfy some of the criteria some of the time, but you can't satisfy all of the criteria all of the time" applies here. Despite your best efforts and planning, there will still be situations when the table will be treated as if it were nonpartitioned. Take, for example, a perfectly valid query submitted by the user community that does not include the attributes of the partition key as part of the selection criteria, or groups by the partition key. In this case, data from the entire table (that is, all partitions) would be scanned in order to satisfy the request.

Select the Type of Partitioning

After you have selected the partition key, the next step in the partitioning process is to decide which type of partitioning you want to implement on the candidate table. Oracle Database 10*g* provides four ways to partition data:

- Range partitioning
- List partitioning
- Hash partitioning
- Composite partitioning

The type of partitioning you choose will depend on the results of your analysis of the candidate table. The commonest type of partitioning is range partitioning and will be covered here in the most detail. Let's look at the characteristics of each.

Range Partitioning   *Range partitioning* has been around the longest of all partitioning types and is the one implemented most often. In most cases, the ranges are based on some date component, such as quarters, months or, in the case of very large data volumes, days. (Theoretically, you can go down to any level of time—hours, minutes, and so on—assuming you have a time component. But the maintenance implications of defining this many partitions make it unrealistic.) The ranges selected will again be based on the results of your analysis of the table, using dates, numeric values, or character values. Following is an example based on the SALES table we saw earlier in the chapter.

NOTE
The partitioning examples presented in this chapter do not address all of the command options available. They are meant to give you a taste of what is available.

To create our SALES table as nonpartitioned, we would use the standard **create table** statement as shown in this listing:

```
create table sales (
    prod_id         number          not null,
    cust_id         number          not null,
    time_id         date            not null,
    channel_id      number          not null,
    promo_id        number          not null,
    quantity_sold   number (10,2)   not null,
    amount_sold     number (10,2)   not null)
tablespace example pctfree 5 initrans 1 maxtrans 255
storage ( initial 65536 minextents 1 maxextents 2147483645);
```

Based on our analysis of the usage patterns and row distribution, we have decided that the optimal partition strategy for this table is based on sales month. We will now redefine the SALES table using **time_id** as our partition key to create monthly partitions for January 2005 to December 2007, inclusive. Creation of data partitions is accomplished using extensions of the **create table** statement. The following listing shows the creation of the table with range partitions. Explanations of the important lines are given in Table 9-4.

```
1 create table sales (
2   prod_id         number          not null,
3   cust_id         number          not null,
4   time_id         date            not null,
5   channel_id      number          not null,
```

```
 6  promo_id        number          not null,
 7  quantity_sold   number (10,2)   not null,
 8  amount_sold     number (10,2)   not null)
 9  storage (initial 65536  minextents 1 maxextents 2147483645)
10  partition by range (time_id)
11  (partition sales_200501 values less than
12                       (to_date('2005-02-01','YYYY-MM-DD'))
13                       tablespace sales_ts_200501,
14  partition sales_200502 values less than
15                       (to_date('2005-03-01','YYYY-MM-DD'))
16                       tablespace sales_ts_200502,
17  partition sales_200503 values less than
18                       (to_date('2005-04-01','YYYY-MM-DD'))
19                       tablespace sales_ts_200503,
...
113 partition sales_200711 values less than
114                      (to_date('2007-12-01','YYYY-MM-DD'))
115                      tablespace sales_ts_200711,
116 partition sales_200712 values less than
117                      (to_date('2008-01-01','YYYY-MM-DD'))
118                      tablespace sales_ts_200712,
119 partition sales_max values less than (maxvalue)
120                      tablespace sales_ts_max);
```

Lines	Important Points
9	Defines the default table-level storage parameters that will apply to all partitions. It is possible to override these defaults at the partition level in favor of specific parameters required for a particular partition.
10	Defines the type of partitioning (for example, **range**) and the partition key (for instance, **time_id**).
11–118	Define each partition based on the values of **time_id** (repetitive lines for Apr 2005 to Oct 2007 omitted for brevity's sake). For each partition, the upper boundary of the partition key value is specified (as defined by the **values less than** clause), as well as the name of the tablespace where the subset is to be stored. Values must be specified in ascending order and cannot overlap. It is good practice to give meaningful names to both the partitions and tablespaces.

TABLE 9-4.   *Explanation of Range Partitioning Syntax*

Lines	Important Points
119–120	Define the default partition for any values of **time_id** that are greater than the last defined partition (for instance, dates greater than June 30, 2006). **maxvalue** is an Oracle keyword that results in a value that is higher than any other possible value of the partition key. It will also include null values if the situation exists.

TABLE 9-4. *Explanation of Range Partitioning Syntax (continued)*

> **NOTE**
> *Lines 11 to 13 define the first partition to hold data where **time_id** is less than February 1, 2005. Our intention in this example is that this first partition will only hold data for January 2005 (our data analysis tells us that there is no data before this date). However, if there happens to be data prior to January 2005, it will also be placed in this partition and may skew the row distribution by placing many more rows than intended in this partition.*

That completes our discussion on range partitioning. Let's now have a look at list and hash partitioning.

List Partitioning   There may be cases when, after your analysis of a candidate table, you decide that range partitioning is not the best fit for your table. Another way to subset your data is to use *list partitioning,* where you group a set of partition key values and assign them to their own tablespace. By using this type of partitioning, you can control the placement of the records in specified partitions, thereby allowing you to group related records together that may not otherwise have a relationship.

As an example, assume we have an INS_COVERAGE table that contains insurance coverages. Our analysis of this table and its usage leads us to decide that we should partition, based on the attribute **cov_type_cd**, into the buckets shown in Table 9-5.

COV_TYPE_CD	Grouping
TERM 65	Life
UL	Life

TABLE 9-5. *Insurance Coverage Groupings*

COV_TYPE_CD	Grouping
ADB	Life
COLA	GIB
GPO	GIB
WP	Disability
DIS	Disability
MF	Investment

TABLE 9-5. *Insurance Coverage Groupings* (continued)

The syntax of the **create table** statement is similar to that for range partitioning. An explanation is provided in Table 9-6.

```
 1 create table ins_coverage (
 2  plan_id           number          not null,
 3  cust_id           number          not null,
 4  time_id           date            not null,
 5  dist_channel_id number          not null,
 6  cov_type_cd       varchar2(50)  not null,
 7  cov_amt           number (10,2) not null,
 8  prem_amt          number (10,2) not null)
 9  storage (initial 65536  minextents 1 maxextents 2147483645)
10 partition by list (cov_type_cd)
11 (partition cov_life values ('TERM 65', 'UL', 'ADB')
12             tablespace cov_life_ts,
13  partition cov_gib values ('COLA', 'GIB')
14             tablespace cov_gib_ts,
15  partition cov_dis values ('WP', 'DIS')
16             tablespace cov_dis_ts,
17  partition cov_inv values ('MF')
18             tablespace cov_inv_ts
19  partition cov_other values(default));
```

TIP
*If you discover missing partition keys values that need to be added to existing partition definitions after the table has been created, you can issue and **alter table abc modify partition xyz add values ('value1', ...).***

Hash Partitioning   If you determine from your table analysis that neither range nor list partitioning is appropriate for your table, but you still want to reap the benefits

Lines	Important Points
10	Defines the type of partitioning (for example, **list**) and the partition key (**cov_type_cd**, for instance). Note that with list partitioning, only one attribute from the table can be chosen as the partition key—in other words, multicolumn partition keys are not permitted.
11–18	Define each partition based on the groups of values of **cov_type_cd**.

TABLE 9-6. *Explanation of List Partitioning Syntax*

offered by partitioning, Oracle Database 10*g* provides a third partitioning option called *hash partitioning*. With hash partitioning, you define up to 16 partition key attributes as well as the number of partitions you want to spread the data across. As long as each partition is on its own physical device and most of the queries use the partition key as a predicate, you should see performance gains. Hash partitioning is useful if the distribution of data is unknown or unpredictable.

The following listing is an example of hash partitioning. Table 9-7 explains the important lines.

```
 1 create table sub_activations (
 2  sub_id            number        not null,
 3  dist_channel_id number          not null,
 4  act_date          date          not null,
 5  deact_date        date          not null,
 6  sales_rep_id      number        not null)
 7  storage (initial 65536  minextents 1 maxextents 2147483645)
 8 partition by hash (sub_id)
 9 partitions 4
10 store in (subact_ts1, subact_ts2, subact_ts3, subact_ts4);
```

Lines	Important Points
8	Defines the type of partitioning (for instance, **hash**) and the partition key (for example, **sub_id**).
9	Specifies the number of partitions over which to spread the data.
10	Specifies the tablespaces into which the partitions will be placed.

TABLE 9-7. *Explanation of Hash Partitioning Syntax*

It is beyond our scope to discuss the hashing algorithm used by Oracle Database 10*g*. We can say, however, that it is based on the number of attributes in the partition key and the number of partitions selected.

Composite Partitioning   The final type of partitioning is a combination of two of the previous types. Combining two types of partitioning is called *composite partitioning*. There are two valid combinations: **range with hash** and **range with list**. Using composite partitioning allows you to take advantage of the features of either hash or list partitioning within the higher groupings of ranges.

A good example of where this type of partitioning is used would be the PHONE_USAGE table we saw in our candidate table analysis. In this case, we have a table that is being loaded with 300 million records per month. We could choose to implement range partitioning by month and then subdivide the monthly partitions into four hash partitions. The following listing shows the SQL syntax that accomplishes this, and Table 9-8 provides the explanation of the important lines.

```
 1 create table phone_usage
 2 (sub_id               number,
 3  call_date            date,
 4  call_type_id         number,
 5  called_location      varchar2(50),
 6  service_carrier_id   number)
 7 storage (initial 65536  minextents 1 maxextents 2147483645)
 8 partition by range (call_date)
 9 subpartition by hash(sub_id)
10 subpartition template(
11  subpartition sub1 tablespace ph_usg_ts1,
12  subpartition sub2 tablespace ph_usg_ts2,
13  subpartition sub3 tablespace ph_usg_ts3,
14  subpartition sub4 tablespace ph_usg_ts4)
15 (partition phoneusg_200601 values less than
16                 (to_date('2006-02-01','YYYY-MM-DD')),
17  partition phoneusg_200602 values less than
18                 (to_date('2006-03-01','YYYY-MM-DD')),
19  partition phoneusg_200603 values less than
20                 (to_date('2006-04-01','YYYY-MM-DD')),
21  partition phoneusg_200604 values less than
22                 (to_date('2006-05-01','YYYY-MM-DD')),
23  partition phoneusg_200605 values less than
24                 (to_date('2006-06-01','YYYY-MM-DD')),
25  partition phoneusg_200606 values less than
26                 (to_date('2006-07-01','YYYY-MM-DD')),
27  partition phoneusg_max values less than (maxvalue));
```

Lines	Important Points
8	Defines the higher-level partitioning type (for example, **range**) and its partition key (for instance, **call_date**).
9	Specifies the secondary partitioning type (in this case, **hash**) and its partition key (here, **sub_id**).
10–14	Specify a template that will be used to define the tablespace names for each subpartition, as well as the tablespace names. The name of each subpartition will be composed of the higher-level partition name concatenated with an underscore, then the subpartition name specified in the template. For example, data for January 2006 will be placed in tablespace **ph_usg_ts1** and divided into four subpartitions called PHONEUSG_200601_SUB1, PHONEUSG_200601_SUB2, PHONEUSG_200601_SUB3, and PHONEUSG_200601_SUB4.
15–27	Specify the ranges for the higher-level partition based on the **call_date** partition key.

TABLE 9-8. *Explanation of Composite Partitioning Syntax*

We've covered all the partitioning types and some of their nuances. Now it's time to look at how we can get an even bigger boost from our partitioned tables using indexing.

Ask the Expert

Q: If the partition key of record in a partitioned table is updated and the new value means that the data belongs to a different partition, does Oracle Database 10g automatically move the record to the appropriate partition?

A: Yes, but the table must have the **enable row movement** option before the update is made. This option is invoked as either part of the **create table** statement, or using an **alter table** statement. Otherwise, the update statement will generate an Oracle error.

Define the Indexing Strategy

Okay, so now you have decided how you are going to partition your data. To really get the most out of partitioning, you will need to look at some indexing strategies. There are two types of indexes applicable to partitioned tables: local and global. Let's take a brief look at each.

Local Partitioned Indexes *Local partitioned indexes* are indexes that are partitioned in the exact same manner as the data in their associated table—that is, they have a direct one-to-one relationship with the data partitions and use the same partition key. This association is illustrated in Figure 9-3; as you can see, each partition has its own associated "local" index. This drawing is based on Figure 9-2, which we saw at the beginning of the chapter. It shows how the data and indexes for each monthly subset are related and then joins it with the concept of the local index.

Because of this relationship, the following points apply to local indexes:

- You cannot explicitly add or drop a partition to/from a local index. Oracle Database 10g automatically adds or drops index partitions when related data partitions are added or dropped. Referring back to Figure 9-3, if we dropped the data partition for January 2005, the corresponding index partition would automatically be dropped as well. Likewise, it we added a new data partition for January 2006, a new index partition would automatically be created.

- One of the advantages of partitioning data is to allow access to other subsets while maintenance is being carried out on another partition. Since local index partitions are in line with the data partitions, this advantage still exists.

- Local partitioned indexes require less maintenance than global indexes.

The SQL syntax for creating a local index is presented in the next listing, which refers to the SALES table we created under the Range Partitioning section. Table 9-9 contains an explanation of the syntax.

```
 1 create index sales_idx_l1 on sales (time_id)
 2 local
 3 (partition sales_idx_200501  tablespace sales_ts_idx_200501,
 4  partition sales_idx_200502  tablespace sales_ts_idx_200502,
 5  partition sales_idx_200503  tablespace sales_ts_idx_200503,
...
37  partition sales_idx_200711  tablespace sales_ts_idx_200711,
38  partition sales_idx_200712  tablespace sales_ts_idx_200712,
39  partition sales_idx_max  tablespace sales_ts_idx_max);
```

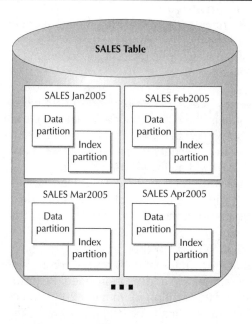

FIGURE 9-3. *Local partitioned index*

Lines	Important Points
2	Specifies that the index is to be **local**. This line alone tells Oracle Database 10*g* that the index is to be partitioned along the same ranges as the data.
3–39	Define the partition names and tablespaces for each partition. These lines are optional, but without them, Oracle Database 10*g* would use the same partition names as the data and would also place the index in the same tablespaces as the data—a situation that is less than ideal for performance!

TABLE 9-9. *Explanation of Local Partitioned Index Syntax*

Ask the Expert

Q: After a table and its local indexes have been defined using range partitioning with a default maxvalue **partition, how can you add more partitions as new subsets of data are received?**

A: Use an **alter table** statement to split the default data partitions, adding your new partition ranges. For example, to add a data partition for January 2008 data in the SALES table in the previous listing, issue the following command:

```
alter table sales
 split partition sales_max at (to_date('2008-02-01','YYYY-MM-DD'))
 into (partition sales_200801 tablespace sales_ts_200801,
     partition sales_max tablespace sales_ts_max);
```

This **alter table** command will result in the default index partition for **sales_idx_l1** to also be split. However, it will use the data partition names (for example, **sales_200801**) and tablespaces (**sales_ts_200801**, for instance); remember in the local index example we explicitly specified the partition names and tablespaces for the index. Therefore, the partition names and tablespaces will need to be adjusted using **alter index** commands, as follows:

```
alter index sales_idx_l1
 rename partition sales_200801 to sales_idx_200801;

alter index sales_idx_l1
 rebuild partition sales_idx_200801 tablespace sales_ts_idx_200801;

alter index sales_idx_l1
 rebuild partition sales_idx_max tablespace sales_ts_idx_max;
```

Some other points about local partitioned indexes:

- They can be unique, but only if the data partition key is part of the index key attributes.

- Bitmap indexes on partitioned tables must be local.

- Subpartitioned indexes are always local.

- They are best suited for data warehouses and decision support systems.

- Local unique indexes also work well in OLTP environments.

Global Partitioned Indexes *Global partitioned indexes* are indexes that are not directly associated with the data partitions. Instead, their partitions are defined independently, and the partition key can be different from the data partition key. This association is illustrated in Figure 9-4. This figure is again based on Figure 9-2, seen at the beginning of the chapter. It shows that the data is partitioned by monthly ranges, with a global index partitioned by product.

One advantage of global indexes is that if partition pruning cannot occur for the data partitions due to the predicates of a query, index partition pruning may still be possible with the global partition index. Global partitioned indexes are available as

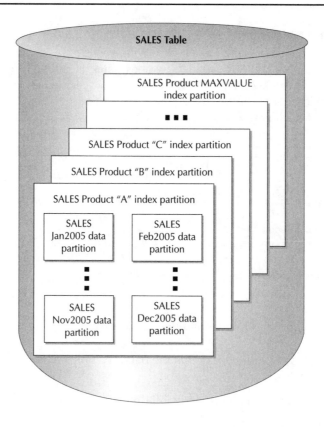

FIGURE 9-4. *Global partitioned index*

either range-based or hash-based. When using range-based global indexes, you must specify a default partition with **maxvalue**. Let's look at an example for creating a global partitioned index and then discuss how it would be used.

Referring again to the PHONE_USAGE table we created in the Composite Partitioning section, we have decided to create a global index on the **call_type_id**. Following is the SQL for this, and the explanation is presented in Table 9-10.

```
 1 create index phone_usg_idx_g1 on phone_usage (call_type_id)
 2 global
 3 partition by range (call_type_id)
 4 (partition ph_usg_idx_g1 values less than (2)
 5                    tablespace ph_usg_ts_idx_1,
 6  partition ph_usg_idx_g2 values less than (3)
 7                    tablespace ph_usg_ts_idx_2,
 8  partition ph_usg_idx_g3 values less than (4)
 9                    tablespace ph_usg_ts_idx_3,
10  partition ph_usg_idx_g4 values less than (5)
11                    tablespace ph_usg_ts_idx_4,
12  partition ph_usg_idx_gmax values less than (maxvalue)
13                    tablespace ph_usg_ts_idx_max);
```

Now, assume the following query is executed against the PHONE_USAGE table:

```
select count(*)
from phone_usage
where call_id = 3;
```

Without the global index we just defined, no partition pruning would occur since the query predicate does not refer to the data partition key **call_date**. But with the global index, only the index entries from the partition **ph_usg_idx_g3** would be scanned and therefore only data records related to those entries would be used in the result set.

Lines	Important Points
2	Specifies that the index is to be **global**.
3	Defines the type of partitioning (here, **range**) for this index and the partition key (**call_type_id**, in this case).
4–13	Define the partition names and tablespaces for each partition.

TABLE 9-10.   *Explanation for Global Partitioned Index Syntax*

Some other points on global partitioned indexes:

- They require more maintenance than local indexes, especially when you drop data partitions.

- They can be unique.

- They cannot be bitmap indexes.

- They are best suited for OLTP systems for direct access to specific records.

Prefixed and Nonprefixed Partition Indexes   In your travels through the world of partitioning, you will hear the terms *prefixed* and *nonprefixed* partition indexes. These terms apply to both local and global indexes. An index is prefixed when the leftmost column of the index key is the same as the leftmost column of the index partition key. If the columns are not the same, the index is nonprefixed. That's all well and good, but what affect does it have?

It is a matter of performance—nonprefixed indexes cost more, from a query perspective, than prefixed indexes. When a query is submitted against a partitioned table and the predicate(s) of the query include the index keys of a prefixed index, then pruning of the index partition can occur. If the same index was nonprefixed instead, then all index partitions may need to be scanned. (Scanning of all index partitions will depend on the predicate in the query and the type of index, global or local—if the data partition key is included as a predicate and the index is local, then the index partitions to be scanned will be based on pruned data partitions.)

Project 9-1   Creating a Range-Partitioned Table and a Local Partitioned Index

Data and index partitioning are an important part in maintaining large databases. We have discussed the reasons for partitioning and shown the steps to implement it. In this project, you will create a range-partitioned table and a related local partitioned index.

Step by Step

1. Create two tablespaces called **inv_ts_2007q1** and **inv_2007q2** using the following SQL statements. These will be used to store data partitions.

```
create tablespace inv_ts_2007q1
   datafile 'inv_ts_2007q1_1.dat' size 10m;

create tablespace inv_ts_2007q2
   datafile 'inv_ts_2007q2_1.dat' size 10m;
```

2. Create two tablespaces called **inv_idx_ts_2007q1** and **inv_idx_2007q2** using the following SQL statements. These will be used to store index partitions.

```
create tablespace inv_idx_ts_2007q1
    datafile 'inv_idx_ts_2007q1_f1.dat' size 10m;

create tablespace inv_idx_ts_2007q2
    datafile 'inv_idx_ts_2007q2_f1.dat' size 10m;
```

3. Create a partitioned table called INVOICE using the following listing, based on the following information:

   a. Define the table with the columns identified in Table 9-11.

   b. Use **order_date** as the partition key, and subset the data into the first and second calendar quarters 2007.

   c. Define the table with the data partitions and tablespaces identified in Table 9-12.

   d. Use the **enable row movement** option:

```
create table invoice (
   invoice_id    number,
   customer_id   number,
   order_date    date,
   ship_date     date)
partition by range (order_date)
(partition INV_2007Q1 values less than
                    (to_date(2007-04-01','YYYY-MM-DD'))
                  tablespace inv_ts_2007Q1,
 partition INV_2007Q2 values less than
                    (to_date('2007-07-01','YYYY-MM-DD'))
                  tablespace inv_ts_2007Q2,
 partition inv_max values less than (maxvalue)
                  tablespace inv_ts_max)
enable row movement;
```

4. Create a local partitioned index called **inv_order_dt_idx** on **call_date** using the following listing as well as the index partitions and tablespaces identified in Table 9-12.

```
create index inv_order_dt_idx on invoice(order_date)
local
(partition inv_idx_2007q1  tablespace inv_idx_ts_2007q1,
 partition inv_idx_2007q2  tablespace inv_idx_ts_2007q2,
 partition inv_idx_max  tablespace inv_idx_ts_max);
```

(continued)

Column Name	Data Type
INVOICE_ID	NUMBER
CUSTOMER_ID	NUMBER
ORDER_DATE	DATE
SHIP_DATE	DATE

TABLE 9-11. *INVOICE Table Columns*

Project Summary

The steps in this project reinforce some of the more common scenarios you will encounter: range-based partitioning and prefixed local partitioned indexes. Separate tablespaces were used for data and indexes, quarterly partitions were defined, a local index was defined, and the **enable row movement** was used to allow the database to automatically redistribute rows to their related partitions in the event of an update to the partition key.

Well, we have certainly covered a lot in this section. Having the background information on these topics will serve you well when maintaining and tuning large databases. Before we move on to the next section, let's take a quick progress check to make sure it all sank in.

	Partition Name	Tablespace Name	Upper Range Limit
Data Partitions	INV_2007Q1	INV_TS_2007Q1	Apr 1, 2007
	INV_2007Q2	INV_TS_2007Q2	July 1, 2007
	INV_MAX	INV_TS_MAX	MAXVALUE
Index Partitions	INV_IDX_2007Q1	INV_IDX_TS_2007Q1	Apr 1, 2007
	INV_IDX_2007Q2	INV_IDX_TS_2007Q2	July 1, 2007
	INV_IDX_MAX	INV_IDX_TS_MAX	MAXVALUE

TABLE 9-12. *INVOICE Table Data and Index Partitions*

Progress Check

1. List at least three DML commands that can be applied to partitions as well as tables.

2. What does partition pruning mean?

3. How many table attributes can be used to define the partition key in list partitioning?

4. Which type of partitioning is most commonly used with a date-based partition key?

5. Which partitioning types cannot be combined together for composite partitioning?

6. How many partition keys can be defined for a partitioned table?

7. Which type of partitioned index has a one-to-one relationship between the data and index partitions?

8. What is meant by a prefixed partitioned index?

CRITICAL SKILL 9.3

Compress Your Data

As you load more and more data into your database, performance and storage maintenance can quickly become concerns. Usually at the start of an implementation of a database, data volumes are estimated and projected a year or two ahead. However, often times these estimates turn out to be on the low side and you find yourself

---

Progress Check Answers

1. The following DML commands can be applied to partitions as well as tables: **delete**, **insert**, **select**, **truncate**, and **update**.

2. Partition pruning is the process of eliminating data not belonging to the subset defined by the criteria of a query.

3. Only one table attribute can be used to define the partition key in list partitioning.

4. Range partitioning is most commonly used with a date-based partition key.

5. List and hash partitioning cannot be combined for composite partitioning.

6. Only one partition key may be defined.

7. Local partitioned indexes have a one-to-one relationship between the data and index partitions.

8. A partitioned index is prefixed when the leftmost column of the index key is the same as the leftmost column of the index partition key.

scrambling for more space in order to load new data. In addition to the partitioning abilities discussed in the previous section, Oracle Database 10*g* has the ability to *compress* your data and indexes to further address the concerns of performance and maintenance.

Compression can be performed at the data or index levels. In this section, we will discuss the options available with Oracle Database 10*g* and their impacts.

Data Compression

With *data compression,* duplicate values in a database block are removed, leaving only a reference to the removed value, which is placed at the beginning of the block. All of the information required to rebuild the data in a block is contained within the block.

By compressing data, physical disk space required is reduced, and disk I/O and memory usage are also reduced, thereby improving performance. However, there are some cases when data compression is not appropriate. The following should be considered when looking at whether or not to compress data:

- Does the table exist in an OLTP or data warehousing environment? Data compression is best suited for data that is updated infrequently or, better yet, is read-only. Since most data in a data warehouse is considered read-only, data compression is more compatible with this type of environment.

- Does the table have many foreign keys? Foreign keys result in a lot of duplicate values in data. Tables with these structures are ideal candidates for data compression.

- How will data be loaded into the table? Even when compression is enabled, data is only compressed during bulk loading (for example, SQL*Loader). If data is loaded using a standard **insert into** statement, the data will not be compressed.

Compressed Data Objects

Compression can be specified for various data-related objects using the **create** or **alter** object commands. Table 9-13 identifies these objects and their first-level parent object, from which default compression properties are inherited if not specified for the base object. For example, if no compression property is specified for a table, it will inherit the property from its tablespace. The same applies to a data partition—if not specified at the partition level, the default property from the table will be used.

Object Type	Compression Property Inheritance Parent
Table	Tablespace
Materialized View	Tablespace
Partition	Table

TABLE 9-13. *Compression Property Inheritance*

The following listing demonstrates the creation of a table with compression enabled. Line 7 contains the keyword **compress** to tell Oracle that data compression is to be enabled.

```
1 create table commission (
2  sales_rep_id     number,
3  prod_id          number,
4  comm_date        date,
5  comm_amt         number(10,2))
6 tablespace comm_ts pctfree 5 initrans 1 maxtrans 255
7 compress;
```

Because compression can be enabled or disabled at different points in an object's lifetime (say, by using an **alter** command), and because the compression action only occurs on new data being loaded, it is possible for an object to contain both compressed and uncompressed data at the same time.

Ask the Expert

Q: Can existing data in a table be compressed and uncompressed?

A: Yes. There are two methods. The first is by using an **alter table** statement such as

```
alter table sales
move compress;
```

The second method is by using the utilities contained in the **dbms_redefinition** package.

Index Key Compression

Index key compression works in a similar manner to data compression in that duplicated values are removed from the index entries, but is a little more complicated and has more restrictions and considerations than data compression, partly due to the way indexes are structured. Since the details of these structures are beyond the scope of this book, we will focus on the benefits of, and the mechanisms for, defining index compression.

Compressing indexes offer the same benefits as data compression—that is, reduced storage and improved (usually) performance. However, performance may suffer during index scans as the burden on the CPU is increased in order to rebuild the key values. One restriction we should mention is that index compression cannot be used on a unique index that has only one attribute.

Enabling index compression is done using the **create index** statement. If you need to compress or uncompress an existing index, you must drop the index first and then re-create it with or without the compression option enabled. The following listing illustrates the syntax for creating a compressed index. Table 9-14 provides an explanation of the syntax.

```
1 create index comm_sr_prod_idx
2  on commission (sales_rep_id, prod_id)
3  compress 1;
```

Using data and index compression can provide substantial benefits in the areas of storage and performance. In the next section, we will look at how to improve query performance using Oracle Database 10*g*'s parallel processing options.

Lines	Important Points
1–2	Specify that the index is to be created on columns **sales_rep_id** and **prod_id**.
3	Specifies that the index is to be compressed, with the number of prefixing (leading) columns to compress. In this case, we used a value of 1 to indicate that duplicate values of the first column, **sales_rep_id**, are to be removed.

TABLE 9-14. *Explanation of Index Compression Syntax*

CRITICAL SKILL 9.4

Use Parallel Processing to Improve Performance

Improving performance, and by this we usually mean query performance, is always a hot item with database administrators and users. One of the best and easiest ways to boost performance is to take advantage of the parallel processing option offered by Oracle Database 10*g* (Enterprise Edition only).

Using normal (that is, serial) processing, the data involved in a single request (for example, user query) is handled by one database process. Using *parallel processing*, the request is broken down into multiple units to be worked on by multiple database processes. Each process looks at only a portion of the total data for the request. Serial and parallel processing are illustrated in Figures 9-5 and 9-6, respectively.

Parallel processing can help improve performance in situations where large amounts of data need to be examined or processed, such as scanning large tables, joining large tables, creating large indexes and scanning partitioned indexes. In order to realize the benefits of parallel processing, your database environment should not already be running at, or near, capacity. Parallel processing requires more processing, memory, and I/O resources than serial processing. Before implementing parallel processing, you may need to add hardware resources. Let's forge ahead by looking at the Oracle Database 10*g* components involved in parallel processing.

Parallel Processing Database Components

Oracle Database 10*g*'s parallel processing components are the *parallel execution coordinator* and the *parallel execution servers*. The parallel execution coordinator is responsible for breaking down the request into as many processes as specified by the request. Each process is passed to a parallel execution server for execution during which only a portion of the total data is worked on. The coordinator then assembles the results from each server and presents the complete results to the requester.

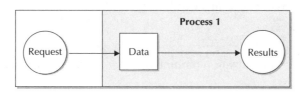

FIGURE 9-5. *Serial processing*

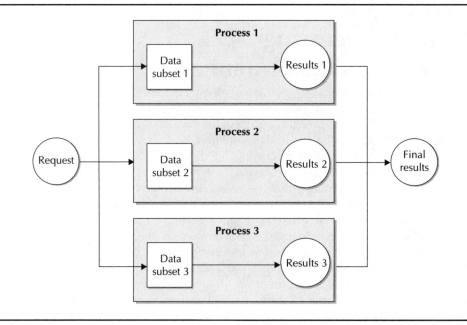

FIGURE 9-6. *Parallel processing*

Parallel Processing Configuration

Generally, not much configuration is required for Oracle Database 10*g* to perform parallel processing. There are, however, a number of configuration options that are required and will affect the effectiveness of parallelism.

To begin with, parallel processing is enabled by default for DDL (for example, **create** and **alter**) and query (for example, **select**) commands, but disabled for DML (say, **insert**, **update**, **delete**, **merge**) commands. If you wish to execute a DML command in parallel mode, you must first issue the following command for the session in which the command is to be executed, as in the following.

```
alter session enable parallel dml;
```

Several database initialization parameters affect parallel processing. These are shown next.

Initialization Parameters

When an Oracle instance starts, the parameters in the initialization file are used to define or specify the settings for the instance. Table 9-15 identifies the initialization parameters that affect parallel processing. In many cases, the default values will provide adequate results for your large database. Specifics of your own environment will influence your decisions on the best values to use.

As you can see from Table 9-15, there are dependencies between parameters. Modifying one may necessitate modifying others. If you modify any of the parallel processing parameters, you may also have to modify the following parameters:

- INSTANCE GROUPS

- PROCESSES

Parameter	Default Setting	Comment
PARALLEL_ADAPTIVE_ MULTI_USER	True	When set to True, enables an adaptive algorithm designed to improve performance in multiuser environments that use parallel processing.
PARALLEL_AUTOMATIC_ TUNING	False	No longer used. Exists for backward compatibility only.
PARALLEL_EXECUTION_ MESSAGE_SIZE	Installation Dependent	Specifies the byte size of messages for parallel processing.
PARALLEL_INSTANCE_ GROUP	Installation Dependent	Used in Real Application Cluster environments to restrict parallel query operations to a limited number of database instances.
PARALLEL_MAX_SERVERS	# of CPUs available to the database instance	Specifies maximum number of parallel processes for the database instance.
PARALLEL_MIN_PERCENT	0	Specifies minimum percentage of parallel processes required for parallel processing. Value is a percentage of PARALLEL_MAX_SERVERS.
PARALLEL_MIN_SERVERS	0	Specifies minimum number of parallel processes for the database instance. Cannot be greater than value of PARALLEL_MAX_SERVERS.
PARALLEL_THREADS_ PER_CPU	Usually set to 2, depending on operation system	Specifies the number of parallel processes per CPU.

TABLE 9-15.   *Initialization Parameters Affecting Parallel Processing*

- SESSIONS

- TRANSACTIONS

Invoke Parallel Execution

Parallel execution can be applied to tables, views, and materialized views. Assuming all necessary configurations have been made, there are several ways to invoke parallel execution. The first way is during table creation (including materialized views), using the **parallel** clause. If the table is being created using the results of a subquery, the loading of the table will be parallelized. In addition, by default, all queries that are executed against the table will be parallelized to the same extent. The next listing shows an example of specifying the parallel option for a table creation.

```
1 create table commission (
2  sales_rep_id     number,
3  prod_id          number,
4  comm_date        date,
5  comm_amt         number(10,2))
6 tablespace comm_ts pctfree 5 initrans 1 maxtrans 255
7 parallel;
```

The import line here is Line 7, specifying the parallel clause. This line could also have included an integer to specify the *degree of parallelism*—that is, the number of processes that are to be used to execute the parallel process. As the degree of parallelism is omitted in this example, the number of processes used will be calculated as number of CPUs × the value of the PARALLEL_THREADS_PER_CPU initialization parameter. The degree of parallelism for a table or materialized view can be changed using an **alter** statement.

Parallel processing can also be invoked when the parallel hint is used in a **select** statement. This hint will override any default parallel processing options specified during table creation. The following listing illustrates the use of the parallel hint. Line 1 contains the parallel hint, specifying the table to be parallelized (commission) and the degree of parallelism (4).

```
1 select /*+ parallel (commission, 4) */
2  prod_id, sum(comm_amt), count(*)
3 from commission
4 group by prod_id;
```

In some cases, Oracle Database 10g will alter how, or if, parallel processing is executed. Examples of these include the following:

■ Parallel processing will be disabled for DML commands (for example, **insert**, **update**, **delete**, and **merge**) on tables with triggers or referential integrity constraints.

■ If a table has a bitmap index, DML commands are always executed using serial processing if the table is nonpartitioned. If the table is partitioned, parallel processing will occur, but Oracle will limit the degree of parallelism to the number of partitions affected by the command.

Parallel processing can have a significant positive impact on performance. Impacts on performance are even greater when you combine range or hash-based partitioning with parallel processing. With this configuration, each parallel process can act on a particular partition. For example, if you had a table partitioned by month, the parallel execution coordinator could divide the work up according to those partitions. This way, partitioning and parallelism work together to provide results even faster.

CRITICAL SKILL 9.5
Use Materialized Views

So far, we have discussed several features and techniques at our disposal to improve performance in large databases. In this section, we will discuss another feature of Oracle Database 10*g* that we can include in our arsenal: materialized views.

Originally called snapshots, *materialized views* were introduced in Oracle8 and are only available in the Enterprise Edition. Like a regular view, the data in a materialized view are the results of a query. However, the results of a regular view are transitory—they are lost once the query is complete and if needed again, the query must be reexecuted. In contrast, the results from a materialized view are kept and physically stored in a database object that resembles a table. This feature means that the underlying query only needs to be executed once and then the results are available to all who need them.

From a database perspective, materialized views are treated like tables:

■ You can perform most DML and query commands such as insert, delete, update and select.

■ They can be partitioned.

■ They can be compressed.

- They can be parallelized.

- You can create indexes on them.

Materialized views are different in other ways and have some interesting features associated with them. Before we talk about those, let's look at some ways to use materialized views.

Uses for Materialized Views

Materialized views are used as a performance enhancing technique. Following are some usage examples. In this section, we will be discussing the first three uses, as they are applicable to our topic of large databases.

- Performing data summarization (for example, sums, averages)

- Prejoining tables

- Performing CPU-intensive calculations

- Replicating and distributing data

In large databases, particularly data warehousing environments, there is always a need to summarize, join, perform calculations, or do all three at once, on large numbers of records for reporting and analysis purposes. To improve performance in the past, a combination of views and physical tables were usually implemented that contained the results of these operations. The summary tables would require some type of extraction, transformation, and load (ETL) process to populate and refresh them. In addition to the base tables containing the detailed data, the users would need to know which combinations of the views and/or summary tables to use. These structures are illustrated in Figure 9-7.

Using materialized views has several advantages over more traditional methods. These include the following:

- Materialized views have a built-in data refresh process, which eliminates the need for custom ETL.

- As we said earlier, the data in materialized views can be partitioned, using the same techniques that apply to tables.

- Materialized views are transparent to the users. This is probably the most attractive feature of using materialized views, and we will expand more on this in the next section when we discuss automatic query rewriting.

Figure 9-8 illustrates summarization using materialized views.

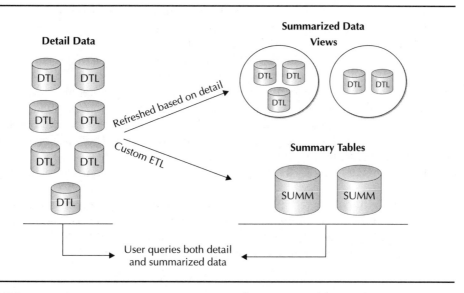

FIGURE 9-7. *Summarization using views and summary tables*

Query Rewrite

Earlier, we stated that one of the benefits of using materialized views was that they are transparent to the users. But what exactly does that mean and how can they be

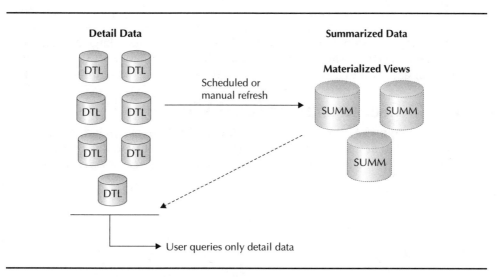

FIGURE 9-8. *Summarization using materialized views*

used if the users can't see them? In fact, because materialized views are so much like tables, you can give the users access to materialized views, but generally this is not done.

Instead, as indicated in Figure 9-8, the users always query the tables with the detail data—they don't usually query the materialized views directly. This is because the query optimizer in Oracle Database 10*g* knows about the materialized views and their relationships to the detail tables and can *rewrite* the query on the fly to access the materialized views instead. This results in huge performance gains without the user having to do anything special—just query the detail data. There is a maintenance benefit of this feature for the user as well: the queries do not have to change to point to different summary tables, as is the case with the more traditional summarization approach.

In order for the query to be rewritten, the structure of the materialized view must satisfy the criteria of the query. The following two listings demonstrate the query rewrite process. Let's assume we need to summarize the COMMISSION table we saw in the data compression section using the following query:

```
select prod_id, to_char(comm_date, 'YYYY-MM'), count(*), sum(comm_amt)
from commission
group by prod_id, to_char(comm_date, 'YYYY-MM');
```

Assume further that a materialized view (called **comm_prod_mv**) exists that contains summarized **commission** data by **sales_rep_id**, **prod_id**, and **comm_date** (full date). In this case, the query would be automatically rewritten as follows:

```
select prod_id, to_char(comm_date, 'YYYY-MM'), count(*), sum(comm_amt)
from comm_prod_mv
group by prod_id, to_char(comm_date, 'YYYY-MM');
```

By rewriting the query to use the materialized view instead, a large amount of data-crunching has been saved and the results will return much more quickly. Let's now turn our attention to determining what materialized views should be created.

When to Create Materialized Views

At this point, you may be asking yourself: "How do I determine what materialized views to create and at what level of summarization?" Oracle Database 10*g* has some utilities to help. These utilities are collectively called the *SQLAccess Advisor* and will recommend materialized views based on historical queries, or based on theoretical scenarios. They can be run from the Oracle Enterprise Manager Grid Control (*OEM*) or by calling the **dbms_advisor** package.

Create Materialized Views

Materialized views are created using a **create materialized view** statement, which is similar to a **create table** statement. This can be performed using SQL*Plus or OEM. The following listing shows a simple example of how to create the **comm_prod_mv** materialized view mentioned earlier and Table 9-16 provides an explanation of the syntax.

```
1 create materialized view comm_prod_mv
2    tablespace comm_prod_mv_ts
3    storage (initial 50k next 50k)
4    refresh complete  next sysdate + 7
5    enable query rewrite
6 as select sales_rep_id, prod_id, comm_date, count(*), sum(comm_amt)
7    from commission
8    group by sales_rep_id, prod_id, comm_date;
```

In the next three sections, we will be discussing some higher-level concepts: Real Application Clusters, Automatic Storage Management, and Grid Computing. But first, a progress check.

Lines	Important Points
2–3	Specify the tablespace and storage parameters.
4	Specifies how and when to refresh the data. In this case, the materialized view will be populated immediately and be completely refreshed every seven days thereafter.
5	Specifies that query rewrite is to be enabled.
6–8	Specify the query that will act as the source of the data.

TABLE 9-16. *Explanation of Materialized View Creation Syntax*

Progress Check ⏱

1. True or False: Tables with many foreign keys are good candidates for compression.

2. Name the two processing components involved in Oracle Database 10*g*'s parallel processing.

3. What is the function of the SQLAccess Advisor?

4. True or False: In order to access the data in a materialized view, a user or application must query the materialized view directly?

5. List the ways in which parallel processing can be invoked.

6. In what situation can index key compression *not* be used on a unique index?

CRITICAL SKILL 9.6

Real Application Clusters: A Primer

When working with large databases, issues such as database availability, performance and scalability are very important. In today's 24/7 environments, it is not usually acceptable for a database to be unavailable for any length of time—even for planned maintenance or for coping with unexpected failures. Here's where Oracle Database 10*g*'s Real Application Clusters (RAC) comes in.

Originally introduced in Oracle9*i* and only available with the Enterprise Edition, Real Application Clusters is a feature that allows database hardware and instances to be grouped together to act as one database using a shared-disk architecture. Following is a high-level discussion on RAC's architecture.

Progress Check Answers

1. True.

2. The Parallel Execution Coordinator and the Parallel Execution Servers.

3. The SQLAccess Advisor recommends potential materialized views based on historical or theoretical scenarios.

4. False. While the end user or application can query the materialized view directly, usually the target of a query is the detail data and Oracle's query rewrite capabilities will automatically return the results from the materialized view instead of the detail table (assuming the materialized view meets the query criteria).

5. Parallel processing can be invoked based on the parallelism specified for a table at the time of its creation, or by providing the parallel hint in a select query.

6. If the unique index has only one attribute, key compression cannot be used.

RAC Architecture

A typical RAC implementation groups multiple Oracle database instances running on multiple machines (or nodes). These nodes communicate with each other and share a common pool of disks. The disks house all of the data files that comprise the database. This architecture is illustrated in Figure 9-9.

Let's look at a few of the key components in Figure 9-9:

- Each node is connected to each other using high bandwidth communications.

- Each node has its own set of log (redo) files.

- The Cluster Manager monitors the status of each database instance in the cluster and enables communication between the instances. This manager is known as the Cluster Synchronization Services (CSS). In previous versions of Oracle, it was just referred to as the "Cluster Manager." When RAC was first introduced, cluster management was performed by third-party software, which is still supported by Oracle Database 10*g*.

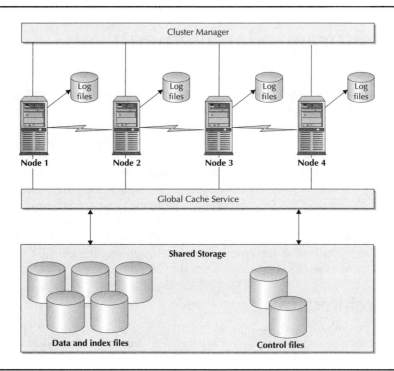

FIGURE 9-7. *Real Application Clusters—conceptual architecture*

- The Global Cache Service controls data exchange between nodes using the *Cache Fusion* technology. Cache Fusion synchronizes the memory cache in each node using high-speed communications. This allows any node to access any data in the database.

- Shared storage consists of data and index files, as well as control files.

This architecture makes RAC systems highly available. For example, if Node 2 in Figure 9-9 fails or requires maintenance, the remaining nodes will keep the database available.

This activity is transparent to the user or application and as long as at least one node is active, all data is available. RAC architecture also allows near-linear scalability and offers increased performance benefits. New nodes can easily be added to the cluster when needed to boost performance.

Administering and maintaining data files on both RAC and single-node systems have always required a good deal of effort, especially when data partitioning is involved. Oracle's solution to reducing this effort is Automatic Storage Management, which we will discuss next.

CRITICAL SKILL 9.7

Automatic Storage Management: Another Primer

In previous versions of Oracle and with most other databases, management of data files for large databases consumes a good portion of the DBA's time and effort. The number of data files in large databases can easily be in the hundreds or even thousands. The DBA must coordinate and provide names for these files and then optimize the storage location of files on the disks. The new *Automatic Storage Management (ASM)* feature in Oracle Database 10*g* Enterprise Edition addresses these issues.

ASM simplifies the management of disks and data files by creating logical groupings of disks into *disk groups.* The DBA need only refer to the groups, not the underlying data files. Data files are automatically named and distributed evenly (striped) throughout the disks in the group for optimal throughput. As disks are added or removed from the disk group, ASM redistributes the files among the available disks, automatically, while the database is still running. ASM can also mirror data for redundancy.

ASM Architecture

When ASM is implemented, each node in the database (clustered or nonclustered) has an ASM instance and a database instance, with a communication link between them. The ASM instance manages and works with the disk groups, and the database instance works with the data files. Figure 9-10 illustrates this architecture.

The following points address the key components in Figure 9-10:

- The ASM instance manages the disk groups and ASM files. The names of the ASM files in each disk group are system generated. The ASM instance maintains a map of data files and disks.

- The database instance accesses the ASM files directly, not the disk groups. In order to do this, the database instance must communicate with the ASM instance to request the names and locations of ASM data files required.

- A database can contain both ASM and non-ASM files and the database instance can access either type.

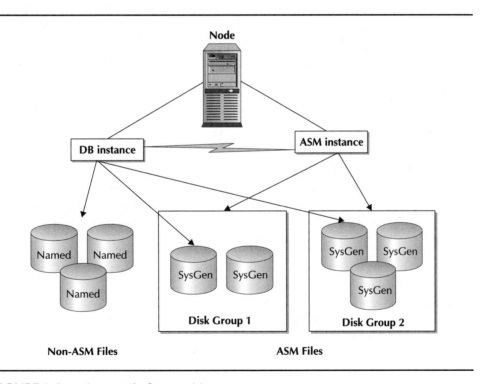

FIGURE 9-8. *Automatic Storage Management*

Ask the Expert

Q: After ASM disk groups are defined, how are they associated with a table?

A: ASM disk groups are referred to during tablespace creation, as in the following example:

```
1 create tablespace ts1
2   datafile +diskgrp1 /alias1;
```

This listing creates tablespace **ts1** in disk group **diskgrp1**. Note that this assumes that both **diskgrp1** and **alias1** have previously been defined.

A table can now be created in tablespace **ts1** and it will use ASM data files.

While ASM can be implemented in a single-node environment, its real power and benefits are realized when used in RAC environments. This powerful combination is the heart of Oracle Database 10*g*'s grid computing database architecture.

CRITICAL SKILL 9.8

Grid Computing: The "*g*" in Oracle Database 10*g*

In this chapter, we have discussed many issues and demands surrounding large databases—performance, maintenance efforts, and so on. We have also discussed the solutions offered by Oracle Database 10*g*. Now we will have a high-level look at Oracle Database 10*g*'s grid-computing capabilities.

NOTE
Oracle Database 10g's grid computing applies to both database and application layers. We will just be scratching the surface of grid computing and focusing on the database components.

The theory behind grid computing is that all parts of the grid (databases, applications, servers, disks, and so forth) work together in a highly integrated fashion, with each component being able to react appropriately to changes in other components in the grid. This results in efficient use of resources, faster response times, high availability, and so on.

The database components of Oracle Database 10*g*'s grid computing provide an infrastructure that brings together multiple servers (RAC) with shared storage (ASM), all tied together using the *Oracle Enterprise Manager (OEM)* Grid Control. Table 9-17 shows how grid computing addresses some of the issues facing large databases.

In order for grid computing to work, a software infrastructure layer needs to be in place to control the hardware and processes, as well as provide some automated maintenance capabilities. This is mainly the function of the OEM and is a core component of the grid. In addition, the Oracle Database 10*g* has the capability to perform some self-management.

Self-Managing Databases

One of the new features of Oracle Database 10*g* is its self-managing capabilities. The components of this feature are as follows:

- **Automatic Workload Repository**   Automatically collects workload and performance statistics to be used for all self-management activities.

Large Database Issue	Grid Components	Benefits
Data volumes	ASM	Reduced maintenance efforts Improved performance through data striping
Number of users and applications	RAC	Multiple nodes available to service requests Improved performance (workload balancing)
Complexity of requests	RAC	Improved performance (workload balancing)
	ASM	Improved performance (data striping)
Database availability	RAC	Multiple nodes available to service requests
Hardware/software costs	RAC and ASM	Use of lower-cost servers and generic disks
Resource management	OEM	Reduced maintenance efforts (aware of all grid components)

TABLE 9-17.   *Large Database Issues Addressed by Grid Computing*

■ **Unified Scheduler** Used to schedule routine administration tasks, as specified by the administrator or based on the information in the Automatic Workload Repository.

■ **Space Manageability** Includes automatic undo management, *Oracle-managed files,* free space management, and multiple block sizes.

■ **Backup and Recovery Manageability** Used to create reusable backup configurations, automate management of backups and logs, and ensure restart within a specified time after system failure. Includes *Recovery Manager* and *Mean Time to Recovery.*

■ **Automatic Database Diagnostic Monitor (ADDM)** Used to diagnose performance bottlenecks.

■ **Server-Generated Alerts** Alerts are sent when the database encounters or anticipates a problem.

■ **Database Resource Manager** Used to prioritize work within the database, ensuring that high priority users or jobs get the resources they need, when they need them.

■ **Advisors** Used to analyze objects and recommend actions. Advisors include

■ **Space Advisors** Segment Advisor and Undo Advisor

■ **Backup and Recovery Advisors** Logfile Size Advisor and MTTR Advisor

■ **SQLAccess Advisor**

■ **SQL Tuning Advisor**

■ **Memory Advisors** Shared Pool Advisor, Buffer Cache Advisor, and PGA Advisor

Grid computing has the potential to offer tremendous benefits in the areas of availability, performance and maintenance, all while reducing costs. Grid computing will be the last in our discussions on design and architectural issues. We'll take a progress check and then explore some of the analytical aspects offered by Oracle Database 10*g* when working with large databases.

Progress Check ⏱

1. In an RAC system, what component connects the nodes to the shared storage?

2. When a disk is added to an ASM disk group, what happens to the existing data in the group?

3. True or False: A database instance in an ASM system accesses the disk groups?

4. What component of a self-managing database contains workload and performance statistics used for self-management activities?

5. What are the database-related components that are part of grid computing?

6. What is the function of the Cluster Manager in RAC systems?

CRITICAL SKILL 9.9

Use SQL Aggregate and Analysis Functions

Once your database has been loaded with data, your users or applications will, of course, want to use that data to run queries, perform analysis, produce reports, extract data, and so forth. Oracle Database 10g provides many sophisticated aggregation and analysis functions that can help ease the pain sometimes associated with analyzing data in large databases.

Progress Check Answers

1. The Global Cache Service (or Cache Fusion) connects the nodes to the shared storage.

2. The existing data is automatically redistributed among all disks in the disk group.

3. False. The database instance communicates with the ASM instance to determine which ASM files to access directly. Only the ASM instance works with the disk groups.

4. The Automatic Workload Repository contains workload and performance statistics used for self-management activities.

5. RAC, ASM, and OEM are the database components that are part of grid computing.

6. The Cluster Manager monitors the status of each database instance in the cluster and enables communication between the instances.

Aggregation Functions

Oracle Database 10*g* provides extensions to the standard SQL **group by** clause of the **select** statement that generate other totals as part of the result set that previously required multiple queries, nested subqueries, or importing into spreadsheet type applications. These extensions are **rollup** and **cube**.

rollup

The **rollup** extension generates subtotals for attributes specified in the **group by** clause, plus another row representing the grand total. The following is an example of the rollup extension, using the SALES table we have seen throughout this chapter:

```sql
select c.cust_gender gender,
       b.channel_class channel_class,
       to_char(a.time_id, 'yyyy-mm') month,
       count(*) unit_count,
       sum(a.amount_sold) amount_sold
from sales a, channels b, customers c
where a.channel_id = b.channel_id
and    a.cust_id = c.cust_id
and    to_char(a.time_id, 'yyyy-mm') between '2001-01' and '2001-02'
group by rollup(c.cust_gender,
                b.channel_class,
                to_char(a.time_id, 'yyyy-mm'));
```

GENDER	CHANNEL_CLASS	MONTH	UNIT_COUNT	AMOUNT_SOLD
F	Direct	2001-01	4001	387000.9
F	Direct	2001-02	3208	365860.13
F	Direct		7209	752861.03
F	Others	2001-01	2486	242615.9
F	Others	2001-02	2056	229633.52
F	Others		4542	472249.42
F	Indirect	2001-01	1053	138395.21
F	Indirect	2001-02	1470	189425.88
F	Indirect		2523	327821.09
F			14274	1552931.54
M	Direct	2001-01	7038	719146.28
M	Direct	2001-02	6180	641192.61
M	Direct		13218	1360338.89
M	Others	2001-01	4310	414603.03
M	Others	2001-02	3751	391792.61
M	Others		8061	806395.64
M	Indirect	2001-01	1851	211947.81
M	Indirect	2001-02	2520	285219.79
M	Indirect		4371	497167.6
M			25650	2663902.13
			39924	4216833.67

In the results, we can see that counts and sums of **amount_sold** are returned at the following levels:

- By GENDER, CHANNEL_CLASS, and MONTH

- Subtotals by CHANNEL_CLASS within GENDER

- Subtotals by GENDER

- Grand total

cube

The **cube** extension takes **rollup** a step further by generating subtotals for each combination of the group by attributes, totals by attribute, and the grand total. The following is an example of the **cube** extension, using the same query we used for **rollup**:

```
select c.cust_gender gender,
       b.channel_class channel_class,
       to_char(a.time_id, 'yyyy-mm') month,
       count(*) unit_count,
       sum(a.amount_sold) amount_sold
from sales a, channels b, customers c
where a.channel_id = b.channel_id
and   a.cust_id = c.cust_id
and   to_char(a.time_id, 'yyyy-mm') between '2001-01' and '2001-02'
group by cube(c.cust_gender,
              b.channel_class,
              to_char(a.time_id, 'yyyy-mm'));
```

GENDER	CHANNEL_CLASS	MONTH	UNIT_COUNT	AMOUNT_SOLD
			39924	4216833.67
		2001-01	20739	2113709.13
		2001-02	19185	2103124.54
	Direct		20427	2113199.92
	Direct	2001-01	11039	1106147.18
	Direct	2001-02	9388	1007052.74
	Others		12603	1278645.06
	Others	2001-01	6796	657218.93
	Others	2001-02	5807	621426.13
	Indirect		6894	824988.69
	Indirect	2001-01	2904	350343.02
	Indirect	2001-02	3990	474645.67
F			14274	1552931.54
F		2001-01	7540	768012.01
F		2001-02	6734	784919.53
F	Direct		7209	752861.03
F	Direct	2001-01	4001	387000.9

F	Direct	2001-02	3208	365860.13
F	Others		4542	472249.42
F	Others	2001-01	2486	242615.9
F	Others	2001-02	2056	229633.52
F	Indirect		2523	327821.09
F	Indirect	2001-01	1053	138395.21
F	Indirect	2001-02	1470	189425.88
M			25650	2663902.13
M		2001-01	13199	1345697.12
M		2001-02	12451	1318205.01
M	Direct		13218	1360338.89
M	Direct	2001-01	7038	719146.28
M	Direct	2001-02	6180	641192.61
M	Others		8061	806395.64
M	Others	2001-01	4310	414603.03
M	Others	2001-02	3751	391792.61
M	Indirect		4371	497167.6
M	Indirect	2001-01	1851	211947.81
M	Indirect	2001-02	2520	285219.79

In the results, we can see that counts and sums of **amount_sold** are returned at the following levels:

- By GENDER, CHANNEL_CLASS, and MONTH
- Subtotals by MONTH within CHANNEL_CLASS
- Subtotals by MONTH within GENDER
- Subtotals by CHANNEL_CLASS within GENDER
- Subtotals by MONTH
- Subtotals by CHANNEL_CLASS
- Subtotals by GENDER
- Grand total

Analysis Functions

Oracle Database 10*g* provides a number of ranking and statistical functions that previously would have required some pretty heavy SQL to perform, or an extract to a third-party application. In this section, we will look at the analysis function available and provide examples of their use where appropriate.

NOTE
Some of the functions in this section are based on complex statistical calculations. Don't be worried if you are unfamiliar with these concepts. It is more important for you to know that these functions exist than it is to understand the theory behind them.

Ranking Functions

Ranking functions provide the ability to rank a row of a query result relative to the other rows in the result set. Common examples of uses for these functions include identifying the top ten selling products for a period, or classifying or grouping a salesperson's commissions into one of four buckets. The ranking functions included in Oracle Database 10g are

- rank
- dense_rank
- cume_dist
- percent_rank
- ntile
- row_number

rank and dense_rank Functions   The simplest ranking functions are **rank** and **dense_rank**. These functions are very similar and determine the ordinal position of each row within the query result set. The difference between these two functions is that **rank** will leave a gap in the sequence when there is a tie for position, whereas **dense_rank** does not leave a gap. The results of the following listing illustrate the difference between the two.

```
select prod_id,
       sum(quantity_sold),
       rank () over (order by sum(quantity_sold) desc) as rank,
       dense_rank () over (order by sum(quantity_sold) desc) as dense_rank
from sales
where to_char(time_id, 'yyyy-mm') = '2001-06'
group by prod_id;

    PROD_ID SUM(QUANTITY_SOLD)       RANK DENSE_RANK
---------- ------------------ ---------- ----------
         24                762          1          1
         30                627          2          2
```

147	578	3	3
33	552	4	4
40	550	5	5
133	550	5	5
48	541	7	6
120	538	8	7
23	535	9	8
119	512	10	9
124	503	11	10
140	484	12	11
148	472	13	12
139	464	14	13
123	459	15	14
131	447	16	15
25	420	17	16
135	415	18	17
137	407	19	18
146	401	20	19

As you can see, the ordinal position 6 does not exist as a value for **rank**, but it does for **dense_rank**. If from this result set you wanted to see the top ten listings for **prod_id**, you would use the original query as a subquery, as in the following listing:

```
select * from
   (select prod_id,
           sum(quantity_sold),
           rank () over (order by sum(quantity_sold) desc) as rank,
           dense_rank () over (order by sum(quantity_sold) desc) as dense_rank
   from sales
   where to_char(time_id, 'yyyy-mm') = '2001-06'
   group by prod_id)
where rank < 11;
```

To see the bottom ten **prod_id**s, use the same query, but change the **order by** option from descending (**desc**) to ascending (**asc**). The next two functions, **cume_dist** and **percent_rank**, are statistical in nature but still part of the family of ranking functions.

cume_dist and percent_rank Functions   The **cume_dist** function calculates the cumulative distribution of a value in a group of values. Since this is not a statistics beginner's guide, we will not attempt to provide the theoretical background on cumulative distribution. However, we can offer these points:

■   The range of values returned by **cume_dist** is always between 0 and 1.

■   The value returned by **cume_dist** is always the same in the case of tie values in the group.

■ The formula for cumulative distribution is

$$\frac{\text{\# of rows with values = value of row being evaluated}}{\text{\# of rows being evaluated}}$$

Looking at the query we used when discussing rank, the following listing calculates the cumulative distribution for **quantity_sold**. The results immediately follow the listing.

```
select prod_id,
    sum(quantity_sold),
    cume_dist () over (order by sum(quantity_sold) asc) as cume_dist
from sales
where to_char(time_id, 'yyyy-mm') = '2001-06'
group by prod_id
order by sum(quantity_sold) desc;
```

```
   PROD_ID SUM(QUANTITY_SOLD)  CUME_DIST
---------- ------------------- ----------
        24                 762          1
        30                 627 .985915493
       147                 578 .971830986
        33                 552 .957746479
        40                 550 .943661972
       133                 550 .943661972
        48                 541 .915492958
       120                 538 .901408451
        23                 535 .887323944
       119                 512 .873239437
       124                 503  .85915493
       140                 484 .845070423
       148                 472 .830985915
       139                 464 .816901408
       123                 459 .802816901
       131                 447 .788732394
        25                 420 .774647887
       135                 415  .76056338
       137                 407 .746478873
       146                 401 .732394366
```

The **percent_rank** function is similar to the **cume_dist** function, but calculates a percentage ranking of a value relative to its group. Again, without getting into the theory, we can make some points about **percent_rank**:

■ The range of values returned by the function is always between 0 and 1.

■ The row with a rank of 1 will have a percent rank of 0.

- The formula for calculating percent rank is

$$\frac{\text{rank of row within its group} - 1}{\text{\# of rows in the group} - 1}$$

The next listing and its results demonstrate the **percent_rank** function using the base query we have been using in this section.

```
select prod_id,
       sum(quantity_sold),
       rank () over (order by sum(quantity_sold) desc) as rank,
       percent_rank ()
            over (order by sum(quantity_sold) asc) as percent_rank
from sales
where to_char(time_id, 'yyyy-mm') = '2001-06'
group by prod_id
order by sum(quantity_sold) desc;
```

PROD_ID	SUM(QUANTITY_SOLD)	RANK	PERCENT_RANK
24	762	1	1
30	627	2	.985714286
147	578	3	.971428571
33	552	4	.957142857
40	550	5	.928571429
133	550	5	.928571429
48	541	7	.914285714
120	538	8	.9
23	535	9	.885714286
119	512	10	.871428571
124	503	11	.857142857
140	484	12	.842857143
148	472	13	.828571429
139	464	14	.814285714
123	459	15	.8
131	447	16	.785714286
25	420	17	.771428571
135	415	18	.757142857
137	407	19	.742857143
146	401	20	.728571429

The ntile Function   The **ntile** function divides a result set into a number of buckets specified at query time by the user, and then assigns each row in the result set a bucket number. The most common number of buckets used are 3 (tertiles), 4 (quartiles), and 10 (deciles). Each bucket will have the same number of rows, except in the case when the number of rows does not divide evenly by the number of buckets. In this case, each of the leftover rows will be assigned to buckets with the lowest bucket numbers until all leftover rows are assigned. For example, if four buckets were specified and the number of rows in the result set was 98, buckets 1 and 2 would have 25 rows each and buckets 3 and 4 would have 24 rows each.

Let's look at an example. Using our base query of **amount_sold** in the SALES table, we want to look at **amount_sold** by product subcategory and rank the amounts into four buckets. Here's the SQL:

```
select b.prod_subcategory,
       sum(a.quantity_sold),
       ntile(4) over (ORDER BY SUM(a.quantity_sold) desc) as quartile
from sales a, products b
where a.prod_id = b.prod_id
and to_char(a.time_id, 'yyyy-mm') = '2001-06'
group by b.prod_subcategory;
```

As you can see in the following results, the number of product subcategories was not evenly divisible by the number of buckets specified (in this case, 4). Therefore, six subcategories were assigned to the first quartile (bucket 1) and five subcategories were assigned to the second, third, and fourth quartiles.

PROD_SUBCATEGORY	COUNT(*)	SUM(A.QUANTITY_SOLD)	QUARTILE
Accessories	3230	3230	1
Y Box Games	2572	2572	1
Recordable CDs	2278	2278	1
Camera Batteries	2192	2192	1
Recordable DVD Discs	2115	2115	1
Documentation	1931	1931	1
Modems/Fax	1314	1314	2
CD-ROM	1076	1076	2
Y Box Accessories	1050	1050	2
Printer Supplies	956	956	2
Memory	748	748	2
Camera Media	664	664	3
Home Audio	370	370	3
Game Consoles	352	352	3
Operating Systems	343	343	3
Bulk Pack Diskettes	270	270	3
Portable PCs	215	215	4
Desktop PCs	214	214	4
Camcorders	196	196	4
Monitors	178	178	4
Cameras	173	173	4

row_number Function   The **row_number** function is a simple function that assigns a unique number to each row in a result set. The numbers are sequential, starting at 1, and are based on the **order by** clause of the query.

We will again use our SALES table query as an example. Using the query from our **ntile** example and adding a new column using **row_count**, we get

```
select b.prod_subcategory,
       sum(a.quantity_sold),
       ntile(4) over (ORDER BY SUM(a.quantity_sold) desc) as quartile,
       row_number () over (order by sum(quantity_sold) desc) as rownumber
       from sales a, products b
where a.prod_id = b.prod_id
and to_char(a.time_id, 'yyyy-mm') = '2001-06'
group by b.prod_subcategory;
```

In the following results, each row is assigned a number, depending on its position defined by the **order by** clause:

PROD_SUBCATEGORY	SUM(A.QUANTITY_SOLD)	QUARTILE	ROWNUMBER
Accessories	3230	1	1
Y Box Games	2572	1	2
Recordable CDs	2278	1	3
Camera Batteries	2192	1	4
Recordable DVD Discs	2115	1	5
Documentation	1931	1	6
Modems/Fax	1314	2	7
CD-ROM	1076	2	8
Y Box Accessories	1050	2	9
Printer Supplies	956	2	10
Memory	748	2	11
Camera Media	664	3	12
Home Audio	370	3	13
Game Consoles	352	3	14
Operating Systems	343	3	15
Bulk Pack Diskettes	270	3	16
Portable PCs	215	4	17
Desktop PCs	214	4	18
Camcorders	196	4	19
Monitors	178	4	20
Cameras	173	4	21

Windowing Functions

Before we get into the details, we need to define a couple of terms: analytic partitioning and analytic window.

- *Analytic partitioning* is the division of the results of an analytic function into groups within which the analytic function operates. This is accomplished using the **partition by** clause of the analytic function. Do not confuse this partitioning with data partitioning discussed earlier in this chapter. Analytic partitioning can be used with any of the analytic functions we have discussed so far.

- An *analytic window* is a subset of an analytic partition in which the values of each row depend on the values of other rows in the window. There are two types of windows: physical and logical. A physical window is defined by a specified number of rows. A logical window is defined by the **order by** values.

Windowing functions can only be used in the **select** and **order by** clauses. They can be used to calculate the following:

- Moving sum

- Moving average

- Moving min/max

- Cumulative sum

- Statistical functions

Let's look at an example of a moving sum function. The following shows the listing and results for calculating the moving sum from our SALES table by product category for a six-month period:

```
select b.prod_category,
       to_char(a.time_id, 'yyyy-mm'),
       sum(a.quantity_sold),
       sum(sum(a.quantity_sold)) over (partition by b.prod_category
                            order by to_char(a.time_id, 'yyyy-mm')
                            rows unbounded preceding) as cume_sum
from sales a, products b
where a.prod_id = b.prod_id
and b.prod_category_id between 202 and 204
and to_char(a.time_id, 'yyyy-mm') between '2001-01' and '2001-06'
group by b.prod_category, to_char(a.time_id, 'yyyy-mm')
order by b.prod_category, to_char(a.time_id, 'yyyy-mm');


PROD_CATEGORY                   TO_CHAR SUM(A.QUANTITY_SOLD)   CUME_SUM
------------------------------- ------- -------------------- ----------
Hardware                        2001-01                  281        281
```

Hardware	2001-02	306	587
Hardware	2001-03	442	1029
Hardware	2001-04	439	1468
Hardware	2001-05	413	1881
Hardware	2001-06	429	2310
Peripherals and Accessories	2001-01	5439	5439
Peripherals and Accessories	2001-02	5984	11423
Peripherals and Accessories	2001-03	5104	16527
Peripherals and Accessories	2001-04	5619	22146
Peripherals and Accessories	2001-05	4955	27101
Peripherals and Accessories	2001-06	5486	32587
Photo	2001-01	2802	2802
Photo	2001-02	2220	5022
Photo	2001-03	2982	8004
Photo	2001-04	2824	10828
Photo	2001-05	2359	13187
Photo	2001-06	3225	16412

As you can see in the results, the moving sum is contained within each product category and resets when a new product category starts. In the past, windowing analysis used to require third-party products such as spreadsheet applications. Having the capabilities to perform these functions right in the database can streamline analysis and report generation efforts.

Other Functions

There are many other functions included with Oracle Database 10*g* that can be used to analyze data in large databases. While we will not be going into any detail for these, they are listed here for completeness:

- Statistical functions, including:
  - Linear regression functions
  - Descriptive statistics functions
  - Hypothetical testing and crosstab statistics functions (contained a new PL/SQL package called **dbms_statistics**)
- **first/last** functions
- **lag/lead** functions
- Reporting aggregate functions
- Inverse percentile functions
- Hypothetical rank and distribution functions

As we stated earlier, we as database administrators do not have to know the theory behind the functions provided by Oracle Database 10*g*, or even how to use their results. However, we should be able to let our users know what capabilities are available. Knowing this, our users will be able to take advantage of these functions and construct efficient queries. In the next section, we will be discussing a new feature in Oracle Database 10*g*—SQL models.

Create SQL Models

One of the more powerful data analysis features introduced in Oracle Database 10*g* is *SQL models*. SQL models allow a user to create multidimensional arrays from query results. Formulas, both simple and complex, can then be applied to the arrays to generate results in which the user is interested. SQL models allow inter-row calculations to be applied without doing expensive self-joins.

SQL models are similar to other multidimensional structures used in business intelligence applications. However, because they are part of the database, they can take advantage of Oracle Database 10*g*'s built-in features of scalability, manageability security, and so on. In addition, using SQL models, there is no need to transfer large amounts of data to external business intelligence applications.

A SQL model is defined by the **model** extension of the **select** statement. Columns of a query result are classified into one of three groups:

- **Partitioning**   This is the same as the analytic partitioning we defined in the Windowing Functions section.

- **Dimensions**   These are the attributes used to describe or fully qualify a measure within a partition. Examples could include product, sales rep id, and phone call type.

- **Measures**   These are the numeric (usually) values to which calculations are applied. Examples could include quantity sold, commission amount, and call duration.

One of the main applications of SQL models is projecting or forecasting measures based on existing measures. Let's look at an example of the **model** clause to illustrate. The listing and its results show an aggregate query using the SALES table:

```
select c.channel_desc, p.prod_category, t.calendar_year year,
       sum(s.quantity_sold) quantity_sold
from sales s, products p, channels c, times t
where s.prod_id = p.prod_id
```

```
and    s.channel_id = c.channel_id
and    s.time_id = t.time_id
and    c.channel_desc = 'Direct Sales'
group by c.channel_desc, p.prod_category, t.calendar_year
order by c.channel_desc, p.prod_category, t.calendar_year;
```

```
CHANNEL_DESC       PROD_CATEGORY                          YEAR QUANTITY_SOLD
----------------   ------------------------------------  ------ -------------
Direct Sales       Electronics                            1998          7758
Direct Sales       Electronics                            1999         15007
...
Direct Sales       Hardware                               2000          1970
Direct Sales       Hardware                               2001          2399
Direct Sales       Peripherals and Accessories            1998         44258
...
Direct Sales       Software/Other                         2000         64483
Direct Sales       Software/Other                         2001         49146
```

In the results, we see the historical aggregate **quantity_sold** for each year by product category for the 'Direct Sales' channel. We can use the **model** clause to project the **quantity_sold**. In the following listing, we will project values for 2002 for the product category Hardware in the channel. The **quantity_sold** will be based on the previous year's value (2001), plus 10 percent. Table 9-18 explains the syntax of the listing.

```
 1 select channel_desc, prod_category, year, quantity_sold
 2 from
 3 (select c.channel_desc, p.prod_category, t.calendar_year year,
 4          sum(s.quantity_sold) quantity_sold
 5  from sales s, products p, channels c, times t
 6  where s.prod_id = p.prod_id
 7  and    s.channel_id = c.channel_id
 8  and    s.time_id = t.time_id
 9  group by c.channel_desc, p.prod_category, t.calendar_year) sales
10 where channel_desc = 'Direct Sales'
11 model
12    partition by (channel_desc)
13    dimension by (prod_category, year)
14    measures (quantity_sold)
15    rules (quantity_sold['Hardware', 2002]
16              = quantity_sold['Hardware', 2001] * 1.10)
17 order by channel_desc, prod_category, year;
```

Lines	Important Points
3–9	Define an in-line select that will be the source for the query. It is basically the same query we started with before the **model** clause.
10	Specifies that we are only going to look at 'Direct Sales' channels.
11	Specifies the **model** clause.
12	Specifies the **partition by** clause (in this case, **channel_desc**).
13	Specifies the **dimension by** clause (here, **prod_category** and **year**). These elements will fully qualify the measure within the **channel_desc** partition.
14	Specifies the **measures** clause (**quantity_sold**).
15–16	Specify the **rules** clause—that is, calculations we want to perform on the measure. In this example, we are referring to a specific cell of **quantity_sold**, described by the dimensions **prod_category** (Hardware) and **year** (2002).

TABLE 9-18. *Explanation of **model** Clause Syntax*

Following are the results of the previous query. Notice that a new row has been added for Hardware in 2002. Its **quantity_sold** is 2638.9, which is the previous year's value (2399) plus 10 percent.

```
CHANNEL_DESC     PROD_CATEGORY                    YEAR QUANTITY_SOLD
---------------- -------------------------------- ------ -------------
Direct Sales     Electronics                      1998           7758
Direct Sales     Electronics                      1999          15007
...
Direct Sales     Hardware                         2000           1970
Direct Sales     Hardware                         2001           2399
Direct Sales     Hardware                         2002         2638.9
Direct Sales     Peripherals and Accessories      1998          44258
...
Direct Sales     Software/Other                   2000          64483
Direct Sales     Software/Other                   2001          49146
```

The **model** clause has many variations and allows for very powerful calculations. Let's point out some of the characteristics and/or features you should be aware of. Supported functionalities include the following:

- Looping (for example, FOR loops)

- Recursive calculations

- Regression calculations

- Nested cell references

- Dimension wildcards and ranges

- The model clause does not update any base table, although in theory you could create a table or materialized view from the results of the query using the **model** clause.

Restrictions include the following:

- The **rules** clause cannot include any analytic SQL or windowing functions.

- A maximum of 20,000 rules may be specified. This may seem like plenty, but a FOR loop is expanded into many single-cell rules at execution time.

Project 9-2 Using Analytic SQL Functions and Models

Once all the database structures have been put in place and data has been loaded, the users will want to analyze it. Knowing what functions are available is important, and so is their use as well, at least to some extent. So, in this project we will walk through a more complex analytical example that includes using the **lag** function and creating a SQL model.

Step by Step

1. Create a view of the SALES table using the following listing. (The SALES table should have been created during your Oracle installation process.) This view will calculate the percentage change (called **percent_chng**) of **quantity_sold** from one year to the next using the **lag** function, summarized by **prod_category**, **channel_desc**, and **calendar_year**.

```
create or replace view sales_trends
as
select p.prod_category, c.channel_desc, t.calendar_year year,
       sum(s.quantity_sold) quantity_sold,
```

```
            round((sum(s.quantity_sold) -
                lag(sum(s.quantity_sold),1)
                    over (partition by p.prod_category, c.channel_desc
                        order by t.calendar_year)) /
                lag(sum(s.quantity_sold),1)
                    over (partition by p.prod_category, c.channel_desc
                        order by t.calendar_year) *
                100 ,2) as percent_chng
from sales s, products p, channels c, times t
where s.prod_id = p.prod_id
and   s.channel_id = c.channel_id
and   s.time_id = t.time_id
group by p.prod_category, c.channel_desc, t.calendar_year;
```

2. Select from the **sales_trends** view using the following listing. Notice that **quantity_sold** and **percent_chng** reset after each **channel_desc**. This is a result of the **lag** function's **partition by** clauses in the view definition.

```
select prod_category, channel_desc, year, quantity_sold, percent_chng
from sales_trends
where prod_category = 'Electronics'
order by prod_category, channel_desc, year;
```

3. Select from the **sales_trends** view using the following listing that contains a **model** clause. In this query, we are projecting **quantity_sold** and **percent_chng** according to the following rules:

   a. Filter the **prod_category** to only select 'Electronics'.

   b. Project for years 2002 to 2006 inclusive.

   c. The projected **quantity_sold** is calculated as the previous year's value plus the average **percent_chng** over the previous three years.

   d. The projected **percent_chng** is the average **percent_chng** over the previous three years.

```
select prod_category, channel_desc, year, quantity_sold, percent_chng
from sales_trends
where prod_category = 'Electronics'
model
    partition by (prod_category, channel_desc)
    dimension by (year)
    measures (quantity_sold, percent_chng)
    rules (
      percent_chng[for year from 2002 to 2006 increment 1] =
          round(avg(percent_chng)[year between currentv()-3 and
                                        currentv()-1], 2),
```

(continued)

```
quantity_sold[for year from 2002 to 2006 increment 1] =
    round(quantity_sold[currentv()-1] *
        (1 + (round(avg(percent_chng)[year between currentv()-3 and
                                      currentv()-1] ,2) / 100))))
order by prod_category, channel_desc, year;
```

4. Notice the projected values for 2002 to 2006 for each **channel_desc**.

Project Summary

The steps in this project build on the discussions we've had on Oracle Database 10g's analytic capabilities. We used the **lag** function to calculate percentage change and used the **model** clause of the **select** statement to project sales five years into the future based on past trends. By going to the next level of examples, we can start to appreciate the significance of these functions and how they can be used.

Oracle Database 10g's analytic functions provide powerful and efficient analysis capabilities that would otherwise require complex SQL and/or third-party tools. All of these functions are part of the core database—ready and waiting to be exploited by your users.

So, now we have come to the end of our discussions on large database features. A great deal of material has been presented in this chapter and we have really only seen the tip of the iceberg! However, you can feel confident that with this background information, you are primed to tackle almost any large database environment out there.

☑ Chapter 9 Mastery Check

1. Which of the following is *not* a valid combination for composite partitioning?

   A. Range partitioning with hash partitioning

   B. List partitioning with hash partitioning

   C. Range partitioning with list partitioning

2. What data population methods can be used on a compressed table that result in the data being compressed?

3. _____ partitioned indexes are defined independently of the data partitions, and _____ partitioned indexes have a one-to-one relationship with the data partitions.

4. Explain the functions of the Parallel Execution Coordinator in parallel processing.

5. For which of the following SQL commands is parallel processing *not* enabled by default?

   A. select

   B. insert

   C. create

   D. alter

6. What is meant by "degree of parallelism"?

7. What new analytic feature can be used to forecast values based on existing measures?

8. What two methods can be used to run the SQLAccess Advisor utilities for materialized views?

9. Which of the following are components of an RAC system? (Select all that apply.)

   A. Parallel Execution Server

   B. Cluster Manager

   C. Shared Storage

   D. ASM Instance

   E. Global Cache Service

10. In a grid computing envrionment, the _____ instance of a node manages the disk groups and maintains a map of data files and disks.

11. _____ partitioning allows you to control the placement of records in specified partitions based on sets of partition key values.

12. What analytic function would you use to assign each row from a query to one of five buckets?

13. What are the database components involved in grid computing?

14. What are the two types of windows that can be used in analytic functions?

15. The _____ automatically collects workload and performance statistics used for database self-management activities.

16. When creating partitioned tables, what option should you use to ensure that rows are redistributed to their correct partition if their partition key is updated?

APPENDIX

Mastery Check Answers

Chapter 1: Database Fundamentals

1. **The _____ background process is primarily responsible for writing information to the Oracle Database 10*g* files.**

   The database writer, or dbwr, background process is primarily responsible for writing information to the Oracle Database 10*g* files.

2. **How many online redo log groups are required to start an Oracle Database 10*g*?**

   B.

   Explanation The minimum number of redo log groups required to start an Oracle Database 10*g* is two though many DBAs add more groups. This increases the fault tolerance of the database.

3. **Of the following four items of information, which one is not stored in Oracle Database 10*g*'s control files?**

   B.

   Explanation The creator of the database is not stored anywhere in the assortment of the Oracle Database 10*g* support files.

4. **What is the function of a default temporary tablespace in the support of the Oracle Database 10*g*?**

   The default temporary tablespace is the location where sessions build intermediary objects to satisfy queries and perform sort operations.

5. **Differentiate between an Oracle Database 10*g* and instance.**

   The database is a collection of files, whereas an instance is a handful of processes working in conjunction with a computer's memory to support access to those files.

6. **Activities such as allocating space in the database and user management are commonly performed by the DBA. What feature in the Oracle Database 10*g* allows some of these secure operations to be carried out by non-DBA users? How are these rights given out?**

   System privileges allow the DBA to give out rights to perform selected secure operations to other Oracle Database 10*g* users. These privileges are given out with a grant statement.

7. **As a user of the Oracle Database 10*g* is created, we often specify a default tablespace. In this context, *default tablespace* means?**

   C.

   Explanation   Often, when one creates a table, the tablespace within which the table resides is not mentioned. The default tablespace feature ensures that tables created in this way always end up in the correct location.

8. **The _____ GUI interface is used to create a new database.**

   The Database Configuration Assistant, or dbca, GUI interface is used to create a new database.

9. **What happens when one tries to store the text "Madagascar" in a field with a specification of varchar2(8)?**

   An Oracle error is returned, and processing of the offending SQL statement terminates.

10. **What is the most common way one uses triggers in the Oracle Database 10*g*? Give an example of this activity.**

    Triggers are most commonly used to perform auditing operations. When an employee's salary is changed, a trigger could record the time, date, and name of the operator who performed the changes.

11. **What programming language, native to the Oracle Database 10*g*, is used to create stored objects such as triggers and functions?**

    D.

    Explanation   PL/SQL, the Oracle Database 10*g* procedural programming language, is what one uses to code items such as triggers and stored procedures.

12. **What is the role of the sysaux tablespace in the Oracle Database 10*g*?**

    The SYSAUX tablespace is a mandatory container that holds an assortment of tables that support some of the administrative tasks related to the Oracle Database 10*g*.

13. **The clob and blob data types differ in all but one of the following three ways. Which one does not apply to the differences between the two data types?**

    C.

    Explanation   As much as possible, system architects stick with the clob rather than the blob data type. It is much easier to work with than its close relative—the blob data type.

14. **There are many ways to replicate data from one node to another. What main feature does Oracle Streams provide that is missing from many other methods?**

    Oracle Streams can keep one node's data in sync with another, an almost insurmountable chore in many do-it-yourself solutions.

15. **What does the acronym SQL stand for?**

    A.

    Explanation   SQL is the industry standard for many relational database systems. Interestingly enough as you become more familiar with its syntax, it reads very much like plain and simple English. This makes it even more attractive as a data retrieval language.

Chapter 2: SQL: The Structured Query Language

1. **DDL and DML translate to _____ and _____, respectively.**

    DDL stands for Data Definition Language. DML stands for Data Manipulation Language.

2. **Which of the following descriptions is true about** insert **statements?**

    B.

    Explanation   Insert statements can *never* have a **where** clause. Every **insert** will create a row, providing it doesn't violate any constraints.

3. **In addition to the two mandatory keywords required to retrieve data from the database, there are three optional keywords. Name them.**

    The optional parts of a **select** statement are the **where** clause, an **order by** statement, and a **group by** statement.

4. **Write a SQL statement to select the customer last name, city, state, and amount sold for the customer represented by customer ID 100895.**

    Possible solutions include any of the Oracle and ANSI join options. The following SQL statement joins the CUSTOMERS and SALES tables using a simple Oracle join:

```
SQL> select cust_last_name, cust_city, cust_state_province, amount_sold
  2  from    customers c, sales s
  3  where  c.cust_id = s.cust_id
  4  and     c.cust_id = 100895;
```

5. **Retrieve a list of all product categories, subcategories, names, and list prices where the list price is greater than $100 while displaying the results for the product category all in uppercase.**

The following statement returns a list of all product categories, subcategories, and names for products with list prices greater than $100. The product categories are also all output in uppercase:

```
SQL> select UPPER(prod_category),
  2           prod_subcategory,
  3           prod_name,
  4           prod_list_price
  5  from     products
  6  where    prod_list_price > 100;
```

6. **Rewrite the query from the previous question and round the amount sold so that there are no cents in the display of the list prices.**

The following SQL statement alters the previous answer to return the list price without cents:

```
SQL> select UPPER(prod_category),
  2           prod_subcategory,
  3           prod_name,
  4           round(prod_list_price,0)
  5  from     products
  6  where    prod_list_price > 100;
```

7. **Retrieve a list of all customer IDs and last names where the customer has more than 200 entries in the SALES table.**

The list of all customer IDs and last names for customers that had more than 200 sales is returned by the following SQL statement:

```
SQL> select c.cust_id, cust_last_name, count(*)
  2  from     customers c, sales s
  3  where    c.cust_id = s.cust_id
  4  group by c.cust_id, cust_last_name
  5  having count(*) > 200;
```

8. **Display the product name of all products that have the lowest list price.**

To display all the product names that have the lowest list price, the following SQL statement would be used:

```
SQL> select prod_name
  2  from     products
  3  where    prod_list_price = (select min(prod_list_price)
  4                               from     products);
```

9. **Create a view that contains all products in the Electronics category.**

   The DDL to create a view with only Electronics products could be created this way:

   ```
   SQL> create view electronics_products
     2  as
     3  select prod_name
     4  from    products
     5  where  prod_category = 'Electronics';
   ```

10. **Sequences provide _____ generated integers.**

    Sequences provide sequentially generated integers. Without this valuable object, sequentially generated numbers could only be produced programmatically.

11. **This referential integrity constraint defines the relationship between two tables. Name it.**

    A foreign key is the referential integrity constraint that relates two tables to each other.

12. **Check constraints enable users to define and enforce rules for:**

    C.

    Explanation   Check constraints enable users to define and enforce rules individually for *one or more columns* within a table. It is not possible to put a check constraint on a table.

13. **Deferred constraints are not checked until this statement is issued.**

    Deferred constraints are not checked until the **commit** keyword statement is executed.

Chapter 3: The Database Administrator

1. **What is the benefit of a role?**

   A *role* is used to group privileges together so that the group (called a role) can be granted to Oracle. Beyond the management savings, think about the savings that are achieved in the catalog. If we give the same 2000 grants to 3000 users, we would have 6,000,000 grants stored in the database. If they were put into a single role, however, there would be only 3000 grants. An extreme example perhaps, but it illustrates the point.

2. **Should a table that is in tens or hundreds of extents be reorged?**

   No.

Explanation   Do not reorg tables unless you need to. The tables' extents are a contiguous set of blocks and if these are large enough, having many extents will not impact performance. You only need to reorg a table when there are a large number of chained rows. You can also consider reorging once your table is in thousands of extents.

3. **What is the preferred method for collecting object statistics?**

In Oracle Database 10g, use an automatic statistics collection whenever possible.

Explanation   Setting the Oracle Database 10g initialization parameter **statistics_level** to typical (the default) allows Oracle to automatically update statistics as a background task. In pre–Oracle Database 10g releases, the DBMS_STATS package should be run manually or can use the **monitoring** keyword in a CREATE or ALTER table. Monitoring and nomonitoring are deprecated in Oracle Database 10g.

4. **What is a segment?**

Each segment is a single instance of a table, partition, cluster, index, or a temporary or undo segment. A segment is broken down further into extents.

5. **What is an extent?**

An extent is a collection of contiguous data blocks that all belong to the same segment. One or more extents can exist for a single segment. New extents can be added to the segment as long as space allows.

6. **Name two reasons for implementing an index.**

Indexes are optional objects built on tables to improve performance and/or to help implement integrity constraints such as primary keys and uniqueness.

7. **How can you place a database in maintenance mode without first shutting it down?**

SYS and SYSTEM users can query the database without stopping the database and performing a subsequent **startup restrict** using the command **alter session quiesce restrict** when the Database Resource Manager option has been set up. The activities of other users continue until they become inactive.

8. **How can we limit the resources that a particular user can consume and how does this work?**

You can use the Profile feature to do some of this, but profiles are now being used more to manage password policies rather than system resources. The preferred approach is to use the Database_Resource_Manager package to limit system resources such as CPU, parallelism, undo pool space, execution time limits, and the number of sessions that can be active for a group.

A resource plan schedule can be used to schedule when groups will be enabled and disabled. Group switching can move a user to another group once a specified threshold has been met.

9. **When managing undo segments, what are the things that you need to think about?**

You need to first determine the length of time that **undo** will need to be retained for. Once you have decided this, you'll need to calculate the **undo** tablespace size based on system activity.

10. **What is likely to happen if you turn on the autoextend property for undo and temporary tablespaces with a maxsize set to unlimited?**

They will continue to grow indefinitely until they eventually use up all of the space in the directory.

11. **What is special about the SYS user account and how does it differ from SYSTEM?**

The SYS account is used as the schema to store the Oracle catalog. This has the DBA role as well as the SYSDBA privilege. The SYSTEM account also has the DBA role but not the **sysdba** privilege.

12. **What are temporary tablespaces used for?**

They store internal data used by Oracle while queries are running. Sort operations make use of the temporary tablespace if there is not enough room in the SGA to perform the sort operation. Data in temporary tablespaces is transient and not persistent. As soon as a transaction has completed, the data in the temporary tablespace can no longer be used. It can be thought of as a scratch pad area for Oracle.

13. **What are the two aspects of security that are covered in Oracle's implementation?**

Two key security aspects that must be implemented are authentication and authorization. Creating a distinct user in Oracle accomplishes authentication in that the user must be authenticated when they enter the database and we must know who they are. Once in the database, they still need to be authorized to access objects and resources. This is accomplished by granting privileges to the user.

14. **Name and describe the types of privileges that can be granted to a user.**

Two types of privileges can be given to a user: system and object privileges. System privileges are used to give authority to overall system objects rather than individual ones. The ability to perform a **create tablespace** is an example of this. Object privileges are a lower-level authority where a named object is granted to a user. Granting select on an individual table is an example of an object privilege.

15. How would you implement your corporate password policy in Oracle?

A profile can be used to implement a password management policy as well as to limit resources for a user. You can specify the number of days after which a user must change their password. You can also establish a policy where a password cannot be used again before a specified number of days has elapsed, and/or the new password must differ from the old by a certain number of changes. A function can also be used to ensure that the user will create a complex password.

Chapter 4: Networking

1. The _____ background process registers the service information to the listener.

The PMON background process registers the service information to the listener.

2. True or False: The LOCAL_LISTENER **parameter should be set to work with port 1521.**

False.

Explanation The **LOCAL_LISTENER** parameter is defined when port 1521 is not used.

3. The _____ is used during installation to configure Oracle Net Services.

The Oracle Net Configuration Assistant is used during installation to configure Oracle Net Services.

4. The _____file can be used to define grant or deny access to the Oracle database server.

The sqlnet.ora file can be used to define, grant, or deny access to the Oracle database server.

5. The _____utility can also be used to test a service.

The tnsping utility can also be used to test a service.

6. A _____ contains a set of parameters that define Oracle Net options on the remote or database server.

A profile contains a set of parameters that define Oracle Net options on the remote or database server.

7. **The ldap.ora file location can be manually specified with the _____ or** TNS_ADMIN **environmental variables.**

   The ldap.ora file location can be manually specified with the *LDAP_ADMIN* or **TNS_ADMIN** environmental variables.

8. **True or False: The easy naming method is a valid naming method.**

   True.

   Explanation The easy naming method is a valid naming method.

9. **The Oracle LDAP directory is called the _____.**

   The Oracle LDAP directory is named the Oracle Internet Directory.

10. **True or False: The Oracle Management Service is a repository of information generated by the Management Agent.**

    False.

    Explanation The Oracle Management Service interfaces with the management agents to process and monitor information. It is not the repository.

Chapter 5: Backup and Recovery

1. **What are some advantages of cold backups, and when would you use them?**

   Cold backups are consistent and very simple to implement. They are useful in situations where the database can be brought down to perform a backup. No recovery is required after a restore from a cold backup, if you choose. You can also perform a cold backup of a database in archivelog mode and perform a recovery of that database. These deliver simplicity and flexibility in cases where you can take a database down to back it up.

2. **What are disadvantages of cold backups?**

   The database is not available during the backup.

3. **Describe the difference between a logical and a physical backup.**

   A physical backup is performed by utilities such as RMAN or by a hot or cold backup, and operates on the underlying database data files. A logical backup, on the other hand, is performed by utilities such as Data Pump Export or Import and allows for a backup or restore to be performed on logical database structures such as tables or indexes.

4. **Name three different types of backups.**

   Three different types of backups are physical hot and cold backups, logical backups as implemented by Data Pump Export/Import, and RMAN backups.

5. What is the difference between an RMAN backup and an RMAN image copy?

Image copies are complete copies of binary data files as they exist in the database. They can be created through a hot or cold backup or by RMAN. Backups are created by RMAN and can only be *used* by RMAN since they are in a proprietary format. Backups compress unused data blocks, while image copies do not.

6. Under what situations should redo logs be restored in a recovery situation?

Redo logs can be restored where a cold backup of a database without archive logging was performed; otherwise, they should not be restored.

7. Name three interfaces that can be used to perform a Data Pump Export and Import.

The three interfaces that can be used to perform Data Pump exports and imports are the command-line interface, a command-line interface that uses a parameter file called **parfile**, and an interactive interface.

8. List some advantages of using RMAN.

RMAN has many advantages, including the following:

- The ability to perform incremental backups.

- The ability to create backup scripts.

- The ability to compress backups so that only blocks that were written to are backed up.

- Its tablespaces are not put into backup mode, so no extra redo is generated.

- Has simplified scripting and management of both files and archive logs.

9. Why would RMAN's recovery catalog be used rather than a control file to implement the repository?

RMAN's recovery catalog has many advantages over using a control file. Some of these are

- Scripts of common tasks can be created and stored.

- All backup information, including file names, are stored in the catalog for a longer period of time if needed.

- Complete reporting capabilities.

- The ability to recover a control file if it has been lost.

- Multiple databases can be managed from one backup location.

10. Are there any disadvantages to an RMAN recovery catalog?

One disadvantage to the recovery catalog is that it must be backed up itself. This is simple since it is a very small schema.

11. How can default settings be set up by you for future runs of RMAN?

Default settings can be set up by you with the RMAN **configure** command. Channels can be configured to achieve optimal performance and other backup configurations can be created to simplify backup and recovery scripts.

12. What is an RMAN backup-set and how does it relate to a backup-piece?

A backup-set is made up of one or more backup-pieces and is what constitutes a full or incremental backup. A backup-piece is a file that is managed by RMAN.

13. Describe the ways in which corrupt blocks can be recovered.

Individual data blocks can be recovered with the database online and available to users. You need to specify which block can be recovered and these can be found in the alert log or the v$backup_corruption or v$copy_corruption views. Block media recovery is only available with RMAN.

14. What are some advantages to incremental image copies?

Incremental image copies save disk space and network resources since the backup files are smaller. They can also speed up recovery when compared to applying archive logs.

15. When performing a recovery from a hot backup, do all files and tablespaces need to be brought forward to the same point in time?

All files and tablespaces (except for files in read-only tablespaces) need to be brought forward to the same point in time.

Chapter 6: PL/SQL

1. Where is PL/SQL executed?

PL/SQL is executed within the confines of the database. It will receive parameters and return data, but all program execution is performed in the database.

2. Which type of PL/SQL statement would you use to increase the price values by 15 percent for items with more than 1500 in stock and by 20 percent for items with fewer than 500 in stock?

B.

Explanation To be able to perform a validation of your data and then perform one task if the condition is met and another when the condition is not met, you must use the IF-THEN-ELSE construct.

3. **What is the** fetch **command used for?**

   The **fetch** command is used to retrieve data from an open cursor that had been opened previously.

4. **What will the following command perform?**

   It will set the value of the variable to 500.

5. **What is wrong with this function definition?**

   The END clause needs to have the same name as the name of the procedure. This value should be raise_price, not lower_price.

6. **What is the advantage of using the %TYPE attribute when defining PL/SQL variables?**

   The advantage of using the %TYPE attribute when defining PL/SQL variables is that it links the definition of the variable to the database definition. It also allows a program to adjust for changes to database structures while impacting the execution of the PL/SQL program.

7. **What Oracle Database 10g facility besides PL/SQL supports exception handling based on error numbers?**

   No other Oracle Database 10g facility besides PL/SQL supports exception handling based on error numbers.

8. **A commit that is issued in a PL/SQL program will commit what?**

   All transactions that are currently pending will be committed, unless the commit is issued within an autonomous transaction.

Chapter 7: Java

1. **True or False: One of the benefits of EJBs is that they combine business and user interface logic.**

   False.

   Explanation EJBs contain business logic, not user interface logic. User interface logic is contained in servlets.

2. **True or False: A benefit of the Oracle JVM is Java's multithreading capability in the database.**

   False.

   Explanation   Try to avoid the Java multithreading capability in the database.

3. **The _____ JDBC driver is used inside of the database.**

   The server-side JDBC driver is used inside of the database.

4. **A _____ can define where additional classes can be found.**

   A resolver specification can define where additional classes can be found.

5. **The _____ command is used to create a Java class file from within Oracle.**

   The **create java source** command is used to create a Java class file from within Oracle.

6. **True or False: SQLJ is the direction Oracle is going in when it comes to writing Java-stored procedures since it's easier to maintain than JDBC.**

   False.

   Explanation   SQLJ is deprecated in Oracle Database 10*g*.

7. **The _____ loads Java source, class, and resource files into the database.**

   The Library Manager loads Java source, class, and resource files into the database.

8. **When writing JDBC, _____ is the first step to be performed.**

   When writing JDBC, registering (loading) a driver is the first step to be performed.

   Explanation   A JDBC driver manages communication between a database and Java applications. Registering the driver is the first step for performing a database operation in a Java program.

9. **True or False: The SQLJ translator converts embedded SQL statements into JDBC code.**

   True.

   Explanation   The SQLJ translator converts embedded SQL code into JDBC code so it can be compiled by the Java compiler.

10. **The _____ script is used to configure the Oracle JVM.**

    The **initjvm.sql** script is used to configure the Oracle JVM.

    Explanation The **initjvm.sql** script loads the Java classes into the Oracle database and sets up the Oracle JVM in the Oracle database.

Chapter 8: XML

1. **XML stands for Extensible _____ Language.**

    XML stands for Extensible Markup Language.

2. **XML documents are in what type of data structure?**

    B.

    Explanation XML documents tag data using a hierarchical structure.

3. **What is the notation used when querying XML documents, which is implemented with Oracle Database 10*g*?**

    XPath is the notation used when querying XML documents.

    Explanation There are plans to base queries using the XQuery standard.

4. **What is a well-formed XML document?**

    A well-formed XML document is syntactically correct (in other words, there are corresponding end tags for every start tag).

5. **Using the** existsnode() **function within a SQL query should return what value if the node exists?**

    D.

    Explanation existsnode() returns a Boolean value: 0 if the node is not found, 1 if it is.

6. **Of the following four methods listed, which is used to store XML documents in Oracle XML DB?**

    D.

    Explanation For XML document management, Oracle has implemented numerous methods that can access Oracle XML DB.

7. **What is used to ensure that an XML document is valid?**

    XML Schema is associated to an XML document that defines the structure and data types the XML document must conform to.

8. **What is the defined data type that is used to store XML documents in Oracle Database 10*g*?**

   XMLType is the defined data type used to store XML documents in Oracle Database 10*g*.

9. **When using** xmlagg() **function to build an XML type, what SQL clause must it be accompanied by?**

   When using **xmlagg()** function to build an XML type, it must be accompanied by a **group by** clause.

   Explanation   The **group by** clause is used to group the result set into a hierarchical structure.

10. **What does the acronym XSLT stand for?**

    C.

    Explanation   XSLT, or Extensible Stylesheet Language, is used to automatically transform XML-tagged documents into multiple display formats such as HTML, or into another XML document.

11. **What does the acronym SQLX stand for?**

    A.

    Explanation   SQLX is the combination of the Structured Query Language used to access relational databases and XPath, which is used to query XML documents.

Chapter 9: Large Database Features

1. **Which of the following is *not* a valid combination for composite partitioning?**

   C.

   Explanation   Range partitioning with list partitioning is *not* a valid combination for composite partitioning.

2. **What data population methods can be used on a compressed table that result in the data being compressed?**

   For data to be compressed, it must be bulk loaded into the table or you can issue an **alter table** statement to compress existing data.

3. _____ **partitioned indexes are defined independently of the data partitions, and** _____ **partitioned indexes have a one-to-one relationship with the data partitions.**

Global partitioned indexes are defined independently of the data partitions, and local partitioned indexes have a one-to-one relationship with the data partitions.Global and local.

4. **Explain the functions of the Parallel Execution Coordinator in parallel processing.**

   The parallel execution coordinator is responsible for breaking down a request into as many processes as specified by the request. After the processes are complete, it then assembles all of the results and presents the complete data set to the requester.

5. **For which of the following SQL commands is parallel processing *not* enabled by default?**

   B.

   Explanation   Parallel processing is *not* enabled by default for **insert**.

6. **What is meant by "degree of parallelism"?**

   "Degree of parallelism" refers to the number of processes that are to be used to execute a parallel process.

7. **What new analytic feature can be used to forecast values based on existing measures?**

   The SQL **model** clause in a **select** statement can be used to forecast values based on existing measures.

8. **What two methods can be used to run the SQLAccess Advisor utilities for materialized views?**

   OEM or **dbms_advisor** package can be used to run the SQLAccess Advisor utilities for materialized views.

9. **Which of the following are components of an RAC system? (Select all that apply.)**

   B, C, E.

   Explanation   Cluster Manager, Shared Storage, and Global Cache Service are all components of an RAC system.

10. **In a grid computing environment, the _____ instance of a node manages the disk groups and maintains a map of data files and disks.**

    In a grid computing environment, the ASM instance of a node manages the disk groups and maintains a map of data files and disks.

11. _____ partitioning allows you to control the placement of records in specified partitions based on sets of partition key values.

    List partitioning allows you to control the placement of records in specified partitions based on sets of partition key values.

12. **What analytic function would you use to assign each row from a query to one of five buckets?**

    ntile is used to assign each row from a query to one of five buckets.

13. **What are the database components involved in grid computing?**

    RAC, ASM, and OEM are the database components involved in grid computing.

14. **What are the two types of windows that can be used in analytic functions?**

    Physical and logical windows are the two types of windows that can be used in analytic functions.

15. **The _____ automatically collects workload and performance statistics used for database self-management activities.**

    The Automatic Workload Repository automatically collects workload and performance statistics used for database self-management activities.

16. **When creating partitioned tables, what option should you use to ensure that rows are redistributed to their correct partition if their partition key is updated?**

    Use **enable row movement** in the **create** table or **alter** table statements to ensure that rows are redistributed to their correct partition if their partition key is updated.

Index

Symbols

!= (inequality) operator, using with where clauses, 45
!= (not equals) operator, using with where clauses, 42
() (parentheses), enclosing subqueries in, 72
:=, significance in PL/SQL, 206
^= (inequality) operator, using with where clauses, 45
+ notation in outer joins, significance of, 61
< (less than) operator, using with where clauses, 45
<= (less than or equal to) operator, using with where clauses, 45
<> (inequality) operator, using with where clauses, 45
= (equality) operator, using with where clauses, 45
> (greater than) operator, using with where clauses, 45
>= (greater than or equal to) operator, using with where clauses, 45
; (semicolon)
    in PL/SQL IF statements, 225
    in SQL statements, 38

A

abort shutdown approach, explanation of, 100
access, controlling with sqlnet.ora file, 154–155
accounts, locking against passwords, 117

ADD_FILE parameter, using with Oracle Data Pump Export, 177
add_months() date function, description of, 54
ADDRESS attribute, setting with dispatchers, 132
ADDRESS parameters in listener.ora, descriptions of, 138
address XML SQL query, definition for, 292
administration tools
    command-line utilities, 149–151
    OEM Central Console, 148
    OEM components, 148
    OEM (Oracle Enterprise Manager), 146
    Oracle Advanced Security option, 151
    Oracle Internet Directory Configuration Assistant, 149
    Oracle Net Configuration Assistant, 148–149
    Oracle Net Manager, 147
    overview of, 146
advisors, role in self-managing databases, 342
aggregation functions
    cube, 345–346
    overview of, 53
    rollup, 344–345
alert logs, backup up, 163
aliases, using with Oracle inner joins, 58–59
alter database command, syntax for, 110
alter statement, using with parallel execution, 330

alter system command, explanation of, 24
alter table abc drop partition xyz command, effect of, 303
alter table command
    compressing data with, 325
    using with data partitions, 317
alter table statements, purpose of, 34
ALTER USER statement, issuing, 114
analysis functions, ranking functions, 347–352
analytic partitioning, explanation of, 353
analytic window, explanation of, 353
analyze statements, purpose of, 34
analyze table command, relationship to partitioned tables, 304
and logical operator, purpose of, 42
ANSI full outer joins, overview of, 65
ANSI inner joins, overview of, 59–61
ANSI natural joins, overview of, 61
ANSI outer joins, overview of, 64–65
applets in Java, features of, 250
arc0 (archiver) background process, description of, 7
architecture and design, DBA's responsibilities for, 91, 109
archive log current command, effect of, 166
archive log management in RMAN, explanation of, 189
archive logs
    backup and recovery considerations, 162
    managing, 110
archived redo logs, backing up, 172–173. *See also* redo logs

arithmetic operators, PL/SQL support for, 204–205
as select keywords, using with create view statements, 78
as statement, using with stored procedures in PL/SQL, 234
ASM (Automatic Storage Management)
architecture of, 338–339
benefits of, 341
description of, 26
overview of, 338
ASM disk groups, associating with tables, 340
authority, granting and taking away, 115–116
avg() aggregate function, description of, 53

B

background processes
explanation of, 3
overview of, 6–7
backup and recovery. *See also* backups; database backup; recovery; RMAN (Recovery Manager); user-managed backups
cold backups, 164–165
DBA's responsibilities for, 91–92
explanation of, 29
hot backups, 165–166
overview of, 158–159
backup and restore optimization in RMAN, explanation of, 190
backup architecture, overview of, 159–160
backup control files, using for recovery, 169–170
backup sets, listing in RMAN, 191
backup types, overview of, 159
backups. *See also* backup and recovery; database backup; recovery; RMAN (Recovery Manager); user-managed backups
of archived redo logs, 172–173
automating, 171
multiplexing in RMAN, 189–190
performing with RMAN, 192–195
BEGIN line in PL/SQL program, significance of, 203
between A and B operator, using with where clauses, 46
between keyword, using with where clauses, 43

binaries in Oracle, backup and recovery considerations, 160
blob data type
versus clob, 15
overview of, 12
block media recovery, performing with RMAN, 191
blocks
backup and recovery considerations, 162
in schemas, 94–95
boolean data type, using in PL/SQL, 208–209
btitle command, effect of, 84
buffer overflow error message, triggering, 235

C

Cache Fusion technology, relationship to RAC, 338
candidate table, analyzing for data partitioning, 305–307
capacity planning, DBA's responsibilities for, 91
CASE statements, using in PL/SQL, 227–228
ceil() numeric function, description of, 52
change management, DBA's responsibilities for, 93
change_password command, using with listeners, 139
channels, allocating automatically with RMAN, 190
character functions, overview of, 51–52
character sets, role in Oracle Net Services, 125
CHECK constraints, description of, 82
checkpoints, backup and recovery considerations, 161–162
CIRCUITS initialization parameter for shared servers, definition of, 131
cjq0 (job queue) background process, description of, 7
ckpt (checkpoint process) background process, description of, 6
CLASS_PATH init.ora parameter, description of, 255
clob data type
versus blob, 15
overview of, 12

close command, using with PL/SQL, 215
Cluster Manager, role in RAC, 337
cman.ora configuration file, description of, 145
cold backups
versus hot backups, 167, 172
overview of, 164–165
recovering from, 167–168
columns
formatting in SQL*Plus, 84
names of, 12
referencing during FOR loops, 216
command-line utilities, overview of, 149–151
comments, adding to PL/SQL programs, 228
comparison operators, using with where clauses, 44–45. *See also* set operators
complete versus incomplete recovery, 168, 170
composite partitioning, explanation of, 313–314
compressing data, 323–326. *See also* index key compression
conditions, including in programs, 222–231
configuration files, syntax for, 144–146
configuration settings, managing with RMAN, 190
connect descriptors
defining, 134–135
example of, 134
Connection Manager. *See* Oracle Connection Manager
connection pooling, overview of, 140
connections
defining, 134–136
maintaining in Oracle Net Services, 126
relationship to Oracle Net Services, 125
testing, 152–153
CONNECTIONS attribute, setting, 132
consistent parameter, using with Import and Export utilities, 184–185
constraints, overview of, 80–83
control files
backup and recovery considerations, 160–161

explanation of, 4
managing, 106
relationship to RMAN
repository, 186–187
using for recovery, 169–170
Conventional-Path mode, running
import and export utilities in, 184
correlated subqueries, using with
joins, 73
corruption checks, performing with
RMAN, 190
count() aggregate function,
description of, 53
create index statements
enabling index compression
with, 326
purpose of, 34
create java class command, effect
of, 266
CREATE JAVA command, effect of,
255
create java resource command,
effect of, 266–267
create java source command, effect
of, 266
create materialized view statement,
effect of, 335
create or replace function
command, effect of, 237
create procedure command, effect
of, 232–233
create table statements
example of, 35
purpose of, 34
using with list partitioning, 311
create table system privilege,
explanation of, 24
create trigger system privilege,
explanation of, 24
create user command, effect of, 113
create user system privilege,
explanation of, 24
create view statement, explanation
of, 78
CREATE_EMPLOYEE package,
example of, 17
CSALTER script, features of, 125
cube function, overview of, 345–346
cume_dist function, example of,
348–349
cumulative backups, RMAN
support for, 192
cursor FOR loop, using with SQL in
PL/SQL programs, 215–216
cursors, using with SQL in PL/SQL
programs, 213–215
customers, deleting, 48

D

data
compressing, 323–326
moving with Oracle Data
Pump, 173–174
data access, determining for
partitioning, 305
data contents, analyzing for data
partitioning, 305
data conversion tools, examples of,
125
data objects, compressing,
324–325
data partitioning
defining indexing strategy for,
315–320
implementing, 305–320
types of, 307–314
data partitioning rationale
manageability, 302–304
overview of, 301–302
performance, 304
data partitions, adding, 317
Data Pump. See Oracle Data Pump
data types
blob, 12
clob, 12
date, 11
number, 10–11
timestamp, 11–12
varchar2, 10
database and instance shutdown,
overview of, 99–101
database backup, writing,
170–172. See also backup and
recovery; backups; recovery;
RMAN (Recovery Manager);
user-managed backups
Database Character Set Scanner
utility, features of, 125
database components, parallel
processing of, 327–328
database objects, managing,
106–108
databases. See also Oracle
Database 10g
associating with instances, 98
backing up with RMAN, 193
controlling access to, 154–155
defining, 2–3
determining state prior to
restoring, 171
exabytes supported by, 29
versus instances, 28–29
large databases, 300
opening, 98–99

operating modes of, 97–101
setting up target databases in
RMAN, 188–189
shutting down, 99–101, 109,
164–165
using XML in, 273–275
data-centric documents, treatment
by XML DB, 274–275
datafiles
backing up with RMAN, 193
backup and recovery
considerations, 162
managing, 110–111
date data type
special formats with, 55–56
using in PL/SQL, 207–208
date data type, overview of, 11
date functions, overview of, 54–55
day-to-day operations
architecture and design, 91
backup and recovery, 91–92
capacity planning, 91
change management, 93
managing database objects, 92
network management, 93
performance and tuning, 92
scheduling jobs, 93
security, 92
storage management, 92
troubleshooting, 93
DBA skill set, overview of, 90–91
DBAs (database administrators)
improving skills of, 109
Java utilities for, 263
opportunities for, 252
responsibilities of, 9–10, 29,
90–93, 109
significance of Java to, 242–245
DBMS_JAVA package, contents of,
256
dbms_profiler facility, explanation
of, 216
dbms_xmlschema.registerSchema(),
example of, 286
dbwr (database writer) background
process
description of, 6
purpose of, 15
DDD format mask for date data
type, description of, 56
DDL (data definition language),
example of, 34–35
declare statement, using with
stored procedures in PL/SQL, 234
dedicated servers, overview of, 128
default settings, managing with
RMAN, 190

default tablespace, role in user environments, 22. *See also* tablespaces; temporary tablespaces

default temporary tablespace, explanation of, 5

default user environments, overview of, 22

deferred constraints, overview of, 83

delete privilege, overview of, 24

delete statements
    example of, 48
    using, 35

dense_rank function, example of, 348

desc statements, using with create view statements, 78

describe command, displaying descriptions of tables with, 35

DESCRIPTION attribute, setting with dispatchers, 132

DESCRIPTION parameters in listener.ora, descriptions of, 138

differential backups, RMAN support for, 192

directory naming methods
    choosing, 144
    easy naming, 143–144
    external naming, 144
    finding information about, 142
    local naming, 143
    and net service alias entries, 143
    overview of, 141

DIRECTORY parameter, using with Oracle Data Pump Export, 176

Direct-Path mode, running import and export utilities in, 184

dispatchers
    relationship to shared servers, 129
    setting, 131–133

DISPATCHERS parameter
    example of, 151
    using with shared servers, 130

distributed management, handling in OEM, 104

DITs (Directory Information Trees), overview of, 141–142

DML (data manipulation language), overview of, 35–36

DNs (distinguished names), overview of, 142

document-centric documents, treatment by XML DB, 274–275

drop table statements
    example of, 35
    purpose of, 34

dropjava utility, example of, 263

dup_val_on_index exception in PL/SQL, explanation of, 217

Dynamic Method, using with directory names, 142

E

easy naming method, overview of, 143–144

EJBs (Enterprise JavaBeans), features of, 251

emca OEM configuration program, advisory about, 27

END line in PL/SQL program, significance of, 203

Enterprise Manager
    Automatic Undo Management view in, 107
        resource group view in, 104
        table definition view in, 96

entity models, linkage to, 81

environmental variables, using with Java, 255

equality (=) operator, using with where clauses, 45

error conditions, handling in PL/SQL, 217–222

error handling Oracle-supplied variables, 220–222

errors, showing in PL/SQL, 233–234

ESTIMATE parameter, using with Oracle Data Pump Export, 176

exabyte, size of, 29

EXCEPTION section of PL/SQL, example of, 217

exceptions in PL/SQL
    creating user-defined exceptions, 219–220
    examples of, 217–218

EXCLUDE parameter
    using with Oracle Data Pump Export, 176
    using with Oracle Data Pump Import, 180

execute command, using with PL/SQL, 234

existsnode() function, using with XML DB queries, 291

EXIT statement, using with loops in PL/SQL, 228–229

exp executable, issuing, 183

expdp utility, using with Oracle Data Pump, 173–176

explicit cursors, explanation of, 214

export syntax, finding, 183–184

Export utility, running, 183–185. *See also* Oracle Data Pump Export

exp.par file, contents of, 178

extents
    backup and recovery considerations, 162
    purpose of, 94–95

external naming, overview of, 144

extract() function, using with XML DB queries, 292

extractvalue() function, using with XML DB queries, 292

F

fetch command, using with PL/SQL, 215

fields, identifying in tables, 12

files, writing SQL*Plus output to, 87

filters, using with Oracle Data Pump Export, 175

firewall access control, overview of, 136

FLASHBACK_SCN and _TIME parameters
    using with Oracle Data Pump Export, 176
    using with Oracle Data Pump Import, 180

floor() numeric function, description of, 52

FOR loops, reference columns during, 216

FOR loops, using in PL/SQL, 229–231

FOREIGN KEY constraints, description of, 82

foreign keys in inner joins, purpose of, 57

forests, role in XML, 277

from clauses
    in ANSI inner joins, 59–60
    in ANSI right outer joins, 64
    role in Oracle inner joins, 57–58

FTP (File Transfer Protocol), description of, 124

full backups, RMAN support for, 192

Full Export mode, using with Oracle Data Pump Export, 174

Full Import mode, using with Oracle Data Pump Import, 178

full outer joins in ANSI, overview of, 65

functions
    aggregate functions, 53
    aggregation functions, 344–346
    analysis functions, 346–352
    creating and using, 237–238
    date functions, 54–55
    example of, 16–17
    nesting, 56
    numeric functions, 52
    overview of, 51
    ranking functions, 347–352
    special formats with date data
        type, 55–56
    string functions, 51–52
    types of, 354–355
    windowing functions, 352–354

G

g in 10*g*, significance of, 25
garbage collection in Oracle JVM,
    overview of, 257
getProperty method, using with
    Java, 259
Global Cache Service, role in RAC,
    338
global partitioned indexes,
    overview of, 318–320
grant statements, purpose of, 34
granting authority, 115–116
greater than (>) operator, using
    with where clauses, 45
greater than or equal to (>=)
    operator, using with where
    clauses, 45
grid computing
    explanation of, 25–27
    large database issues addressed
        by, 341
    overview of, 340–342
group by clauses
    overview of, 67–68
    using with rollup functions, 344
group by statements, role in SQL
    statements, 37

H

hash partitioning, explanation of,
    311–313
having clauses, overview of, 68
hot backups
    versus cold backups, 167
    overview of, 165–166
    recovering from, 168
    SQL script for, 171–172

HTML (hypertext markup
    language), sample tags in, 272
HTML versus XML documents, 275
HTTP (Hypertext Transport
    Protocol), description of, 124

I

IF logic structures, using in PL/SQL,
    223–225
IF/THEN construct, using in
    PL/SQL, 223–225
IF/THEN/ELSE construct, using in
    PL/SQL, 225–226
IF/THEN/ELSEIF construct, using in
    PL/SQL, 226–227
Image Copies, performing with
    RMAN, 194
immediate shutdown approach,
    explanation of, 100
imp executable, issuing, 184
impdp utility, using with Oracle
    Data Pump, 173–174, 178–179
implicit cursors, explanation of, 214
import syntax, finding, 183
Import utility, running, 183–185.
    See also Oracle Data Pump
    Import
in operator, using with where
    clauses, 45
INCLUDE parameter
    using with Oracle Data Pump
        Export, 176
    using with Oracle Data Pump
        Import, 181
incomplete versus complete
    recovery, 168, 170
incremental backups, RMAN
    support for, 192, 194
INDEX attribute, setting, 132
index key compression, overview of,
    326. *See also* compressing data
index partitions, example of, 322
indexes, overview of, 19
indexing strategy, defining for data
    partitioning, 315–320
inequality (!=) operator, using with
    where clauses, 45
inequality (^=) operator, using with
    where clauses, 45
inequality (<>) operator, using with
    where clauses, 45
initcap() string functions,
    description of, 52
initialization parameters, effect on
    parallel processing, 329–330

init.ora file
    backing up, 160
    setting dispatchers in, 132
inner joins, overview of, 57–62
insert privilege, overview of, 23
insert statements
    example of, 36–37
    using, 35
instance and database shutdown,
    overview of, 99–101
instance configuration, performing
    in OEM, 102
instances
    associating databases with, 98
    versus databases, 28–29
    explanation of, 3
integrity constraints, types of, 82
intersect operator, overview of,
    75–76

J

J2EE (Java 2 Platform, Enterprise
    Edition), features of, 248–249
J2EE server, features of, 249
J2SE (Java 2 Platform, Standard
    Edition), features of, 248
JAR (Java ARchive) files, contents
    of, 264
Java. *See also* Oracle Database
    10*g* JVM
    applets in, 250
    configuring for Oracle Database
        10*g*, 254–255
    disadvantages of, 246–247
    EJBs (Enterprise JavaBeans) in,
        251
    environmental variables for, 255
    explanation of, 29
    getting up to speed on, 268
    initialization parameters for,
        254–255
    in Oracle, 256–257
    and Oracle Database 10*g*, 252
    in Oracle architecture, 247
    overview of, 245–247
    platform-independence of, 247
    relationship to n-tiered
        architectures, 251
    servlets in, 250–251
    session space in, 254
    significance to Oracle DBAs,
        242–245
    support for multithreading, 257
    three-tier support of, 247
    writing standalone applications
        in, 250

Java classes, loading, 264
Java objects, creating in Oracle
  Database 10*g*, 266–267
Java programs
    embedding SQL statements
      into, 261–262
    types of, 249
Java utilities, examples of, 263
JAVA_HOME init.ora parameter,
  description of, 255
java_max_sessionspace_size
  parameter, explanation of, 254
java_pool_size parameter, using
  with Oracle JVM, 254
JavaBeans, features of, 250
Java-stored procedures, overview
  of, 262–264
JDBC drivers, overview of,
  258–259
JDBC (Java DataBase Connectivity)
    overview of, 258
    using, 259–260
job queue (cjq0) background
  process, description of, 7
job scheduling, DBA's
  responsibilities for, 93
joins
    correlated subqueries with, 73
    inner joins, 57–61
    outer joins, 61–65
    overview of, 57
    self-joins, 66–67
JSP (JavaServer Pages), features of,
  250–251

K

keys, role in inner joins, 57

L

large databases
    explanation of, 300
    managing, 302–304
    relationship to grid computing,
      341
LARGE_POOL_SIZE initialization
  parameter for shared servers,
  definition of, 131
last_day() date function, description
  of, 54
LD_LIBRARY_PATH init.ora
  parameter, description of, 255

LDAP (Lightweight Directory
  Access Protocol), relationship to
  directory naming, 141
ldap.ora configuration file
    description of, 145
    using with directory names, 142
left outer joins in ANSI, overview
  of, 64–65
length() string functions, description
  of, 52
less than (<) operator, using with
  where clauses, 45
less than or equal to (<=) operator,
  using with where clauses, 45
lgwr (log writer) background
  process, description of, 6
like '%tin%' operator, using with
  where clauses, 46
like command, using with where
  clauses, 44
list partitioning, explanation of,
  310–312
LISTENER attribute, setting, 132
listener commands, executing, 149
Listener Control utility, features of,
  149
LISTENER parameter in listener.ora
    advisory about, 139
    description of, 138
listener.ora file
    example of, 138, 144–145
    protocol examples for, 139
listeners. *See also* Oracle Net
  Listener
    defining multiple listeners, 140
    displaying information from, 150
    setting passwords for, 139
    stopping, 149
loadjava utility, example of, 263
local naming method, overview of,
  143
local partitioned indexes, overview
  of, 315–318
locations, defining in Oracle Net
  Services, 127
log records, archiving after hot
  backups, 166
logical backup and recovery,
  explanation of, 159
logical operators, PL/SQL support
  for, 205
loops, using in PL/SQL, 228–231
lower() string functions, description
  of, 51
LSNRCTL prompt, generating, 149

M

managing database objects, DBA's
  responsibilities for, 92
materialized views
    creating, 335
    guidelines for, 334–335
    overview of, 331–332
    and query rewrite, 333–334
    uses for, 332–333
max() aggregate function,
  description of, 53
MAX_DISPATCHERS initialization
  parameter for shared servers,
  definition of, 130
MAX_SHARED_SERVERS
  initialization parameter for shared
  servers, definition of, 131
maxvalue, specifying default
  partitions with, 319
metadata, moving with Oracle
  Data Pump, 173–174
min() aggregate function,
  description of, 53
minus operator, overview of, 76
MM format mask for date data type,
  description of, 56
MML (Media Management Layer),
  role in RMAN, 187
mod() numeric function,
  description of, 52
model clause
    syntax for, 357
    variations of, 358
model extension, using with select
  statement, 355–356
Month format mask for date data
  type, description of, 56
months_between() date function,
  description of, 54
mount phase, explanation of, 98
MULTIPLEX attribute, setting, 132
multiplexing backups in RMAN,
  189–190
multithreading, Java support for, 257

N

Named Pipes protocol, description
  of, 124
naming methods
    directory naming, 141
    DITs (Directory Information
      Trees), 141–142
    DNs (distinguished names), 142
    overview of, 140

native Java compiler, features of, 256
natural joins in ANSI, overview of, 61
nested functions, overview of, 56
Net Listener. *See* Oracle Net Listener
net service alias entries, relationship to directory naming, 143
Net Services. *See* Oracle Net Services
network bandwidth, optimizing in Oracle Net Services, 124–125
network communication stack, diagram of, 123
network management, DBA's responsibilities for, 93
network protocols, overview of, 123–124
NETWORK_LINK parameter
    using with Oracle Data Pump Export, 177
    using with Oracle Data Pump Import, 181
networking
    explanation of, 29
    in multitiered environments, 155–156
networks, diagram of, 126
NLS_LANG environmental variable, purpose of, 125
no_data_found exception in PL/SQL, explanation of, 217
nodes
    in RAC, 337
    in XML, 277
nomount phase, explanation of, 98
nonprefixed partition indexes, overview of, 320
not between A and B operator, using with where clauses, 46
not equals (!=) operator, using with where clauses, 42
not in operator, using with where clauses, 45
NOT NULL constrained columns, possible entries in, 83
n-tiered architectures, advantages of, 251
ntile function, example of, 350–351
NULL constraints, description of, 82
number data type
    integer and decimal digits in, 25
    length of field determined in, 15
    overview of, 10–11
    using in PL/SQL, 207

number fields, storing values in, 25
numeric functions, overview of, 52

O

object privileges, working with, 23–25
objects. *See also* stored objects
    creating, 118–119
    sequences as, 80
OEM Central Console, features of, 148
OEM (Oracle Enterprise Manager)
    benefits of, 341
    components of, 148
    distributed management in, 104
    features of, 146
    instance configuration in, 102
    versus Oracle Net Manager, 147
    overview of, 101–102
    Resource Consumer Groups in, 102–103
    schema, security, and storage management in, 103
    startup of, 27–28
    Tools option in, 105–106
    user sessions in, 102
    warehouse features in, 105
offline backups, RMAN support for, 193
ojvmjava utility, example of, 263
on statements, using with ANSI inner joins, 59–60
online backups, RMAN support for, 193
online redo logs, explanation of, 4
open command, using with PL/SQL, 215
open phase, explanation of, 98
operators. *See* comparison operators; set operators
or logical operator, purpose of, 42
ORA* errors, examples of, 217
Oracle Advanced Security option, features of, 151
Oracle Application Server 10g, features of, 267
Oracle architecture, Java in, 247
Oracle binaries, backup and recovery considerations, 160
Oracle Connection Manager, overview of, 135–136
Oracle Data Pump, features of, 173–174

Oracle Data Pump Export. *See also* Export utility
    example of, 181–182
    parameters for, 175
    using, 174–178
Oracle Data Pump Import. *See also* Import utility
    parameters for, 179–181
    using, 178–182
Oracle Database 10g. *See also* databases
    background processes in, 3
    creating Java objects in, 266–267
    instances in, 3
    operating modes of, 97–101
    relationship to Java, SML, and Web Services, 252
    self-managing capabilities of, 341–342
    shutting down, 3
    starting, 3
    storing XML in, 283–287
Oracle Database 10g architecture
    background processes in, 6–7
    control files in, 4
    default temporary tablespaces in, 5
    diagram of, 7
    online redo logs in, 4
    spfiles (system parameter files) in, 6
    SYSAUX tablespaces in, 5
    SYSTEM tablespaces in, 5
    undo tablespaces in, 5–6
Oracle Database 10g infrastructure
    overview of, 93
    schemas, 94–96
    storage structures, 97
Oracle Database 10g JVM. *See also* Java
    components of, 257
    garbage collection in, 257
    overview of, 256
Oracle Database Configuration Assistant, using with Java, 254
Oracle DBAs. *See* DBAs (database administrators)
Oracle Internet Directory Configuration Assistant, features of, 149
Oracle Java products
    Oracle Application Server 10g, 267
    Oracle JDeveloper 10g, 267–268
Oracle JDeveloper 10g, features of, 267–268

Oracle JVM, initialization
parameters for, 254–255
Oracle Management Agent,
features of, 148
Oracle Management Repository,
features of, 148
Oracle Management Service,
features of, 148
Oracle Net Configuration Assistant,
features of, 148–149
Oracle Net Listener, overview of,
137–139. *See also* listeners
Oracle Net Manager
controlling database access
with, 155
features of, 147
Oracle Net Services
character sets in, 125
connections in, 125
defining locations in, 127
maintaining connections in, 126
network protocols in, 123–124
optimizing network bandwidth
in, 124–125
overview of, 122–123
Oracle network communication
stack, diagram of, 123
Oracle network, overview of, 126
Oracle Resource Manager,
description of, 26
Oracle sample database, tables in,
39–41
Oracle Scheduler, description of, 26
Oracle Streams, description of, 26
Oracle XML DB. *See* XML DB
repository
ORA-20000: ORU-10027 error,
triggering, 235
order by statements
example of, 50–51
using with correlated
subqueries and joins, 73
others exception in PL/SQL,
explanation of, 218
outer joins, overview of, 61–62
owner parameter, using with
Import and Export utilities, 185

P

packages, overview of, 17
parallel execution, invoking,
330–331
PARALLEL parameter
using with Oracle Data Pump
Export, 177

using with Oracle Data Pump
Import, 181
parallel processing
configuring, 328–330
of database components,
327–328
effect of initialization
parameters on, 329–330
overview of, 327
parameter files. *See* spfiles (system
parameter files)
parameters, setting and resetting, 84
parentheses (()), enclosing
subqueries in, 72
PARFILE parameter, 174, 185
using with Oracle Data Pump
Export, 177
using with Oracle Data Pump
Import, 181
PART_MASTER table, creating
synonym for, 21
part_master table definitions, 13
partition keys, identifying, 307
partition pruning, explanation of,
304
partitioning. *See* data partitioning
password authentication, setting for
listeners, 139
passwords, locking accounts
against, 117
PATH init.ora parameter,
description of, 255
pattern searches, using where
clauses with, 44
percent_rank function, example of,
349–350
performance
DBA's responsibilities for, 92
improving with parallel
processing, 327–331
physical backup and recovery,
explanation of, 159
PL/SQL
architectural diagram of, 201
assigning values to variables in,
206
calling procedures in, 239–240
CASE statements in, 227–228
characters supported by, 204
explanation of, 29
features of, 200–202
handling error conditions in,
217–222
IF logic structures in, 223–227
logical operators supported by,
205

loops in, 228–231
Oracle products used with, 201
program control decision matrix
in, 224
program structure of, 202–203
PL/SQL block, form of, 202–203
PL/SQL character set
arithmetic operators, 204
characters supported by, 204
PL/SQL data types
boolean, 208–209
date, 207–208
number, 207
overview of, 204–209
varchar2, 207
PL/SQL programs
adding comments to, 228
calling, 239–240
getting feedback from, 211
SQL in, 213–215
writing to access databases,
259–260
pmon (process monitor)
background process, description
of, 6
PMON, relationship to Oracle Net
Listener, 137
POOL attribute, setting, 132
ports, defining dispatchers for,
132–133
power() numeric function,
description of, 52
precision, relationship to number
data type, 10
prefixed partition indexes,
overview of, 320
PRIMARY KEY constraints,
description of, 82
primary keys in inner joins,
purpose of, 57
private synonym, explanation of, 21
privileges
for Java-stored procedures, 264
managing for database users,
115–119
working with object and system
privileges, 23–25
procedures. *See also* stored
procedures
calling in PL/SQL, 239–240
overview of, 16
PRODUCTS table, contents of, 41
products.xml, storing in Oracle
XML DB, 289
profiles, using, 117, 154–155

program control in PL/SQL, overview of, 223–231

Progress Check
for "Backup and Recovery," 163, 182–183
for "Creating Essential Objects, 118–119
for "The Database Administrator," 97, 112
for "Database Fundamentals," 18, 22
for "Java," 252–253
for "Large Database Features," 323, 336, 343
for "Networking," 136–137
for "PL/SQL," 210, 222, 236
for "SQL: Structured Query Language," 49, 71
for "XML," 282–283, 294

PROTOCOL attribute, setting with dispatchers, 132

pseudo-column variables, explanation of, 220–221

public synonym, explanation of, 21

Q

Q format mask for date data type, description of, 55

queries, using with XML, 291–292

QUERY parameter
using with Oracle Data Pump Export, 177
using with Oracle Data Pump Import, 181

query rewrite, relationship to materialized views, 333–334

QUEUESIZE parameter in listener.ora, description of, 139

R

RAC (Real Application Clusters)
architecture of, 337–338
benefits of, 341
description of, 26
overview of, 336

raise_application_error function, using with PL/SQL, 217

range partitioning
explanation of, 308–310
syntax for, 309–310

range searches, using where clauses with, 42–43

range with hash partitioning, explanation of, 313–314

range with list partitioning, explanation of, 313–314

ranking functions
cume_dist, 348–349
ntile, 350–351
overview of, 347
percent_rank, 349–350
rank and dense_rank, 347–348
row_number, 352

read-only tablespaces, backing up, 167

records, identifying in tables, 12

recovery. See also backup and recovery; backups; recovery; RMAN (Recovery Manager); user-managed backups
from cold backups, 167–168
guidelines for, 168
from hot backups, 168
performing with RMAN, 194–195
seven steps to, 169
using backup control files for, 169–170

recovery catalogs
setting up, 188–189
using with RMAN, 187

redo logs. See also archived redo logs
backing up, 172–173
backup and recovery considerations, 161
managing, 106

redundancy versus recovery windows in RMAN, explanation of, 191

relational databases
concepts related to, 12–13
explanation of, 29

relational view, creating for XML, 294–295

relationships between tables, example of, 14

remap parameters, using with Oracle Data Pump Import, 181

reorg of objects, advisory about, 93

replace() string functions, description of, 51

reporting in RMAN, 191–192

repository
defining with naming methods, 140–144
role in RMAN, 186

resolver specifications for Java-stores procedures, overview of, 264

Resource Consumer Groups, selecting in OEM, 102–103

RESOURCE_VIEW, using with XML, 288

restore operations, performing with RMAN, 194–195

resync command, effect of, 187

reuse_datafiles parameter, using with Oracle Data Pump Import, 181

REVERSE clause, using with FOR loops in PL/SQL, 229–230

revoke statements, purpose of, 34

right outer joins in ANSI, overview of, 64–65

RMAN (Recovery Manager). See also backups; backup and recovery; database backup; recovery; user-managed backups
architecture of, 186–188
archive log management in, 189
backup and restore optimization in, 190
block media recovery in, 191
configuration and default settings in, 190
corruption and verification checks in, 190
features of, 159, 185–186
multiplexing backups in, 189–190
performing backups in, 192–195
performing restore and recovery operations with, 194–195
redundancy versus recovery windows in, 191
reporting in, 191–192
stored scripts in, 189
trial recovery in, 191

roles
creating and granting, 116–117
overview of, 22

rollback commands, using with delete statements, 48–49

rollup function, overview of, 344–345

round() numeric function, description of, 52

row_number function, example of, 352

rownum = 1, including when using implicit cursors, 214

rows
retrieving to meet multiple criteria, 41–42
in tables, 12

rpad() string functions, description of, 52

rules clause, relationship to model clause, 358

S

SALES table, creating as nonpartitioned, 308

sbt tape, role in RMAN, 188

scale, relationship to number data type, 10

Schema Export mode, using with Oracle Data Pump Export, 174

Schema Import mode, using with Oracle Data Pump Import, 178

schema objects, overview of, 108

schemas
    logical schema structures, 95–96
    in OEM, 103
    segments, extents, and blocks, 94–95

SDP (Sockets Directory Protocol), description of, 124

search lists, using where clauses with, 43–44

security
    DBA's responsibilities for, 92
    in OEM, 103

segments
    backup and recovery considerations, 162
    purpose of, 94–95

select keywords, role in SQL statements, 37

select privilege, overview of, 23

select statements
    example of, 37–38
    issuing, 37–38
    using, 35

self-joins, overview of, 66–67

self-managing databases component, features of, 341–342

semicolon (;)
    in PL/SQL IF statements, 225
    in SQL statements, 38

sequences, overview of, 79–80

serial processing, diagram of, 327

server processes, characteristics of, 127

servers
    dedicated servers, 128
    shared servers, 129–131

SERVICE attribute, setting, 132

services command, example of, 150–151

services, support for, 127

servlets in Java, features of, 250–251

session multiplexing, overview of, 136

SESSIONS attribute, setting, 131–132

set commands
    ending, 83
    example of, 151

set keyword, using with update statements, 46–47

set linesize command, effect of, 83

set operators. *See also* comparison operators
    intersect, 75–76
    minus, 76
    overview of, 74
    union, 74–75
    union all, 75

shared servers
    monitoring with views, 133–134
    overview of, 129–131

shared_pool_size parameter, using with Oracle JVM, 254

SHARED_SERVER_SESSIONS initialization parameter for shared servers, definition of, 131

SHARED_SERVERS initialization parameter for shared servers, definition of, 131

SHNEW schema
    creating with Oracle Data Pump Import, 182
    role in Export utility, 185

show errors command, using with PL/SQL, 233–234

smon (system monitor) background process, description of, 6

SOAP (Simple Object Access Protocol), integration into Web Services, 243

space, managing, 109–111

spfiles (system parameter files)
    backup and recovery considerations, 160
    explanation of, 6
    reading startup parameters from, 15

SQL models, creating, 355–358

SQL statement components, 37
    DDL (data definition language), 34–35
    DML (data manipulation language), 35–36

SQL statements
    embedding into Java programs, 261–262

for tablespace quotas, 20

SQL (Structured Query Language)
    explanation of, 29
    in PL/SQL programs, 213–215

SQL syntax for local partitioned indexes, 315–316

SQL*Plus
    executing SQL statements in, 38
    formatting output with, 83–84
    writing PL/SQL programs in, 210–212

SQLFILE parameter, using with Oracle Data Pump Import, 181

SQLJ, using, 261–262

sqlnet.ora configuration file
    contents of, 154
    description of, 145

SQLX queries, important points related to, 279–280

SQL/XML standard, overview of, 276–281

sqrt() numeric function, description of, 52

START_JOB parameter, using with Oracle Data Pump Export, 177

startup
    explanation of, 25
    forcing, 99

startup command, effect of, 98

startup restrict command, effect of, 99

Static Method, using with directory names, 142

status command, example of, 150

storage management
    DBA's responsibilities for, 92
    in OEM, 103

stored objects. *See also* objects
    functions, 16–17
    overview of, 14
    packages, 17
    procedures, 16
    triggers, 16
    views, 15–16

stored procedures, creating, 232–236. *See also* procedures

stored scripts in RMAN, explanation of, 189

string functions, overview of, 51–52

subqueries, overview of, 72–73

substr() string functions, description of, 52

sum() aggregate function, description of, 53

synonyms, overview of, 21

SYS account, using, 112

SYSAUX table space, explanation of, 5

sysdate date function, description of, 54

sysdba privilege, granting, 112

SYSMAN account, purpose of, 112

system limits, implementing with profiles, 117

system privileges, working with, 24–25

SYSTEM tablespace, explanation of, 5

T

Table Export mode, using with Oracle Data Pump Export, 174

Table Import mode, using with Oracle Data Pump Import, 179

table structure, analyzing for data partitioning, 305

tables
    associating ASM disk groups with, 340
    describing, 35
    example of, 12
    joining, 57–62
    in Oracle sample database, 39–41
    relating to part_master relational database, 13–14
    relationships between, 14
    working with, 12–14

Tablespace Export mode, using with Oracle Data Pump Export, 174

Tablespace Import mode, using with Oracle Data Pump Import, 179

tablespace quotas, overview of, 20

tablespaces. *See also* default tablespace; temporary tablespaces
    backing up, 165–166
    backing up with RMAN, 194
    backup and recovery considerations, 162
    explanation of, 5
    managing, 110

target databases, setting up in RMAN, 188–189

TCP.* parameters for sqlnet.ora file, descriptions of, 154

TCP/IP (Transmission Control Protocol/Internet Protocol), description of, 123

TCP/IP with SSL (Secure Sockets Layer), description of, 123

temporary tablespaces. *See also* default tablespace; tablespaces
    advisory about autoextending of, 110
    role in default user environments, 22

TICKS attribute, setting, 132

timestamp data type, example of, 11–12

title command, effect of, 84

TNS listener error, occurrence of, 137

to_char conversion function, explanation of, 55

too_many_rows exception in PL/SQL, explanation of, 217

Tools option in OEM, explanation of, 105–106

trace files, backup and recovery considerations, 163

trailing spaces in varchar2 columns, dealing with, 25

transactional shutdown approach, explanation of, 100

transactions, explanation of, 4

transform() function, using with XSLT, 296

TRANSPORT_TABLESPACES (TTS) parameter
    using with Oracle Data Pump Export, 177
    using with Oracle Data Pump Import, 181

Transportable Tablespace Export mode, using with Oracle Data Pump Export, 175

Transportable Tablespace (TTS), using with Oracle Data Pump Import, 179

trial recovery, performing with RMAN, 191

triggers, overview of, 16

troubleshooting, DBA's responsibilities for, 93

trunc commands, using with delete statements, 48–49

truncate statements, purpose of, 34

tsnames.ora configuration file, description of, 145

TSPITR (Tablespace Point In Time Recovery), explanation of, 166

tuning, DBA's responsibilities for, 92

U

Undo management, overview of, 107

Undo segments, backup and recovery considerations, 161

undo tablespaces
    advisory about autoextending of, 110
    explanation of, 5–6
    purpose of, 15

Unicode character sets, considering, 125

union all operator, overview of, 75

union operator, overview of, 74–75

UNIQUE constraints, description of, 82

update privilege, overview of, 24

update statements
    example of, 46–47
    using, 35

updatexml() function, effect of, 290–291

user environments, overview of, 22

user sessions, managing in OEM, 102

user-defined exceptions, creating in PL/SQL, 219–220

user-managed backups, types of, 164. *See also* backup and recovery; backups; database backup; recovery; RMAN (Recovery Manager)

users
    creating, 113
    editing, 114
    granting authority to, 115–116
    managing, 112–114
    overview of, 20

using statements, role in ANSI inner joins, 59–61

V

value() function, role in updating XML documents, 290–291

value_error exception in PL/SQL, explanation of, 218

values, assigning to variables in PL/SQL, 206, 209

varchar2 data type
    example of, 10
    using in PL/SQL, 207

variables
    assigning values to in PL/SQL, 206

error handling Oracle-supplied
  variables, 220–222
variables, assigning values to in
  PL/SQL, 209
verification checks, performing
  with RMAN, 190
views
  example of, 15–16
  monitoring shared servers with,
    133–134
  using, 78–79

W

warehouse features, availability in
  OEM, 105
Web Services
  justification for use of, 244
  and Oracle Database 10g, 252
  technologies integrated into,
    243–244
WebDAV (WWW Distributed
  Authoring Protocol), description
  of, 124
when others exception, using in
  PL/SQL, 221
where clauses
  with != (not equals) operator, 42
  in ANSI inner joins, 59–60
  in ANSI right outer joins, 64
  example of, 41
  operators used with, 44–45
  with pattern searches, 44
  with range searches, 42–43
  with search lists, 43–44

using update statements with,
  46–47
using with delete statements, 48
using with DML statements, 47
where clauses, role in SQL
  statements, 37, 57–58
WHILE loops, using in PL/SQL, 229
windowing functions, overview of,
  352–354
WSDL (Web Services Description
  Language), description of, 244
WW format mask for date data
  type, description of, 56

X

xdburitype() function, using with
  XML DB, 289
XML data, loading, 286–287
XML documents, updating,
  290–291
XML (Extensible Markup Language)
  creating from data stored in
    Oracle, 276–281
  creating relational view of,
    294–295
  explanation of, 29
  integration into Web Services,
    244
  and Oracle Database 10g, 252
  overview of, 272
  storing in Oracle Database 10g,
    283–287
  uses of, 273–275
  using in databases, 273–275
  using simple queries with,
    291–292

XML DB repository
  features of, 274
  overview of, 284
  path-based access to, 289–290
  querying documents in, 291–292
XML listings, creating, 281–282
XML Schema, registering, 284–286
XML versus HTML documents, 275
xmlagg() function, using in SQLX,
  279–281
xmlattributes() function, using in
  SQLX, 277, 279
xmlelement() function, using in
  SQLX, 277, 279–280
xmlforest() function, using in SQLX,
  277–280
XPath syntax, using with
  updatexml() function, 290
xsi:schemaLocation attribute,
  purpose of, 285
XSLT (Extensible Stylesheet
  Language Transformations), using
  for programmatic access, 296

Y

Y format masks for date data type,
  description of, 55
YEAR format mask for date data
  type, description of, 55

Z

ZERO_DIVIDE exception in
  PL/SQL, explanation of, 218

INTERNATIONAL CONTACT INFORMATION

AUSTRALIA
McGraw-Hill Book Company
Australia Pty. Ltd.
TEL +61-2-9900-1800
FAX +61-2-9878-8881
http://www.mcgraw-hill.com.au
books-it_sydney@mcgraw-hill.com

CANADA
McGraw-Hill Ryerson Ltd.
TEL +905-430-5000
FAX +905-430-5020
http://www.mcgraw-hill.ca

GREECE, MIDDLE EAST, & AFRICA
(Excluding South Africa)
McGraw-Hill Hellas
TEL +30-210-6560-990
TEL +30-210-6560-993
TEL +30-210-6560-994
FAX +30-210-6545-525

MEXICO (Also serving Latin America)
McGraw-Hill Interamericana Editores
S.A. de C.V.
TEL +525-1500-5108
FAX +525-117-1589
http://www.mcgraw-hill.com.mx
carlos_ruiz@mcgraw-hill.com

SINGAPORE (Serving Asia)
McGraw-Hill Book Company
TEL +65-6863-1580
FAX +65-6862-3354
http://www.mcgraw-hill.com.sg
mghasia@mcgraw-hill.com

SOUTH AFRICA
McGraw-Hill South Africa
TEL +27-11-622-7512
FAX +27-11-622-9045
robyn_swanepoel@mcgraw-hill.com

SPAIN
McGraw-Hill/
Interamericana de España, S.A.U.
TEL +34-91-180-3000
FAX +34-91-372-8513
http://www.mcgraw-hill.es
professional@mcgraw-hill.es

UNITED KINGDOM, NORTHERN,
EASTERN, & CENTRAL EUROPE
McGraw-Hill Education Europe
TEL +44-1-628-502500
FAX +44-1-628-770224
http://www.mcgraw-hill.co.uk
emea_queries@mcgraw-hill.com

ALL OTHER INQUIRIES Contact:
McGraw-Hill/Osborne
TEL +1-510-420-7700
FAX +1-510-420-7703
http://www.osborne.com
omg_international@mcgraw-hill.com

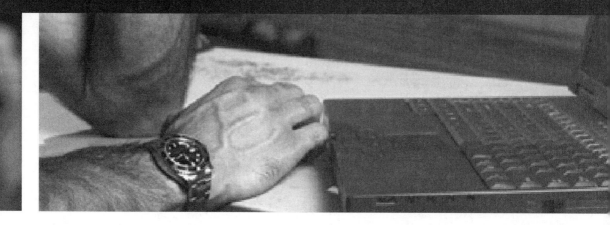

GET YOUR FREE SUBSCRIPTION
TO ORACLE MAGAZINE

Oracle Magazine is essential gear for today's information technology professionals. Stay informed and increase your productivity with every issue of *Oracle Magazine*. Inside each free bimonthly issue you'll get:

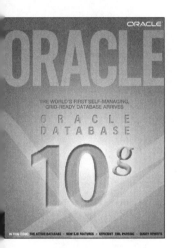

- Up-to-date information on Oracle Database, Oracle Application Server, Web development, enterprise grid computing, database technology, and business trends
- Third-party vendor news and announcements
- Technical articles on Oracle and partner products, technologies, and operating environments
- Development and administration tips
- Real-world customer stories

IF THERE ARE OTHER ORACLE USERS AT YOUR LOCATION WHO WOULD LIKE TO RECEIVE THEIR OWN SUBSCRIPTION TO ORACLE MAGAZINE, PLEASE PHOTOCOPY THIS FORM AND PASS IT ALONG.

ORACLE
MAGAZINE

Three easy ways to subscribe:

① Web
Visit our Web site at otn.oracle.com/oraclemagazine. You'll find a subscription form there, plus much more!

② Fax
Complete the questionnaire on the back of this card and fax the questionnaire side only to +1.847.763.9638.

③ Mail
Complete the questionnaire on the back of this card and mail it to P.O. Box 1263, Skokie, IL 60076-8263

ORACLE®

FREE SUBSCRIPTION

○ **Yes, please send me a FREE subscription to *Oracle Magazine*.**   ○ **NO**

To receive a free subscription to *Oracle Magazine*, you must fill out the entire card, sign it, and date it (incomplete cards cannot be processed or acknowledged). You can also fax your application to +1.847.763.9638.
Or subscribe at our Web site at otn.oracle.com/oraclemagazine

○ From time to time, Oracle Publishing allows our partners exclusive access to our e-mail addresses for special promotions and announcements. To be included in this program, please check this circle.

○ Oracle Publishing allows sharing of our mailing list with selected third parties. If you prefer your mailing address not to be included in this program, please check here. If at any time you would like to be removed from this mailing list, please contact Customer Service at +1.847.647.9630 or send an e-mail to oracle@halldata.com.

signature (required) _____ date _____

X

name _____ title _____

company _____ e-mail address _____

street/p.o. box _____

city/state/zip or postal code _____ telephone _____

country _____ fax _____

YOU MUST ANSWER ALL TEN QUESTIONS BELOW.

① WHAT IS THE PRIMARY BUSINESS ACTIVITY OF YOUR FIRM AT THIS LOCATION? (check one only)
- ☐ 01 Aerospace and Defense Manufacturing
- ☐ 02 Application Service Provider
- ☐ 03 Automotive Manufacturing
- ☐ 04 Chemicals, Oil and Gas
- ☐ 05 Communications and Media
- ☐ 06 Construction/Engineering
- ☐ 07 Consumer Sector/Consumer Packaged Goods
- ☐ 08 Education
- ☐ 09 Financial Services/Insurance
- ☐ 10 Government (civil)
- ☐ 11 Government (military)
- ☐ 12 Healthcare
- ☐ 13 High Technology Manufacturing, OEM
- ☐ 14 Integrated Software Vendor
- ☐ 15 Life Sciences (Biotech, Pharmaceuticals)
- ☐ 16 Mining
- ☐ 17 Retail/Wholesale/Distribution
- ☐ 18 Systems Integrator, VAR/VAD
- ☐ 19 Telecommunications
- ☐ 20 Travel and Transportation
- ☐ 21 Utilities (electric, gas, sanitation, water)
- ☐ 98 Other Business and Services

② WHICH OF THE FOLLOWING BEST DESCRIBES YOUR PRIMARY JOB FUNCTION? (check one only)
Corporate Management/Staff
- ☐ 01 Executive Management (President, Chair, CEO, CFO, Owner, Partner, Principal)
- ☐ 02 Finance/Administrative Management (VP/Director/ Manager/Controller, Purchasing, Administration)
- ☐ 03 Sales/Marketing Management (VP/Director/Manager)
- ☐ 04 Computer Systems/Operations Management (CIO/VP/Director/ Manager MIS, Operations)

IS/IT Staff
- ☐ 05 Systems Development/ Programming Management
- ☐ 06 Systems Development/ Programming Staff
- ☐ 07 Consulting
- ☐ 08 DBA/Systems Administrator
- ☐ 09 Education/Training
- ☐ 10 Technical Support Director/Manager
- ☐ 11 Other Technical Management/Staff
- ☐ 98 Other

③ WHAT IS YOUR CURRENT PRIMARY OPERATING PLATFORM? (select all that apply)
- ☐ 01 Digital Equipment UNIX
- ☐ 02 Digital Equipment VAX VMS
- ☐ 03 HP UNIX
- ☐ 04 IBM AIX
- ☐ 05 IBM UNIX
- ☐ 06 Java
- ☐ 07 Linux
- ☐ 08 Macintosh
- ☐ 09 MS-DOS
- ☐ 10 MVS
- ☐ 11 NetWare
- ☐ 12 Network Computing
- ☐ 13 OpenVMS
- ☐ 14 SCO UNIX
- ☐ 15 Sequent DYNIX/ptx
- ☐ 16 Sun Solaris/SunOS
- ☐ 17 SVR4
- ☐ 18 UnixWare
- ☐ 19 Windows
- ☐ 20 Windows NT
- ☐ 21 Other UNIX
- ☐ 98 Other
- 99 ☐ None of the above

④ DO YOU EVALUATE, SPECIFY, RECOMMEND, OR AUTHORIZE THE PURCHASE OF ANY OF THE FOLLOWING? (check all that apply)
- ☐ 01 Hardware
- ☐ 02 Software
- ☐ 03 Application Development Tools
- ☐ 04 Database Products
- ☐ 05 Internet or Intranet Products
- 99 ☐ None of the above

⑤ IN YOUR JOB, DO YOU USE OR PLAN TO PURCHASE ANY OF THE FOLLOWING PRODUCTS? (check all that apply)
Software
- ☐ 01 Business Graphics
- ☐ 02 CAD/CAE/CAM
- ☐ 03 CASE
- ☐ 04 Communications
- ☐ 05 Database Management
- ☐ 06 File Management
- ☐ 07 Finance
- ☐ 08 Java
- ☐ 09 Materials Resource Planning
- ☐ 10 Multimedia Authoring
- ☐ 11 Networking
- ☐ 12 Office Automation
- ☐ 13 Order Entry/Inventory Control
- ☐ 14 Programming
- ☐ 15 Project Management
- ☐ 16 Scientific and Engineering
- ☐ 17 Spreadsheets
- ☐ 18 Systems Management
- ☐ 19 Workflow

Hardware
- ☐ 20 Macintosh
- ☐ 21 Mainframe
- ☐ 22 Massively Parallel Processing
- ☐ 23 Minicomputer
- ☐ 24 PC
- ☐ 25 Network Computer
- ☐ 26 Symmetric Multiprocessing
- ☐ 27 Workstation

Peripherals
- ☐ 28 Bridges/Routers/Hubs/Gateways
- ☐ 29 CD-ROM Drives
- ☐ 30 Disk Drives/Subsystems
- ☐ 31 Modems
- ☐ 32 Tape Drives/Subsystems
- ☐ 33 Video Boards/Multimedia

Services
- ☐ 34 Application Service Provider
- ☐ 35 Consulting
- ☐ 36 Education/Training
- ☐ 37 Maintenance
- ☐ 38 Online Database Services
- ☐ 39 Support
- ☐ 40 Technology-Based Training
- ☐ 98 Other
- 99 ☐ None of the above

⑥ WHAT ORACLE PRODUCTS ARE IN USE AT YOUR SITE? (check all that apply)
Oracle E-Business Suite
- ☐ 01 Oracle Marketing
- ☐ 02 Oracle Sales
- ☐ 03 Oracle Order Fulfillment
- ☐ 04 Oracle Supply Chain Management
- ☐ 05 Oracle Procurement
- ☐ 06 Oracle Manufacturing
- ☐ 07 Oracle Maintenance Management
- ☐ 08 Oracle Service
- ☐ 09 Oracle Contracts
- ☐ 10 Oracle Projects
- ☐ 11 Oracle Financials
- ☐ 12 Oracle Human Resources
- ☐ 13 Oracle Interaction Center
- ☐ 14 Oracle Communications/Utilities (modules)
- ☐ 15 Oracle Public Sector/University (modules)
- ☐ 16 Oracle Financial Services (modules)

Server/Software
- ☐ 17 Oracle9*i*
- ☐ 18 Oracle9*i* Lite
- ☐ 19 Oracle8*i*
- ☐ 20 Other Oracle database
- ☐ 21 Oracle9*i* Application Server
- ☐ 22 Oracle9*i* Application Server Wireless
- ☐ 23 Oracle Small Business Suite

Tools
- ☐ 24 Oracle Developer Suite
- ☐ 25 Oracle Discoverer
- ☐ 26 Oracle JDeveloper
- ☐ 27 Oracle Migration Workbench
- ☐ 28 Oracle9*i*/AS Portal
- ☐ 29 Oracle Warehouse Builder

Oracle Services
- ☐ 30 Oracle Outsourcing
- ☐ 31 Oracle Consulting
- ☐ 32 Oracle Education
- ☐ 33 Oracle Support
- ☐ 98 Other
- 99 ☐ None of the above

⑦ WHAT OTHER DATABASE PRODUCTS ARE IN USE AT YOUR SITE? (check all that apply)
- ☐ 01 Access
- ☐ 02 Baan
- ☐ 03 dbase
- ☐ 04 Gupta
- ☐ 05 IBM DB2
- ☐ 06 Informix
- ☐ 07 Ingres
- ☐ 08 Microsoft Access
- ☐ 09 Microsoft SQL Server
- ☐ 10 PeopleSoft
- ☐ 11 Progress
- ☐ 12 SAP
- ☐ 13 Sybase
- ☐ 14 VSAM
- ☐ 98 Other
- 99 ☐ None of the above

⑧ WHAT OTHER APPLICATION SERVER PRODUCTS ARE IN USE AT YOUR SITE? (check all that apply)
- ☐ 01 BEA
- ☐ 02 IBM
- ☐ 03 Sybase
- ☐ 04 Sun
- ☐ 05 Other

⑨ DURING THE NEXT 12 MONTHS, HOW MUCH DO YOU ANTICIPATE YOUR ORGANIZATION WILL SPEND ON COMPUTER HARDWARE, SOFTWARE, PERIPHERALS, AND SERVICES FOR YOUR LOCATION? (check only one)
- ☐ 01 Less than $10,000
- ☐ 02 $10,000 to $49,999
- ☐ 03 $50,000 to $99,999
- ☐ 04 $100,000 to $499,999
- ☐ 05 $500,000 to $999,999
- ☐ 06 $1,000,000 and over

⑩ WHAT IS YOUR COMPANY'S YEARLY SALES REVENUE? (please choose one)
- ☐ 01 $500, 000, 000 and above
- ☐ 02 $100, 000, 000 to $500, 000, 000
- ☐ 03 $50, 000, 000 to $100, 000, 000
- ☐ 04 $5, 000, 000 to $50, 000, 000
- ☐ 05 $1, 000, 000 to $5, 000, 000

100103

Sound Off!

Visit us at **www.osborne.com/bookregistration** and let us know what you thought of this book. While you're online you'll have the opportunity to register for newsletters and special offers from McGraw-Hill/Osborne.

We want to hear from you!

Sneak Peek

Visit us today at **www.betabooks.com** and see what's coming from McGraw-Hill/Osborne tomorrow!

Based on the successful software paradigm, Bet@Books™ allows computing professionals to view partial and sometimes complete text versions of selected titles online. Bet@Books™ viewing is free, invites comments and feedback, and allows you to "test drive" books in progress on the subjects that interest you the most.

OSBORNE DELIVERS RESULTS!] OSBORNE
www.osborne.com